LINUX
MULTIMEDIA GUIDE

LINUX
MULTIMEDIA GUIDE

JEFF TRANTER

O'REILLY™

Bonn · *Cambridge* · *Paris* · *Sebastopol* · *Tokyo*

Linux Multimedia Guide
by Jeff Tranter

Copyright © 1996 O'Reilly & Associates, Inc. All rights reserved.
Printed in the United States of America.

Published by O'Reilly & Associates, Inc., 101 Morris Street, Sebastopol, CA 95472.

Editor: Andy Oram

Production Editor: Nicole Gipson Arigo

Printing History:

>   September 1996:   First Edition.

This book is printed on acid-free paper with 85% recycled content, 15% post-consumer waste. O'Reilly & Associates is committed to using paper with the highest recycled content available consistent with high quality.

ISBN: 1-56592-219-0

TABLE OF CONTENTS

Table of Contents

PART THREE

CHAPTER TWELVE
HYPERMEDIA APPLICATIONS   145

CHAPTER THIRTEEN
GAMES   155

PART FOUR

CHAPTER FOURTEEN
PROGRAMMING SOUND DEVICES   163

Examples

Examples

PREFACE

Multimedia: a hot topic in the computer industry today, or so say the trade journals. But how much is truth, and how much is just media hype? Admittedly much of what one reads in the press is driven by corporate marketing departments, but in my opinion the underlying technology is important for two main reasons. First, multimedia brings together a number of different areas of computer science and computer hardware that in the past were separate. As is often the case, the synergy that occurs when these technologies are combined results in a whole that is more powerful than the sum of its individual parts.

Second, this combination of technologies opens up new possibilities for computing, leading to new applications and making computers more accessible to those with little technical background. Multimedia allows people to interact with computers and each other in new ways, offering the potential to extend the computer from being a specialized tool for an elite few into an "information appliance" that will affect, and hopefully enrich, all of our lives.

Unfortunately, UNIX-compatible systems have been largely ignored when it comes to multimedia. I believe this situation has come about for two main reasons. First, UNIX systems have traditionally had little or no hardware support for multimedia, having come from a multiuser, time-sharing environment in which most users interacted with the system using character-based terminals. Second, UNIX systems have until recently been expensive, both for the computer hardware and for software applications. Because of these two drawbacks, multimedia developers did not see a large enough market for UNIX multimedia applications, especially for home use, and instead concentrated on the much larger DOS PC platform.

Linux is changing all this. Developed by Finnish university student Linus Torvalds and an informal volunteer team of programmers around the world, Linux is a free, full-featured 32-bit UNIX compatible operating system that runs on low-cost and powerful PC hardware. Linux supports many multimedia devices, most notably the majority of the popular CD-ROM drives and sound cards. Add to that a number of powerful software development tools, many from the GNU project, and you have a powerful software development environment for multimedia.

The explosion of Linux has generated an army of software developers looking for interesting applications to create—and multimedia is one of the new software frontiers to explore. I hope this book helps encourage the development of these applications.

Linux is based on a number of standards, making it generally compatible with other UNIX systems. The Linux sound device drivers can also be used with several other Intel-based UNIX systems, including Interactive, SCO, BSD, and SVR4, so much of the information in this book is directly applicable to those systems as well.

Linux also runs on a number of different computer architectures including DEC Alpha, MIPS, PowerPC, Motorola 68K, and Sun SPARC. This book is aimed at the Intel processor version of Linux, because it is by far the most common and supports the most multimedia devices. However, much of the information should be relevant to the other architectures as well.

At the time of writing, the latest stable version of the Linux kernel was 2.0. Given the rapid pace of development, new versions will undoubtedly be available by the time you read this, but the examples used should work with little or no changes (the most likely changes to the kernel being bug fixes, support for new devices, and ports to new computer platforms).

History of This Book

In my professional life as a software engineer, I use workstations running UNIX on a daily basis. I postponed buying a PC for home use, mainly because I dreaded the thought of being tied to a single-tasking proprietary system with unfamiliar tools. I looked at a number of low-cost UNIX clones for the PC, but after learning of Linux, I realized that it looked like the best match for my interests. I broke down and bought a system, installed Linux on it, and have never looked back.

As time went on, I installed the inevitable upgrades (more RAM to run the X Window System, more disk space to run applications), and in early 1994 I bought a sound card. I spent several weeks reading documentation (which mostly consisted of little more than README files), configuring the kernel sound drivers, and finding applications that supported sound under Linux. The process was somewhat confusing, due to the lack of documentation and a lot of unfamiliar terminology. In an effort to help others who were struggling with the same problems, I wrote the Linux Sound HOWTO document and made it freely available on the Internet.

About six months later I purchased a CD-ROM drive to go with my sound card. Again I waded through the README files, compiling and testing a number of applications. At the end of all this, I wrote the Linux CD-ROM HOWTO.

The HOWTO documents were intended to be a temporary solution to the lack of real documentation. I received considerable feedback from other users that the HOWTOs were useful, but that more detailed information was still needed, particularly on applications and programming.

At the same time I had written a number of articles for the publication *Linux Journal*, and was looking for a challenging new project. I approached O'Reilly with the idea of doing a book on multimedia under Linux, and they immediately welcomed the idea. Well, the project was indeed challenging, and I learned a lot more about multimedia in the process. A year later, this book is the result.

Overview

This book is primarily aimed at users interested in developing new multimedia applications under Linux. It's meant to be a practical book describing applications and tools that exist today. The reader is assumed to have a basic familiarity with Linux or other UNIX-like operating systems, and to be comfortable with concepts such as C programming, *make* files, and text editing. A knowledge of multimedia programming and hardware is not a prerequisite—these topics will be covered extensively.

Less experienced users who are not yet programmers can still benefit from this book, but will need to supplement their knowledge with some of the other reference material given in Appendix B. Most examples will use C, but some approaches to multimedia development that do not require traditional programming, such as HTML, will also be covered.

The book is divided into five parts. Part I is an overview of basic multimedia technology, covering concepts such as sound, video, and CD-ROM hardware and software. These basics are prerequisites to understanding the material that comes later in the book.

Part II, the user's guide, describes how to configure Linux for sound and CD-ROM hardware, a necessary step before running multimedia applications. Included are checklists for diagnosing problems, and answers to many common questions.

Part III gives an overview of the types of multimedia applications available for Linux, including sound, video, and hypermedia. This section should give you a flavor for the types of applications that currently exist, and possibly trigger some ideas for new ones that you can develop.

Developing new multimedia applications requires software programming. Part IV is the programmer's guide, covering the software details of the sound and CD-ROM devices under Linux, and the various toolkits available for developing multimedia applications. I develop several working multimedia applications to further illustrate the concepts.

Finally, Part V, the appendixes, includes a glossary of terms, an index, and an extensive list of further references on multimedia topics. Linux- and multimedia-related World Wide Web and Internet ftp sites are also given here, including sites containing all of the example software listings and multimedia applications developed in the book.

Conventions Used in This Book

The following is a list of the typographical conventions used in this book.

italic

> is used for program names, command names, URLs, filenames, function names, for emphasis, and to introduce new terms.

`constant width`

> indicates computer software listings, short snippets of code, fully functional example programs, a series of commands, or output displayed on a computer screen.

`constant width bold`

> shows user input, to distinguish it from output.

Example Programs

You can obtain the source code for the programs presented in this book from O'Reilly & Associates through their Internet server.

The example programs in this book are available electronically in a number of ways: by ftp, Ftpmail, BITFTP, and UUCP. The cheapest, fastest, and easiest ways are listed first. If you read from the top down, the first one that works for you is probably the best. Use ftp if you are directly on the Internet. Use Ftpmail if you are not on the Internet, but can send and receive electronic mail to Internet sites (this includes CompuServe users). Use BITFTP if you send electronic mail via BIT-NET. Use UUCP if none of the above works.

FTP

To use ftp, you need a machine with direct access to the Internet. A sample session is shown, with what you should type in **boldface**.

```
% ftp ftp.uu.net
Connected to ftp.uu.net.
220 FTP server (Version 6.21 Tue Mar 10 22:09:55 EST 1992) ready.
Name (ftp.uu.net:joe): anonymous
331 Guest login ok, send domain style email address as password.
Password: yourname@domain.name (use your user name and host here)
230 Guest login ok, access restrictions apply.
ftp> cd /published/oreilly/linux/multimedia
250 CWD command successful.
ftp> binary (Very important! You must specify binary transfer for compressed files.)
200 Type set to I.
ftp> get examples.tar.gz
200 PORT command successful.
150 Opening BINARY mode data connection for examples.tar.gz.
226 Transfer complete.
ftp> quit
221 Goodbye.
%
```

The file is a compressed tar archive; extract the files from the archive by typing:

```
% gzcat examples.tar.gz | tar xvf -
```

Some systems require the following tar command instead:

```
% gzcat examples.tar.gz | tar xof -
```

If *gzcat* is not available on your system, use separate *gunzip* and *tar* or *shar* commands.

```
% gunzip examples.tar.gz
% tar xvf examples.tar
```

Ftpmail

Ftpmail is a mail server available to anyone who can send electronic mail to and receive it from Internet sites. This includes any company or service provider that allows email connections to the Internet. Here's how you do it.

You send mail to *ftpmail@online.ora.com*. In the message body, give the ftp commands you want to run. The server will run anonymous ftp for you and mail the files back to you. To get a complete help file, send a message with no subject and the single word "help" in the body.

The following is a sample mail session that should get you the examples. This command sends you a listing of the files in the selected directory and the requested example files. The listing is useful if there's a later version of the examples you're interested in.

```
% mail ftpmail@online.ora.com
Subject:
reply-to username@domain.name      (Where you want files mailed)
```

```
open
cd /published/oreilly/linux/multimedia
mode binary
uuencode
get examples.tar.gz
quit
.
```

A signature at the end of the message is acceptable as long as it appears after "quit."

BITFTP

BITFTP is a mail server for BITNET users. You send it electronic mail messages requesting files, and it sends you back the files by electronic mail. BITFTP currently serves only users who send it mail from nodes that are directly on BITNET, EARN, or NetNorth. BITFTP is a public service of Princeton University. Here's how it works.

To use BITFTP, send mail containing your ftp commands to *BITFTP@PUCC*. For a complete help file, send HELP as the message body.

The following is the message body you send to BITFTP:

```
FTP   ftp.uu.net   NETDATA
USER   anonymous
PASS   myname@podunk.edu  Put your Internet email address here (not your BITNET address)
CD /published/oreilly/linux/multimedia
DIR
BINARY
GET   examples.tar.gz
QUIT
```

Once you've got the desired file, follow the directions under ftp to extract the files from the archive.

UUCP

UUCP is standard on virtually all UNIX systems and is available for IBM-compatible PCs and Apple Macintoshes. The examples are available by UUCP via modem from UUNET; UUNET's connect-time charges apply.

You can get the examples from UUNET whether you have an account there or not. If you or your company has an account with UUNET, you have a system some where with a direct UUCP connection to UUNET. Find that system, and type:

```
uucp uunet\!~/published/oreilly/linux/multimedia/examples.tar.gz
yourhost\!~/yourname/
```

The backslashes can be omitted if you use the Bourne shell (sh) instead of csh. The file should appear some time later (up to a day or more) in the directory

/usr/spool/uucppublic/`yourname`. If you don't have an account, but would like one so that you can get electronic mail, contact UUNET at 703-204-8000.

It's a good idea to get the file */published/oreilly/ls-lR.Z* as a short test file containing the filenames and sizes of all the files available.

Once you've got the desired file, follow the directions under ftp to extract the files from the archive.

We'd Like to Hear from You

We have tested and verified all of the information in this book to the best of our ability, but you may find that features have changed (or even that we have made mistakes!). Please let us know about any errors you find, as well as your suggestions for future editions, by writing:

O'Reilly & Associates, Inc.
101 Morris Street
Sebastopol, CA 95472
1-800-998-9938 (in the US or Canada)
1-707-829-0515 (international/local)
1-707-829-0104 (FAX)

You can also send us messages electronically. To be put on the mailing list or request a catalog, send email to:

nuts@ora.com   (via the Internet)
uunet!ora!info (via UUCP)

To ask technical questions or comment on the book, send email to:

bookquestions@ora.com (via the Internet)

Acknowledgments

Linux is a terrific platform for multimedia, due in a large part to the kernel device drivers. Hannu Savolainen is the primary developer of the Linux sound driver. I believe that Linux offers better support for sound than any other UNIX-compatible operating system.

I'd also like to single out the efforts of Eberhard Moenkeberg, who wrote the SBPCD kernel drivers for Panasonic and several other CD-ROM drives, and whose software was used as the basis for many other kernel drivers.

My thanks go to the technical reviewers who spent long hours poring over the first draft: Dave Fowler, Dana Peters, and Marc Seguin.

Thanks also to the editing, production, and management staff at O'Reilly & Associates. Andy Oram was the technical editor. Nicole Gipson Arigo was the copyeditor and project manager. Clairemarie Fisher O'Leary and Sheryl Avruch performed quality control checks. Seth Maislin wrote the index, with assistance from Cynthia Grabke. Erik Ray, Ellen Siever, and Lenny Muellner worked with the tools to create the book. Chris Reilley helped with the illustrations, Nancy Priest designed the interior book layout, and Edie Freedman designed the front cover. Steve Abrams and Darcell Burton provided production assistance.

Finally, this book is dedicated to the thousands of Linux activists around the world who are responsible for making Linux a success.

INTRODUCTION TO MULTIMEDIA

Part I of the book is an introduction to multimedia, starting with a definition and a discussion of multimedia technologies and applications.

We then delve into three of the key multimedia technologies: digital audio, CD-ROM, and computer graphics. Part I concludes with a look at hypertext and related technologies.

By the end of this part of the book you should have a good understanding of multimedia concepts and the technology behind multimedia systems and applications. These ideas are prerequisites to the later sections, which will cover installation and configuration of multimedia hardware under Linux, currently available multimedia applications, and multimedia programming.

If you are already familiar with multimedia you may wish to skim through this part of the book, but I urge you not to skip it entirely as it covers some issues that are specific to Linux.

CHAPTER ONE
MULTIMEDIA AND LINUX

The term *multimedia* is bandied about a lot these days, but what does it really mean? In this first chapter I'll start by defining the word and the technologies that it encompasses. I'll describe some of the areas where multimedia is being used today, and look at one detailed example. I'll conclude with a discussion of why Linux is a good computing platform for multimedia.

Let's start off with a definition. My dictionary doesn't define multimedia, but it lists the prefix "multi" as meaning "many" or "more than one."

"Media" is the plural of "medium," which has a number of definitions. Here are a few that look promising: "a means of effecting or conveying something," "a channel of communication," and "a mode of artistic expression." Another is "a condition in which something may function or flourish." Let's hope so.

A Working Definition

In reference to computers, multimedia means different things to different people, but most would agree that it incorporates a number of common characteristics:

- Clearly, it makes use of computers.

- It often involves *continuous* media such as sound and moving images.

- It relates to more than one physical sense (sound, sight),[*] making it appeal to more than one type of learning.

- It places demands on processing power, bandwidth, and storage capacity.

- It often involves the synchronization of several data streams.

---

[*] Arguably, the use of a mouse or joystick as a pointing device could be considered using the sense of touch.

3

For the purposes of this book, here is my working definition:

> *Multimedia is the simultaneous use of more than one means of communication or technology in order to convey information.*

I like to think of multimedia as making use of two powerful concepts, both of which are independent and complement each other. The first is the use of computer graphics, including still images and moving video, and of computer-generated sound, including speech and music.

The second is hypertext, sometimes called *hypermedia* when extended to include more than just printed information. Hypertext is based on electronic documents with "links" to other documents. The largest and probably most well known hypermedia system is the World Wide Web, which spans thousands of computer systems around the world.

Multimedia Technologies

Many of these multimedia ideas have been around for some time, but they have only recently become practical and affordable for widespread use because of a number of new technological breakthroughs. Some of the key technologies used to achieve this are:

- CD-ROM and other high density mass storage devices

- Data compression techniques, for computer data as well as methods specifically optimized for sound and video

- Low-cost personal computers, with fast processors, large amounts of memory and disk storage, and high-resolution bitmapped displays

- Computer sound and music, produced using digital sampling techniques

- Networking, both local and wide area, including the Internet and high speed networks based on technologies such as ISDN and ATM

Multimedia Applications

By taking these multimedia concepts and using the aforementioned technologies, one can build some useful applications. Here are some examples of where multimedia is being used today:

Computer-based training
   Multimedia can make training interactive, intuitive, and personalized.

Music
   This category includes the creation of music with the aid of computers as well as appreciation (listening to music created by others).

Collaborative tools

These tools help users share ideas and information, even over long distances.

Games

Several popular games make use of multimedia technologies to immerse the player in a virtual world.

General dissemination of information

This includes standalone kiosk applications as well as distributed systems like the World Wide Web.

Let's look at a concrete example of a specific, real, multimedia application. If some of the terms used aren't familiar to you, don't worry, we'll be covering them later.

I recently set up a hypertext information system using technology from the World Wide Web. The goal is to make existing information from a number of sources more readily available to a group of users (primarily software designers) on a large computer network. The information consists mainly of documents that exist in various formats on different computer systems. Users want to be able to access the system from multiple operating systems: several flavors of UNIX workstations running the X Window System, VT100 terminals, dial-up access via modems, and PCs running Microsoft Windows.

I use the *Mosaic* hypertext browser program as the primary tool—it provides an intuitive, graphical point-and-click interface with virtually no learning curve, and is available for most platforms. For text-based users, the *Lynx* browser is used.

Mosaic supports hypertext documents written in HTML, the native format used by the World Wide Web. The existing documents can in most cases be converted to HTML using filter programs (some examples: UNIX manpages, FrameMaker documents, GNU *info* pages, and even a format used by a proprietary text processing system). Some new HTML documents were created from scratch and others were left as plain ASCII text.

Users on machines that support NFS can read the files directly; for others, an HTTP server is set up to provide access via TCP/IP.

With Mosaic, hypertext links make browsing documents fast; you just click on a link to move to another page or document. Users can print or email pages to others, and even make personal annotations for later reference. A user's favorite documents can be accessed from a "hot list."

However, my system goes beyond just text. Many documents incorporate graphics in-line with the text. One user provided me with some ray-traced images of a company logo to make some of the pages more visually appealing. I also include support for viewing larger graphics and animations with external viewer programs. For example, a collection of the Linux HOWTO documents was obtained from an Internet archive site and made available—these were already in HTML format. Users can view a GIF file image of Linus Torvalds, and by clicking on a hypertext link, hear Linus' voice revealing how he pronounces "Linux" (thereby ending a long-standing debate).

Users are also able to add to the system by adding links to their own personal home pages, which often include personal information such as hobbies, current projects, a résumé, and a picture.

The same system provides access to Usenet news, hypertext links to obtain files using ftp, and, as Internet access was added, the capability of accessing other information systems such as *Gopher*, *Archie*, and WAIS.

The HTTP server makes it possible to create live documents that are generated on request, such as a current index of all documents available in a software repository. Clicking on the document name invokes a program to view it. Also supported are online tools. For example, by entering an employee's name in a text field, you can see his or her telephone number, email address, and location from a corporate database. Future plans include using this fill-out form's capability to perform online surveys, filling out electronic time sheets, or submitting reports of software defects directly into a problem management system. Most of these applications can be programmed using a freely available script language such as Perl or Tcl. More sophisticated tools incorporating graphics, animation, and sound may use the new Java language, or be implemented in C or C++.

All of the tools to implement this system are freely available. No traditional programming is required, other than writing some shell scripts, building the necessary tools from the source distributions, and a basic knowledge of HTML. Some time later a connection to the World Wide Web was added to the system, extending the amount of information available by several orders of magnitude, with no need for additional training or tools.

Linux and Multimedia

Suppose you've decided that you want to undertake a multimedia project. Why is Linux a good platform to use? Let me argue my case.

Linux is a true 32-bit operating system that makes use of all of the hardware features of 386 (and later) processors. For those familiar with operating system concepts, I can tell you that it supports multitasking, virtual memory, shared libraries, demand loading, shared copy-on-write executables, sophisticated memory management, and TCP/IP networking. To the less technically oriented, what that ultimately means is that you can efficiently and reliably run many large software programs.

Linux is low cost—the source and binaries are distributed freely. You can obtain the files over the Internet or from an electronic bulletin board system (BBS) at no cost. Multimedia developers will likely want to invest in a CD-ROM drive, in which case a 2 CD Linux distribution with over a gigabyte of software can be purchased for as little as US$20.

Most of the popular hardware devices are supported. Specifically for multimedia, support exists for most graphics cards, the majority of popular sound cards, and virtually all CD-ROM drives.

Highly compatible with most UNIX systems (being based on the IEEE POSIX standards with extensions from AT&T System V, SunOS, and BSD), Linux is able to use many existing applications with little or no porting. Users familiar with UNIX-like systems should feel right at home.

Linux has a large and rapidly growing user base. No one knows how many users exist, but one estimate[*] places it at between 650,000 and 17 million users world wide. Linux is very popular with universities and students, who are often on a limited budget. When these students graduate and enter the work force, their experiences with Linux may have an influence on their choice of computing platforms for their working life.

UNIX was originally designed to be a pleasant platform for software development. Linux is true to this spirit, and includes sophisticated compilers, debuggers, editors, and other development tools.

To be fair, some relative weaknesses exist with Linux as a multimedia platform. Currently there is a lack of polished and commercial multimedia tools. So users typically have to use lower-level toolkits and programming languages to develop multimedia applications. This is changing however; many commercial applications are being ported to Linux and offered with the same level of support as other platforms (and often at a lower cost).

The fast pace of Linux development means that users who try to stay on the "bleeding edge" can spend considerable time compiling new kernels, debugging new features, and trying to keep up-to-date with the latest developments. Most users should find it straightforward to select a stable Linux distribution and find it every bit as reliable (if not more so) than commercial operating systems. While most users do not find it necessary, it is possible to purchase commercial support for Linux from a number of third parties.

What Lies Ahead

Another way of looking at Multimedia is the merging of three traditionally disparate technologies: computing, broadcasting (or publishing), and communication.

I can't help feeling that there's a certain irony in a book about multimedia—a technology that some predict will make the printed page obsolete. I'm betting against that, but I do believe multimedia will make computers more effective, enjoyable, easier to use, and open to new applications.

In this first chapter I've discussed what multimedia encompasses and where it can be used. In the rest of Part I we will look at four of the key multimedia

---

* Harald Alvestrand, the "Linux Counter," *linux-counter@uninett.no*, May 1996.

technologies in more detail, starting with audio in Chapter 2, *Digital Audio*. In Chapter 3, *CD-ROM*, I examine compact disc read-only memory, an important storage technology, and one that has links with audio as well. Chapter 4, *Graphics and Video*, covers computer graphics, both still images as well as animations and video. Chapter 5, *Hypertext, Hypermedia, and the World Wide Web*, rounds out Part I with a more detailed examination of hypertext and related technologies.

CHAPTER TWO
DIGITAL AUDIO

To the uninitiated, the technology of computer audio can seem to be fraught with a confusing array of jargon taken from both the electronics and music industries. In this chapter I'll concentrate on digital audio, covering buzzwords related to sound generation, sound card hardware, and sound file formats. If you are considering the purchase of a sound card, this chapter concludes with general suggestions for selecting sound hardware to meet your requirements.

What Can a Sound Card Do?

The typical PC hardware is capable of producing a beep from a small speaker and little more.[*] For real audio generation you need to purchase a sound card. What can you do with it? Well, a typical sound card can perform some or all of these functions:

- Generate music and sound effects

- Record and save digitized sound to a file

- Play back digitized sound files

- Play an audio CD using a CD-ROM drive

- Control external MIDI devices such as synthesizers or drum machines

- Provide an interface to CD-ROM or SCSI storage devices

- Provide a joystick interface

---

[*] Actually, in Chapter 8, *The CD-ROM Driver*, I'll show that with some creative software it can do more, but not very well.

9

- Support volume and tone controls

- Allow you to record or play back audio from external devices

I'll cover some of the more unfamiliar terms shortly.

Digital Sampling

Sound is produced by variations in air pressure. Pressure is an *analog* property; that is, it can take on any value over a continuously variable range. Figure 2-1(a) shows a plot of a hypothetical sound as a function of time, much as one might see using a device such as an oscilloscope connected to a microphone. At a given position in space the air pressure varies over time above and below the average value as sound waves pass through the air. The sound may be speech, music, or a complex mixture of the two, but at any instant in time it is described by a single value.

Computers work with numbers and can store only discrete values. For this reason they are more correctly known as *digital** computers. In order to convert sound to a form that a computer can process and store, it must undergo a process called analog to digital conversion. Similarly, producing sound from a computer file or data in memory requires a process of digital to analog conversion. The devices that perform this (often a single chip) are known as Digital to Analog Converters (D/A or DAC) and Analog to Digital Converters (A/D or ADC).

The process of analog to digital conversion is also known as *sampling*. The quality of a digital sample, that is, how well it represents the original signal, is mostly dependent on two factors: sampling rate and sample size.

Figure 2-1(b) shows the analog waveform being digitized. The waveform must be sampled at regular intervals to determine its value over time. The rate at which the value is measured and converted to discrete samples is called the *sampling rate*, expressed in samples per second, or more often (and less accurately) in Hertz.

Figure 2-2 illustrates the effect of sampling rate. In (a) you see the original waveform. Using a relatively high sampling rate, as in (b), the result after digital to analog conversion resembles the shape of the original waveform quite closely. In (c) you see the effect of halving the sampling rate—some of the peaks and valleys are no longer as apparent. There may be a discernible difference between the original and reproduced sounds. In (d) the sampling rate is again reduced, resulting in even more distortion of the signal.

If the sampling rate is too low, then important information about the original sound waveform will be lost. The *sampling theorem* states that in order to accurately reproduce a signal, you must use a sampling rate at least twice as high as the highest frequency component of the signal you wish to reproduce.

---

* Analog computers have been built, but have not been popular for reasons I won't explain here. You might find one in a museum.

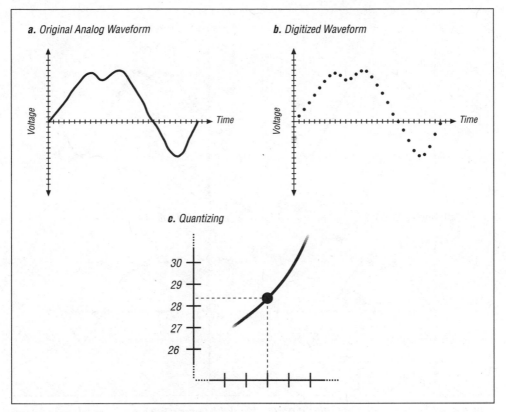

Figure 2–1: Analog to digital conversion

Why then would one not always use a very high sampling rate? As the rate increases, the amount of information stored increases proportionally, so that high sampling rates imply that more memory and disk space is required to store the sound data. Also, the complexity (and therefore cost) of the analog to digital hardware increases as sample rates go up.

The other important factor is sample size. As a sound is converted from analog to digital form (a process known as quantizing) it must be represented as a discrete number. The sample size is the range of values that each quantized sample can take. A common sampling size is 8 bits; in this case each sample must be represented by one of 2^8 or 256 values. If the analog waveform lies between two values, it must be rounded off. In Figure 2-1(c) you see an expanded view of one sample from the analog waveform. The value lies between 28 and 29 units. The analog to digital converter must round off the measurement to one of these two discrete values. Thus there is some error, known as a *quantizing error*, or *quantizing distortion*, involved in A/D conversion. If we had used a 16-bit analog to digital converter, we would have a range of 2^{16} or 65536 values to choose from,

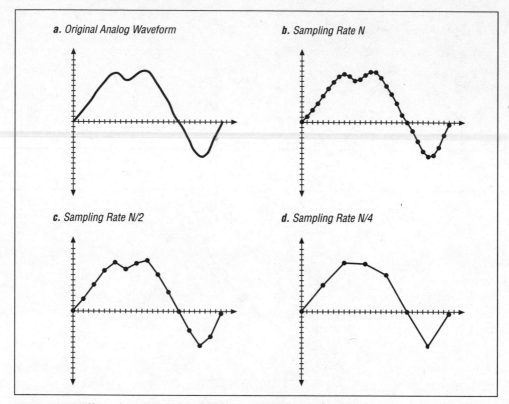

Figure 2–2: Effect of sampling rate on analog to digital conversion

rather than 256. There would be more values for the analog to digital converter to choose from between 28 and 29 units, and the quantizing error would be reduced.

With a larger sample size the range of sound values that can be represented is also larger. Usually called *dynamic range*, this means that both very loud and very quiet sounds can be accurately represented.

Why not then use a large sample size? Again, the amount of storage needed increases (e.g., we need to store 16 rather than 8 bits for each sample). More important, for each additional bit of sample size, our A/D conversion must be twice as accurate, which means that it is more expensive. Making accurate samples also takes time, so there is a trade-off between the sample size and sampling rate. The most common sample sizes are 8 and 16 bits, because these fit nicely into the 8 bit bytes of memory used by most computers.

Enough theory, let's do some simple back-of-the-envelope calculations to get some idea of what sample rate and size mean in real terms.

Modern telephone switching systems typically store speech in digital form. A sampling rate of 8 kHz (8000 samples per second) and a sample size of 8 bits are typical. These values are also comparable to what a sound card could use to store speech data to a file. In order to store 10 seconds of speech data, the amount of space required would be:

10 seconds x 8000 samples/sec x 8 bits/sample = 640,000 bits or 80 Kilobytes

This value is certainly manageable for disk or even memory storage. At this rate, a high density floppy disk could hold approximately 3 minutes of speech. However, it would not be very acceptable for music, since according to the sampling theorem, only frequencies up to 4 kHz would be accurately reproduced. Music can contain frequencies as high as the human ear can perceive, somewhere between 10 and 20 kHz, depending on the listener.

How about a music CD? Audio compact discs use a sampling rate of 44100 samples per second and a sample size of 16 bits. They also store two channels of data (i.e., stereo). A typical 60-minute CD would then contain:

60 mins x 60 secs/min x 44100 samples/sec x 2 bytes/sample x 2 channels = 635,040,000 bytes or about 600 megabytes

This wouldn't fit on a floppy, and probably not even on your hard disk. It is, not surprisingly, typical of the amount of storage you get on a CD-ROM (about 640 megabytes).

There are some techniques that can reduce these storage requirements. Sound data typically has a lot of redundancy and can be compressed, either using compression algorithms such as those used for computer data, or specialized algorithms specifically optimized for sound data.

The coding schemes mentioned above were assumed to be linear; that is, the digitized values were proportional to the sound intensity. Research shows that the human ear is less able to detect differences in sound level for very loud and very quiet sounds. *Companding* is a technique whereby a modified logarithmic scale is used for encoding, allowing a greater range of values to be represented in a smaller sample size (with more quantizing error at the very high and very low levels). A common companding algorithm is known as μ-law,[*] which effectively stores about 12 bits of data in 8-bit samples. Some sound cards have hardware support for μ-law, reducing the overhead of performing the encoding and decoding in software. Digital telephone systems in North America commonly use μ-law encoding.[†]

There are other parameters that influence sound quality, such as noise, frequency response, and various types of distortion. These are rather technical and mainly of interest to hardware engineers so they won't be covered further.

---

[*] μ is the Greek letter mu, pronounced "mew."
[†] European systems use a slightly different format known as A-law, presumably adapted to the European ear. This format is not commonly used for computer audio.

In summary, digital sampling is one of the newer techniques for producing sound, having been made affordable by recent advances and cost reductions in hardware, especially memory and D/A converters. Its primary advantage is flexibility. Any sound can be digitized, including human speech, music, or sound effects that don't exist in nature. A sampling synthesizer, for example, can use samples recorded from a real musical instrument, such as a piano. Sounds can also be manipulated by computer software once they are stored in digital form. Most modern electronic music instruments use sampling techniques.

FM Synthesis

Many sound cards provide hardware for producing sounds using FM synthesis. FM synthesis is an older technique than digital sampling and is based on modifying simple waveforms and combining them using different combinations of several mathematical operations.

The synthesizer hardware provides a number of voices—the number of simultaneously playable notes—typically between 6 and 20. Each voice is defined in terms of several waveform oscillators (known as *operators*), which are combined to produce a specific sound. FM synthesizers are characterized by the number of voices and operators, and often provide different operating modes that trade off one against the other.

The basic idea is to start with oscillators, hardware circuits that generate sine, triangle, or other simple waveforms with specific frequencies and amplitudes. These are then changed by combining them with another waveform, a process usually called *modulation*.

Figure 2-3 shows a simple example. In (a) we start with a simple sine wave, a signal that is easy to generate but does not produce a very interesting sound on its own. In (b) a second waveform is generated that has a characteristic shape, defined by the attack, decay, sustain, and release parameters. This waveform will be used as an envelope to modulate the sine wave. An electronic circuit combines signals (a) and (b), essentially multiplying them together. The resulting waveform, having a much more complex shape, is shown in (c). By varying the base waveform and the parameters of the modulation envelope, a sound can be produced that is similar to a musical instrument such as a piano.

FM synthesis chips allow several waveforms to be combined in various ways (e.g., added or subtracted). Other effects such as feedback, chorus, echo, and delay can then be added, allowing many different types of sounds to be produced.

The synthesizer parameter settings for a specific sound are known as a *patch* and libraries of these are stored on disk as patch files.[*]

---

[*] The term *patch* dates back to the time when synthesizers were not computer-based, consisting of a complex array of waveform generators, filters, and other hardware devices. The user manually connected the system together using short cables known as *patch cords* to

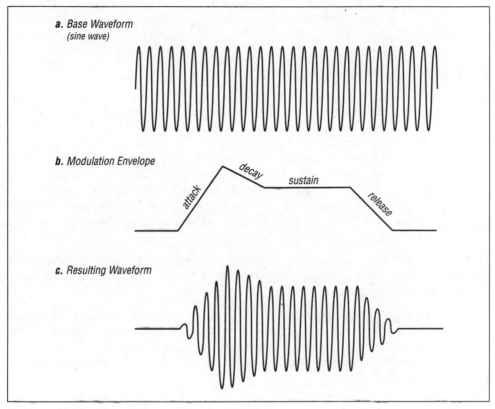

a. Base Waveform
(sine wave)

b. Modulation Envelope

c. Resulting Waveform

Figure 2-3: FM synthesis

If this sounds like a convoluted way to produce the sound of a musical instrument, you are getting the right idea. Most users will obtain and use a predefined set of standard patches, and never change them. A typical patch file defines 128 melodic and 47 percussive instruments, providing quite a wide range of sounds.

The advantage of FM synthesis is that it requires reasonably simple hardware (typically integrated into a single chip) and little software overhead to produce. The main disadvantage is that determining the patch parameters is something of a black art. Producing realistic instrument sounds is difficult, and the results often leave something to be desired.

Professional music systems have generally moved to sampling techniques, but FM synthesis is still useful for backwards compatibility with older equipment and for providing basic sounds with little CPU overhead.

---

obtain the desired sound. Changing patches took minutes or even hours—not very practical in a live concert setting. Anyone remember the Moog synthesizer?

Many sound cards provide both FM synthesis and sampling hardware, and a common approach is to use the FM synthesizer for music, leaving the sampling hardware available for speech or sound effects.

Wavetable Synthesis

Traditional digital sampling is limited because only one D/A converter (or two for systems that support stereo) is available for generating sound, allowing only one sound sample to be played at a time. FM synthesizers, on the other hand, typically have a number of independent sound voices, but, as mentioned in the previous section, the sound quality is poorer. A newer technique known as *wavetable synthesis* combines the best of both. Multiple independent voices are provided, but each voice uses digital sampling, with dedicated RAM provided for downloading the digital samples into memory on the sound card. Once the samples are downloaded, they can be played, combined, and modified using hardware effects with little CPU overhead.

Thus, this technique combines the flexibility and realism of digital sampling with the reduced software complexity and overhead of FM synthesis. Sound cards using wavetable synthesis can also emulate FM synthesizers.

The disadvantage of this technique is that cards supporting wavetable synthesis are currently more expensive. They are also not fully software compatible with the older FM sound cards, a concern if they are to be used with older software applications. The price is coming down, however, as the circuitry becomes integrated into single chip devices.

Mixing

Mixing refers to the process of combining or adding audio signals. Virtually all sound cards provide some mixing capability. Typically you can select from a number of inputs, such as:

- an FM synthesizer

- a sampling D/A converter

- an external line level input

- an external microphone

- a CD-ROM audio input

The mixer combines signals from each input and sends them to one or more outputs. The proportions in which each of the signals are combined (the *gains*) can be controlled, as well as an overall output level control. Stereo devices offer separate controls of the left and right channels—strictly an analog process. You can digitize signals and add them together using software techniques, but mixers generally do this entirely in hardware, without any ongoing computer processing.

I've been talking about software-controlled mixing here. Some cards provide a manual hardware volume control, and many speakers do as well. Some cards provide bass and treble tone controls (which are not strictly mixing functions).

Sound File Formats

The basic idea behind storing sampled sound data to a file is to preserve the digital samples as sequential, time-ordered values. If the data has more than one channel (e.g., stereo) then the samples are usually interleaved. The so-called *raw* file format does this function.

However, given a raw sound file, there is no simple way of determining what type of data the file contains. Therefore, most sound files also contain a header that describes the data in the file, typically including such parameters as:

- Sampling rate
- Sample size
- Number of channels
- Coding format (e.g., linear or μ-law, integer or floating point, signed or unsigned, little-endian or big-endian[*] representation)
- Other miscellaneous information such as a description of the sound data, author and copyright information, etc.

These formats are sometimes referred to as *self-describing* formats. The data may also use some form of compression to reduce the file size.

Sound files are also commonly given (and known by) file extensions that indicate the file format. Let's look at three common formats.

The AU format is common on UNIX workstations, and was originally developed by Sun Microsystems. It uses one channel of 8-bit samples with μ-law encoding. The original Sun workstations supported only an 8 kHz sample rate, so this is the most common. Newer machines also support higher rates. The files may have a header describing the sampling parameters, or they may contain just the raw data. Linux has a special sound device, */dev/audio*, which directly supports this data format, mainly for compatibility with software developed on Sun workstations. The same file format is used on NeXT computers, with the SND file extension.

The VOC format was developed by Creative Labs, maker of SoundBlaster sound cards. This format is reasonably sophisticated and flexible. A file header describes the sampling parameters. A simple type of compression is used that removes periods of silence from the samples.

---

* Little-endian and big-endian refer to whether bits increase in value from right to left or from left to right.

The WAV format developed by IBM and Microsoft is the standard sound file format for Windows. This format is relatively complex and self-describing.

Note that there are utility programs that can convert sound files from one format to another. I'll look at these in Chapter 10, *Applications for Sound and Music*.

MIDI

If you've ever played with, or maybe even written, software to turn your computer into an "electronic organ," you were probably somewhat frustrated with the results when using a computer keyboard like a piano.

On the other hand, if (like me) you have no formal training to play the piano, you may have bought one of those low cost electronic music keyboards thinking you could produce music. The individual notes are impressive, but putting them together in real-time is another matter. If only you could control talent from your computer.

MIDI stands for *Musical Instrument Digital Interface*, and as the name suggests, is a standard hardware and software protocol for allowing electronic musical instruments and computers to communicate with each other. Devices that conform to the MIDI interface can be connected together and communicate over a MIDI bus, a bidirectional serial interface. This method is analogous to the way devices such as modems, mice, and printers can communicate with a computer using an RS-232 serial interface.

Events such as key presses (I'm talking about music keyboards here) are sent as commands over the MIDI bus, allowing the control of devices in real time. MIDI is commonly used to connect and control professional music equipment such as synthesizers, keyboards, drum machines, and even lighting equipment.

A typical MIDI message might contain the following information:

• Which MIDI device the message originated from

• Whether a key was pressed or released

• Which key was pressed

• How hard the key was pressed (or more precisely, the velocity; usually this controls volume)

MIDI files are a standardized way of storing MIDI events in a computer. They can represent the "notes" of a song or the configuration of MIDI devices. You can produce a MIDI file by recording the events from a MIDI keyboard, or creating it on a computer using a MIDI editor program. The files are portable and can be played back on another computer system.

Many sound cards provide a MIDI port, sometimes as an option. Using the port you can communicate with and control MIDI devices. You can "play" synthesizers using MIDI commands or capture music keyboard events and store them as a MIDI file for later playback or editing. MPU-401 is an industry standard for smart MIDI interface cards; some sound boards are compatible with this, others provide only a subset of the functionality.

With suitable software you can also use the on-board FM or wavetable synthesizer of a sound card to play MIDI files. In this case no MIDI bus or MIDI devices are involved.

MIDI events describe the notes, but not the sound of the instrument producing them. A MIDI file played on different systems will probably sound different. The *General MIDI* specification extends the definition to standardize on a number of instruments (or patches) that conforming devices need to provide. The specification only gives names to the patches, for example, "Acoustic Grand Piano." It doesn't describe exactly what they should sound like; that specification is left up to the implementor.

New revisions of the MIDI specification are being developed. Some areas being addressed are creating a level of compatibility between MIDI devices from different vendors and increasing the data rate on the bus.

Adagio

MIDI is not meant to be a human-readable format. Adagio is a music description language developed at Carnegie Mellon University. Musical scores can be composed using Adagio software and played using the appropriate tools. Programs to convert between Adagio and MIDI files are also available.

MOD Files

MIDI and Adagio describe songs in terms of note events, but do not fully describe the sounds used. MOD files (an abbreviation for module files) are a self-contained format for describing a melody as well as the sound samples used to play the song. You use a MOD file editor to create a music composition and a MOD file player to play it. The format was originally developed on and tailored for the Commodore Amiga computer, but MOD software is available for other platforms as well, including Linux.

The advantage of the MOD file format is that it completely describes a song in a flexible and reasonably compact format (typically 30K to 300K bytes in size). The main disadvantage is that generating the effects needed for MOD files in real time requires a lot of CPU processing power, unless they can be performed in hardware. Because the files use a number of fixed, small samples, there is only limited capability to support effects such as vocals. Soundcards using wavetable synthesis offer a distinct advantage here.

A wealth of free MOD files are available on electronic bulletin board systems and Internet archive sites, produced by amateur and semi-professional musicians.

MPEG Audio

MPEG is a working group formed under ISO to define standards for digital video and audio compression. The audio portion of MPEG uses sophisticated algorithms optimized for digital audio that allow quite high compression rates (theoretically up to 22:1 but typically about 6:1). It is called a lossy algorithm because the original data is not reproduced exactly, but a listener should not be able to hear the difference.

Several levels of MPEG audio standards are under development. The lower levels require considerable processing to perform real-time compression and playback, but are just within the reach of PCs and workstations to perform in software. Some commercial and freeware decoding software is available. Higher levels require specialized encoder/decoder hardware.

Other proprietary sound file compression schemes have been developed and sold by computer vendors. An advantage of MPEG is that it is an open specification developed under the auspices of the International Organization for Standardization, an independent standards body. MPEG is slated to be used for applications such as CD-I, CD Video, digital radio, HDTV, and DBS satellite transmission.

A group known as the Internet Underground Music Archive (IUMA) is using the Internet to distribute music in MPEG audio format. Their goal is to maintain a publicly accessible, fast Internet site that archives the music, artwork, and text of any musician, group, or band that wishes their music to be internationally and freely distributed. With the Internet experiencing tremendous growth, they expect the Internet Underground Music Archive to be accessible to the majority of people with computers by the late 1990s.

MPEG encoder and decoder hardware is currently priced beyond the reach of most non-professional users, but is expected to become affordable in the near future as it becomes integrated into single-chip devices.

Miscellaneous Functions

Most sound cards provide a number of additional useful functions, including audio input and output ports, a joystick port, and SCSI and CD-ROM interfaces. You also obviously need speakers for sound output and a microphone for recording live sound.

Some Representative Sound Files

Table 2-1 shows some of the key parameters for a number of typical sound files, for comparison purposes. The first sound file in the table was obtained by directly reading the raw digital data from an audio CD. The file was subsequently converted to other formats using a sound file conversion utility. The MIDI and MOD entries were distinct files, representative of their type.

Table 2-1: Example Sound Files

File Type	Sample Size	Sampling Rate	Duration	File Size	Comments
wav	16 bit	44 kHz	10 secs	1770K	stereo, sampled from CD
wav	8 bit	22 kHz	10 secs	221K	mono
voc	8 bit	22 kHz	10 secs	221K	mono
raw	8 bit	22 kHz	10 secs	221K	raw 8-bit linear samples
au	8 bit	8 kHz	10 secs	80K	µ-law
mod	8 bit	varies	4 mins	280K	MOD file
mid	n/a	n/a	2 mins	15K	MIDI file

Sound Card Comparison

Many sound cards are available, and more are appearing on the market all the time. Which is best? The answer is—it depends. No one card is best; you need to look at a number of factors; most can be summarized as cost, compatibility, and application. You might want to install more than one sound card in your system.

Obviously the amount of money you wish to spend will limit the choice of cards you can consider. Keep in mind you will also need accessories such as speakers, a microphone, and possibly cables to connect to other devices. There is virtually no upper limit on the price you can pay for a sound card.

You need to look at the compatibility of the sound card with the software you intend on using. The Linux kernel supports many, but not all cards. You need to use a supported model, or one that is hardware-compatible with a supported card.

Many sound card "clones" are claimed by the vendors to be compatible with others, but often they are compatible only under MS-DOS using the drivers that the vendors supply. The cards will likely not work under Linux unless special kernel drivers are written for them or they are 100% compatible at the register level.

You always have the option of writing a Linux driver yourself, but even if you are up to the challenge, you will need programming documentation from the sound card vendor; this information is often not available or is included only with the purchase of an expensive software developer's kit. There are also a few software applications under Linux that only work with specific sound cards; check the applications you plan to use (if known) to see if there are any such limitations. Compatibility with other operating systems you run may also be a consideration.

Many users also want to use the sound card under MS-DOS or other operating systems. You should check that appropriate software drivers for the sound card are provided by the manufacturer or operating system vendor. If there are specific software applications you'll be using, make sure they support your sound card.

Another factor to consider is your application. If you want the card mainly for adding sound effects to games, then high sound quality is likely not a priority, and a low-cost card should suffice. If you are a semi-professional musician, then high sound quality and a MIDI interface are likely important to you. You should also think about the future; some sound cards offer options that can be added later, such as a CD-ROM interface.

Table 2-2 lists a number of popular sound cards supported under Linux, and compares their basic features. The cards compared are the SoundBlaster, SoundBlaster Pro, and SoundBlaster 16 from Creative Labs, Gravis UltraSound, and ProAudioSpectrum 16. The intent here is to provide some basis of comparison, not to recommend any one sound card over another. When interpreting the data in the table, keep in mind that some cards exist in different versions or with options that have slightly different capabilities, and that parameters such as the number of operators and voices vary depending on the operating mode selected. Many features have been omitted.

I will offer a few general recommendations when selecting sound hardware. Unless your budget is severely strained, you should opt for a 16-bit rather than 8-bit card. There is little difference in price (in fact by the time you read this, 8-bit cards may be almost unobtainable). As discussed previously, wavetable is the best overall sound card technology. However, if you want compatibility with the most MS-DOS applications (especially games), a SoundBlaster or 100% compatible is generally the best choice.

Table 2–2: Sound Card Comparison

	Sound-Blaster	Sound-Blaster Pro	Sound-Blaster 16	Gravis Ultra-sound	ProAudio Spec-trum 16
Digital Playback:					
sample size (bits)	8	8	16	16	16
maximum sampling rate	44K	44K	44K	44K	44K
channels	1	2	2	2	2
Digital Recording:					
sample size (bits)	8	8	16	8	16
maximum sampling rate	12K	44K	44K	44K	44K
channels	1	2	2	2	2
FM Synthesis:					
number of voices	11	11/20	11/20	n/a	11/20
number of operators	2	4/2	4/2	n/a	4/2

Table 2-2: Sound Card Comparison (continued)

	Sound-Blaster	Sound-Blaster Pro	Sound-Blaster 16	Gravis Ultra-sound	ProAudio Spec-trum 16
Wavetable Synthesis:					
number of voices	n/a	n/a	n/a	32	n/a
Other Features:					
MIDI interface	N	Y	Y	Y	N
CD-ROM interface	N	Y	Y	N	Y
joystick port	Y	Y	Y	N	N

CHAPTER THREE

CD-ROM

CD-ROM (Compact Disc Read-Only Memory) is another key technology for multimedia. Its primary use is as a medium for delivery of multimedia data. In this chapter I'll review some of the terms and key concepts that are prerequisites for understanding how to develop your own multimedia applications.

What Can a CD-ROM Drive Do?

Most computer users have at least one hard disk drive as the primary mass storage device, a floppy drive for data transfer with other systems, and maybe a tape drive for archival purposes. How does a CD-ROM drive fit into the storage hierarchy?

The main advantage of CD-ROM storage is the large amount of data capacity (I'll have more to say about this shortly). It provides reasonably fast access time (generally in between floppy and hard disk speeds) and lower cost per megabyte than floppy or hard disk. The media is also very reliable.

A CD mounted on a workstation running Linux can export the data to other machines in a network using NFS or other networking protocols.

A side benefit of CD-ROM is compatibility with audio CD technology. So this brings the price of the hardware down. But it also adds versatility, as most CD-ROM drives are capable of playing audio CDs, either through headphones or a sound card. CD-ROM is therefore ideal for many multimedia applications, because of the large storage capacity needed for sound and graphics files.

CD-ROM Technology

CD-ROM is a mass storage technology that uses an optical laser to read microscopic "pits" on the thin metal layer of a plastic disc. The physical format is identical to that used for audio compact discs. Because it uses optical methods, it cannot be damaged by magnetic fields. As there is no physical contact with the disk, the life of the media is quite long—probably longer than a human lifetime, and possibly as long as 1000 years.

CD-ROMs provide read-only storage, and can be manufactured in high volume at low material cost (less than US$1 per disc).

The maximum storage capacity of a single disk is approximately 650 megabytes, equivalent to over 500 high density 3.5" floppy disks or roughly 250,000 typed pages.

First generation drives (known as single-speed drives), provide a transfer rate of approximately 150 kilobytes per second. Double-speed drives are commonly available, and triple, quadruple, and higher speed drives have been introduced. Single speed is essentially obsolete; you might consider buying one if it is available at a very low cost and if speed is not important to you, but they are not suitable for multimedia applications (they work fine for playing audio CDs, though).

Most drives support a single CD, but there are multi-disc players that support 6, 12, or even more than 100 discs, although only one is loaded at any one time. These are sometimes called jukeboxes.

A minor point on nomenclature: although this is not universally followed, a common convention is to use the word "disk" to refer to read/write media such a floppies and hard drives, and "disc" to refer to read-only media.

Some of the CD-ROM standards are known by the colors of the published books. The "Red Book" is a common name for the Compact Disc Digital Audio standard. "Yellow Book" is the standard for computer-based CD-ROM. "Green Book" is the CD-I standard. "Orange Book" is the standard for write-once compact discs, and "White Book" covers video CDs.

CD-ROM Interfaces

Some CD-ROM drives use a proprietary (i.e., vendor-unique) interface between the computer and drive. Often the interface is included as part of a sound card, reducing the overall cost and avoiding the need to fill an extra bus slot. Users who do not wish to buy a sound card can buy a low-cost interface card that provides only the CD-ROM interface circuitry normally found on the sound card.

The main disadvantage of this scheme is that the sound card interface often limits your choice of CD-ROM drives, and may only support a single device. However, some of these interfaces do support multiple drives per interface card (and some also support multiple interface cards).

The interface circuitry on the sound card is minimal, much like the IDE floppy and hard disk drives, leading some people to incorrectly refer to them as IDE CD-ROM drives.

Many CD-ROM drives use the Small Computer Systems Interface, the same SCSI interface popular with hard disk drives, tape drives, and many other peripherals. SCSI offers good performance and the ability to add multiple devices. You can also choose drives from any one of many vendors, and in the future upgrade to a faster or larger drive (or keep the drive when you upgrade the computer).

SCSI interfaces are generally more expensive than proprietary interfaces, and a separate SCSI controller card is needed. Some sound cards do provide the interface, however, avoiding the need for a separate controller card.

It should be noted that some sounds cards use a "SCSI-like" interface with a special interface card. These are typically not fully SCSI-compatible and not suitable for use with other SCSI devices.

The IDE (or ATA) standard for hard disk drives has been extended to add more functionality; the new standard is called ATAPI or enhanced IDE. Many ATAPI CD-ROM drives are now on the market. These provide much the same advantages as IDE hard drives: low cost and good performance. Like SCSI, they also offer the ability to support multiple devices and large device sizes. ATAPI CD-ROM drives typically connect to the same disk controller used for hard and floppy drives and are currently the most popular choice for PC systems.

Filesystems

Like hard disks, CD-ROM drives are formatted with a filesystem. Unlike hard drives, however, the filesystem types are standardized and portable across most operating systems.

The original CD-ROM filesystem was unofficially called High Sierra. After it was adapted as an official ISO standard, with a few minor modifications, it was designated ISO 9660. Many people use the two terms interchangeably. The ISO 9660 filesystem is something of a "least common denominator" format. Filenames are limited to the MS-DOS style 8+3 character format, all uppercase. There can be up to eight levels of subdirectories.

For UNIX-compatible systems like Linux, these restrictions are, well, too restrictive. The *Rock Ridge Interchange Protocol* (RRIP) uses some undefined fields in the ISO 9660 format to support UNIX features such as long filenames, symbolic links, and more levels of subdirectories. Virtually all CD-ROMs use the ISO 9660 filesystem, and many support the Rock Ridge extensions. A few other filesystems are in use, most notably the Apple Macintosh HFS and Sun Microsystems file systems.

There are also "hybrid" CDs, which provide several filesystems (e.g., both ISO 9660 and HFS filesystems) on the same disc, making them usable on different computer systems.

The Inheriting File System (IFS) is a Linux kernel driver that allows you to mount multiple filesystems at the same point. It is similar to the Translucent File System provided under SunOS. A read-only CD-ROM filesystem and a read/write hard disk directory can be mounted at a common point. All CD-ROM data can be accessed, while at the same time new files can be added to any of the directories being stored on the hard disk. Files can also be modified or deleted, which is useful for systems that are primarily CD-ROM-based but that require some file changes. For example, you could mount the directory */etc* from a live CD-ROM filesystem and still retain the ability to change files such as */etc/HOSTNAME* that require local modification.

Finally, it should be noted that the capability of reading CD-ROM filesystems is entirely dependent on the operating system, and not the CD-ROM drive itself. Thus, there are no "Macintosh HFS" compatible CD-ROM drives; to the hardware it is just data.

Specialized Uses

CD-ROM discs are physically the same as those used for audio CD, although the data is stored somewhat differently. Most, but not all, CD-ROM drives support playing audio CDs.[*] These drives typically provide an analog sound output that can be fed into a sound card and played through speakers. Note that when you read an audio disc, a CD-ROM drive runs at the speed of a single speed drive. Don't buy a quad speed drive and use it only for playing audio CDs!

Some multimedia CDs contain both an ISO 9660 format filesystem as well as one or more audio CD tracks. Such CDs are sometimes called hybrid discs, although the term is also used to refer to discs with more than one type of filesystem. These CDs provide one way to implement sound in a multimedia application, but accessing digital and audio data at the same time is not generally feasible. This system is more practical for an application that first loads a program or data from CD-ROM, then switches to using the CD for audio playback.

When playing audio CDs, the CD-ROM drive is using an analog signal output. Some drives also support reading the data from audio CDs in digital form. The data can then be saved to disk as a sound file, producing an exact digital copy. But before you run out and copy your CD collection to hard disk, keep in mind the storage requirements we calculated in Chapter 1, *Multimedia and Linux*.

There are software applications that play audio CDs in a CD-ROM drive using a graphical user interface that operates much like a consumer CD player. You can click on graphical play, stop, skip, and other buttons to control the player.

CD-I stands for Compact Disc-Interactive, a standard for discs that are intended to be used with a standalone playback machine for consumer use that supports audio and video. The disc contains data and the software to run on the playback unit.

---

* Some audio CD players will attempt to play CD-ROMs containing computer data. The noise produced is essentially random and very loud. Turn down the volume before trying this!

CD-I discs are not intended for running directly on PCs, but rather on the embedded CD-I processor. (CD-I processors in a PC card are becoming available, though, which would allow you to run a CD-I disc on a PC.)

PhotoCD is a process developed by Kodak whereby photographic images are digitized using a scanner and stored on a CD-ROM disc. The images can be retrieved and viewed on a computer using appropriate software. Many photo labs now offer PhotoCD as an alternative to conventional film prints. A laser burns the data into a dye layer on the disc (which has a distinctive gold color). Up to 100 images can be stored on a disc and each image is stored in five different resolutions, from 128 by 192 pixels to 2048 by 3072 pixels, at 24 bit color resolution. Depending on whether the display device is a television monitor, a personal computer, or a workstation with a large 24-bit display, an appropriate image size and resolution can be chosen.

There is a more expensive variant called ProPhotoCD, which also stores images, but at 4096 by 6144. This resolution provides a higher image quality suitable for professional photographic work.

New images can be subsequently added to a PhotoCD. Because the data on disc cannot be changed, a new index area is written each time the CD is updated. Reading the new data requires a CD-ROM drive that supports these "multisession" discs.

Writable CD-ROM drives can be used to create "one off" discs using the same technology as PhotoCDs. The drives are significantly more expensive than read-only drives, but prices are dropping. These can be cost effective for low-volume applications, or to produce a master that will subsequently be duplicated in volume after testing.

CHAPTER FOUR

GRAPHICS AND VIDEO

When conveying information, there is often no substitute for the visual medium. As the saying goes, "a picture is worth a thousand words." Many concepts are difficult to describe in print, and are best shown using pictures, diagrams, and graphs.

Moving images, with sound added, take this concept one step further. Sadly perhaps, those people raised in our television-based society may relate best to video-based information. Unlike television however, computer-based video can be interactive. The user can stop, rewind, fast forward, or view in slow motion if desired, making it particularly applicable to multimedia-based training.

In this chapter I discuss video technology, starting with graphics, then moving on to animation and full-motion video.

Graphics Basics

When in graphics mode, virtually all modern computers use bitmapped displays, in which the dots or pixels that make up the image are mapped into corresponding bits in memory. This memory is usually on a video card, and is called *video memory*, or a *frame buffer*, to distinguish it from the computer's main memory.

For a simple monochrome display, each pixel is either black or white, so a single bit can define the state. Figure 4-1 illustrates how the video memory is mapped into a two-dimensional array of pixels on the screen. In this 640 by 480 pixel display, one bit of video memory is mapped to a single pixel.

Even though the display can only present black and white, by using an alternating pattern of black and white pixels the human eye will perceive intermediate shades of gray. This process, known as *dithering*, is commonly used by dot matrix and laser printers to represent grayscale images. The disadvantage of dithering is the loss of resolution due to a need for several pixels to represent each "gray" value.

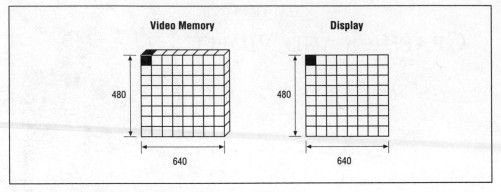

Figure 4–1: Monochrome display

A true grayscale display can handle several shades of intensity between black and white. In this case several bits of memory are used to define the shade of gray for each pixel. This idea can be conceptualized as a third dimension, so that the video memory now consists of a number of *bit planes*. Figure 4-2 shows a monochrome display with 4 bits per pixel, allowing 2^4 or 16 different gray levels. With a digital video monitor, these four pixel values may directly correspond to four hardware signals on the video hardware. Most modern video monitors are analog devices, accepting a continuously variable input level. In this case, the video card would use a digital to analog converter to adapt the pixel values in video memory to a suitable level for the monitor.

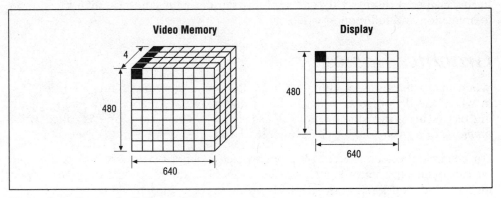

Figure 4–2: Grayscale display

Color displays are produced by combining the three primary colors red, green, and blue, in various combinations. Figure 4-3 shows a system with 24-bit planes, 8 bits for each of the red, green, and blue color levels. Each pixel takes on any of 2^{24} or roughly 16 million colors. The system would utilize three digital to analog converters.

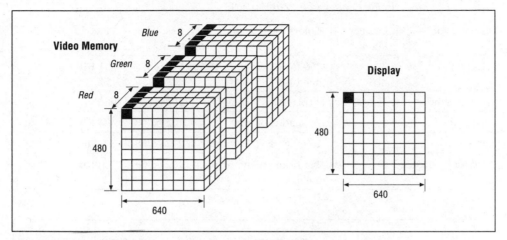

Figure 4-3: Color display

The problem with the previous example is the large amount of video memory required—in this case, 3 bytes per pixel. Many video systems use what is known as a *palette* (sometimes called a colormap or color lookup table). In this case, fewer bits are stored per pixel. The pixel values are used as indexes into a lookup table of colors. Figure 4-4 shows a system with 8 bits per pixel, indexing into a 24-bit palette with 256 entries. With this system we can still choose from 16 million different colors, but only 256 unique colors can be displayed simultaneously. Memory requirements are reduced from the system in Figure 4-3 by almost a factor of 3. The disadvantages are the reduced number of simultaneous colors and the extra software complexity required to maintain the lookup tables.

As with monochrome displays, dithering can be used to simulate additional colors by using alternating patterns of pixels that average out to the desired color. The disadvantage is the loss in resolution and the extra processing required to calculate the appropriate pixel values.

Table 4-1 shows how the different video displays compare in their usage of video memory, for two common video resolutions.

Table 4-1: Video Display Comparison

Display Type	Bits Per Pixel	Colors	Resolution	Video Memory
monochrome	1	2 (black and white)	640x480	38 KB
grayscale	4	16 shades of gray	640x480	150 KB
color	24	16 million	640x480	900 KB

Table 4–1: Video Display Comparison (continued)

Display Type	Bits Per Pixel	Colors	Resolution	Video Memory
color with palette	8	256 from palette of 16 million	640x480	301 KB
monochrome	1	2 (black and white)	1024x768	96 KB
grayscale	4	16 shades of gray	1024x768	384 KB
color	24	16 million	1024x768	2.3 MB
color with palette	8	256 from palette of 16 million	1024x768	769 KB

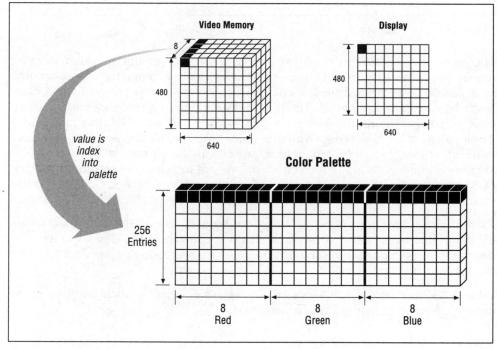

Figure 4–4: Color display with palette

Users of 8-bit pixel depth video cards are probably accustomed to the phenomenon called "color flashing" or "technicolor." When displaying several graphic images simultaneously, the windowing system may change the colormap to fit the window with the current focus, causing the colors in the other windows to change wildly. As the cost of video memory and graphics controller chips come down, 24-bit displays like the one in Figure 4-3 are becoming more affordable, and this effect is becoming a relic of the past.

Under the X Window System, the program *xdpyinfo* will display a lot of information about your video hardware including the number of bitplanes and the number of colormaps.

If you are shopping for a video card and comparing advertised specifications, watch out for an area of possible confusion. An *n* bit video card may refer to a card with *n* bits per pixel, or it may refer to a card that fits into a slot with an *n* bit data bus. For example, a video card that uses the PCI bus may be referred to as a "32-bit video card," even though it may only support 8 bits per pixel. Similarly, a 24-bit per pixel video card may be designed for a 16-bit wide ISA bus slot.

Graphics Formats

The obvious way of storing a computer image in a file is to simply save a representation of the video memory; these are usually called bitmap or raster files. An obvious improvement is to add some header information to the file to indicate the size of the image and the pixel depth.

Compression Techniques

The key problem with bitmap files is the amount of storage required. Compression techniques can reduce the size dramatically. A simple but effective compression scheme is run-length encoding. Graphics images often contain sequences of pixels with the same color value. Rather than storing each pixel, run-length encoding stores the length of the repeated data, followed by the value to be repeated.

Other techniques, similar to those used for compressing binary files, can also be used on graphics images. All of these techniques are lossless—that is, the original data can be exactly recovered when uncompressed. For many graphics applications, minor differences can be tolerated. So-called lossy algorithms have been developed specifically for graphics that provide very high compression ratios, at the expense of some degradation from the original image. In some cases the user can control the trade-off between compression ratio and degradation as a parameter when compressing the file.

Fractal compression is a recent technique based on fractals. Anyone familiar with the Mandelbrot set has seen the intricate and complex images that are produced by a simple algorithm. If an inverse transformation for an image could be found, then a simple fractal equation might describe a complex image. One of the pioneers of fractals and iterated function systems, Michael Barnsley, has formed a company to develop and market fractal-based compression. The company initially reported extremely high compression rates.

While the company has so far kept most of its results confidential, it appears that the initial claims for fractal compression were based on a few manually constructed examples and were not representative of the general case. Time will tell if fractal compression is superior to other more traditional techniques.

Non-Bitmapped Formats

Other file formats are used for graphics that are not based on arrays of pixels.

Vector files describe drawings using mathematical equations and are commonly used for CAD systems (which often use pen-based plotters for output).

Metafiles can combine both bitmapped and vector graphics data.

Page Description Languages (PDL) describe the layout of a printed page containing graphics and text. PostScript is the most common PDL, and is implemented as a stack-based interpretive language somewhat like the computer language Forth. PDL provides an efficient and reasonably portable way of describing documents.

Some Representative Image Formats

Table 4-2 lists the characteristics of some representative graphics files. The original image was taken from a PhotoCD and stored in various formats.

Table 4–2: Example Graphics Files

File Extension	File Size	Compression Ratio	Comments
pcd	4,907,008	n/a	PhotoCD (5 resolutions)
bmp	1,179,702	1:1	raw bitmap (768x512)
gif	333,437	4:1	GIF
jpeg	7,329	161:1	1% quality
jpeg	11,830	100:1	5% quality
jpeg	19,131	62:1	10% quality
jpeg	59,997	20:1	50% quality
jpeg	91,862	13:1	75% quality
jpeg	224,874	5:1	95% quality
ppm	1,179,704	1:1	portable pixmap
ppm	4,797,291	5 times larger	portable pixmap (ASCII)
rgb	1,175,492	1:1	Iris
tif	1,179,800	1:1	TIFF
ps	2,394,708	2 times larger	PostScript
Z	1,013,495	1:1	bmp file run through *compress*
gz	957,079	1:1	bmp file run through *gzip*

The original PhotoCD file contains an image in five resolutions, ranging from 192x128 to 3072x2048. The 768x512 image was used for the conversions. The file used 24-bit color resolution.

The second column of the table shows the file sizes in bytes, while the third indicates the amount of compression relative to a bitmap file. The plain bitmap format was chosen as the reference because it just contains raw data. A compression ratio of 2:1 indicates a file that is half as large as the uncompressed version, while 1:1 indicates no significant compression.

The GIF format gives reasonable compression (mostly because the GIF format stores only 8-bit colors). GIF uses Lempel-Ziv compression and is very good for images that contain many pixels of the same color such as line drawings or presentation graphics. The maximum of 256 different colors is rarely a problem with these types of images. It is a lossless format.

JPEG gives very good compression. There was no noticeable degradation of this image until the 10% quality level (5% had considerable degradation and at 1% the image was virtually unrecognizable). JPEG is a lossy compression scheme, and works best for images such as photographs that contain many colors and non-geometric objects. Unlike GIF, it supports 24-bit color. JPEG is less suited to line graphics, where the errors in compression and uncompression may be visible as irregularities in lines and other regular objects.

Portable pixmap (PPM) is a standardized color bitmap format that includes a small header, hence it is only a few bytes larger than a plain bitmap file. The ASCII portable pixmap format represents the image using printable ASCII numbers, and is five times larger (this format is useful for sending images by electronic mail).

Iris and TIFF formats are essentially the same size as the bitmap. PostScript is roughly twice as large as bitmap, mainly because it represents images as bits converted to ASCII. The image is also monochrome (but typically uses dithering).

Compressing the bitmap file using the standard compression utilities *compress* and *gzip* reduces it only by about 20%, illustrating that graphics-specific compression schemes are much more effective than general purpose compression tools.

Graphics formats are important to multimedia, but are equally applicable to other imaging technologies such as FAX. Utilities exist for converting between virtually all of the image formats. Some of the more sophisticated techniques (JPEG, fractal compression) are sometimes encoded or decoded using dedicated hardware.

Full-Motion Video

Full-motion video is a logical extension to graphic images. Displaying a series of images over time produces the illusion of animation. In addition to horizontal and vertical resolution and number of colors, an important specification for animation is the *frame rate*—the number of images that are displayed per unit of time. A common standard for comparison is 30 frames per second, the rate used for North American television systems.

Another distinction that can be made is animation versus video. Animation generally refers to images that consist of diagrams, line drawings, and the like. They typically demand fewer colors and a lower frame rate. Images from television or motion pictures are generally classified as video.

A very simplistic approach to animation is to string together a number of graphic images, displaying them sequentially. Obviously this will require a lot of data to be transferred, limiting the frame rate that can be achieved. As a simple example, a 640x480 image with 8 bits per pixel requires about 300K of storage. At 30 frames per second, the data being transferred is roughly 9 megabytes per second. This is significantly faster than can be achieved with a typical hard disk drive. We need to reduce the frame rate, reduce the image size, or use some form of compression.

Imagine a video sequence showing a person's face as they are speaking. The background portions of the video images will be essentially unchanged if the camera position does not move. Adjacent frames will tend to be similar, so compression techniques based on the changes from one image to another can reduce the file size, and thus the amount of data to be transferred. Lossy compression algorithms optimized for video can also be used. With these algorithms, the data rate is compressed down to a level that can be met by a double-speed CD-ROM drive.

It is also useful to include sound information in the same file as the animation. In order to allow the sound to be produced in synchronization, the sound and video are usually *interleaved*. A small quantity of video data is followed by the accompanying quantity of audio data, then the next piece of video data, and so on.

In general, software-based approaches to decompression are limited in size, frame rate, and image quality. Hardware-based approaches are needed for anything approaching NTSC video quality, the North American television standard. Decompression hardware, sometimes referred to as video codecs, is rapidly coming down in price. We may soon see today's videocassette replaced by video CD technology, just as the vinyl record album has been supplanted by CD digital audio.

A Sampling of Video File Formats

Table 4-3 lists the specifications for a few representative video files.

MPEG refers to a series of standards for digital video and audio developed by the Moving Pictures Experts Group. MPEG-1 offers approximately the same resolution as NTSC video. Using sophisticated compression algorithms, it can compress a 320x240 full-motion video data stream down to 1.5 megabits per second, a data rate that can be accommodated by a single speed CD-ROM drive. MPEG-2 is designed for higher resolution video for broadcast television and video on demand systems, using a 720x480 resolution. This requires a higher data rate, but offers audio and video quality comparable to VCR systems.

QuickTime is a video and animation format developed by Apple Computer. Initially available only for Apple Macintosh systems, viewers are also now available for other operating systems. QuickTime files can support sound as well as video.

AVI (Audio-Video Interleaved) is the animation and video format developed by Microsoft for Windows. AVI supports a number of different compression schemes and varying resolutions. Sound is also supported.

FLC is an animation format used by the Autodesk Animator software package, which runs under MS-DOS.

Table 4–3: Example Video Files

File Type	Image Resolution	Frames	Duration	File Size	Comments
mpg	192x144	683	2 mins	2MB	MPEG-1 video
mov	128x84	1045	40 secs	3MB	QuickTime video
flc	452x339	62	20 secs	758 KB	FLC animation
avi	160x120	206	20 secs	1.5MB	AVI video

In Chapter 11, *Applications for Graphics and Animation*, I'll look at applications for displaying these files.

CHAPTER FIVE

HYPERTEXT, HYPERMEDIA, AND THE WORLD WIDE WEB

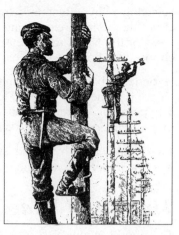

U p to now I've focused on some specific technologies: sound, CD-ROM, and video. These are important, and individually they can and have been used on their own for computer applications. But to truly be considered multimedia, we need something more, something like hypertext.

Hypertext and Hypermedia

Traditional computer text is based on the familiar printed page metaphor. Documents are essentially laid out like books, for users to read through in a sequential manner. You may be able to search for text, but there is no easy way to backtrack to where you were reading before the search.

Most computer files are straight text, and are generally stored in one file, or as a collection of files on one computer system. There may be provision for graphics, but not for audio or video. How often do you print out a computer file to read it?

More than 30 years ago, a new type of document was envisioned that broke away from the printed page metaphor. *Hypertext* refers to a document that contains traditional text as well as *links* to other parts of the document, or other documents. The reader can move around the document by selecting the links, or backtrack to places that have been previously visited. The linked documents may be physically distributed across different computers or networks. The ability to follow hypertext links at will allows the reader to find information in a non-linear, interactive fashion, more attuned to the way in which people work and think.

As a hypothetical example, we could imagine reading a hypertext document about the history of computing. Part of the document might refer to Linux, and mention that it was written by Linus Torvalds, a student at the University of Helsinki, Finland. A hypertext link from the word "Finland" might point to another article describing this country, mentioning that one of Finland's chief exports is herring.

Selecting a hypertext link from the word "herring" could bring up information about that animal, explaining that it is a gregarious edible fish found in the colder areas of the North Atlantic. After this brief foray into ichthyology, the reader might choose to follow the links back to the original text concerned with computers.

Hypertext that includes multimedia information such as sound, graphics, and video, is sometimes referred to as *hypermedia*. In our hypothetical example above, a hypermedia system might have allowed us to hear Linus Torvalds' voice, see a map of Finland, and view a short video showing herring being caught.

Two commercial hypertext systems that many readers may be familiar with are Apple's HyperCard and the Microsoft Windows help system.

The World Wide Web

The World Wide Web is a distributed hypertext system, originally designed at CERN, the European center for particle physics. The system is distributed over the Internet, the global "network of networks" that includes thousands of individual computer networks and millions of computers.

The World Wide Web is a powerful medium that allows developers to make their hypermedia information readily available to many users. It's also easy to use and is being extended constantly, making it a good structure for multimedia in general.

To access the Web, you use a program known as a viewer or browser. Most browsers offer an intuitive graphical user interface, so there is virtually no learning curve to use the system. One of the first popular browsers was *Mosaic*, developed by the National Center for Supercomputing Applications (NCSA) in the USA. A number of other browsers are available now, with varying capabilities, running on almost every conceivable computing platform.

The Web browser runs as a client program, communicating with a Web server, in most cases using HyperText Transfer Protocol (HTTP). HTTP is the method by which users request information, and the Web server responds to their requests. The server returns the information in a machine-independent format, and also provides security controls to control access to information. Users normally do not have to concern themselves with the underlying HTTP protocol, as the Web browser programs take care of this task.

Most browsers are graphical, with the ability to display in-line graphics. For file formats that cannot be directly handled, external viewers are called. The browser typically looks at the file extension to determine what viewer to use (e.g., ".ps" for PostScript, ".au" for sound, ".mpg" for MPEG video).

Every hypertext page on the Web can be identified using a Uniform Resource Locator, or URL. The URL defines the protocol to use, the address of the computer system, and a UNIX-style pathname to the destination. Figure 5-1 shows the format of a URL and lists some examples.

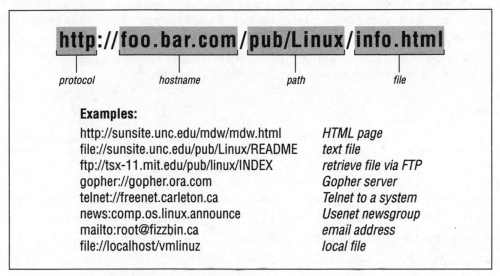

Figure 5–1: The Uniform Resource Locator (URL)

If omitted, the fields assume default values, and relative pathnames can be used. Users typically use URLs when pointing their Web browsers to a site. URLs are also used within hypertext links to point to other Web pages.

HTML

Most World Wide Web hypertext documents themselves are written in HyperText Markup Language (HTML), a simple language for describing the information contained in hypertext pages and the links between pages. Even though the markup language is quite simple, it is surprisingly powerful. HTML itself directly supports only text and graphics,* but URLs can point to multimedia objects such as sound files, videos, and animations, which can be viewed using external programs. HTML also supports links to information accessed using other protocols such as ftp, Telnet, Usenet news, and electronic mail.

Using the Common Gateway Interface (CGI), HTML pages can be generated by programs that run on an HTTP server, allowing the creation of dynamic content based on user input. Users of the Web do not need to know HTML, but creating Web pages generally requires a knowledge of the language, although there are tools to aid in the editing process.

---

* There are some proprietary extensions to HTML to support playing of sound and simple animation but these are not part of the official HTML specification and are not supported by most Web browsers.

The World Wide Web is growing quickly in popularity, and the cost of connecting to the Internet is going down as the number of users is expanding. Many commercial, government, and educational sites are scrambling to get on the Web.

We will see in Chapter 17, *Using Toolkits for Multimedia Programming*, how HTML can be used for developing standalone multimedia systems.

MIME

MIME (Multipurpose Internet Mail Extensions) is a standard for attaching multimedia information to electronic messages. Initially intended for electronic mail, MIME is now being used on the World Wide Web and other areas. In the past, many software vendors developed their own mutually incompatible protocols for transferring multimedia information by mail. MIME is a freely available, vendor-independent specification that makes all compliant systems compatible.

Some of the formats supported by MIME are:

- Non-ASCII character sets
- Graphic images
- Animations
- Sound
- File attachments
- PostScript
- HTML hypertext links

MIME offers a standard means of extending electronic mail beyond a simple text-based mode of communication. Most World Wide Web browsers use the MIME configuration files to map file types to appropriate multimedia viewer programs.

Hyper-G

Hyper-G is an attempt to solve some limitations of the current HTML-based World Wide Web technology. The current Web architecture is limited in its support for full-text search tools and user authorization. One approach is to link the Web to database systems such as Gopher servers, but these are still a collection of individual databases. Search engines that make use of databases generated by "web-crawlers" are having more difficulty staying current as the size of the Web increases. More sophisticated tools are needed to organize the information in these multiple databases in a coherent fashion.

Researchers at Graz University of Technology in Austria are developing the Hyper-G system as a replacement for the World Wide Web that addresses these issues while building on what has been learned from the Web. It still supports links to the WWW and Gopher systems. Using Hyper-G, data distributed across many databases can be combined and searched for. There are facilities to control authorization—who can read data and who can change it.

Hyper-G is at a pre-release stage but is currently being used at some universities and commercial sites. *Harmony* is a Mosaic-like browser for Hyper-G that runs on X11 systems.

It is still too soon to know if Hyper-G will become the successor to the World Wide Web, but it does offer a number of interesting capabilities, making it something to watch in the future.

VRML

VRML stands for Virtual Reality Modeling Language, a standardized language for describing three-dimensional scenes containing objects. The language describes the object's position, dimensions, color, textures, and possibly even higher-level behaviors. As well as describing scenes, the language supports hypertext links (using URLs) to other entities.

VRML essentially extends the Web to support three-dimensional graphics and sound, which is a new and exciting area of multimedia development. The VRML language is evolving at a rapid pace.

Java

The developers of Java at Sun Microsystems have described the language as "a simple, object-oriented, distributed, interpreted, robust, secure, architecture-neutral, portable, high-performance, multithreaded, dynamic, buzzword-compliant, general-purpose programming language."

The idea behind Java is to extend the capabilities of the Internet by allowing users to write small applications (called *applets*) in the Java language that can be downloaded and executed locally by any Web browser program that supports Java.

Java syntax is based on a simplified subset of the C++ language. Unlike C++, the language has no pointers and implements garbage collection. The source code is compiled into a machine independent format that is portable across all Java language interpreters. Security features guard against applets that perform undesired functions (e.g., deleting files on a local disk).

Java is ideal for creating applications that go beyond what is possible with HTML: animation, sound, and interaction with the user are possible. Many Web browsers now directly support Java. Developed at Sun Microsystems, the language specification and source code for the development kit are being made freely available.

Java is being predicted to be the major programming language for developing portable multimedia applications in the future. Vendors that have licensed Java include Netscape, IBM, Borland, Adobe, Silicon Graphics, and Microsoft.

SGML

Related to HTML is SGML, the Standard Generalized Markup Language. An ISO standard, SGML is a standardized way of describing the structure and format of documents. A Document Type Definition, or DTD, is written in SGML and defines a specific document type. Using the structure defined by a DTD, tools are written to format or translate documents between different formats. This book was written using a DTD known as DocBook, a standard for computer documentation and technical books. Many of the Linux HOWTO documents are written using a DTD specifically designed for the purpose. This system allows the same document source files to be formatted in HTML, ASCII text, and PostScript, using a number of text-processing tools.

SGML is expected to become more popular, as desktop publishing tools move away from proprietary file formats that are not interchangeable. HTML is defined by an SGML DTD, and also bears a resemblance to the SGML language (but it is not, strictly speaking, a subset).

HyTime

HyTime is Hypermedia/Time-based Structuring Language, ISO/IEC/ANSI standard 10744. It is a language for describing the structure of hypermedia documents and can be considered an extension of SGML. HyTime adds to SGML support for the addressing of document objects, the ability to describe the relationships between document objects, and the numeric measurement of objects. The objects can include true multimedia such as sound and video clips.

HyTime has been used as the framework for SMDL, the Standard Music Description Language (ISO/IEC Draft standard 10743). In addition, the U.S. Department of Defense is using HyTime to develop databases of technical information for weapons systems.

SMSL

Standard Multimedia Scripting Language (SMSL) is a standard being developed to add multimedia support to SGML document authoring tools. Current SGML tools support the creation of documents that incorporate hypertext links to multimedia objects such as graphics, audio, and video clips, but only as external entities. Unlike multimedia authoring systems, the SGML system has no control over the operation of the external viewer programs.

SMSL will use HyTime as the means for extending SGML to control the scheduling, measurement, and rendering of multimedia objects. It will provide an object-oriented interface between the programming languages that support multimedia services and the SGML/HyTime documents. This feature will allow authors to develop interactive multimedia documents making use of full-motion video, for example, through the use of HyTime pointers, allowing SGML authors to go beyond simple hypertext documents to create true multimedia.

SMSL is being developed under the auspices of the ISO SC18/WG8 and ANSI X3V1 standards committees.

PART TWO

USER'S GUIDE

Part II of the book looks at installation and configuration of multimedia hardware and the corresponding Linux kernel drivers. We start with a general discussion of the hardware requirements for multimedia under Linux. Subsequent chapters focus on sound, CD-ROM, and joystick interfaces.

CHAPTER SIX

GENERAL HARDWARE REQUIREMENTS

Before we look at the primary multimedia devices—sound cards and CD-ROM drives—let's review the other parts of your computer system that are not traditionally multimedia components, but are needed for running or developing multimedia applications.

Hard Disk Storage

It seems you can never have enough disk storage capacity. As I showed with some calculations in Part I, multimedia sound and video files can require a significant amount of disk space. It is easy to underestimate hard disk storage requirements, particularly for multimedia development, so for new purchases it is wise to buy some extra capacity (as a rule of thumb I'd recommend buying double what you expect to need). If you have an IDE drive that is several years old, you also may see significant speed improvements by upgrading it to a newer model.

Note that a CD-ROM drive can actually reduce your hard disk storage requirements by allowing more files to be offloaded to CD. For example, source code for applications from archive sites need not be kept online if available on a Linux CD-ROM. Many Linux distributions also offer an installation option that leaves most files on CD, at a cost in performance.

For many sound, graphics, and video data files, compression also helps reduce disk storage requirements. This process can be done as needed on a per-file basis or by using one of the more automated compression systems available for Linux. You definitely should keep your disk partitions below 90% capacity to avoid performance degradation.

Finally, don't forget to periodically back up your critical data to another medium such as floppy disk or tape. More than one Linux software project has been delayed because of data loss—usually due to human error—and no backups.

Memory

Like disk storage, the more main memory available to Linux, the better. Linux is very efficient in its use of memory, particularly when compared to UNIX workstations based on RISC processors. The bare minimum for Linux is four megabytes of memory. It is just barely possible to run the X Window System with such a system, but performance will be poor. A more realistic minimum is eight megabytes, and sixteen will make quite an improvement, particularly if you are doing software development. Remember, you can never have too much memory, as the Linux kernel will always use any extra for its dynamic disk cache.

If you are short on memory, a number of things can be done. Probably the most common solution is not to run the X11 windowing system. Even if you need X for testing multimedia applications—if you are editing or performing memory-intensive functions such as compiling a new kernel—it may pay to quit from X and use the text-based virtual consoles.

The kernel has drivers for all devices. The hardware-dependent software needed to control the devices is implemented in the Linux kernel so applications can access the hardware in a portable way. Linux also offers another unique way to save memory: its support for loadable kernel modules. Traditionally on UNIX systems all device drivers are compiled into the kernel. Even rarely used drivers (e.g., for a tape drive used only for backups) must always reside in the kernel taking up memory that can't be swapped out to disk like user programs. Under Linux, most device drivers may be compiled optionally as modules that can be dynamically loaded and unloaded when desired. More recently, support has been added for a program called *kerneld*, which automatically loads and unloads drivers when needed. For example, when a user issues the command to mount a CD-ROM drive, the kernel will automatically load the appropriate CD-ROM device driver and the ISO 9660 filesystem driver. If a driver has not been used for a period of time, the kernel will automatically unload it from memory.

Loadable kernel modules offer a number of other advantages; you can consult the documentation for more information.

Processor

Obviously the faster processors will improve performance, but surprisingly the type and speed of processor is usually not as important as memory on a Linux system. A system that starts swapping due to lack of memory will be slow no matter what processor it uses.

If you have a 386 or 486SX processor and are contemplating the addition of a separate floating point unit, keep in mind that only a very few specific floating point intensive tasks will yield significant improvement. For multimedia development, the two most common examples are ray tracing and converting sound files from one format to another.

Video

Most multimedia applications for Linux run under the X Window System. A resolution of 1024x768 pixels with 256 colors is about the practical minimum for doing multimedia work. Much better is 1280x1024 with 16-bit color. At these higher resolutions, a larger monitor (17-inch) is highly recommended, if you can afford it.

An accelerated video card also makes a big performance improvement, but make sure when purchasing a new system that the card is supported by the XFree86 X server software.

Miscellaneous

A few other pieces of hardware should round out your multimedia system. A mouse is mandatory for running X, and a three-button model works best under most window managers (two-button mice are also supported). A low-cost joystick is also useful as an alternate input device. You'll need a 3.5" floppy disk drive and a modem for transferring data to other systems. Finally, if you have any money left in your budget, you might want to investigate a tape drive for backup storage.

TIP　　　Linux supports most, but not all, popular hardware devices. If you're contemplating the purchase of a new system, check the latest Linux HOWTO documents, especially the "Hardware Compatibility" and "XFree86" HOWTOs. Other useful sources of information are Usenet newsgroups, BBS systems, and local Linux user groups. The ideal situation is to find a computer vendor that is familiar with Linux and can ensure you that the system is compatible.

The MPC Standards

When software vendors began developing the first multimedia applications for personal computers, they soon realized that the great variation in PC hardware configurations made it difficult to ensure that the applications would run on any given machine.

The Software Publishers Association (SPA), a consortium of PC software companies, formed a working group in order to establish common standards for multimedia. The idea was to define a minimum set of specifications for multimedia PCs.

Any conforming system should be able to run applications designed for the standard, now known as the Multimedia Personal Computer, or MPC, standard.

The first specification, MPC level 1, came out in 1991. Reflecting the first generation multimedia technology for PCs, level 1 is now generally considered obsolete. The standard was updated and released as MPC level 2 in 1993. Changes reflected the capability of newer hardware technology and the requirements of more sophisticated multimedia applications. Two years later the MPC level 2 standard was starting to show its age. In 1995 MPC level 3 was released, reflecting the current state of the art.

Technically Linux systems cannot meet the MPC standard because it specifies a Microsoft Windows and DOS operating environment. The hardware portion of the standard is useful though, particularly as a guide for assessing a complete system's multimedia capability. However, even if your system is not compliant with any MPC levels, it may still be usable for multimedia under Linux.

Table 6-1 lists some of the major components of the MPC specifications. Keep in mind that these are minimum requirements. It is interesting to see how multimedia technology has progressed over a period of less than five years.

Table 6–1: Summary of MPC Specifications

	Level 1	Level 2	Level 3
CPU:	16 MHz 386SX	25 MHz 486SX	75 MHz Pentium
Memory:	2 MB	4 MB	8 MB
Hard disk:	30 MB	160 MB	540 MB
CD-ROM:	single speed	double speed	quad speed
Sound:	8-bit D/A, A/D 11/22 kHz sampling 6 voice FM synthesizer MIDI playback	16-bit D/A, A/D 44 kHz sampling 8 voice FM synthesizer MIDI playback	16-bit D/A, A/D 44 kHz sampling wavetable synthesizer MIDI playback
Video:	640x480 16 colors	640x480 64K colors	MPEG playback at 352x240 30 fps 15-bit color
Other:	101 key keyboard 2-button mouse MIDI interface joystick	101 key keyboard 2-button mouse MIDI interface joystick	101 key keyboard 2-button mouse MIDI interface joystick

As well as setting standards, the Multimedia Working Group is also developing a set of conformance tests for MPC level 3. A system must pass the conformance tests in order to be branded as MPC level 3 compliant.

CHAPTER SEVEN

THE LINUX SOUND DRIVER

I n this chapter we will look at how to get your sound card working under
Linux, a prerequisite to running or developing multimedia applications that use
audio.

The Linux kernel includes a driver* for a number of popular sound cards. The
same driver also can be used under several other UNIX compatible operating systems that run on personal computers including FreeBSD, NetBSD, SCO, AT&T system V, and Interactive UNIX. The primary author is Hannu Savolainen of Helsinki,
Finland.

The pace of Linux software development is rapid, and support for new hardware
and features is constantly being added. I maintain a freely available document
called the Linux Sound HOWTO, one of a series of Linux guides on various topics.
This document is updated regularly and should be consulted for the latest information on sound card installation, supported sound cards, and frequently asked questions. Appendix B, *Linux Resources*, in this book lists some sources for obtaining a
copy of the Sound HOWTO.

Supported Hardware

In order to use the Linux sound card drivers you need a supported sound card. A
large number of PC sound cards are available, and many of them have a unique
programming interface at the hardware level. Most sound cards are supplied with
device drivers for MS-DOS, but these are of no use under Linux because it uses a
completely different architecture. Thus, Linux device drivers must be written for
each sound card, and because Linux is developed primarily by volunteers in their
spare time, it is virtually impossible to support all sound cards on the market.

---

* The sound driver has variously been known by the names Voxware, TASD, and USS Lite.
See Chapter 14, *Programming Sound Devices*, for more information.

Fortunately, a reasonably high degree of similarity exists among the most popular sound cards, and thanks to some creative programming, the Linux sound drivers are able to support the majority of cards in use today. Table 7-1 lists sound cards supported under Linux at the time of this writing; if your card is not listed here, don't despair, it still may be usable under Linux.

Table 7-1: Sound Cards Supported by Linux

Manufacturer	Models
AcerMagic	S23
AdLib	AdLib
Advanced Gravis	Ultrasound, ACE, Max, 16-bit option
ATI	Stereo F/X
Aztech	Sound Galaxy 8-bit, Lyra, Nova, Pro16, NX Pro16
Cardinal	DSP16
Creative Labs	SoundBlaster 1.0, 2.0, Pro, 16, 16ASP, AWE32
Crystal	CS4231- and CS4248-based cards
Diamond	LX series
Ensoniq	SoundScape
Logitech	SoundMan 16, SoundMan Games, SoundMan Wave
MAD16	Pro (OPTi 82C929)
MediaTriX	AudioTriX Pro
Media Vision	Jazz16
Microsoft	Windows Sound System, Personal Sound System
Mozart	OAK OTI-601
Orchid	SW32
Pro Audio	Spectrum 16, Studio 16
Pro Sonic	16
Reveal	some models
Roland	MPU-401 MIDI interface
Texas Instruments	TM4000M Notebook
ThunderBoard	ThunderBoard
Turtle Beach	Maui, Tropez
various	MIDI interfaces based on 6850 UART chip
various	FM Synthesizers based on Yamaha OPL-2,3,4 chips

First, support for your card may have been added to Linux since this book was written. Reading the previously mentioned Sound HOWTO document is a good way to check for more recent information.

Second, if your card is claimed by the manufacturer to be compatible with one of the supported sound cards, it may work. However, to work under Linux it must be compatible at the hardware register level. Some cards described as "100% Sound-Blaster compatible" are only compatible when using an MS-DOS TSR driver program, which is not usable under Linux. If you are uncertain, the best approach is just to try it out and experiment with different options.

The "Troubleshooting" section later in this chapter offers some hints for getting compatible cards to work.

The PC Speaker Sound Driver

If you don't have a sound card in your system you have one other option for supporting sound under Linux. Michael Beck has written a kernel driver that is mostly compatible with the sound card driver but uses only the PC's internal speaker. As you might expect, the performance and sound quality are not up to the level of a sound card, and results vary from system to system, but it does produce intelligible sound. It supports a digital to analog converter device for sound output and a simple mixer. It even pretends to support 16-bit stereo so you can run applications such as *DOOM*.

Sound input is not supported, nor is there any support for the FM synthesizer device provided by most sound cards. You will also find that the driver consumes a lot of CPU processing time, slowing down other applications.

The PC speaker sound driver is not part of the standard kernel distribution; you have to obtain it separately. At the time of this writing the latest version was 0.9b, available from *ftp://ftp.informatik.hu-berlin.de/pub/os/linux/hu-sound/*. You can find copies at most of the major Linux archive sites listed in Appendix B.

The PC speaker sound driver package includes instructions for installation and configuration. The basic installation process consists of:

1. Unpacking the distribution (using *tar*)

2. Applying a kernel patch (using the *patch* program)

3. Configuring and building a new Linux kernel

4. Creating the device files (using the included script)

5. Rebooting with the new kernel

Included in the distribution is a sample sound file and some utilities. The *pcsel* program allows you to control functions of the driver such as selecting the type of output device (i.e., speaker or one of the D/A circuits), which printer port to use, and whether to support stereo. A copy of the *vplay* program for playing sound files is also included.

The PC speaker driver can take over most of the functions of the normal sound card driver. Alternatively, if you have a sound card, the PC speaker driver can co-exist with the sound card driver.

If you are serious about multimedia, you will want to purchase a sound card, but in the meantime the PC speaker driver is one way to try some of the concepts in this book.

Installation

Configuring Linux to support sound involves the following steps:

1. Installing the sound card

2. Configuring and building the kernel for sound support

3. Creating the device files

4. Booting the Linux kernel and testing the installation

The next sections cover each of these steps in detail.

Installing the Sound Card

If you have not already done so, install your sound card hardware following the manufacturer's instructions. If you are not comfortable working with the inside of your system, you might want to ask someone for assistance or have your dealer perform the installation.

Linux has no special installation requirements. If the sound card works under another operating system such as MS-DOS, then it should be ready to go under Linux.

Older sound cards usually have switch or jumper settings to select functions such as IRQ, DMA channel, and I/O address. If you are unsure of what settings to use, the factory defaults are generally a good choice. Try to avoid conflicts with other devices such as Ethernet cards, SCSI host adaptors, and serial and parallel ports.

Newer sound cards generally set their configuration parameters in software without jumpers. If you are using such a card under another operating system, use the same settings under Linux to reduce the likelihood of problems.

TIP   Whether you set them by hardware jumpers or configure them in software, keep a record of your sound card settings for later reference. You will need them whenever you configure a new kernel.

Configuring the Kernel

When initially installing Linux you likely used a precompiled kernel. These kernels usually do not provide sound support, so it is best to recompile the kernel yourself with the drivers you need. You also may want to recompile the kernel in order to upgrade to a newer version or to free up memory resources by minimizing the size of the kernel.

The sound drivers are included in the source distribution for the Linux kernel. When you installed Linux on your system you almost certainly were given the opportunity to install the kernel source. You will also need to have installed the Linux software development tools, most notably the GNU C compiler and linker.

Under the popular Slackware distribution of Linux, for example, the kernel source code is included on the "Q" series of floppy disks and the software development tools on the "D" series (these names are also used when installing from CD-ROM). If you didn't load these packages when originally setting up your Linux system, you should go back and install them now before proceeding further. If you don't have these files or wish to install a more recent version, you can obtain them from an Internet archive site or BBS system.

The details of building the Linux kernel vary slightly depending on the kernel revision and the Linux distribution you installed. I will be concentrating on the aspects of configuring the kernel that are related to the sound driver.

TIP   If you have not recompiled the kernel before, you may wish to consult other documentation such as the Linux Kernel HOWTO or *Running Linux (Second Edition)*, which is published by O'Reilly & Associates, Inc.

The first time you configure the kernel for sound support it is a good idea to check all of the README files included with the kernel sound drivers, particularly information specific to your card type. The documentation files can be found in the kernel sound driver directory, usually installed in */usr/src/linux/drivers/sound*.

The usual procedure for building the kernel is to log in as *root*, move to the kernel source directory, and configure the kernel using the commands:

```
% cd /usr/src/linux
% make config
```

The kernel configuration program will now prompt you with a number of kernel device drivers and options. You should answer "y" (yes) or "n" (no) as appropriate for your system. Just pressing the Enter key will accept the default value (shown in the prompt as an uppercase letter).

TIP   There are two alternative ways to configure the kernel. A graphical kernel configuration program that runs under the X Window System can be invoked with **make xconfig**. A menu-based system that requires only text displays is available as **make menuconfig**. You may find these easier to use than the command line–based configuration method.

Near the end of the kernel configuration you will be prompted:

```
Sound card support (CONFIG_SOUND) [Y/m/n/?]
```

You should answer "y" to enable the sound driver in the kernel. The second option, entering "m," will build the sound driver as a loadable module that will not reside in the compiled kernel itself but that can be loaded and unloaded on demand. I recommend first installing and testing the sound driver as part of the kernel. If you want to explore the loadable module option, you should consult the documentation that comes with the module's package. If you don't see the "m" option shown above, you probably have an older version of the kernel that pre-dates module support. Entering "n" to the prompt will cause sound support not to be compiled in to the kernel. Entering "?" will cause some descriptive help text to be displayed.

You should next see the sound configuration program being compiled and run, and it will then ask you what sound card options you want. Be careful when answering these questions since answering a question incorrectly may prevent some later ones from being asked. Don't enable support for a sound card that you do not have installed as this will only use more memory and possibly cause incorrect operation.

I list here a brief description of each of the configuration dialog options. Answer "y" (yes) or "n" (no) to each question. The default answer is shown first and in uppercase so that "[Y/n/?]" means "y" by default and "[N/y/?]" means the default is "n". To use the default value, just use the Enter key, but remember that the default value isn't necessarily correct for your system. At most prompts you can enter "?" to view a short description of what this option is about.

Note also that not all questions may be asked. The configuration program may disable some questions depending on earlier choices. It may select some options automatically as well. Also, the configuration program will attempt to determine if you select options that are meaningless or contradictory, and notify you of the fact. The details will vary slightly depending on the kernel version you are using, but the following is typical of the questions with which you should be prompted.

```
Configuring Sound Support
Old configuration exists in '/etc/soundconf'. Use it [Y/n/?]
```

You will see this message if you have previously configured the kernel for sound support. Entering "y" will allow you to use the previously saved sound configuration. This option is useful if you are recompiling the kernel repeatedly and do not want to keep entering the sound configuration data. Unless you are certain that the previous sound configuration is correct, then you should enter "n" here.

```
ProAudioSpectrum 16 support [N/y/?]
```

Answer "y" only if you have a ProAudio Spectrum 16, ProAudio Studio 16, or Logitech SoundMan 16. Don't enable this if you have some other card made by Media-Vision or Logitech since they are not PAS16 compatible.

```
SoundBlaster (SB, SBPro, SB16, clones) support [N/y/?]
```

Answer "y" if you have any type of SoundBlaster card made by Creative Labs or a 100% hardware-compatible clone. For an unknown card you may answer "y" if the card claims to be SoundBlaster compatible, and hope that it will work.

```
Generic OPL2/OPL3 FM synthesizer support [N/y/?]
```

Answer "y" if your card has an FM chip made by Yamaha (OPL2/OPL3/OPL4). Answering "y" is usually a safe and recommended choice, however some cards may have software (TSR) FM emulation. Enabling FM support with these cards may cause trouble (I don't currently know of any such cards, however).

```
Gravis Ultrasound support [N/y/?]
```

Answer "y" if you have a GUS, GUS MAX, or other card made by Advanced Gravis.

```
MPU-401 support (NOT for SB16) [N/y/?]
```

Be careful with this question. The MPU401 interface is supported by almost all sound cards. However, some natively supported cards have their own driver for MPU401. Enabling the MPU401 option with these cards will cause a conflict. Also, enabling MPU401 on a system that doesn't really have a MPU401 could cause some trouble. If your card was in the list of supported cards, look at the card-specific instructions in the *Readme.cards* file. It's safe to answer "y" if you have a true Roland MPU401 MIDI interface card.

```
6850 UART Midi support [N/y/?]
```

In most cases you should answer "n" to this question. Only very rarely is the 6850 UART MIDI interface found on sound cards. You'll know if you have such a card.

```
PSS (ECHO-ADI2111) support [N/y/?]
```

Answer "y" only if you have Orchid SW32, Cardinal DSP16, or some other card based on the PSS chipset (AD1848 codec, ADSP-2115 DSP chip, and Echo ESC614 ASIC CHIP).

```
16 bit sampling option of GUS (_NOT_ GUS MAX) [N/y/?]
```

Answer "y" if you have installed the 16-bit sampling daughtercard on your GUS. Answer "n" if you have a GUS MAX. Enabling this disables GUS MAX support.

```
GUS MAX support [N/y/?]
```

Answer "y" only if you have a Gravis UltraSound MAX card.

```
Microsoft Sound System support [N/y/?]
```

Answer "y" if you have the original Windows Sound System card made by Microsoft or the Aztech SG16 Pro or NX16 Pro. You may also answer "y" if your card was not listed earlier in the configuration process. For cards having native support, consult the card-specific instructions in the file *Readme.cards*. Some drivers have their own MSS support and enabling this option will cause a conflict.

```
Ensoniq Soundscape support [N/y/?]
```

Answer "y" if you have a sound card based on the Ensoniq SoundScape chipset, which includes some cards being manufactured by Ensoniq, Spea, and Reveal.

```
MediaTriX AudioTriX Pro support [N/y/?]
```

Answer "y" if you have the AudioTriX Pro.

```
Support for MAD16 and/or Mozart based cards [N/y/?]
```

Answer "y" if your card has a Mozart (OAK OTI-601) or MAD16 (OPTi 82C928 or 82C929) audio interface chip. These chips are currently quite common so it's possible that many no-name cards have one of them. In addition, the MAD16 chip is used in some cards made by known manufacturers such as Turtle Beach (Tropez), Reveal (some models), and Diamond (most recent ones).

```
Support for Crystal CS4232 based (PnP) cards [N/y/?]
```

Enter "y" if you have a sound card of this type.

```
Support for Turtle Beach Wave Front (Maui, Tropez) synthesizers [N/y/?]
```

Enter "y" if you have a Turtle Beach Maui or Tropez sound card.

```
Audio Excel DSP 16 initialization support [N/y/?]
```

Enable this if you have an Audio Excel DSP16 card. The configuration program then asks some questions about the higher-level services. It's recommended that you answer "y" to each of these questions. Answer "n" only if you know you will not need the option.

```
/dev/dsp and /dev/audio support (usually required) [N/y/?]
```

Answering "n" disables */dev/dsp* and */dev/audio*—A/D and D/A converter devices. Answer "y" unless you want to disable these devices for some uncommon reason.

```
MIDI interface support [N/y/?]
```

Answer "y" if you want support for controlling devices over the MIDI bus. This option also affects any MPU401 and/or General MIDI compatible devices.

```
FM synthesizer (YM3812/OPL-3) support [N/y/?]
```

Answer "y" here unless you know your card does not support FM synthesis.

```
Do you want support for the mixer of SG NX Pro  [N/y/?]
```

Enable this if you have a Sound Galaxy NX Pro. This card is SoundBlaster-compatible but has some additional mixer functions that this option supports.

```
Do you want support for the MV Jazz16 (ProSonic etc.)  [N/y/?]
```

Enable this option if you have this type of sound card.

```
Do you have a Logitech SoundMan Games [N/y/?]
```

Enable this if you have a Logitech SoundMan Games sound card. Do not enable it if you have any other type of Logitech sound card.

```
/dev/sequencer support [N/y/?]
```

Answering "n" disables */dev/sequencer* and */dev/music* devices, the on-board MIDI synthesizers.

After the above questions, the configuration program prompts for the card-specific configuration information. Usually just a set of I/O addresses and IRQ and DMA channel numbers are asked. With some cards the program asks for some files to be used during initialization of the card. These are used by cards wtih a DSP chip or microprocessor that must be initialized by downloading a program (microcode) file to the card. In some cases this file is written to a header file by the *config* program and then included in the driver during compilation. Again, read the information in the file *Readme.cards* pertaining to your card type. Here is an example for a SoundBlaster Pro card:

```
I/O base for SB
Possible values are: Check from manual of the card
The default value is 220
Enter the value: 220
I/O base for SB set to 220.

SoundBlaster IRQ
Possible values are: Check from manual of the card
The default value is 7
Enter the value: 5
SoundBlaster IRQ set to 5.

SoundBlaster DMA
Possible values are: 0, 1 or 3
The default value is 1
Enter the value: 1
SoundBlaster DMA set to 1.
```

```
SoundBlaster 16 bit DMA (_REQUIRED_for SB16, Jazz16, SMW)
Possible values are: 5, 6 or 7
The default value is 5
Enter the value: 5
SoundBlaster 16 bit DMA (_REQUIRED_for SB16, Jazz16, SMW) set to 5.

MPU401 I/O base of SB16, Jazz16 and ES1688
Possible values are: Check from manual of the card
        (0 disables this feature)
The default value is 0
Enter the value: 0

SB MPU401 IRQ (SB16, Jazz16 and ES1688)
Possible values are: Check from manual of the card
        (-1 disables this feature)
The default value is -1
Enter the value: -1

Audio DMA buffer size
Possible values are: 4096, 16384, 32768 or 65536
The default value is 65536
Enter the value: 65536
The DMA buffer size set to 65536
```

After answering these questions you will see:

```
The sound driver is now configured.
Save copy of this configuration to '/etc/soundconf' [Y/n/?]
```

Normally you enter "y" here. Then, if you need to reconfigure the kernel to change other device drivers, you have the option of using this saved configuration.

After configuring the kernel for sound support you will continue to see prompts for some additional kernel configuration options. When that process is completed you are ready to move on to compiling and installing the new kernel. Again, this is dependent on which Linux distribution you use, and whether you boot your system from floppy or a boot loader such as LILO. A typical procedure is to do **make clean** followed by **make dep**. You would then run **make zlilo** (if you use the LILO boot loader) or **make zdisk** if you boot from floppy disk. You can expect the kernel compilation process to take anywhere from about 10 minutes to several hours depending on the speed of your system.

Creating the Device Files

The kernel uses device files to identify which device drivers to use. The device files are created using the *mknod* command. Each device type is associated with a unique number, known as the major number. A second number, the minor number, can be used to identify multiple devices of the same type. The major and minor numbers are used by the kernel to identify which kernel driver should be used for the device.

The first time the kernel sound driver is configured you need to create the sound device files. The easiest way to do this task is to cut the short shell script from the end of the file *Readme.linux* in the directory */usr/src/linux/drivers/sound*, and run it as user *root*.

WARNING   A potential security issue arises with sound cards. If you have a microphone attached to your system and are running in a networked environment, it is conceivable that other users could remotely log on to your system and eavesdrop on what was being said or annoy you by playing sound files. If this is a concern, you should either restrict the permissions on the sound device files or ensure that the microphone is disconnected when not in use.

If your device entries already exist, you might want to ensure they are correct. If they are not, or if you are in doubt, run the above script, and it will replace any existing entries with correct ones.

Some older Linux distributions provided install scripts that created incorrect sound device files. You may also have a */dev/MAKEDEV* script for creating device files. Using the script included with the kernel sound driver is preferred since it should always be up to date with the latest supported sound devices.

After running the script your sound device files should look something like this (run a command such as *ls -l /dev | more* to check):

```
lrwxrwxrwx   1 root           11 Aug 22 00:01 audio -> /dev/audio0
crw-rw-rw-   1 root     14,    4 Aug 22 00:01 audio0
crw-rw-rw-   1 root     14,   20 Aug 22 00:01 audio1
lrwxrwxrwx   1 root            9 Aug 22 00:01 dsp -> /dev/dsp0
crw-rw-rw-   1 root     14,    3 Aug 22 00:01 dsp0
crw-rw-rw-   1 root     14,   19 Aug 22 00:01 dsp1
crw-rw-rw-   1 root     14,    2 Aug 22 00:01 midi00
crw-rw-rw-   1 root     14,   18 Aug 22 00:01 midi01
crw-rw-rw-   1 root     14,   34 Aug 22 00:01 midi02
crw-rw-rw-   1 root     14,   50 Aug 22 00:01 midi03
crw-rw-rw-   1 root     14,    0 Aug 22 00:01 mixer
crw-rw-rw-   1 root     14,   16 Aug 22 00:01 mixer1
crw-rw-rw-   1 root     14,    8 Aug 22 00:01 music
crw-rw-rw-   1 root     14,   17 Aug 22 00:01 patmgr0
crw-rw-rw-   1 root     14,   33 Aug 22 00:01 patmgr1
crw-rw-rw-   1 root     14,    1 Aug 22 00:01 sequencer
lrwxrwxrwx   1 root           10 Aug 22 00:01 sequencer2 -> /dev/music
crw-rw-rw-   1 root     14,    6 Aug 22 00:01 sndstat
```

The time and date stamps will obviously vary on your system. Pay particular attention to the device names and the major and minor device numbers listed in the fourth and fifth columns. File ownership and permissions should also match the above.

Normally the configuration you used when building the kernel will be acceptable to the sound card driver. It is also possible to pass parameters on the kernel command line (e.g., from LILO) to configure the sound driver. These are defined in the file *Readme.linux*. It should rarely be necessary to use these, they are mainly intended for developers of Linux boot disks to create a kernel that supports multiple types of sound cards.

Booting Linux and Testing the Installation

You should now be ready to boot the new kernel and test the sound drivers. Follow your usual procedure for installing and rebooting the new kernel.

TIP   When testing a new kernel, keep a copy of the previous working kernel in case of problems. Either set up LILO to allow booting from the backup kernel, or make a boot floppy (or both).

During booting, check for a message such as the following on powerup (if they scroll by too quickly to read, you should be able to retrieve them with the *dmesg* command):

```
Sound initialization started
snd2 <SoundBlaster Pro 3.2> at 0x220 irq 5 drq 1
snd1 <Yamaha OPL-3 FM> at 0x388 drq 0
Sound initialization complete
```

This display should match your sound card type and jumper settings (if any).

The driver may also display some error messages and warnings during boot. Watch for these when booting the first time after configuring the sound driver.

Next you should check the device file */dev/sndstat*. Reading the sound driver status device file can provide additional information on whether the sound card driver initialized properly. Typical output should look something like this:

```
% cat /dev/sndstat
Sound Driver:3.5.2-960330 (Tue May 21 19:08:17 EDT 1996 root,
Linux fizzbin 2.0.0 #1 Tue May 21 19:22:57 EDT 1996 i386
Kernel: Linux fizzbin 2.0.0 #1 Tue May 21 19:22:57 EDT 1996 i386
Config options: a80002

Installed drivers:
Type 1: OPL-2/OPL-3 FM
Type 2: SoundBlaster
Type 6: SoundBlaster 16bit
Type 7: SB MPU

Card config:
SoundBlaster at 0x220 irq 5 drq 1,5
```

```
(SB MPU at 0x0 irq 1 drq 0)
OPL-2/OPL-3 FM at 0x388 irq 0 drq 0

Audio devices:
0: SoundBlaster Pro 3.2

Synth devices:
0: Yamaha OPL-3

Midi devices:
0: SoundBlaster

Timers:
0: System clock

Mixers:
0: SoundBlaster
```

Now you should be ready to play a simple sound file. Obtain a sample sound file[*] and send it to the sound device as a basic check of sound output.

```
% cat endoftheworld >/dev/dsp
% cat crash.au >/dev/audio
```

(Make sure you don't omit the ">" in the commands above.)

Now you can verify sound recording. Connect a microphone to the sound card and speak into it while executing this command:

```
% dd bs=8k count=4 <dev/audio >sample.au
4+0 records in
4+0 records out
```

Then play it back using:

```
% cat sample.au >/dev/audio
```

If these tests pass, you can be reasonably confident that the sound D/A and A/D hardware and software are working. If you experience problems, refer to the next section of this chapter.

Troubleshooting

If you still encounter problems after following the instructions in the previous section, here are some things to check. The checks are listed in increasing order of complexity. If a test fails, solve the problem before moving to the next stage.

---

[*] See Chapter 10, *Applications for Sound and Music*, and Appendix B, *Linux Resources*, for some sources of sound files.

Make Sure You Are Really Running the Kernel You Compiled

You can check the date stamp on the kernel to see if you are running the one that you compiled with sound support. You can do this with the *uname* command:

```
% uname -a
Linux gollum 2.0.0 #1 Tue May 21 19:22:57 EDT 1996 i586
```

or by displaying the file */proc/version*:

```
% cat /proc/version
Linux version 2.0.0 (root@gollum) (gcc version 2.7.0) #1 Tue May 21
19:22:57 EDT 1996
```

If the date stamp doesn't seem to match when you compiled the kernel, then you are running an old kernel. Did you really reboot? If you use LILO, did you re-install it (typically by running */etc/lilo/install*)? If booting from floppy, did you create a new boot floppy and use it when booting?

Make Sure the Sound Drivers Are Compiled Into the Kernel

You can see what drivers are compiled in by looking at */proc/devices*:

```
% cat /proc/devices
Character devices:
 1 mem
 4 tty
 5 cua
 6 lp
14 sound
15 Joystick

Block devices:
 2 fd
 3 hd
25 sbpcd
```

What we are looking for here is character device 14, labeled "sound". If the sound device is not listed then something went wrong with the kernel configuration or build. Start the installation process again, beginning with configuration and building of the kernel.

Did the Kernel Detect Your Sound Card During Booting?

Make sure that the sound card was detected when the kernel booted. If your sound card was not found, then something is wrong. Make sure it really is installed. You should have seen a message during the boot. If the messages scrolled off the screen, you can usually recall them using the command:

```
% dmesg
```

or

```
% tail /var/adm/messages
```

If the sound card works under DOS then you can be reasonably confident that the hardware is working, so it is likely a problem with the kernel configuration. Either you configured your sound card as the wrong type or wrong parameters, or your sound card is not compatible with any of the Linux kernel sound card drivers. Recheck the configuration options and/or try some different options.

One possibility is that your sound card is one of the so-called "compatible" types that require initialization by the DOS driver. Try booting DOS and loading the vendor-supplied sound card driver. Then soft-boot Linux using Control-Alt-Delete. Make sure that the card I/O address, DMA, and IRQ settings for Linux are the same as those used under DOS. Read the *Readme.cards* file from the sound driver source distribution for hints on configuring your card type.

If your sound card is not listed in this document, it is possible that the Linux drivers do not support it. You can check with some of the references listed in Appendix B for assistance.

Can You Read Data from the DSP Device?

Try reading from the */dev/audio* device using the *dd* command listed earlier in this document. The command should run without errors. If this does not work, then a possible cause is the device file. Make sure that the device files in the */dev* directory have the correct major and minor numbers as listed previously. Check that the permissions on the device file allow reading and writing.

If you can play back but not record, obtain a mixer program and use it to set the input device and level.

A remote possibility is a hardware problem. Try testing the sound card under DOS, if possible, to determine if this could be the case.

When All Else Fails

If you still have problems, here are some final suggestions for options to try:

- Carefully re-read this chapter.

- Read the latest Sound HOWTO document and the kernel source README files.

- If you have access to Usenet news, post a question to one of the *comp.os.linux* newsgroups.

- Send a question to the Sound channel of the Linux mailing list (see Appendix B for details).

- Try using the most recent Linux kernel (there will typically be both a stable kernel and a development kernel).

- Contact your computer dealer.

- Contact the sound card manufacturer.

- Send mail to the author of the sound driver.

- Send mail to the author of the Linux Sound HOWTO.

CHAPTER EIGHT

THE CD-ROM DRIVER

I n this chapter I cover how to configure Linux to support a CD-ROM drive. In addition to the Sound Card HOWTO, I maintain the Linux CD-ROM HOWTO. You can obtain more up-to-date information on CD-ROM drives by consulting this document, which is freely available from the Internet and several other sources (see Appendix B, *Linux Resources*).

Supported Hardware

As I discussed in Chapter 3, *CD-ROM*, CD-ROM drives can be categorized into three types: SCSI, Enhanced IDE, and proprietary. Linux supports most drives of all three types.

The SCSI interface is well defined, and drives that conform to the standard should work fine under Linux. Technically you need a drive that uses a block size of 512, or 2048 bytes; this includes the vast majority of CD-ROM drives on the market. You also need a supported SCSI controller card. Most popular SCSI controllers, both dedicated cards and those provided on sound cards, are supported. Some CD-ROMs include a controller card with a special interface that is not fully SCSI-compatible (e.g., it may not support adding other SCSI devices on the bus). This type will most likely not work under Linux.

The Linux SCSI HOWTO document, referenced in Appendix B, has the most up-to-date information on which controllers are supported and how to set them up.

Like SCSI, Enhanced IDE or ATAPI drives are based on an ANSI standard, and any conforming drives should work under Linux. This interface type is the most common for drives being sold today.

The third category, proprietary drives, is more problematic to support because each interface is unique. These drives were initially the most popular because of their low cost, with the interfaces usually provided on a sound card. Each type of interface requires a specific Linux kernel device driver to support it. To further complicate matters, the same drives can be sold under various brand names, and vendors may switch drive types.

Table 8-1 lists the proprietary CD-ROM drives that were supported under Linux as of the time of this writing, along with the kernel driver that works with each drive.

Table 8-1: Supported Proprietary CD-ROM Drives

Manufacturer	Model	Kernel Driver
Panasonic	CR-521, CR-522, CR-523	sbpcd
Panasonic	CR-562, CR-563	sbpcd
Creative Labs	CD-200, CD-200F	sbpcd
IBM	External ISA	sbpcd
Longshine	LCS-7260	sbpcd
Teac	CD-55A	sbpcd
Sony	CDU-31A, CDU-33A	cdu31a
Sony	CDU-531, CDU-535	sonycd535
Aztech	CDA268-01A	aztcd
Conrad	TXC	aztcd
CyCDROM	CR520ie, CR940ie	aztcd
Orchid	CDS-3110	aztcd
Okano/Wearnes	CDD110	aztcd
GoldStar	R420	gscd
Philips/LMS	CM206	cm206
Mitsumi	CRMC LU005S	mcd/mcdx
Mitsumi	FX001	aztcd
Optics Storage	Dolphin 8000AT	optcd
Sanyo	H94A	sjcd

If your drive is not listed here, it may still be supported under Linux. Make sure that your drive really is a proprietary interface. Most vendors are now shipping enhanced IDE/ATAPI models. Don't assume that, for example, if your drive is made by Creative Labs then it is one of the proprietary drives listed in the table. Particularly if it is a quad speed or faster model, it is probably an enhanced IDE interface and should use the ide-cd kernel driver.

Some CD-ROM drives connect directly to the PC parallel port. These are not currently supported under Linux. The interfaces tend to be proprietary, and the manufacturers do not release the information necessary to write a driver.

Because new device drivers are continually being written for Linux, someone may have added support for your drive since this book was written. If you are running an older Linux kernel you may need to upgrade. The CD-ROM HOWTO document is a good place to check for information on newly supported drives.

A number of supported drives are also sold under different brand names. For example, some of the Panasonic drives have been sold under the names Creative Labs, Matsushita, and Kotobuki. You may have to do some experimentation to determine if your drive is compatible.

Finally, because all of the Linux source code is freely available, you have the option of writing your own drivers, or even contracting someone else to do this for you. Generally the largest barrier to this option is not the programming effort, but the difficulty of obtaining the necessary documentation from the manufacturer. In some cases the vendor will only release the information under a non-disclosure agreement, in which case the driver can't be made freely available.

Installation

Configuring Linux to support a CD-ROM drive involves the following steps:

1. Installing the hardware

2. Configuring and building the Linux kernel with the appropriate device drivers

3. Creating the device files and setting boot time parameters

4. Booting the Linux kernel

5. Mounting the media

The next sections cover each of these steps in detail.

Installing the Hardware

Follow the manufacturer's instructions for installing the hardware or have your dealer perform the installation. The details will vary depending on whether the drive is internal or external and on what type of interface used. Linux needs no special installation requirements. You may need to set jumpers on the drive and/or interface card for correct operation; some of the kernel drivers include *README* files that include this information (look in the directory that is called */usr/src/linux/Documentation/cdrom*).

TIP	Keep a record of the CD-ROM interface settings for IRQ and I/O addresses, if known. You will need them whenever you configure a new kernel.

If your drive is already installed and working under another operating system, then no hardware or configuration changes should be needed.

Configuring the Kernel

When initially installing Linux from CD-ROM you probably will be using a boot and/or root disk provided as part of a Linux distribution. If possible, you should choose a boot disk with the kernel driver for your CD-ROM device type. Once Linux has initially been installed, most users will want to compile their own kernel. I will mention here some issues that are specific to CD-ROM drives. The Linux Kernel HOWTO and the O'Reilly book *Running Linux (Second Edition)* have more information on building the Linux kernel.

Obviously, you need to compile in support for your CD-ROM drive when you go through the initial **make config** step of building the kernel. There is also a graphical configuration tool invoked using **make xconfig** and a menu-based text tool invoked by **make menuconfig**. I'll describe the command-line configuration program because it is more commonly used and easier to describe in words.

If you have an ATAPI CD-ROM drive, enable it when answering the following questions:

```
Enhanced IDE/MFM/RLL disk/cdrom/tape support
Enhanced IDE/MFM/RLL disk/cdrom/tape support
    (CONFIG_BLK_DEV_IDE) [Y/n/?] y
    (CONFIG_BLK_DEV_IDE) [Y/n/?] y
  Use old disk-only driver on primary interface
  Use old disk-only driver on primary interface
    (CONFIG_BLK_DEV_HD_IDE) [N/y/?] n
    (CONFIG_BLK_DEV_HD_IDE) [N/y/?] n
  Include IDE/ATAPI CDROM support
  Include IDE/ATAPI CDROM support
    (CONFIG_BLK_DEV_IDECD) [N/y/?] y
    (CONFIG_BLK_DEV_IDECD) [N/y/?] y
```

For SCSI CD-ROM drives, enable these options:

```
SCSI support (CONFIG_SCSI) [N/y/m] y
SCSI support (CONFIG_SCSI) [N/y/m] y
...
...
SCSI CDROM support (CONFIG_BLK_DEV_SR) [N/y/m] y
SCSI CDROM support (CONFIG_BLK_DEV_SR) [N/y/m] y
```

If you have a multi-disc CD changer (jukebox) enable this option:

```
Probe all LUNs on each SCSI device (CONFIG_SCSI_MULTI_LUN) [N/y/?] y
Probe all LUNs on each SCSI device (CONFIG_SCSI_MULTI_LUN) [N/y/?] y
```

Also enable support for your SCSI host adaptor when prompted:

```
Adaptec AHA152X support (CONFIG_SCSI_AHA152X) [N/y/m] y
Adaptec AHA152X support (CONFIG_SCSI_AHA152X) [N/y/m] y
```

For proprietary interface CD-ROM drives, enable the appropriate driver. First answer "y" to:

```
Support non-SCSI/IDE/ATAPI drives (CONFIG_CD_NO_IDESCSI) [Y/n/?] y
Support non-SCSI/IDE/ATAPI drives (CONFIG_CD_NO_IDESCSI) [Y/n/?] y
```

Then you can use Table 8-1 to determine the driver to use for your model. For example, for a Sony CDU-31A drive, you would answer yes to:

```
Sony CDU31A/CDU33A CDROM support (CONFIG_CDU31A) [N/y/m/?] y
Sony CDU31A/CDU33A CDROM support (CONFIG_CDU31A) [N/y/m/?] y
```

Virtually all CD-ROMs use the ISO 9660 filesystem, so you also must enable:

```
ISO9660 cdrom filesystem support (CONFIG_ISO9660_FS) [Y/m/n/?] y
ISO9660 cdrom filesystem support (CONFIG_ISO9660_FS) [Y/m/n/?] y
```

You then should follow the usual procedure for building the kernel and installing it. Don't boot with the new kernel until you create the device files and set up any boot-time parameters as described in the next section.

TIP   The ISO 9660 filesystem and many of the CD-ROM drivers can be built as loadable kernel modules. This process is described in the modules documentation and Kernel HOWTO. It is recommended that you first get your CD-ROM drive working as a traditional kernel driver before building it as a module.

If a drive type listed in Table 8-1 doesn't appear to be supported by your kernel, you likely need to upgrade to a newer version (several of the drivers are only offered in the 1.3 and later kernels). You may need to use a driver that is distributed separately from the kernel source code, which usually involves patching the kernel. Again, the Kernel HOWTO explains this process.

Creating the Device Files

The kernel uses device files to identify which device driver to use. If you are running a standard Linux distribution you may have created the necessary device files during installation. Under Slackware Linux, for example, there is a menu-based *setup* tool that includes CD-ROM setup, and most systems have a */dev/MAKEDEV* script. If you don't use these methods, you can use the more manual procedure listed in this section. No matter what method you choose, it is recommended that you at least verify the device files against the information in this section.

The device files are created using the *mknod* command. Each device type is associated with a unique number, known as the *major number*. A second number, the *minor number*, can be used to identify multiple devices of the same type. The major and minor numbers are used by the kernel to identify which kernel driver should be used for the device.

In subsequent sections the commands needed to create the device files for each CD-ROM device type are listed. This should be done as user *root*. Note that some Linux distributions may use slightly different CD-ROM device names from those listed here.

It is recommended that you also create a symbolic link called */dev/cdrom* that points to the CD-ROM device to make it easier to remember. For example, for a Panasonic CD-ROM drive, which we'll see later uses a device file name of */dev/sbpcd*, the link would be created using

```
% ln -s /dev/sbpcd /dev/cdrom
% ln -s /dev/sbpcd /dev/cdrom
```

If you want users other than *root* to be able to play audio CDs, you will need to set the protection on the device file (the real file, not the symbolic link to it) to allow all users to read and write. Following the example above, this would be:

```
% chmod 666 /dev/sbpcd
% chmod 666 /dev/sbpcd
% ls -l /dev/sbpcd
% ls -l /dev/sbpcd
brw-rw-rw-  1 root     disk     25,   0 Jul 18  1994 /dev/sbpcd
brw-rw-rw-  1 root     disk     25,   0 Jul 18  1994 /dev/sbpcd
```

This setup allows any user to access and control the CD-ROM drive. It is up to you if you want to permit this. You must choose which permissions to allow. As CD-ROMs are read-only devices, these permissions aren't a major breach of system security.

When booting Linux, the device drivers attempt to determine whether the appropriate devices are present, typically by probing specific addresses. Many of the drivers auto-probe at several addresses, but because of differences in configuration, possible device conflicts, and hardware limitations, the drivers sometimes need help identifying the addresses and other parameters. Most drivers support an option on the kernel command line to pass this information to the device driver. This can be done interactively, or more commonly, configured into your boot loader. With LILO, for example, you would add an *append* command such as the following to your */etc/lilo.conf* file:

```
append = "sbpcd=0x230,SoundBlaster"
append = "sbpcd=0x230,SoundBlaster"
```

See the LILO documentation for more information.

In the next section I discuss issues specific to individual device drivers. For each driver I list:

- The author's name and email address
- Whether multisession drives are supported
- Whether multiple drives are supported
- If the driver can be built as a kernel-loadable module
- If the driver can directly read frames of digital audio
- If the driver performs auto-probing on boot
- The device file name and major number
- The configuration file (found in */usr/include/linux*)
- The relevant kernel configuration option (This line lists the question you must answer "yes" to when you configure the kernel.)
- Documentation (found in */usr/src/linux/Documentation/cdrom*)

I then list any additional information that is specific to the driver. You will probably want to read only the section relevant to your drive type.

Sbpcd driver

Principal author: Eberhard Moenkeberg (*emoenke@gwdg.de*)
Multisession support: yes (but not CD-52x drives)
Multiple drive support: yes
Loadable module support: yes
Reading audio frames: yes (CR-562, CR-563, and CD-200 only)
Auto-probing: yes
Device file: */dev/sbpcd*, major 25
Configuration file: *sbpcd.h*
Kernel config option: Matsushita/Panasonic/Creative . . . support?
README file: */usr/src/linux/Documentation/cdrom/sbpcd*

This is the kernel driver for proprietary interface CD-ROM drives sold under a variety of brand names. It accepts a kernel command line of the form

```
sbpcd=io-address,interface-type
sbpcd=io-address,interface-type
```

where *io-address* is the base address of the device (e.g., 0x230), and *interface-type* indicates the type of interface to the drive, one of SoundBlaster,

LaserMate, or SPEA. See the README file for hints on what interface type to use for different configurations. Using **sbpcd=0** disables auto-probing, disabling the driver.

The device file can be created using

```
% mknod /dev/sbpcd b 25 0
% mknod /dev/sbpcd b 25 0
```

Up to four drives per controller are supported. The next three drives on the first controller would use minor device numbers 1 through 3. If you have more than one controller, create devices with major numbers 26, 27, and 28, up to a maximum of 4 controllers (therefore, 16 CD-ROM drives in total; hopefully enough for most users).

WARNING   A common error is to assume that any CD-ROM drive that connects to a SoundBlaster card should use this kernel driver. Most CD-ROM drives being sold by Creative Labs are now EIDE/ATAPI drives and will not work with this driver; they should use the ATAPI driver instead.

Sonycdu535 driver

Principal author: Ken Pizzini (*ken@halcyon.com*)
Multisession support: no
Multiple drive support: no
Loadable module support: yes
Reading audio frames: no
Auto-probing: no
Device file: */dev/sonycd535, major 24*
Configuration file: *sonycd535.h*
Kernel config option: Sony CDU535 CD-ROM support?
README file: */usr/src/linux/Documentation/cdrom/sonycd535*

This driver accepts a kernel command line of the form

```
sonycd535=io-address
sonycd535=io-address
```

where *io-address* is the base address of the controller (e.g., 0x320). Alternatively, you can set the address in the file *sonycd535.h* and compile it in.

The device file can be created using

```
% mknod /dev/sonycd535 b 24 0
% mknod /dev/sonycd535 b 24 0
```

Some Linux distributions use */dev/sonycd* for this device. Older versions of the driver used major device number 21; make sure your device file is correct. This driver was previously distributed as a patch but is now part of the standard kernel. See the README file for more information on this driver.

Cdu31a driver

> Principal author: Corey Minyard (*minyard@wf-rch.cirr.com*)
> Multisession support: yes
> Multiple drive support: no
> Loadable module support: yes
> Reading audio frames: yes
> Auto-probing: no
> Device file: */dev/cdu31a*, major 15
> Configuration file: *cdu31a.h*
> Kernel config option: Sony CDU31A/CDU33A CD-ROM support?
> README file: */usr/src/linux/Documentation/cdrom/cdu31a*

This driver accepts a kernel command line of the form

```
cdu31a=io-address,irq,PAS
cdu31a=io-address,irq,PAS
```

The first number is the base address of the card (e.g., 0x340). The second is the interrupt number to use (0 means to use polled input/output). The optional third parameter should be "PAS" if the drive is connected to a ProAudioSpectrum 16 sound card, otherwise it's left blank. The device file can be created using

```
% mknod /dev/cdu31a b 15 0
% mknod /dev/cdu31a b 15 0
```

See the file *cdu31a* for more information on this driver. Also see the Web page created by Jeffrey Oxenreider (*zureal@infinet.com*) that covers a lot of common problems with these drives—*http://www.limited.net/~zureal/cdu31a.html*.

Aztcd driver

> Principal author: Werner Zimmermann (*zimmerma@rz.fht-esslingen.de*)
> Multisession support: yes
> Multiple drive support: no
> Loadable module support: yes
> Reading audio frames: no
> Auto-probing: no
> Device file: */dev/aztcd0*, major 29
> Configuration file: *aztcd.h*
> Kernel config option: Aztech/Orchid/Okano/Wearnes (non-IDE) CD-ROM support?
> README file: */usr/src/linux/Documentation/cdrom/aztcd*

This driver accepts a kernel command line of the form

```
aztcd=io-address
aztcd=io-address
```

where the parameter is the base address of the card (e.g., 0x340).

The device file can be created using

```
% mknod /dev/aztcd0 b 29 0
% mknod /dev/aztcd0 b 29 0
```

See the README file for more information on this driver.

Gscd driver

Principal author: Oliver Raupach (*raupach@nwfs1.rz.fh-hannover.de*)
Multisession support: yes
Multiple drive support: no
Loadable module support: yes
Reading audio frames: no
Auto-probing: no
Device file: */dev/gscd0*, major 16
Configuration file: *gscd.h*
Kernel config option: Goldstar R420 CD-ROM support?
README file: */usr/src/linux/Documentation/cdrom/gscd*

This driver accepts a kernel command line of the form

```
gscd=io-address
gscd=io-address
```

specifying the base address of the card (e.g., 0x340).

The device file can be created using

```
% mknod /dev/gscd0 b 16 0
% mknod /dev/gscd0 b 16 0
```

See the README file and the World Wide Web site *http://linux.rz.fh-hannover.de/~raupach/goldstar.html* for more information on this driver.

Mcd driver

Principal author: Martin Harriss (*martin@bdsi.com*)
Multisession support: no
Multiple drive support: no
Loadable module support: yes
Reading audio frames: no
Auto-probing: no
Device file: */dev/mcd*, major 23

Configuration file: *mcd.h*
Kernel config option: Standard Mitsumi CD-ROM support?
README file: */usr/src/linux/Documentation/cdrom/mcd*

This is the older driver for Mitsumi that has been available for some time. You might want to try the newer *mcdx* driver, which has some new features but is still considered experimental.

This driver accepts a kernel command line of the form

```
mcd=io-address,irq
mcd=io-address,irq
```

specifying the base address of the card (e.g., 0x340) and the IRQ request number used. The device file can be created using

```
% mknod /dev/mcd b 23 0
% mknod /dev/mcd b 23 0
```

See the README file for more information on this driver.

Mcdx driver

Principal author: Heiko Schlittermann (*heiko@lotte.sax.de*)
Multisession support: yes
Multiple drive support: yes
Loadable module support: yes
Reading audio frames: no (not supported by hardware)
Auto-probing: no
Device file: */dev/mcdx0*, major 20
Configuration file: *mcdx.h*
Kernel config option: Experimental Mitsumi support?
README file: */usr/src/linux/Documentation/cdrom/mcdx*

This is a new driver for Mitsumi drivers. The older and possibly more stable *mcd* driver is still available.

This driver accepts a kernel command line of the form

```
mcdx=io-address,irq
mcdx=io-address,irq
```

specifying the base address of the card (e.g., 0x340) and the IRQ request number used. The device file can be created using

```
% mknod /dev/mcdx0 b 20 0
% mknod /dev/mcdx0 b 20 0
```

WARNING   If you recently bought a Mitsumi CD-ROM drive, don't assume that it should use this kernel driver. Most Mitsumi models are now EIDE/ATAPI drives and should use the *idecd* kernel driver.

See the README file for more information on this driver.

Cm206 driver

Principal author: David A. van Leeuwen (*david@tm.tno.nl*)
Multisession support: yes
Multiple drive support: no
Loadable module support: yes
Reading audio frames: no
Auto-probing: yes
Device file: */dev/cm206cd*, major 32
Configuration file: *cm206.h*
Kernel config option: Philips/LMS CM206 CD-ROM support?
README file: */usr/src/linux/Documentation/cdrom/cm206*

The driver accepts a kernel command line of the form

```
cm206=io-address,irq
cm206=io-address,irq
```

where the first number is the base address of the card (e.g., 0x340) and the second is the interrupt channel number.

The device file can be created using

```
% mknod /dev/cm206cd b 32 0
% mknod /dev/cm206cd b 32 0
```

See the README file for more information on this driver.

Optcd driver

Principal author: Leo Spiekman (*spiekman@dutette.et.tudelft.nl*)
Multisession support: yes
Multiple drive support: no
Loadable module support: yes
Reading audio frames: no
Auto-probing: no
Device file: */dev/optcd0*, major 17
Configuration file: *optcd.h*
Kernel config option: Experimental Optics Storage ... CD-ROM support?
README file: */usr/src/linux/Documentation/cdrom/optcd*

The driver accepts a kernel command line of the form

```
optcd=io-address
optcd=io-address
```

to specify the base address of the card (e.g., 0x340). The device file can be created using

```
% mknod /dev/optcd0 b 17 0
% mknod /dev/optcd0 b 17 0
```

See the README file for more information on this driver.

Sjcd driver

Principal author: Vadim V. Model (*vadim@rbrf.msk.su*)
Multisession support: no
Multiple drive support: no
Loadable module support: yes
Reading audio frames: no
Auto-probing: no
Device file: */dev/sjcd*, major 18
Configuration file: *sjcd.h*
Kernel config option: Experimental Sanyo H94A CD-ROM support?
README file: */usr/src/linux/Documentation/cdrom/sjcd*

The driver accepts a kernel command line of the form

```
sjcd=io-address,irq,dma
sjcd=io-address,irq,dma
```

indicating the base address, interrupt, and DMA channel to be used (e.g., sjcd=0x340,10,5). The device file can be created using

```
% mknod /dev/sjcd b 18 0
% mknod /dev/sjcd b 18 0
```

See the README file for more information on this driver.

SCSI driver

Principal author: David Giller
Multisession support: yes (depending on drive)
Multiple drive support: yes
Loadable module support: yes
Reading audio frames: yes (depending on drive)
Auto-probing: yes
Device file: */dev/scd0*, major 11
Configuration file: *cdrom.h*

Kernel config option: SCSI CD-ROM support?
README file: */usr/src/linux/Documentation/scsi.txt*

There are kernel command line options specific to each type of SCSI controller. See the Linux SCSI HOWTO for more information. Multiple drives are supported (up to the limit of the maximum number of devices on the SCSI bus). Create device files with major number 11 and minor numbers starting at zero:

```
% mknod /dev/scd0 b 11 0
% mknod /dev/scd0 b 11 0
% mknod /dev/scd1 b 11 1
% mknod /dev/scd1 b 11 1
```

IDECD driver

Principal author: Scott Snyder (*snyder@fnald0.fnal.gov*)
Multisession support: yes
Multiple drive support: yes
Loadable module support: no
Reading audio frames: yes
Auto-probing: yes
Device file: */dev/hd[a-h]*, major 22
Configuration file: *cdrom.h*
Kernel config option: Include support for IDE/ATAPI CD-ROMs?
README file: */usr/src/linux/Documentation/cdrom/ide-cd*

This is the driver for ATAPI CD-ROMS. The driver accepts a kernel command line of the form

```
hdx=cdrom
hdx=cdrom
```

where **hdx** can be any of *hda* through *hdh*, or simply *hd* for the "next" drive in sequence. The parameters for each IDE controller also can be specified with a command line of the form

```
idex=io-address,ctl,irq
idex=io-address,ctl,irq
```

The first parameter is the IDE interface, named *ide0* through *ide4.* The second is the base address of the interface, and the third is the control address (normally the base address plus 0x206). The fourth parameter is the interrupt number. Only the first parameter is mandatory. See the README file for more details.

TIP   Most CD-ROM drives now use the IDE/ATAPI interface. If you are uncertain which kernel driver to use, this is the best one to try first.

Booting Linux and Testing the Installation

Once the kernel is built and the device files created you can reboot. Watch for a message such as the following indicating that the CD-ROM has been found by the device driver (the message will vary depending on the drive type):

```
SBPCD: Trying to detect a SoundBlaster CD-ROM drive at 0x230.
SBPCD: Trying to detect a SoundBlaster CD-ROM drive at 0x230.
SBPCD: - Drive 0: CR-562-x (0.76)
SBPCD: - Drive 0: CR-562-x (0.76)
SBPCD: 1 SoundBlaster CD-ROM drive(s) at 0x0230.
SBPCD: 1 SoundBlaster CD-ROM drive(s) at 0x0230.
SBPCD: init done.
SBPCD: init done.
```

If the bootup messages scroll by too quickly to read, you should be able to retrieve them using the commands *dmesg* or *tail /var/adm/messages* (you may have to run as *root*).

If the drive is not found, then a problem has occurred. See the "Troubleshooting" section later in this chapter.

Mounting, Unmounting, and Ejecting Devices

To mount a CD-ROM, insert a disc in the drive, close the tray, and run the *mount* command as *root*. Assuming that you have created a symbolic link called */dev/cdrom* to your device file and that an empty directory */mnt* exists, then the following command will mount an ISO 9660 formatted CD-ROM:

```
% mount -t iso9660 -r /dev/cdrom /mnt
% mount -t iso9660 -r /dev/cdrom /mnt
```

The CD now can be accessed under the directory */mnt*. Note that although */mnt* is commonly used as a temporary mount point, some Linux distributions use */mnt/cdrom* instead. For a permanent installation you might want to use a more appropriate name like */cdrom*.

The *mount* command has many other options. You can read the *mount(8)* manual page for details.

You can add an entry to */etc/fstab* to automatically mount a CD-ROM when Linux boots or to specify parameters to use when it is mounted; see the *fstab(5)* manual page. The "user" option, in particular, is useful because it allows non-*root* users to mount and unmount discs (subject to some restrictions).

To unmount a CD-ROM, use the *umount* command as *root*:

```
% umount /mnt
% umount /mnt
```

The disc can be unmounted only if no processes are currently accessing the drive (including having their default directory set to the mounted drive). You can then eject the disc. Most drives have an eject button; there is also a standalone *eject* program that will eject CD-ROMs under software control.

WARNING   You should not eject a CD-ROM while it is mounted (this may or may not be possible depending on the type of drive). Unlike floppies, there is no danger of corrupting the data on the disc, but you may confuse the kernel device driver and obtain incorrect data.

The *sbpcd* driver can automatically eject a CD-ROM when it is unmounted and insert the CD tray when a disc is mounted. You can turn this feature off when compiling the kernel or by using a software command.

Note that to play audio CDs you should not try to mount them. Also, after playing an audio CD you may not be able to mount a CD-ROM. You need to send a CD audio "stop" command (using a CD player program) before trying the mount. This problem only appears to occur with some device drivers.

TIP   For an automated method of mounting and unmounted removable media, including CD-ROMs, you can use the *Supermount* package by Stephen Tweedie (*sct@dcs.ed.ac.uk*). This package is available at the ftp site *ftp://sunsite.unc.edu/pub/Linux/patches/diskdrives/*.

Troubleshooting

If you can't get your CD-ROM drive to work, try each of the following checks in order.

Make Sure You Really Are Running the Kernel You Compiled

You can check the date stamp on the kernel to see if you are running the one that you compiled with CD-ROM support. You can do this with the *uname* command:

```
% uname -a
% uname -a
Linux fizzbin 2.0.0 #1 Wed Mar 27 20:11:05 EST 1996 i386
Linux fizzbin 2.0.0 #1 Wed Mar 27 20:11:05 EST 1996 i386
```

or by displaying the file */proc/version*:

```
% cat /proc/version
% cat /proc/version
Linux version 2.0.0 (root@fizzbin) (gcc version 2.7.0) #1
Linux version 2.0.0 (root@fizzbin) (gcc version 2.7.0) #1
    Tue May 21 19:22:57 EDT 1996
    Tue May 21 19:22:57 EDT 1996
```

If the date stamp doesn't seem to match when you compiled the kernel, then you are running an old kernel. Did you really reboot? If you use LILO, did you re-install it (typically by running */etc/lilo/install*)? If booting from floppy, did you create a new boot floppy and use it when booting?

Make Sure the Proper Drivers Are Compiled Into the Kernel

You can see what drivers are compiled in by looking at */proc/devices*:

```
% cat /proc/devices
% cat /proc/devices
Character devices:
Character devices:
 1 mem
 1 mem
 2 pty
 2 pty
 3 ttyp
 3 ttyp
 4 tty
 4 tty
 5 cua
 5 cua
 6 lp
 6 lp
 7 vcs
 7 vcs
14 sound
14 sound
15 Joystick
15 Joystick

Block devices:
Block devices:
 2 fd
 2 fd
 3 ide0
 3 ide0
25 sbpcd
25 sbpcd
```

First look for your CD-ROM device driver. These are all block devices, in this case you can see that the *sbpcd* driver is present.

Also make sure that ISO 9660 filesystem support was compiled in, by looking at
/proc/filesystems:

```
% cat /proc/filesystems
% cat /proc/filesystems
        ext2
        ext2
        msdos
        msdos
nodev   proc
nodev   proc
        iso9660
        iso9660
```

You can also see what input/output port addresses are being used by a driver with
the file */proc/ioports*:

```
howto % cat /proc/ioports
howto % cat /proc/ioports
0000-001f : dma1
0000-001f : dma1
0020-003f : pic1
0020-003f : pic1
  ...
  ...
0230-0233 : sbpcd
0230-0233 : sbpcd
  ...
  ...
03f7-03f7 : floppy DIR
03f7-03f7 : floppy DIR
03f8-03ff : serial(auto)
03f8-03ff : serial(auto)
```

If any of the drivers you thought you compiled in are not displayed, then something went wrong with the kernel configuration or with the build. Start the installation process again, beginning with configuration and building of the kernel.

Did the Kernel Detect Your Drive During Booting?

Make sure that the CD-ROM device was detected when the kernel booted. You
should have seen a message on bootup. If the messages scrolled off the screen,
you can usually recall them using the command:

```
% dmesg
% dmesg
```

or

```
% tail /var/adm/messages
% tail /var/adm/messages
```

If your drive was not found, then something is wrong. Make sure it is powered on and all cables are connected. If your drive has hardware jumpers for addressing, check that they are set correctly (e.g., drive 0 if you have only one drive). ATAPI CD-ROMS should be jumpered as "single" or "master," and not "slave" when only one IDE device is attached to an interface. If the drive works under DOS, then you can be reasonably confident that the hardware is working.

Not all kernel drivers use auto-probing, and in any case the probing is not always reliable. Use the kernel command-line option listed for your kernel driver type. You may want to try several different values if you are not sure of the address or other parameters. LILO can be (and usually is) configured to allow you to enter the parameters manually when booting.

If you have a system with a "Plug and Play" BIOS, you may need to disable it using your system setup program. At the time of this writing, Linux did not yet support Plug and Play devices but it was in development.

Another possibility is that you used the wrong kernel driver for your CD-ROM drive. Some documentation may refer to proprietary interfaces as IDE, leading some to mistakenly believe they are ATAPI drives.

Another possibility is that your drive (or interface card) is one of the so-called compatible types that requires initialization by the DOS driver. Try booting DOS and loading the vendor-supplied DOS device driver. Then soft-boot Linux using Control-Alt-Delete.

If your drive is not listed in this document, it is possible that there are no drivers for it available under Linux. You can check with some of the references listed in Appendix B for assistance.

Can You Read Data from the Drive?

Try reading data from the CD-ROM drive. Typing the following command should cause the drive activity light (if present) to come on, and if the device is in working order, no errors should be reported. Use whatever device file is appropriate for your drive and make sure a CD-ROM is inserted; use Control-C to exit.

```
% dd if=/dev/cdrom of=/dev/null bs=2048
% dd if=/dev/cdrom of=/dev/null bs=2048
^C
^C
124+0 records in
124+0 records in
124+0 records out
124+0 records out
```

If this works, then the kernel is communicating with the drive and you can move on to the next step. If not, then a possible cause is the device file. Make sure that the device file in the */dev* directory has the correct major and minor numbers as listed previously for your drive type. Check that the permissions on the device file allow reading and writing.

A remote possibility is a hardware problem. Try testing the drive under DOS, if possible, to determine if this could be the case.

Can You Mount the Drive?

If you can read from the drive but cannot mount it, first verify that you compiled in ISO 9660 filesystem support by reading */proc/filesystems*, as described previously. Make sure you are mounting the drive with the *-t iso9660* and *-r* options and that a reliable CD-ROM (not audio CD) is inserted in the drive. You normally must mount drives as user *root*.

With ATAPI CD-ROM drives you may need to mount specifying a block size of 2048 bytes. Add the option *-o block=2048* to the mount parameters. Make sure that the mount point exists and is an empty directory.

If you are automatically mounting the CD-ROM on bootup, make sure that you have correct entries in the */etc/fstab* file. Some Linux install programs have been known to create incorrect entries.

If you are running the *syslog* daemon, there may be error messages from the kernel that you are not seeing. Try using the *dmesg* command:

```
% dmesg
% dmesg
SBPCD: sbpcd_open: no disk in drive
SBPCD: sbpcd_open: no disk in drive
```

There may also be errors logged to files in */var/adm*, depending on how your system is configured.

Debugging Audio Problems

If the drive works with CD-ROMs, but not for playing audio CDs, here are some possible solutions.

You need an application program to play audio CDs. Some applications may be broken or may not be compatible with your drive. Try other applications or try recompiling them yourself.

A few of the CD-ROM kernel drivers do not support playing audio CDs. Check the appropriate README file or source code comments to see if that is the case.

Check if the audio can be played through the headphone jack. If so, then the problem is most likely related to your sound card. Use a mixer program to set the input device and volume levels. Make sure you have installed an audio cable from the CD-ROM drive to the sound card and that the kernel sound card driver is installed and working.

When All Else Fails

If you still have problems, here are some final suggestions for things to try:

- Carefully re-read this chapter.

- Read the latest Linux CD-ROM HOWTO document and the kernel source README files.

- Post a question to one of the *comp.os.linux* or other Usenet newsgroups.

- Send a question to the Linux mailing list.

- Try using the latest Linux kernel.

- Contact your computer dealer.

- Contact the CD-ROM manufacturer.

- Send mail to the author of the relevant kernel driver.

- Send mail to the author of the Linux CD-ROM HOWTO.

CHAPTER NINE

THE JOYSTICK DRIVER

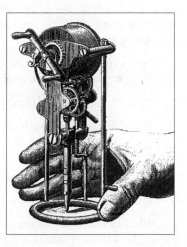

A common input device used by multimedia applications, most notably games, is the standard PC analog joystick. A device driver for Linux is available that supports the joystick port provided on most game, multifunction input/output, and sound cards. In this chapter I describe what is needed to configure the joystick driver under Linux.

The joystick driver assumes the interface uses the standard joystick input/output address 0x201. More than one joystick interface card is not supported. If you have both a multifunction I/O card with a joystick interface and an interface on a sound card, make sure that one of the interfaces is disabled or there will be a conflict.

Most joystick interfaces support two joysticks. Often, to connect more than one joystick requires a special "Y" cable that splits the single joystick connector into two. Most three axis joysticks are also accommodated (the third axis, typically used as a throttle control for flight simulator programs, uses one of the axes from the second joystick input). Only two buttons per joystick are supported.

Installation

The joystick driver is not part of the standard kernel distribution; you have to obtain it separately. At the time of writing, the latest version was 0.8.0, available from *ftp://sunsite.unc.edu/pub/Linux/kernel/patches/console/joystick-0.8.0.tar.gz*. You can also find it at most of the major Linux archive sites listed in Appendix B, *Linux Resources*.

The driver is a loadable kernel module, so you need the module utilities (standard with most Linux distributions) in order to be able to load and unload it. Running as a module has several benefits: it can be loaded and unloaded as needed to save memory, and building the driver does not require recompiling the kernel or rebooting the Linux system.

The package includes instructions for installation and configuration. The basic installation process consists of:

1. Unpacking the distribution (using *tar*)

2. Installing the */usr/include/linux/joystick.h* header file

3. Compiling the driver

4. Creating the device files (using the included script)

5. Loading the driver into a running Linux kernel

Included in the distribution is a program for testing the joystick driver, and a utility for calibrating the values read by the driver against your joystick.

Some of the applications described in Part III make use of a joystick, and Chapter 15, *Programming Joystick Devices*, describes how to program the joystick device under Linux.

PART THREE

A SURVEY OF MULTIMEDIA APPLICATIONS

The range of tools and applications that can be used to create multimedia on Linux is impressive, particularly when you consider that most of them are available free on the Internet.

In Part III we review some of these multimedia applications. The intent is to give you an appreciation of what exists, so I offer only an overview of the features and capabilities, rather than detailed instructions for running and using them. An understanding of what some current multimedia applications can do will be useful in Part IV when we develop new applications of our own.

Except where noted otherwise, all of the applications for Linux are freely available either as part of Linux distributions or from Internet and BBS archive sites.

CHAPTER TEN

APPLICATIONS FOR SOUND AND MUSIC

I will begin this chapter with a look at applications related to audio. I've somewhat arbitrarily divided the applications into a number of different categories. Except where noted otherwise, all of the applications for Linux are freely available as part of Linux distributions or from Internet and BBS archive sites. The primary site for each application is listed with its description, though in most cases, you can also find the application on many other sites. Appendix B, *Linux Resources*, lists a number of popular Linux archive sites on the Internet. The contents of these sites are also included on many Linux CD-ROM distributions.

I've listed the primary author of each package, with an email address, if available. In many cases, a number of people have worked on a software package, and sometimes the current maintainer may be different from the author. Check the documentation that comes with each package for the latest status. Use discretion when contacting developers by email. Many receive a high volume of messages from people asking for assistance and have only a limited amount of time to devote to developing and supporting free software.

Some of the applications include ready-to-run binaries, but more often you will need to compile them from source code. They should compile and run cleanly, but occasionally you may experience some problems, which happen for a number of reasons. Binaries compiled for different versions of the kernel sound driver may not be compatible with your version. You also may run into binaries linked with versions of shared libraries that do not exist on your system. Recompiling from source code generally solves these problems.

The location of files can vary from one Linux distribution to another (although this situation is improving with the adoption of the Linux File System Standard). The author of the distribution may have made assumptions about the location of header files that may not be valid for your system. You may have to tweak some of the *make* files to get them to work. In some cases, changes to libraries, system header files, and even the C compiler can cause errors when building the software that will require source code changes.

Some applications have undergone considerable testing, while others may be an inexperienced programmer's first foray into multimedia. Usually the documentation will indicate if the author considers his creation to be stable or a "use at your own risk" alpha release. Often the author or other Linux users are happy to help if you have questions.

Multimedia is a new area and solving these problems is "part of the game" with Linux and should be considered a learning opportunity.

Digital Audio

I include in this category any applications that are related to digitized or sampled sound. These programs are useful for three distinct purposes. First, you can use them as tools to create and modify sound files to be used by other applications. Second, you can call the applications from other multimedia programs in order to add sound support to them. For example, *Mosaic* needs to call an external tool to play sound samples linked to Web pages. Third, you can study the source code and adapt it for use in new applications. Most of these applications are released under the GNU General Public License, which, among other things, allows you to use the source code to create a derived work, provided that it is released under the same policy.

The applications offer a user interface that generally falls in one of three categories. Some make use of a command-line interface, the traditional way for tools to operate under UNIX-like operating systems. This interface is powerful because it allows the applications to be used as building blocks that can be called from shell scripts or other applications.

Some tools offer a graphical user interface that runs under the X Window System. This graphical interface is usually more intuitive to use and makes the application interactive.

Interfaces in the third category make use of the *termcap* or *curses* libraries. This category fits somewhere in the middle—the applications are text-based but can be interactive, making use of the terminal's text capabilities. By using color and character graphics, the developer may implement a pseudo-graphical interface.

Here are some examples of what digital audio applications can do:

- Record sound from a microphone or other audio source and save it to a sound file (at various sample sizes and sampling rates and using different sound file formats).

- Play back a digitized sound file using a sound card.

- Allow the user to edit a sound waveform (usually graphically) with the capability of adding, removing, and duplicating portions of the sound file, combining different sound samples, adjusting volume levels, and adding effects such as echo and filtering.

- Convert sound files from one format to another (e.g., from μ-law to WAV format).

- Allow sound waveforms to be visualized graphically in the time or frequency domains, either from a sound file or using real-time data from a sound card.

The following sections outline some of the most basic tools that any multimedia user or developer needs.

srec/splay/vrec/vplay

> Authors: Hannu Savolainen (*hannu@voxware.pp.fi*) and Michael Beck
> (*beck@informatik.hu-berlin.de*)
> Available from: *ftp://sunsite.unc.edu/pub/Linux/kernel/sound/snd-util-3.0.tar.gz*

The *snd-util* package, put together by Hannu Savolainen, author of the kernel sound driver, is a collection of some basic sound utilities. In the early days of Linux development, these were the only sound applications available.

The package includes the programs *srec* and *splay*. These two programs (actually one program invoked by two different names) provide rudimentary capability for recording and playback of digitized sound files. The tools are command line–based.

srec records sound, writing the raw data to a file or standard output if no filename is specified. *splay* will play the same raw sound data back. The input device that is used for recording and the levels for record and playback depend on the current mixer settings. You can use a mixer program to set these.

For example, to record 10 seconds of audio at a 22 kHz sampling rate and 8-bit sample size, one could use the following command:

```
srec -t 10 -s 22000 sound.raw
```

The file can then be played back using:

```
splay -s 22000 sound.raw
```

These tools are simple but useful for basic sound recording and playback. The *vrec* and *vplay* programs extend the functionality further, supporting sound files in two of the more popular sound file formats: Creative Labs VOC and Microsoft WAV.

Hannu Savolainen wrote the *splay* and *srec* programs. Michael Beck wrote *vrec* and *vplay*.

wavedit

> Author: Aaron Goldstein (*ag4z@andrew.cmu.edu*)
> Available: *ftp://sunsite.unc.edu/pub/Linux/apps/sound/editors/wavedit-v0.1.tgz*

wavedit is a simple waveform editor that graphically displays the shape of a sound file and allows the user to make changes with a mouse using cut, paste, and copy functions. You also can play the waveform or save it to a disk file.

wavedit is written in C++ and uses the *svgalib* graphics library to enable it to run on a Linux virtual console.

sox

> Author: Lance Norskog (*thinman@netcom.com*)
> Available from: *ftp://sunsite.unc.edu/pub/Linux/apps/sound/convert/*
> *Lsox-linux.tar.gz*

sox (the name stands for SOund eXchange) is a powerful utility for converting sound files from one format to another and for performing some basic audio effects. It understands all of the common sound formats and provides the ability to manipulate nonstandard types.

The original *sox* program was ported to Linux by Greg Lee (*lee@uhunix.uhcc.hawaii.edu*). He also added some enhancements, including the programs *play* and *pplay*, aliases for *sox* that can play sound files.

sox is an invaluable tool if you have any need to convert between sound file formats. It is also one of the few utilities that runs much more quickly if a math coprocessor is present.

WAVplay

> Author: Andre Fuechsel (*af1@irz.inf.tu-dresden.de*)
> Available from: *ftp://sunsite.unc.edu/pub/Linux/apps/sound/players/*
> *wavplay021w1.tar.z*

WAVplay is a graphical sound recording and playback tool. You can record sound, see it displayed graphically, and play it back. *WAVplay* has a facility for selecting portions of the waveform and zooming the display, but has no sound editing capabilities.

Figure 10-1 shows the user interface, which is based on the Athena widgets toolkit for X11.

Also included are the command-line utilities *play* and *record* for sound recording and playback.

Edwin N. Strickland

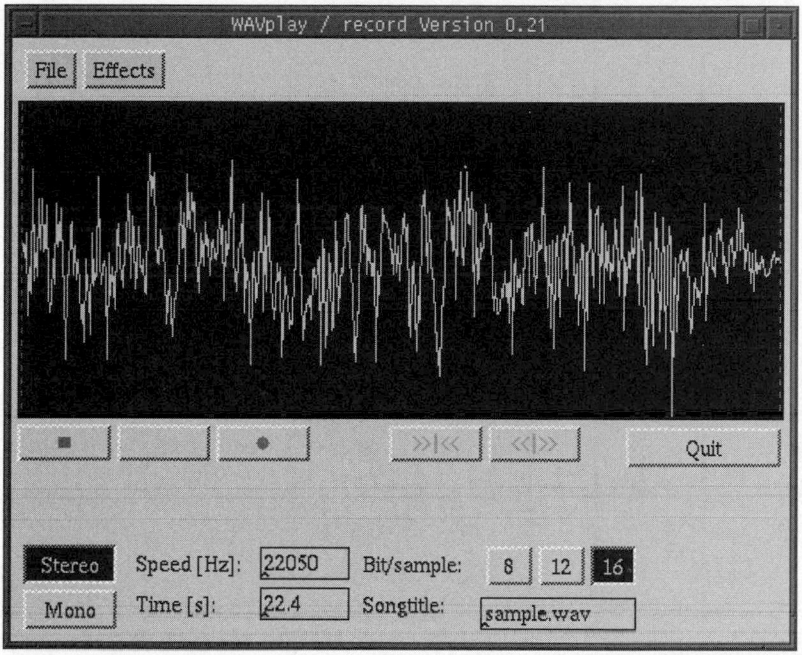

Figure 10–1: WAVplay

Sound Studio

Author: Paul D. Sharpe (*een2pds@sun.leeds.ac.uk*)
Available from: *ftp://sunsite.unc.edu/pub/Linux/apps/sound/players/
studio.0.1.tgz*

Sound Studio is a full-featured graphical sound recording, playback, and editing tool that runs under the X Window System. Paul Sharpe developed the tool as a third-year university project and has made it freely available on the Internet. Figure 10-2 shows the main window of the user interface.

Sound Studio lets you record and play back sound files. The sound waveform can be viewed and edited from the GUI using the mouse. All mixer functions can also be controlled from this tool. Online help is provided, as well as a comprehensive manual in PostScript format.

The tool was created specifically for Linux using the *Tcl/Tk* toolkit and some C code. It calls the *sox* program for some of the underlying functions such as sound file conversion and effects. This utility is one of the most comprehensive tools of its type for Linux and obviously represents several months of development effort.

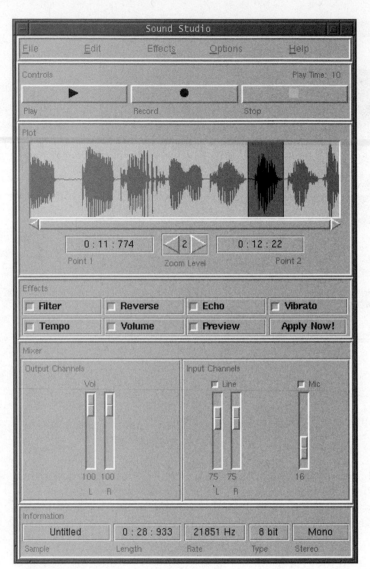

Figure 10-2: Sound Studio

MiXViews

Author: Douglas Scott (*MixViews@ccmrc.ucsb.edu*)
Available from: *ftp://ftp.ccmrc.ucsb.edu/pub/MixViews*

MiXViews is a comprehensive graphical sound editing, processing, and analysis tool that runs under the X Window System. *MiXViews* presents the user with a graphical representation of sound data. It can read and write data using most common sound file formats, as well as record and play back using a sound card directly. You can edit the sound data by selecting portions of the waveform with the mouse and using functions such as cut, paste, and delete.

The utility also supports effects such as mixing, filtering, scaling of amplitude and frequency, and combining waveforms. Using a Fast Fourier Transform option the sound data can also be viewed in the frequency domain. Figure 10-3 shows an example of the user interface.

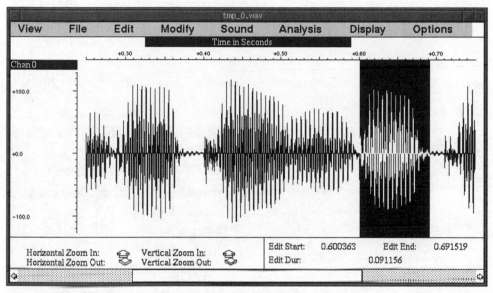

Figure 10-3: MiXViews

MiXViews runs under X on Linux and several other workstation UNIX platforms. It was implemented using the *InterViews* toolkit. Written in C, it uses the MVC (Model-View-Controller) paradigm of object-oriented programming. All of the source code is freely available on the archive site; precompiled binaries are also available for users who do not wish to rebuild it themselves.

Mixers

A mixer program allows the user to control the mixer device provided on most sound cards. If you do any type of sound recording or playback, you need a mixer program to select the input channel and volume levels.

As with the tools in the previous section, mixer programs are offered with command line–, graphical–, and *curses*– or *termcap*–based user interfaces. If GUI-based, the particular toolkit used to implement the mixer influences the look and feel of the interface. Many users prefer the text-based programs, as some graphical mixers are very large and take considerable time to start up, and they consume much real estate on the display.

Sound cards vary in the functions provided in their mixer circuitry. A properly implemented mixer will query the hardware for its capabilities and only allow the user to change settings that are valid.

Some other useful features to look for in a mixer program include support for selecting the recording inputs, the ability to lock the left and right channels together for stereo channels, and the ability to save mixer settings to a file for later recall.

Quite a number of audio mixer programs have been written for Linux. It seems to be a popular application to write as a first multimedia program.

Figure 10-4 is a screen shot illustrating some of the mixer programs described in this section.

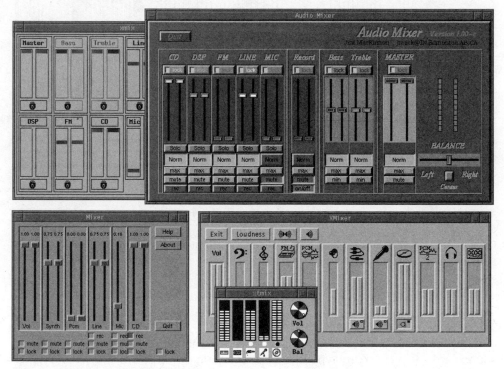

Figure 10–4: Some mixer programs

xmixer (multimedia)

Author: Olav "Mac" Wolfelschneider (*wosch@rbg.informatik.th-darmstadt.de*)
Available from: *ftp://sunsite.unc.edu/pub/Linux/apps/sound/*
multimedia-2.1.tar.gz

Olav's multimedia package includes *xmixer*, an X11-based mixer. It sports a nice graphical user interface based on a custom toolkit that produces a small executable.

aumix

Author: Savio Lam (*lam836@cs.cuhk.hk*)
Available from: *ftp://sunsite.unc.edu/pub/Linux/apps/sound/mixers/*
aumix-0.2.tar.gz

aumix is a text-based mixer that uses the *ncurses* library to implement a color display with sliders and controls implemented using graphics characters. Also included is the prototype of a simple audio level meter program called *dbmeter*.

cam

Author: Jan Vandenberghe (*jvdbergh@uia.ua.ac.be*)
Available from: *ftp://sunsite.unc.edu/pub/Linux/apps/sound/mixers/*
cam-0.7.tar.gz

The *cam* program uses *aumix* as a starting point. It is a color *ncurses*-based mixer. The author extended the tool to add support for stereo channels, online help, and the ability to load and save mixer settings to a file. It can also run as a purely command line–based tool.

The author explains the name in the README file: "CPU stands for Computerfreaks Playing around on University. It is a computer club some friends and I started. I took the name CPU's Audio Mixer because the child has got to have a name."

setmixer

Author: Michal Jaegermann (*michal@ellpspace.math.ualberta.ca*)
Available from: *ftp://sunsite.unc.edu/pub/Linux/apps/sound/mixers/*
setmix-0.4.tar.gz

setmixer is a simple command line–oriented mixer, intended as a convenient way to initialize your sound card when the system boots. It supports all functions including stereo.

A typical use of the tool, to set both channels of master volume to 100% and the CD input to 77% and 78% for the left and right channels respectively, would look like this:

```
% setmixer vol 100 cd 77,78
% setmixer -V
    vol - 100,100
  synth - 75,75
    pcm - 75,75
   line - 75,75
    mic - 16
     cd - 77,78
```

xamixer

Author: Jim MacKinnon (*jmack@IN.Edmonton.AB.CA*)
Available from: *ftp://sunsite.unc.edu/pub/Linux/apps/sound/mixers/
            xamixer1.00c-src.tgz*

xamixer is a comprehensive graphical mixer that runs under X. It was implemented using the freely available *XForms* toolkit. Just about every conceivable mixer feature is supported including a number of buttons for shortcuts such as setting channels to maximum and minimum gain.

xamixer is provided in source form and a precompiled binary for those who don't have the *XForms* toolkit installed.

xfmix

Author: Radek Doulik (*rodo@earn.cvut.cz*)
Available from: *ftp://sunsite.unc.edu/pub/Linux/apps/sound/mixers/
            xfmix-0.2.tar.gz*

xfmix is another X11-based graphical mixer implemented using the *XForms* toolkit. One unique feature is its online help. The version I reviewed was the initial alpha-level release, and did show some warning messages during operation, but was quite usable nevertheless.

xmix

Author: Hal Brand (*brand@netcom.com*)
Available from: *ftp://sunsite.unc.edu/pub/Linux/apps/sound/mixers/
            xmix-2.1.tar.gz*

xmix is a graphical mixer for X. It uses the Athena widget set. While functional, the user interface is not as polished as some of the other toolkits. By linking the program with the 3D Athena widget library (or using the supplied precompiled binary) the program has a more Motif-like three-dimensional appearance.

xmmix

Author: Ti Kan (*ti@amb.org*)
Available from: *ftp://sunsite.unc.edu/pub/Linux/apps/sound/mixers/*
        xmmix-1.1.tar.gz

xmmix is yet another X11 graphical mixer program; this one is based on the Motif toolkit. It is portable to a number of PC-based UNIX systems that support the Linux kernel sound drivers.

In order to build *xmmix* you need the Motif toolkit. Motif is a commercial product available for Linux from a number of vendors, and must be purchased. No pre-compiled binary for *xmmix* is supplied.

xtmix

Author: Martin Denn (*mdenn@unix-ag.uni-kl.de*)
Available from: *ftp://sunsite.unc.edu/pub/Linux/apps/sound/mixers/xtmix02.tgz*

xtmix is a small graphical mixer, running under X. Unlike some of the other programs reviewed here, it takes up little real estate on your display.

xvmixer

Author: Hannu Savolainen (*hannu@voxware.pp.fi*)
Available from: *ftp://sunsite.unc.edu/pub/Linux/kernel/sound/snd-util-3.0.tar.gz*

These last two mixer programs are by Hannu Savolainen, the author of the kernel sound driver. His *snd-util* package includes a number of basic sound utilities, including two mixer programs.

mixer is a simple command-line mixer program meant mainly to illustrate sound programming. A few examples are shown below:

```
% mixer
Usage: mixer { vol|synth|pcm|line|mic|cd } <value>
  or   mixer { +rec|-rec } <devicename>
% mixer vol
The mixer vol is currently set to 98:100.
% mixer vol 100
Setting the mixer vol to 100:100.
% mixer vol 10:20
Setting the mixer vol to 10:20.
% mixer vol 100
Setting the mixer vol to 100:100.
```

xvmixer is a graphical program that uses the *XView* toolkit for X11. It's quite simple (about 300 hundred lines of C code) but does the job.

Music Applications

I consider music applications to be any tools used for the composing and play-back of music, rather than just simple sound samples. These applications are most often used with files in formats such as MIDI, MOD, and Adagio.

As we discussed in Chapter 2, *Digital Audio*, one can play MIDI files directly using a sound card. You can also control MIDI devices external to the sound card using a MIDI interface.

One issue that is often important to developers who need to play music as part of a multimedia application is CPU overhead. Playing MOD files, for example, can take a good portion of a computer's resources. If an application plays a MOD file as background music for a multimedia application, performance of the rest of the program may be unacceptable. Two solutions to reducing this overhead are using FM synthesis (which is of poorer quality but often acceptable) or using a wavetable sound card (which is more expensive and limits the hardware that the application will run on).

Some multimedia developers are tempted to invent their own song file format. An issue to keep in mind is that with the popular formats for music files such as MOD and MIDI, one can find literally thousands of songs on the Internet. If you invent your own format, you will have to compose your own songs (or write a conver-sion tool).

In reviewing the applications described in the upcoming sections, you will see that most are utilities for playing song files. There are few free software tools for com-posing and editing songs. I'd particularly like to see a tool for composing MOD files using a graphical user interface. Here is a good opportunity for some new multimedia applications.

Adagio

> Author: Greg Lee (*lee@uhunix.uhcc.hawaii.edu*)
> Available from: *ftp://tsx-11.mit.edu/pub/linux/packages/sound/adagio05.tar.gz*

This package contains several utilities for playing and manipulating Adagio and MIDI files. Much of the program code is from a toolkit written at Carnegie Mellon University, with changes needed to allow it to be compiled under Linux. Included are the following programs:

mp
> plays MIDI files or converts them to Adagio scores

xmp
> version of *mp* with X11 graphical user interface

ad

plays an Adagio score or creates a file of MIDI information than can be sent to the *tracks* program

tracks

adds header information to one or more files created with *ad* to form a standard MIDI file

midt

disassembles MIDI files

tm

assembles one or more MIDI dumps produced by *midt*

setfm

downloads patch files to the sound driver

This package also includes the Carnegie Mellon MIDI Toolkit manual and some FM synthesizer patch files.

playmidi

Author: Nathan Laredo (*laredo@gnu.ai.mit.edu*)
Available from: *ftp://sunsite.unc.edu/pub/Linux/apps/sound/players/
playmidi-2.3.tgz*

playmidi is a text-based MIDI file player. It can play to a GUS sound card, external MIDI device, or an FM synthesizer such as that found on a SoundBlaster card. It can also play Creative Labs Music (CMF) and Microsoft RIFF (RMI) files.

playmidi uses the *curses* library to support an optional real-time color display of the notes being played. *xplaymidi* is a variant that runs under X11 with a graphical display, and *splaymidi* uses an SVGALIB-based graphical display. Both of the graphical versions show the words to the songs in a real-time "Karaoke mode" if the MIDI file contains the lyrics. Figure 10-5 shows *xplaymidi* in operation.

Sample MIDI files and all of the necessary FM patches for standard MIDI instruments are included.

TiMidity

Author: Tuukka Toivonen (*titoivon@snakemail.hut.fi*)
Available from: *ftp://sunsite.unc.edu/pub/Linux/apps/sound/players/
timidity-0.2h.tgz*

TiMidity converts MIDI song files to WAV format sound files. It uses Gravis Ultrasound-compatible instrument patch files to generate the digital data. The audio data can be played in real time to a sound card or stored as a disk file. It can produce 8- and 16-bit sound data with selectable sampling rate.

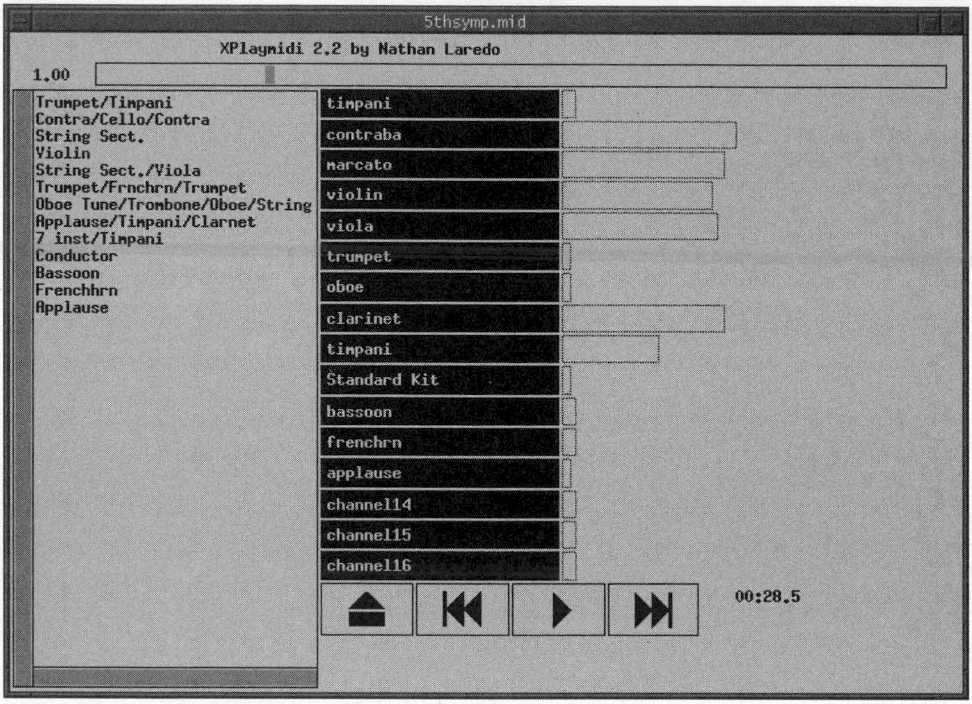

Figure 10–5: XPlaymidi

To use the utility you need MIDI patch files. If you have a GUS sound card, you should have received these patch files with it. If not, you can obtain freely available patches off the Internet from several sources listed in the *TiMidity* distribution. You don't need a GUS card to use this utility.

The user interface is selectable between command line, interactive *curses*-based text, or X11. Also included is a utility for creating patches from WAV files.

Tclmidi

> Author: Mike Durian (*durian@boogie.com*)
> Available: *ftp://sunsite.unc.edu/pub/Linux/apps/sound/midi/tclmidi-3.1d.tar.gz*

Tclmidi is an interpreter for the Tcl language with additional commands for working with MIDI files. Commands are provided to read, write, and manipulate MIDI files from Tcl. It also records from and plays back to external MIDI devices if the included device driver for MPU-401 compatible MIDI interface cards is used. The driver is a kernel-loadable module (it doesn't use the Linux kernel MIDI drivers). It also works on BSD/386, NetBSD, and SVR4 systems. *Tclmidi* optionally can be built with support for the Tk GUI toolkit. The package includes manpages, some example and contributed programs, and some test scripts.

MOD File Players

A number of players for MOD files have been written for Linux. Most offer a simple command-line interface, but a few have a graphical interface as well.

Some players have been written specifically to take advantage of the wavetable synthesis hardware on GUS sound cards. This feature significantly reduces the amount of processing required to play the files. Some of these programs can play files that are in compressed or archived formats, which is also a handy feature.

A number of different file types are generally referred to as "mods." Most programs support playing a subset of types. Some of the common ones, known by the names of the programs used to generate them, are:

- Composer 669
- Fast Tracker
- MED
- MOD (4, 6, or 8 channels; 15 or 31 samples)
- Multi Tracker (MTM)
- Noise Player
- Pro Tracker
- Scream Tracker III (S3M)
- Sound Tracker
- Star Trekker
- Take Tracker
- Ultra tracker (ULT)

Table 10-1 summarizes some of the available players for Linux. All of these can be found at *ftp://sunsite.unc.edu/pub/Linux/apps/sound/players/*.

Table 10–1: Linux MOD File Player Comparison

Name	File	Features
gmod/xgmod	gmod+x-2.1.tgz	compressed/archived files, GUS only, GUI
jol	jol-v0.1-bin+src.tgz	low CPU usage, written in C++
mod	mod-v0.8.tgz	stereo, compressed/archived files, GUS only, GUI
nspmod	nspmod-0.1.tar.gz	stereo, good sound, low CPU usage
pmod	pgmod-1.25b.tgz	GUS only, uses own driver

Table 10–1: Linux MOD File Player Comparison (continued)

Name	File	Features
s3mod	s3mod-v1.09.tar.gz	stereo, 16-bit support, GUS or non-GUS support
tracker	tracker-4.3-linux.tar.gz	stereo, run-time commands, stable and reliable
yampmod	yampmod-0.1.tar.gz	4 channel MODs only, low CPU overhead

With all these choices, which program should you use? If you have a GUS, you should get one of the programs designed for it. For non-GUS cards, *tracker* is a good choice for overall file compatibility and sound quality. It also runs on just about every computer platform including the Amiga on which MOD files originated. If you have a slower machine, *nspmod* or *jol* may be better as they require fewer CPU resources.

sod

> Author: Russell Marks (*mr216@gre.ac.uk*)
> Available: *ftp://sunsite.unc.edu/pub/Linux/apps/sound/players/sod2-1.0.tar.gz*

sod is a player for sound files in CSF format, which is a sound file format similar to MOD files invented by Russell Marks and Graham Richards. Like MOD files, CSF is based on using digitized 8-bit sound samples that are scaled and mixed in software to produce different notes. Unlike MODs, CSF files are in a relatively simple ASCII format that can be created using any text editor. There is no practical limit to the number of channels and the number of simultaneous notes that can be played per channel. Playback can be at any sampling rate, at 8- or 16-bit sampling width.

The *sod* program can play back to a sound card in real time or write the samples to a file. The package comes with some example song files and about a hundred instrument samples. It is a purely command line–oriented tool. The processing requirements to play the files are comparable to MOD files, although you can control this by varying the sampling rate and using buffered playback.

glib

> Author: Marc Espie (*espie@ens.fr*)
> Available: *ftp://sunsite.unc.edu/pub/Linux/apps/sound/editors/glib19f.tar.gz*

glib is a text-based librarian and patch editor for electronic synthesizers. *Xgl* is an X-based (*XView*) interface, which provides the means to modify wave envelopes graphically.

glib has support for the original SoundBlaster 2-operator FM synthesizer chip and the newer 4-operator OPL-3 chip found on cards such as the SoundBlaster Pro, and has limited support for the Gravis Ultrasound and the Kawaii K1 MIDI synthesizer.

Included is a document on programming the AdLib/SoundBlaster FM music chips by Jeffrey Lee (*jlee@smylex.uucp*). It was originally written by Tim Thompson, and many others have contributed to it. The Linux package was put together by Greg Lee.

Jazz

> Author: Per Sigmond (*Per.Sigmond@hiagder.no*)
> Available from: *ftp://sunsite.unc.edu/pub/Linux/apps/sound/midi/*
>   *jazz-src-v25a.tar.gz*

Jazz is a full-featured MIDI sequencer with an X11 graphical interface. With it you can load, edit, and save musical compositions in standard MIDI file format.

Jazz controls external MIDI devices (not sound cards) using its own device driver. It currently supports only the Roland MPU-401 MIDI interface card. You need the freely available *WxWindows* GUI toolkit to compile the source code.

Version 1 of *Jazz* was written by Andreas Voss (*andreas@avix.rhein-neckar.de*).

maplay

> Author: Tobias Bading (*bading@cs.tu-berlin.de*)
> Available from: *ftp://sunsite.unc.edu/pub/Linux/apps/sound/players/*
>   *maplay1_2.tar.gz*

maplay is an MPEG audio player that runs under Linux as well as Sun, SGI, and DEC workstations. It can decode and play back MPEG audio level I and II streams (level III may be added in future). *maplay* is written in C++.

maplay supports playback only to 16-bit sound cards. You also need a fast machine: real-time stereo decoding requires a Pentium class system. Slower machines can decode the MPEG stream to an audio file for later playback.

Louis P. Kruger (*lpkruger@tucson.princeton.edu*) added Linux support to *maplay*.

plany

> Author: Walter Reynolds (*ciswgrx@gsusgi2.gsu.edu*)
> Available from: *ftp://sunsite.unc.edu/pub/Linux/apps/sound/players/plany.tar.gz*

plany (for "play any") is a frontend interface to other sound file player programs. It allows you to display a list of music files such as MIDI, MOD, and WAV format files. You can select files or lists of files to be played in sequence using a *curses*-based interface and single-key commands.

plany uses a simple configuration file to match files to the appropriate player program, either by the filename suffix or strings within the file. It can also uncompress and unarchive files before playing. Finally, it remembers the location of the files and an optional song rating, in a per-user database file.

plany is a simple program, but very convenient for playing song files of different types.

Tickle Music

Author: Shannon Hendrix (*shendrix@pcs.cnu.edu*)
Available from: *ftp://sunsite.unc.edu/pub/Linux/apps/sound/players/*
      tmusic-1.0.tar.gz

Tickle Music is a graphical frontend to music file players for MIDI and MOD files. It uses the Tcl/Tk toolkit. You can browse directories, selecting files to be played in a play list. The tool then lets you play a queue of song files using the appropriate player for the file type. Figure 10-6 shows a screen shot of Tickle Music in operation.

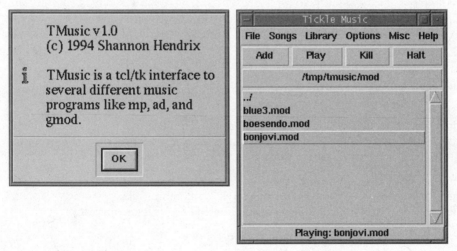

Figure 10–6: Tickle Music

Network Audio Programs

In this section I look at a number of programs designed for supporting audio over a network, either a one-way radio-like broadcast system, or two-way real-time communication between users. In order to use any of these packages, you need to be on the Internet or a network with at least two machines.

The ability to communicate using voice communications either over a local area network or the Internet is a relatively recent phenomenon and has attracted much interest. It remains to be seen whether the Internet can compete with traditional telephone networks.

Cyber Radio 1

Author: John Selbie (*jselbie@cis.ufl.edu*)
Available from: *ftp://sunsite.unc.edu/pub/Linux/apps/sound/CyberRadio1.tar.gz*

Cyber Radio 1 is a software package used at Georgia Tech to broadcast the campus radio station over the Internet. A server program digitizes audio and broadcasts it over the network. A client program running on other systems then accepts the audio and plays it back using the machine's audio device.

The system has been tested on Linux, Sun SPARC, BSD, and SGI UNIX systems. It is small and very simple to configure and is said to be quite good for music programming. It uses 8 kHz μ-law encoded sound data.

radio

Author: Guido van Rossum (*Guido.van.Rossum@cwi.nl*)
Available from: *ftp://sunsite.unc.edu/pub/Linux/apps/sound/talk/*
radio204linux.tar.gz

radio is another program for broadcasting audio over a network. It runs on most workstation platforms that support audio, including Linux.

The package consists of two programs. Users run *radio* to listen to programming. The program *broadcast* is used for transmitting audio to clients' machines. Multiple transmitters are supported.

radio sends 8 kHz μ-law encoded sound. Two variants of ADPCM compression are optionally supported. The uncompressed audio is reported to take about 1% of the total available bandwidth of a typical Ethernet network.

The tool is command line–oriented. A separate program, *tuner*, has a graphical user interface using Motif.

mtalk

Author: (*misch@elara.fsag.de*)
Available from: *ftp://sunsite.unc.edu/pub/Linux/apps/sound/talk/mtalk-0.4.tgz*

mtalk is a simple program for sending two-way audio over a network. It sends 8 kHz μ-law encoded data, either the plain 8-bit data or encoded using GSM compression. It uses the TCP protocol, or can operate via the *term* program (useful if you are connected to the Internet via a modem).

The package consists of a user-level program that is used to initiate a communication and a server daemon program that starts automatically on the calling end. The voice connection is one-way only, due to limitations of the Linux kernel sound driver, so it operates in a press-to-talk mode like radio. The user interface is command line–based.

mtalk uses its own proprietary protocol, so users on each end must use the same software package.

ztalk

> Authors: Scott Doty (*scott@cs.santarosa.edu*) and W. Richard Jhang
> (*feinmann@cs.mcgill.ca*)
> Available from: *ftp://sunsite.unc.edu/pub/Linux/apps/sound/talk/*
> *ztalk03+vm.tar.gz*

ztalk is a "voice mail" system for sending audio messages over a network. It works somewhat like electronic mail: audio messages can be composed and sent from a command line–oriented tool. On the receiving end the program can view, select, and play back stored messages.

ztalk was originally based on source code from *mtalk*. It uses GSM encoding (and optionally, no compression). The tool provides address book and alias features, and online help. It uses TCP and will run through the *term* program.

xztalk

> Author: Liem Bahneman (*roland@cac.washington.edu*)
> Available from: *ftp://sunsite.unc.edu/pub/Linux/apps/sound/talk/*
> *xztalk-1.3.tar.gz*

xztalk is a graphical user interface for the *ztalk* program. It needs the Motif X11 toolkit to build it (a precompiled binary is supplied). You also need to have installed the *xtalkd* program. Like *ztalk*, it supports *term*.

TCP_Talk

> Author: Arnaud Louet
> Available from: *ftp://sunsite.unc.edu/pub/Linux/apps/sound/talk/*
> *TCP_talk051.tgz*

TCP_Talk is another two-way audio talk program. It supports half-duplex communication with variable sampling rates and bits per sample. Three optional compression schemes and two simple encryption algorithms are offered. It uses a command-line interface and is implemented using client and server programs.

CyberPhone

Author: Matthew Krokosz and Greg Foglesong (*cyberphone@magenta.com*)
Available from: *ftp://sunsite.unc.edu/pub/Linux/apps/sound/talk/*
cyberphone_0.4.5-lnx.tar.z

CyberPhone is a commercial software package for real-time audio communications over the Internet. A user can call other users directly or use a server program that manages the status of users and allows calls to be placed by selecting names from a phone book.

The program features a graphical Motif user interface running under X11. A connection to the Internet is needed, either a direct connection or SLIP or PPP access using a 14.4 kbps or faster modem. Also required are a 16-bit sound card and microphone. The protocol uses silence removal and supports two compression algorithms.

CyberPhone is available for Linux and Sun workstations. It is a commercial product with a free demonstration version, but the full product requires registration and payment. It is distributed in binary format only.

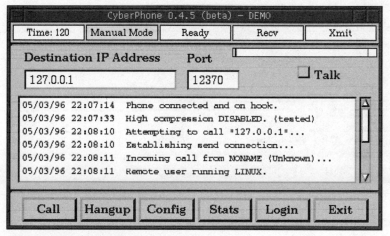

Figure 10–7: CyberPhone

Figure 10-7 shows a screen shot of the *CyberPhone* main window. More information can be found at CyberPhone's home page on the World Wide Web at *http://magenta.com/cyberphone/*.

RealAudio

Author: Progressive Networks, Inc. (*beta@realaudio.com*)
Available from: *http://www.realaudio.com/*

Progressive Networks has developed the *RealAudio* protocol and software for sending low bandwidth real-time audio over the Internet. Web sites use a RealAudio server to broadcast audio to users who play it back using a player program. The server software is sold commercially while executable versions of the player programs are freely downloadable from the Progressive Networks Web site. The server normally works via a Web browser such as Mosaic or Netscape. RealAudio players are available for all major computer platforms including Linux.

The RealAudio protocol is geared toward users with a low-bandwidth Internet connection, typically a modem link. Sound is monophonic, with quality said to be comparable to AM radio at 14.4 kbps or FM radio at 28.8 kbps. Figure 10-8 shows the user interface for the Linux version, which was in beta test at the time of this writing.

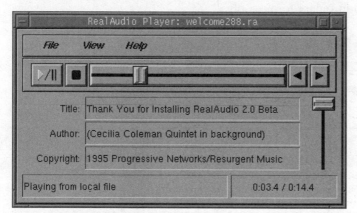

Figure 10–8: RealAudio

Incidently, it is quite obvious looking at the user interface that it was built using the XForms toolkit, which we'll look at in Chapter 17, *Using Toolkits for Multimedia Programming*.

Speech Applications

This section looks at some applications related to the synthesis, analysis, and recognition of human speech. Many of these programs are only at the prototype stage, but they offer an interesting glimpse of what may be the future of computer interfaces.

Speaking of speech, one of the endless debates in the Linux world is, how exactly do you pronounce the word *Linux*? After much discussion on Usenet, Linus Torvalds provided the definitive answer by generating sound files of himself speaking the answer. At *ftp://ftp.funet.fi/pub/OS/Linux/PEOPLE/Linus/SillySounds/* (also on most other Linux archive sites) can be found two small sound files, one in English and one in Swedish (Linus' native tongue), featuring the creator of Linux saying "Hello, this is Linus Torvalds, and I pronounce Linux, Linux."

speak

> Author: Rob Hooft (*hooft@EMBL-Heidelberg.DE*)
> Available from: *ftp://sunsite.unc.edu/pub/Linux/apps/sound/speech/*
> *speak-1.0.tar.gz*

Take a public-domain program written by the U.S. Naval Research Laboratory in 1976 that converts English text to a series of 42 different sound phonemes. Record all the phonemes as small digitized sound files. Then write a small program that accepts text, calls the conversion library, and plays the phonemes through a sound card. That's the concept behind the *speak* package.

The resulting playback actually sounds pretty terrible. The phonemes are fixed so they don't change pitch or volume, or run together smoothly. It can be amusing to try a command like:

```
% fortune | tee /dev/tty | scat
```

then try to guess, without looking at the screen, what it was saying. I couldn't understand it, but maybe you will have better luck.

speak was originally written for Sun workstations by John A. Wasser and was subsequently modified for Linux by Rob Hooft.

rsynth

> Author: Nick Ing-Simmons (*nicki@lobby.ti.com*)
> Available from: *ftp://sunsite.unc.edu/pub/Linux/apps/sound/speech/*
> *rsynth-2.0.tgz*

Rob Hooft was disappointed with the results from the *speak* program so he ported another speech synthesis system to Linux: *rsynth*. It also makes use of a number of freely available software libraries to put together a speech synthesizer. Unlike *speak*, it creates the phonemes at run time using a sophisticated algorithm that models the human vocal tract. The result is output that is much more intelligible.

The downside of the more complex algorithm is that it takes longer to generate the speech. The calculations are floating point–intensive, so a 386 or 486SX system with no math coprocessor is very slow—on the order of one minute to generate each word. On a system with a floating-point unit the speed is much more reasonable, roughly one second per word or less. You can also vary the sampling rate, or send the output to a sound file for later playback.

OGI Speech Tools

> Author: Center for Spoken Language Understanding (*tools@cse.ogi.edu*)
> Available from: *ftp://sunsite.unc.edu/pub/Linux/apps/sound/speech/ ogi-speech.tar.gz*

The *OGI speech tools* package contains tools to do speech processing (e.g., graphical display, neural networks for speech recognition, vector quantization, and a library of often-used functions). It was developed at the Center for Spoken Language Understanding. The Linux package was put together by Tilo Schuerer (*tilo@cs.TU-Berlin.DE*).

This software is primarily designed for researchers studying computational linguistics, speech compression, recognition, and applications of neural networks. The graphical tools run under X11, and the documentation is in the form of manpages and TEX manuals.

ears

> Author: Ralf W. Stephan (*ralf@ark.franken.de*)
> Available from: *ftp://sunsite.unc.edu/pub/Linux/apps/sound/speech/ ears-0.23.tar.gz*

ears (Easy Automatic Recognition of Speech) is a simple speech-recognition system. It can recognize individual words spoken into a sound card and display them as text. At least, that's the theory. *ears* is speaker-dependent and therefore needs to be trained by the user for the words to be recognized using the included *train_ears* program. It can handle only a limited number of words and does not support continuous speech; the user must utter the words individually. It is written in C++.

I found the speech recognition quite accurate provided that I took care to speak clearly. If I spoke a word that had not been learned, it usually indicated that the word was not recognized rather than incorrectly matching it to a known word. Speaking more quickly, slowly, or in a different tone of voice caused the accuracy to be greatly reduced. It recognizes only the speech of the person who trained it.

The author has plans to write a speech-driven shell program that would allow users to run programs using voice commands. An early prototype is included.

Audio CD Players

A number of programs have been written to support playing audio CDs using a CD-ROM drive. Some make use of a graphical interface that closely resembles the appearance and functionality of a consumer audio CD player. Table 10-2 summarizes the features of some of the programs available for Linux. All of these programs can be found at the sites *ftp://sunsite.unc.edu/pub/Linux/apps/sound/cds/* or *ftp://sunsite.unc.edu/pub/Linux/X11/xutils/cdplayers/*.

Table 10–2: Audio CD Player Program Comparison

Name	File	Features
cdplayer	CDplayer-2.0.tar.gz	volume control and eject
tkcd	CDplayer-2.0.tar.gz	X11, runs over *cdplayer*, database
workbone	WorkBone-2.3.tar.gz	interactive commands
xplaycd	multimedia-2.0.tar.gz	X11, database, playlists, volume
workman	WorkMan-1x-1.2.2a.tar.gz	X11, database, playlists, volume
cdp	cdp-0.33.tgz	interactive commands, database
cdtool	cdtool-1.0.tgz	database
playcd	playcd-0.91.tar.gz	interactive commands, small
xcd	xcd-1.3-src.tar.gz	X11, database
xcdplayer	xcdplayer-2.3a.tgz	X11, database, small
xmcd	xmcd-1.4.tar.gz	X11, database, many features
xmitsumi	xmitsumi-0.75.tar.gz	X11, written for Mitsumi drives
xworkbone	xworkbone-0.1.tar.gz	X11, simple, based on workbone

Several of these programs support databases of discs. These allow the user to see the name of a disc and the tracks on it. One of the first graphical CD player programs with a database was *Workman*; its database format is supported by several of these programs while others use proprietary formats.

You may encounter problems using a CD database obtained from other users. CD player programs use the length of each track to identify the disc. Different pressings of the same CD can result in slightly different track times, causing a disc to not match the database. Some programs allow some tolerance in mismatching to help alleviate this, while others require an exact match.

Figure 10-9 shows a screen shot of some of the CD player programs that run under the X Window System.

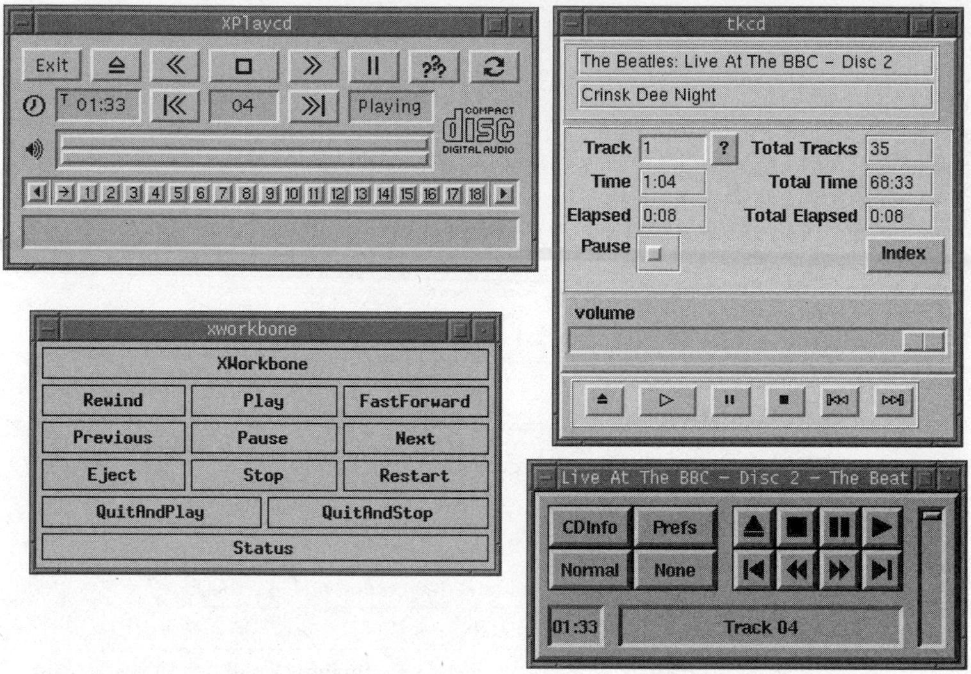

Figure 10–9: Some audio CD player programs

Miscellaneous

I conclude this chapter with some applications that don't quite fit into any of the other categories. They illustrate how multimedia can be used to implement new applications that are unlike anything that previously existed.

cthugha

> Author: Harald Deischinger (*k3096e5@cxmeta.edvz.uni-linz.ac.at*)
> Available from: *ftp://sunsite.unc.edu/pub/Linux/apps/sound/*
> *cthugha-L-0.7.src.tgz*

cthugha is hard to describe in words; you have to see it. A technical description is "audio input seeded image processing." The program accepts sound input, typically from an audio CD player. It uses the sound data to display constantly changing color images. The author describes it as "an oscilloscope on acid" and "the 90's version of the lava lamp."

Originally written for MS-DOS, the distribution listed here is a Linux port with a version that runs on the console using *svgalib* graphics and an alternate version that runs under X11. Also included is a server program, which can export the sound data from a machine with a sound card to other machines on a network. The program supports about 50 command-line options and run-time parameters for adjusting the display, and you can also design your own effects via data files.

The program has its own World Wide Web page (*http://www.afn.org/˜cthugha/*), Usenet news group (*alt.graphics.cthugha*), and an internal mailing list (send email containing the text "join cthugha" to *fileserv@torps.apana.org.au*).

cthugha is free for noncommercial use but the author would appreciate receiving a postcard to "register" your copy. Commercial users should register the software for US$50 or (preferably) by sending the author two audio CDs.

tune

> Author: Kirat Singh (*ksingh@fas.harvard.edu*)
> Available from: *ftp://sunsite.unc.edu/pub/Linux/apps/sound/tune-1.1.tar.gz*

tune is a small utility that reads audio from a sound card, performs a Fast Fourier Transform (FFT) on it, and displays the name of the musical note corresponding to the dominant frequency. The author wrote it to assist in tuning a guitar. *tune* is written in C++ and uses a freely available math library for the FFT calculations. Both source and precompiled binary are supplied.

freq

> Author: Philip VanBaren (*phillipv@eecs.umich.edu*)
> Available from: *ftp://sunsite.unc.edu/pub/Linux/apps/sound/freqs/freq51.tar.gz*

freq is a software spectrum analyzer program. It accepts input from a sound card, performs a Fast Fourier Transform, and displays the data as a plot of amplitude versus frequency. The source code can be compiled for several platforms including Linux with SVGA graphics and the X Window System. Figure 10-10 shows the X11 version.

You can control various parameters using command-line options or at run-time using keyboard commands.

svgafft

> Author: Andrew Veliath (*drewvel@eideti.com*)
> Available from: *ftp://sunsite.unc.edu/pub/Linux/apps/sound/freqs/*
> *svgafft-0.2b.tar.gz*

svgafft is another spectrum analyzer program for Linux. This one supports only the VGA display, although an X version is planned. In addition to the usual line graph, this program features a number of other interesting displays including an LED-style colored bar graph with peak display and a three-dimensional plot. Extensive command-line and run-time options are available for adjusting the display.

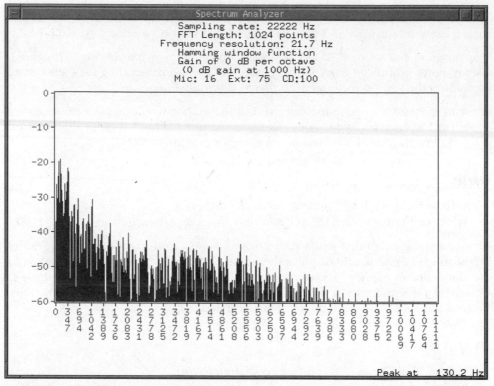

Figure 10–10: Freq spectrum analyzer

svgafft is written in C++ with an FFT library written in, believe it or not, FORTRAN. The GNU *f2c* FORTRAN to C translator, included with most Linux distributions, works fine as a substitute for a FORTRAN compiler.

cdda2wav

Author: Heiko Eissfeldt (*heiko@colossus.escape.de*)
Available from: *ftp://sunsite.unc.edu/pub/Linux/apps/sound/cds/
cdda2wav0.3alpha.src.tar.gz*

The *cdda2wav* utility reads digital data from an audio CD and writes it to a sound file in WAV format. This process effectively allows making an exact copy of audio from a CD.

The utility only works with CD-ROM drives that support reading the digital audio data. It supports both SCSI commands for reading digital audio and Linux-specific *ioctl* functions. Command-line parameters let you select the position on CD, the sample size, sampling rate, and many other parameters.

CHAPTER ELEVEN

APPLICATIONS FOR GRAPHICS AND ANIMATION

I n this chapter I look at some of the available applications related to multimedia graphics, animation, and video that run under Linux. I've somewhat arbitrarily divided the applications into categories.

The information in this chapter is only a sampling of the applications available for Linux. Most programs written for UNIX systems running the X Window System will compile and run under Linux with little or no porting. The intent here is to highlight only a few representative packages of each type. To explore further information, see Appendix B, *Linux Resources*, which lists some sources for more applications.

For each program I list the author and the primary site where the application can be found on the Internet. In some cases an alternate site is listed, usually a version that has been ported to or simply compiled for Linux systems for the convenience of other Linux users.

Because ftp sites are constantly changing and reorganizing, the file locations, and particularly the file names, are all subject to change. Some of the utilities are also included in Linux distributions available on the Internet, on CD-ROM, or on floppy disk.

Graphics Viewers

Applications in this category are those used primarily for displaying graphics images. Some also provide the capability for manipulating the images. Most run under the X Window System, but some support the PC video display directly. You can use these applications to review images that will be used in multimedia applications and to perform simple image manipulation and file conversion.

xloadimage

Author: Jim Frost (*jimf@centerline.com*)
Available from: *ftp://ftp.x.org/R5contrib/xloadimage.4.1.tar.gz*
Alternate site: *ftp://sunsite.unc.edu/pub/Linux/X11/xapps/graphics/viewers/ xloadimage.4.1.tgz*

xloadimage is a simple utility for loading images into an X window (including the root window). It reads about 20 of the more common image formats. Also offered are some image manipulation functions such as clipping, brightening, dithering, gamma correction, scaling, and smoothing. A unique feature is an interactive help facility. *xloadimage* is purely command line–based with no graphical user interface other than the window that displays the image.

xli

Author: Graeme Gill (*graeme@labtam.oz.au*)
Available from: *ftp://ftp.x.org/contrib/applications/xli.1.16.tar.gz*
Alternate site: *ftp://sunsite.unc.edu/pub/Linux/X11/xapps/graphics/ viewers/xli-linux.1.15.lsm*

xli is an enhanced version of the *xloadimage* utility. It offers essentially the same functions, but supports several additional file formats. The package includes documentation on how to extend *xli* for new image types and has a short text file that presents a good explanation of gamma correction. Alex Kent (*alex@nmt.edu*) built the precompiled Linux version found on sunsite.

xv

Author: John Bradley (*bradley@cis.upenn.edu*)
Available from: *ftp://ftp.cis.upenn.edu/pub/xv/xv-3.10a.tar.gz*
Alternate site: *ftp://sunsite.unc.edu/pub/Linux/X11/xapps/graphics/viewers/ xv-3.10.tgz*

xv is my all-around favorite image viewer and conversion tool. It supports over a dozen common file formats (both for loading and saving) and several image manipulation functions and effects. All functions can be performed using the intuitive graphical user interface, usually eliminating the need to refer to a manual or use command-line options. Figure 11-1 shows *xv* in action.

A unique feature is the "Visual Schnauzer" for browsing using small thumbnail images. *xv* also has a sophisticated color editor and even an ASCII/hex file viewer. Documentation includes a comprehensive (100-page) manual in PostScript form.

The distribution policy for *xv* is rare for the UNIX world: shareware. The author requests a registration fee of US$25. Volume discounts are available for larger sites. Note that, unlike most shareware software, the source code is made available, and the unregistered version is not crippled in any way.

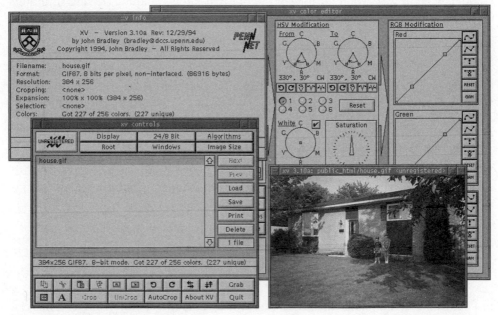

Figure 11-1: The xv image viewer

xv compiles cleanly under Linux. If you have been using it for some time, be sure you are running the latest 3.10 version; it has a number of nice improvements over the 3.0 release.

Ghostscript/Ghostview

Ghostscript author: L. Peter Deutsch, Aladdin Enterprises (*ghost@aladdin.com*)
Ghostview author: Tim Theisen, University of Wisconsin
　　　　　(*ghostview@cs.wisc.edu*)
Available from: *ftp://prep.ai.mit.edu/pub/gnu/*
Aladdin version: *ftp://ftp.cs.wisc.edu/ghost/aladdin/ghostscript-3.53.tar.gz*

Ghostscript is by far the most robust, complete, and widely used of the few freely available PostScript interpreters and viewers. It provides drivers for various devices including an X11 window, other graphics file formats, and many common ink jet and dot matrix printers.

Its primary use is for viewing PostScript files, but it is also useful as a conversion tool and for driving non-PostScript printers (I routinely use it to effectively turn my low-cost ink jet printer into a PostScript device). Color is supported, and the package includes the 35 standard PostScript fonts as well as a number of others. For users who do not run X, there is a *Ghostscript* driver available for PC VGA displays running under Linux.

Ghostview is an X11 frontend for *Ghostscript* that allows loading, saving, printing, selecting pages, and other functions using a graphical user interface.

Two versions of *Ghostscript* exist. Most Linux systems come with GNU *Ghostscript* which is released under the GNU GPL. Aladdin *Ghostscript* is also freely download-able and usable but is released under a different license that prohibits commercial distribution. Both versions have a common heritage—the GNU version of *Ghostscript* is the Aladdin version with a time lag of one year. Being newer, the Aladdin *Ghostscript* version typically has more functionality. For example, the current Aladdin *Ghostscript* has fully functional level 2 PostScript and PDF interpreters, whereas GNU *Ghostscript* has only fragmentary level 2 and no PDF.

These packages are quite large and take time to configure and compile. Fortunately most Linux distributions include them. Precompiled binaries are also available on most Linux archive sites.

xpdf

> Author: Derek B. Noonburg (*derekn@vw.ece.cmu.edu*)
> Available from: *ftp://ftp.andrew.cmu.edu/pub/xpdf/*

PDF files are a common means of delivering documentation from commercial hardware and software vendors. Adobe offers a free file viewer, but unfortunately it is not available for Linux systems.

xpdf is a freely available viewer for PDF files that runs under X. It supports hyper-text links and can also produce PostScript output. The program runs on most UNIX systems and is available as source code or precompiled binaries for most plat-forms, including Linux.

ImageMagick

> Author: John Cristy
> Available from: *ftp://ftp.x.org/contrib/applications/ImageMagick/*
> *ImageMagick-3.7.5.tar.gz*
> Alternate site: *ftp://sunsite.unc.edu/pub/Linux/X11/xapps/graphics/*
> *ImageMagick-3.7.4.2-elf.tgz*

ImageMagick is a suite of utilities for viewing and manipulating images. Included are the following:

display
> a menu-driven image display program

animate
> displays a series of images in sequence

montage
>   tiles images to create a composite image

import
>   captures an X window to a graphics file

mogrify
>   performs image transformations

identify
>   describes characteristics of image files

convert
>   image file conversion utility

ImageMagick runs under X11 and requires a number of other graphics libraries in order to be compiled. All in all it's a very powerful set of utilities. The latest information can be found on the *ImageMagick* Web page, which is located at *http://www.wizards.dupont.com/cristy/ImageMagick.html*.

pcdview

>   Author: Gerd Knorr (*kraxel@cs.tu-berlin.de*)
>   Available from: *ftp://sunsite.unc.edu/pub/Linux/apps/graphics/viewers/ pcdview.tar.gz*

pcdview is a simple viewer for PhotoCD images using the Linux VGA display. It only supports displaying the 768x512 resolution images at 800x600 display resolution. A 16-bit per-pixel graphics card is required for color display; otherwise it uses grayscale. A "slide show" mode displays a series of images in sequence. The utility is fast and simple, and offers an alternative for users who do not run the X Window System.

xpcd

>   Author: Gerd Knorr (*kraxel@cs.tu-berlin.de*)
>   Available from: *ftp://sunsite.unc.edu/pub/Linux/X11/xapps/graphics/viewers/ xpcd-0.3.3.tar.gz*

xpcd is an X11-based viewer for PhotoCD files. When invoked, it displays a list of the images from a mounted PhotoCD. Individual images or an overview of all images can be displayed in grayscale. The complete images at any of five resolutions can then be extracted and viewed using an external program such as *xv*.

A useful feature of *xpcd* is the ability to select a region of an image using the mouse, and then extract only that portion of the image. This feature allows using the highest resolution images when "zooming in" on regions of interest. It also shows off the high degree of resolution obtained using PhotoCD images.

xpcd normally reads files directly from a mounted PhotoCD; it can also read files on a normal filesystem. It uses the *hpcdtoppm* utility to convert the images to a form that can be accepted by external viewer programs.

zgv

> Author: Russell Marks (*mr216@gre.ac.uk*)
> Available from: *ftp://sunsite.unc.edu/pub/Linux/apps/graphics/viewers/*
> *zgv2.7-src.tar.gz*

zgv is a viewer for GIF, JPEG, PBM, PGM, PPM, BMP, and TGA files on standard VGA and most SVGA displays. It offers a full-screen file-selector frontend that is similar to the Visual Schnauzer of *xv* (it reads and saves compatible thumbnail files).

The program is fast, easy to use, and offers many features including mouse support, a slide show option, and interactive viewing commands. *zgv* is a good choice for a viewer if you don't normally run the X Window System or have a system with limited memory.

Graphics Editors

In this section I include utilities for creating and editing images using a graphical user interface. You can use these to create images for multimedia applications.

One common distinction with these programs is to categorize them as either paint or draw programs. A paint program typically allows you to create images using a paintbrush metaphor, offering various choices of color and brush shape and size. Like a real painting, once an object (such as a line, circle, or polygon) has been placed on the canvas it becomes part of the image and can no longer be manipulated independently. The image is generally stored as a bitmap. Paint programs are useful for artistic drawings or those primarily without geometric shapes, as they allow the user fine control over the color of individual pixels.

The draw programs provide tools for placing objects of various types (such as lines, rectangles, splines, and text). After an object has been placed on the drawing, it still remains an independent entity that can be moved, scaled, and reshaped. Objects can overlap, in which case they can be placed behind or in front of other objects. The image is stored in a way that retains the characteristics of each individual object. Draw programs are more suited to technical drawings that consist primarily of geometric shapes.

bitmap

> Author: Davor Matic
> Available from: *ftp://ftp.x.org/*

bitmap is the standard bitmap file editor included as part of the MIT X distribution. Bitmaps do not store color information and are most commonly used for icons.

bitmap works like a paint program and is very easy to use. It is normally included with Linux distributions that include the X Window System.

pixmap

Author: Lionel Mallet (*Lionel.Mallet@sophia.inria.fr*)
Available from: *ftp://ftp.x.org/contrib/applications/pixmap/pixmap2.6.tar.gz*

This program is a pixmap editor, similar to the X11 *bitmap* program, but for colored images. Pixmaps are most commonly used under X for colored icons. When compiling you have a choice of using the Motif or freely available Athena widget interfaces. It requires the XPM library (typically included in Linux X distributions). The package includes a manpage and reference card in LATEX format.

xfig

Author: Brian Smith (*bvsmith@lbl.gov*)
Available from: *ftp://ftp.x.org/contrib/applications/drawing_tools/xfig/*
　　　　　　xfig.3.1.4.tar.gz

xfig is a menu-driven tool that allows the user to draw and manipulate objects interactively using an X11 interface. The resulting pictures can be saved, printed on PostScript printers, or converted to a variety of other formats (for example, to allow inclusion in LATEX documents).

This program is very comprehensive, yet easy to use. It is suitable for producing mechanical, architectural, and electronic diagrams. It provides all of the usual geometric shapes, including spline curves. Objects can be grouped and aligned. It offers support for color and an undo function. Many example drawings are included. The related package, *transfig*, can be used to convert the output to other common image file formats.

tgif

Author: William Chia-Wei Cheng (*william@cs.ucla.edu*)
Available from: *ftp://sunsite.unc.edu/pub/Linux/X11/xapps/graphics/draw/*
　　　　　　tgif-2.15pl6bin.tar.gz

tgif is an Xlib-based two-dimensional drawing facility that runs under X11. It supports the hierarchical construction of drawings and provides easy navigation between sets of drawings. A unique feature is the ability to export drawings as Prolog language files.

This tool is very large and comprehensive (expect it to take some time to compile from source). It offers much the same features as *xfig*: many primitive objects with support for grouping. It can import and export drawings in encapsulated PostScript, XBM, and XMP formats. Undo and redo are provided, and drawings can span multiple pages.

An interesting feature is the ability to associate an object with an action (e.g., a shell script) to be executed when the object is selected. The graphical user interface is easy to use and sports tear-off menus.

xpaint

Author: David Koblas (*koblas@netcom.com*)
Available from: *ftp://sunsite.unc.edu/pub/Linux/X11/xapps/graphics/draw/ xpaint-2.4.4.tar.gz*

xpaint is a paint program for X with a graphical user interface. It supports reading and writing all of the most common image formats. Drawing tools offer all of the usual objects such as points, lines, circles, and rectangles. More sophisticated features include different brush types, area flood fill, spray can, and patterns.

The tool provides an online help system. It supports color and offers a number of special graphics effects such as image sharpening, smoothing, edge detection, and embossing. Several images can be edited simultaneously. Figure 11-2 shows a typical session using *xpaint*.

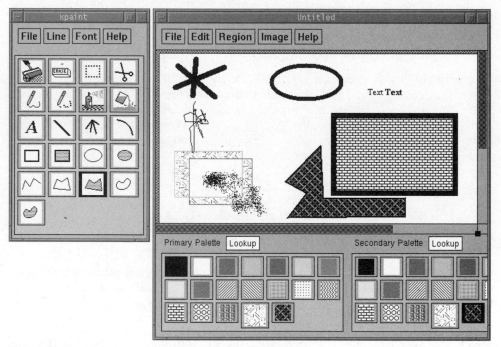

Figure 11-2: xpaint

xpaint is included with X11 in most Linux distributions, or you can use the precompiled Linux version listed above.

idraw

idraw is part of the *InterViews* X11 toolkit that I will explore further in Chapter 17, *Using Toolkits for Multimedia Programming*. A structured drawing program, it supports all common graphics primitives such as circles, rectangles, and text. Objects can be grouped and a top-to-bottom stacking order defined. Color is supported.

idraw saves files in PostScript, so they can be directly printed or displayed by other tools (but it can't load arbitrary PostScript files). *idraw* is included as a part of most Linux distributions. Figure 11-3 shows a figure being created in *idraw*.

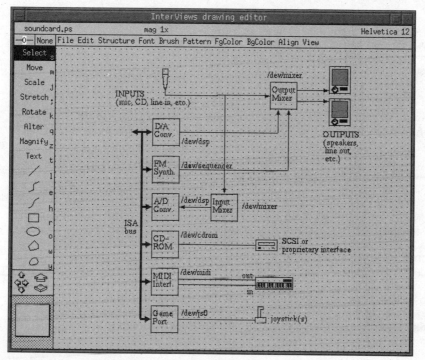

Figure 11-3: idraw

Satan Paint

Author: Jonathan Clark (*jc@npc.ece.utexas.edu*)
Available from: *ftp://sunsite.unc.edu/pub/Linux/apps/graphics/spaint.tar.gz*

Satan Paint is a drawing program with a graphical user interface. It provides most of the expected features: a mouse-based interface with the ability to draw points, lines, circles, and rectangles in 8-bit color. It offers some simple graphics effects, it has an undo feature, and it can import and export most common graphics file formats as well as its own native format.

The program also offers some more unique features. An alternate version runs directly on VGA graphics cards. A script language allows all of the graphics functions to be performed in a non-interactive programmed mode. It also offers some simple animation functions intended to assist in creating the small images (or sprites) used in developing games programs. A series of images can be edited simultaneously, displayed in sequence, or morphed.

Satan Paint runs on a number of different platforms and is distributed in precompiled binary form only.

The GIMP

Authors: Spencer Kimball (*spencer@xcf.berkeley.edu*),
      Peter Mattis (*petm@xcf.berkeley.edu*)
Available from: *ftp://ftp.xcf.berkeley.edu/pub/gimp*
Alternate site: *ftp://sunsite.unc.edu/pub/Linux/X11/xapps/graphics/gimp/*
      gimp-0.54.1.tar.gz

The GIMP, or The General Image Manipulation Program, is a graphical image manipulation and drawing utility. It supports all of the common image file formats from 8 to 24 bits of color. *The GIMP* offers many different tools for drawing and selecting portions of an image. Various transformations and effects can be produced with multiple levels of undo and redo.

The program can be extended using external programs (called plug-ins) to support other file formats and effects. It comes with a number of plug-ins; users can also write their own.

The tool runs under X and has an intuitive, professional-looking user interface based on the Motif toolkit.

The GIMP is released as source code under the GNU GPL. Building it requires the Motif toolkit, but precompiled statically linked Linux binaries are available for users without Motif. It runs on most UNIX systems and is developed under Linux. At the time of this writing, it was still considered a beta release.

Image Conversion Tools

Programs in this category are intended for converting between file formats, although some of these tools can perform some image manipulation functions as well. They are primarily command line–oriented. Many of these are also offered as graphics libraries that can be used within your own applications to make it easier to display images.

JPEG Utilities

Author: ported to Linux by Rob Hooft (*hooft@chem.ruu.nl*)
Available from: *ftp://sunsite.unc.edu/pub/Linux/apps/graphics/convert/
jpeg-V4a-bin.tar.z*

This item is a package of utilities for converting to and from JPEG format files. The original source code can be found at *ftp://ftp.cs.columbia.edu/jpeg/src/*.

FBM Utilities

Author: Michael Mauldin, ported to Linux by Rob Hooft (*hooft@chem.ruu.nl*)
Available from: *ftp://sunsite.unc.edu/pub/Linux/apps/graphics/fbm-1.0-bin.tar.z*

This program is a collection of utilities for manipulating Fuzzy PixMap (FBM) files, a graphics format developed by Michael "Fuzzy" Mauldin. It is a precompiled Linux version; the original source code can be found at the ftp site *ftp://nl.cs.cmu.edu/usr/mlm/ftp/*.

TIFF Tools

Author: ported to Linux by Rob Hooft (*hooft@chem.ruu.nl*)
Available from: *ftp://sunsite.unc.edu/pub/Linux/apps/graphics/
tiff-tools-3.3A.tar.gz*

These utilities are used for manipulating TIFF format graphics files. The original source and documentation is at *ftp://sgi.com/graphics/tiff/*.

PBM Utilities

Author: ported to Linux by Rob Hooft (*hooft@chem.ruu.nl*)
Available from: *ftp://sunsite.unc.edu/pub/Linux/apps/graphics/convert/
netpbm-Mar1994-bin.tar.gz*

PBM utilities is a precompiled version of the portable bitmap toolkit for Linux. It's a comprehensive set of utilities comprising over 120 programs, which are able to convert between almost every known graphic file format. It also provides tools to perform some image manipulation and effects. The original author is Jef Poskanzer (*jef@acme.com/jef@well.sf.ca.us*).

hpcdtoppm

Author: Hadmut Danisch (*danisch@ira.uka.de*)
Available from: *ftp://sunsite.unc.edu/pub/Linux/apps/graphics/convert/
hpcdtoppm.linux.tar.gz*

hpcdtoppm (following the naming convention used by the PBM utilities) accepts PhotoCD files and converts them to the portable bitmap format. It also supports conversion to PostScript. The utility can extract any of the image resolutions contained with a PhotoCD file, and in conjunction with the PBM utilities, image resolutions can then be converted to any other format.

Image Generation Tools

In this category are applications for creating images using algorithmic or programmed methods rather than interactive drawing. They are of use both for individual images as well as animations.

POV-Ray

> Author: the POV-Ray team
> Available from: *ftp://ftp.povray.org/*

POV-Ray is the "Persistence Of Vision" ray tracing package, a utility for rendering photo-realistic images. Probably the most popular ray tracer under Linux, it was developed by a team of talented programmers and made freely available. It also runs on many other computer platforms including most UNIX systems, MS-DOS, Amiga, and the Apple Macintosh.

POV-Ray uses an ASCII scene description language similar to C. It comes with many predefined material textures and example scene files. The output file is in 24-bit color. It has some support for images and for producing animations.

POV-Ray can be easier to use than some other rendering packages because all functions are performed by the same program and it is well documented by an extensive user manual (100 pages in PostScript form).

The Linux port of POV-Ray is available in source form and as a precompiled binary. Images optionally can be displayed in an X11 window or directly using the VGA display during rendering. More information can be found on the POV-Ray Web site at *http://www.povray.org/*.

Radiance

> Author: Berkeley Labs (*GJWard@lbl.gov*)
> Available from: *ftp://sunsite.unc.edu/pub/Linux/apps/graphics/rays/*
> *Radiance2R4.tar.gz*

Radiance is a rendering package developed at Lawrence Berkeley Laboratory in California and EPFL in Switzerland. Technically, it is not a ray-tracing package; it renders using the radiosity technique. The package includes documentation (including a tutorial), sample scene files, and some utilities. Images can be displayed in an X window during rendering.

The program also runs on many workstation platforms including NeXT and Apple A/UX. A related package, *trad*, is a Tk-based graphical frontend to *Radiance*. For more information, see *http://radsite.lbl.gov/radiance/HOME.html*.

Midnight Modeller

Author: David Taylor (UNIX port by Michael Lamertz and Joerg Hessdoerfer)
Available from: *ftp://sunsite.unc.edu/pub/Linux/apps/graphics/rays/pov/ mnmlinux-pl2.tgz*

Writing scene files for POV-Ray can be tedious. The usual method is to sketch the objects on graph paper and use a lot of trial and error to determine the coordinates in three dimensions. *Midnight Modeller* is a program that allows you to interactively construct a scene in three dimensions using wire frame graphics. Little or no knowledge of the underlying scene description language is needed, and immediate feedback of the image is obtained.

Originally an MS-DOS program, the Linux version runs under X. It supports all POV-Ray features including the more complex objects and is fully menu-driven. Written to work with POV-Ray, it also allows importing and exporting models in several file formats. Figure 11-4 shows a *Midnight Modeller (mnm)* screen.

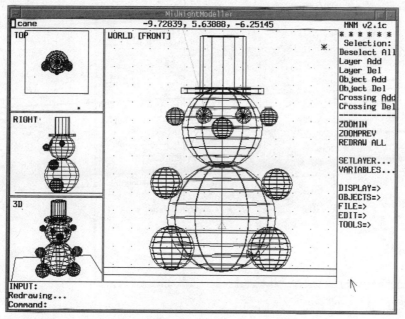

Figure 11-4: The Midnight Modeller

137

Aero

Author: Andreas Ziegler et al. (*aziegler@hermes.informatik.uni-stuttgart.de*)
Available from: *ftp://sunsite.unc.edu/pub/Linux/apps/graphics/rays/*
      aero_1.5.0_src.tar.gz

Aero is a modeler that simulates dynamic systems of objects in three dimensions. You use the interactive graphical design tool to define systems made up of objects such as spheres, cylinders, rectangular solids, and planes. Objects can be assigned material, color, texture, mass, and the effects of gravity and other forces. You can connect the objects using rods, joints, springs, and dampers. *Aero* then models the positions of the objects over time in three dimensions. You can view the animation within the tool using wire frame graphics, and then export each frame as a POV-Ray scene file, which can then be rendered. Using other animation tools, the images can be combined into an animation file in a format such as MPEG.

The package includes documentation and several examples, some of them quite complex. Figure 11-5 is representative of a typical *Aero* screen.

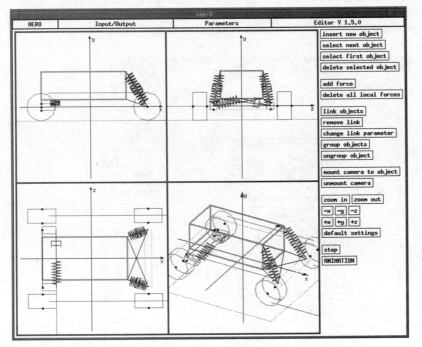

Figure 11–5: The Aero Modeler

XWarp

Authors: Luca Maranzano, Guido Cardino, Roberto Surlinelli
(*calamaro@dist.dist.unige.it*)
Available from: *ftp://sunsite.unc.edu/pub/Linux/X11/xapps/graphics/ XWarp-1.00.tgz*

XWarp is a utility for distorting or "warping" an image in GIF format. The program displays an image with a grid overlayed (actually two—one source and one destination grid, only one of which is displayed at any one time). The user can move points on the grid to define the warping. The program then modifies the image according to the grids. The effect is similar to pressing a piece of Silly Putty onto newspaper to create an image, then stretching the putty to change it. You could, for example, make a person's nose bigger or ears pointed. It can be a lot of fun.

XWarp runs under X11 with an XView (OpenLook) user interface and comes with some example images.

xmorph

Author: Michael J. Gourlay (*gourlay@ucsu.colorado.edu*)
Available from: *ftp://sunsite.unc.edu/pub/Linux/X11/xapps/graphics/ xmorph-14nov95.tgz*

xmorph is a digital image warping or "morphing" program that runs under X11. To use it, load two images such as two different people's faces. Next, manually adjust a mesh or grid over each image to define how the images will be warped. The utility then creates an image that is in between the two original images.

xmorph supports automatically creating a series of images that can then be combined into an animation. Usage is described by an online help system.

The Linux binaries were compiled by Todd Huss (*thuss@moose.uvm.edu*). The original source is part of the MIT X11 contrib distribution and can be found at *ftp://ftp.x.org/contrib/*.

sis

Author: Joerg Bakker (*bakkerjg@cip11.mathematik.uni-stuttgart.de*)
Available from: *ftp://sunsite.unc.edu/pub/Linux/apps/graphics/sis.tar.gz*

sis stands for Single Image Stereogram, the three-dimensional images made popular by the "Magic Eye" books and posters. *sis* reads in a depth or contour map, a file in which depth information is represented by shades of gray. The input must be in TIFF or TGA format. *sis* then produces a three-dimensional image file that can be viewed on the screen or sent to a printer. Several sample depth map files are included with the package. You can also generate your own using ray tracing software such as POV-Ray.

By default, *sis* uses a random pattern of black and white dots for the background pattern of the image. You can also use a color image file as the background, which will be tiled as needed.

Video and Animation Viewers

These program are used for displaying various types of animation and video files.

flip

Author: John Remyn (*boogyman@xs4all.hacktic.nl*)
Available from: *ftp://sunsite.unc.edu/pub/Linux/apps/graphics/viewers/flip03.tgz*

flip is a viewer for FLI and FLC animation files. It uses the VGA display directly via the *svgalib* graphics library. It is simple, small (about 11K), fast, and works well. In the same directory on sunsite is the file *robotrk.fli.gz*, an example FLI file which can be used to test *flip*.

mpeg_play

Author: Lawrence Rowe, Ketan Patel, Brian Smith
Available from: *ftp://sunsite.unc.edu/pub/Linux/apps/graphics/viewers/*
mpeg_play-2.3-src.tar.gz

mpeg_play is the MPEG-1 video decoder developed at the University of California, Berkeley. It runs on just about any UNIX platform that supports X11 and an 8-, 24-, or 32-bit per-pixel display. All decoding is done in software, and there is no support for audio. Several dithering algorithms are offered.

Version 2.2 offers a graphical user interface using the Motif toolkit. You will need the Motif shared library in order to run the precompiled Linux binary listed above. The older version 2.0 has a simpler interface that does not require Motif. If you do not have Motif, then get this version. If you prefer an XView GUI, you can try the *xvmpeg* package, which can be found at the following ftp site: *ftp://sunsite.unc.edu/pub/Linux/X11/xapps/graphics/viewers/xvmpg1a.tgz*.

The original source for *mpeg_play* can be found at the following ftp site: *ftp://mm-ftp.cs.berkeley.edu/pub/mpeg/play/mpeg_play-2.1-src.tar.gz*. A number of sample MPEG streams can be found at the same site. *mpeg_play* is also part of the MIT X11 contrib distribution.

vgamp

Author: Gwoho Liust (*20c@ucrmath.ucr.edu*)
Available from: *ftp://sunsite.unc.edu/pub/Linux/apps/graphics/viewers/*
vgamp-1.0.tar.gz

vgamp is an MPEG-1 video player that uses the Linux VGA display (not X11). It supports the 320x200 256-color VGA mode only.

vgamp is based on the Berkeley *mpeg_play* but has been completely rewritten, with critical routines coded in assembly language and optional optimization for 486 machines. This results in a frame rate typically double that of *mpeg_play*.

The original program has a problem with not restoring the VGA display properly to text mode. You should install the patch from the file *svgamp-1.0.patch* to correct this problem.

xanim

Author: Mark Podlipec (*podlipec@wellfleet.com*)
Available from: *ftp://ftp.shell.portal.com/pub/podlipec/xanim27062.tar.Z*

xanim is a player for animation files that runs under X11. The version listed here supports several popular formats: FCI, FLC, IFF, GIF, DL, Amiga MovieSetter, Utah Raster Toolkit RLE images and animations, AVI, Quicktime, JFIF images, and MPEG-1.

xanim supports most features and variants of these file formats, with only a few exceptions (it does not support AVI compression using the Intel Indeo video codec, for example).

Sound is supported for file formats that include audio data. It can also play a WAV format sound file simultaneously for files that do not have sound in the animation file.

xanim runs on most UNIX platforms including Linux. It offers a graphical user interface with VCR-like controls that is built using the Motif, Athena, or Athena 3D toolkits. Precompiled Linux binaries can be found on sunsite. It is also part of the MIT X contrib distribution.

In my opinion, this is the best overall animation player program for Linux (although MPEG support is still weak). It does require a fast machine for playing the larger video files and sound simultaneously. For more information see "The Xanim Home Page" at *http://www.portal.com/~podlipec/home.html*.

Video and Animation Generation Tools

These tools allow you to create an animation file from a series of separate image files. Note that some of the viewer programs listed earlier support a simple form of animation by directly loading a sequence of images.

mpeg2codec

Author: MPEG Software Simulation Group (*MPEG-L@netcom.com*)
Available from: *ftp://sunsite.unc.edu/pub/Linux/apps/graphics/convert/
mpeg2codec_v1.1a-src+bin.tgz*

This package provides software-based MPEG-2 video encoder and decoders. The encoder program, *mpeg2enc*, accepts a group of files in YUV or PPM format along with a parameter file and encodes them into an MPEG-1 or MPEG-2 video stream. *mpeg2dec* does the reverse: it accepts an MPEG file and produces a series of separate image files corresponding to each frame. The decoder can also display directly to an X11 window.

The tools are configurable but not fast. They were written as a portable reference implementation for instructional purposes rather than an optimized one. Other utilities, like *mpeg_play*, are more suitable if a fast MPEG-1 player is desired.

The package includes considerable documentation. The original source code can be found at *ftp://ftp.mpeg.org/pub/mpeg/mssg/*. The version listed above was pre-compiled for Linux by Todd Huss (*thuss@moose.uvm.edu*).

mpeg_encode

Authors: Lawrence Rowe, Kevin Gong, Ketan Patel, Dan Wallach
Available from: *ftp://sunsite.unc.edu/pub/Linux/apps/graphics/convert/
mpeg_encode-1.3-src+bin.tgz*

mpeg_encode is the Berkeley MPEG video encoder. It accepts PPM or YUV format image files as input and produces an MPEG-1 file. It can optionally perform the CPU-intensive encoding in parallel on a number of networked machines.

Compared to the SSG encoder described previously, *mpeg_encode* appears to me to be more configurable and better optimized for speed. Included is a manpage and a short user's guide. The version here was compiled for Linux by Todd Huss (*thuss@moose.uvm.edu*). The original source is available from *ftp://mm-ftp.CS.Berkeley.EDU/*.

mpeg_util

Author: Andy Hung (*achung@cs.stanford.edu*)
Available from: *ftp://sunsite.unc.edu/pub/Linux/apps/graphics/convert/
mpeg_util.tgz*

Yet another MPEG encoder and decoder, *mpeg_util* was developed by the Portable Video Research Group at Stanford University. It was written for functionality and completeness, not speed. The decoder only produces files; there is no display support. Documentation includes a 50-page PostScript manual. All of the source can be found at *ftp://havefun.stanford.edu/pub/mpeg/*.

pvquant

Author: Frank van der Hulst (*frank@whare.cavebbs.welly.gen.nz*)
Available from: *ftp://sunsite.unc.edu/pub/Linux/apps/graphics/rays/*
pvquant-1.60.tgz

This package offers a number of utilities useful for animation using POV-Ray, pre-compiled for Linux. The following are included:

animdat
    generates POV scene files for animation

animfli
    creates FLI animation from a series of ray traced images

octree
    color quantization utility

pvq
    animation creation script

It also includes two sample POV scene files. The original source code is from *ftp://nic.funet.fi/pub/msdos/graphics/graphics/pv3dv060.zip*.

sceda

Author: Denis McLaughlin (*denism@cyberus.ca*)
Available from: *http://www.cyberus.ca/~denism/sceda/sceda.html*

sceda is a constraint-oriented three-dimensional modeler. It also provides support for splined keyframe animation. Animated objects have their position, their rotation, and their scale smoothly interpolated across multiple keyframes via a modified spline function.

Wire frame animations can be performed from within *sceda*. The frames can be exported to scene description files for rendering programs such as POV-Ray and *Radiance*. A script file for performing rendering is also generated.

The author develops under Linux, but it should be portable to any UNIX-like system that supports X11. *sceda* is based on Stephen Chenney's constraint-based modeler *sced*.

CD-ROM Mastering Tools

One of the final steps in creating your own CD-ROM is to generate an ISO 9660 filesystem master containing all of the desired files and directories. This can be written to tape, to removable hard disk, or to a CD-ROM created using a CD writer, a special CD-ROM drive that supports writable CDs. The advantage of the latter is that it results in a disc that can be read and tested using any CD-ROM drive. After testing, the master can be sent to a CD manufacturing facility for mass production.

While it is by no means a straightforward process, there are tools that can be used under Linux to assist in creating your own CD-ROM.

In addition to the tools, there is a CD Writer mini-HOWTO document written by Matt Cutts (*cutts@ms.uky.edu*) that outlines the steps he went through to create a CD-ROM using a recordable CD-ROM drive under Linux. It can be found at *ftp://sunsite.unc.edu/pub/Linux/docs/HOWTO/mini/CD-Writer*.

mkisofs

> Author: Eric Youngdale (*ericy@cais.com*)
> Available from: *ftp://tsx-11.mit.edu/pub/linux/BETA/cdrom/mkisofs-1.03.tar.gz*

mkisofs is a premastering program to generate an ISO 9660 filesystem. As ISO 9660 is a somewhat special filesystem in which files are never removed, added, or modified, this program does more than create an empty filesystem. It also populates it with files from a directory tree on another filesystem.

Typically it is used to generate an ISO 9660 filesystem on hard disk, which can be used as the image for data that will be placed on a CD-ROM. This data could then be sent by tape or removable hard disk to a CD-ROM vendor for mastering, or used in conjunction with the *cdwrite* program to write to a recordable CD-ROM drive.

mkisofs supports the Rock Ridge extensions and comes with some debugging and checking tools. It is used by Yggdrasil Computing to produce their Linux CDs.

cdwrite

> Author: Adam J. Richter (*adam@yggdrasil.com*)
> Available from: *ftp://tsx-11.mit.edu/pub/linux/BETA/cdrom/private/mkisofs/*
> *cdwrite-1.3.tar.gz*

cdwrite is a utility for copying an ISO 9660 filesystem image to a CD-ROM writer. It is written to work with Philips drives, but may work with other types of SCSI-writable CD-ROM drives with some changes. This program is used by Yggdrasil Computing to master their Linux CDs.

CHAPTER TWELVE

HYPERMEDIA APPLICATIONS

In this chapter, I'll review some of the hypertext browsers available for Linux. While the applications were primarily designed for accessing the World Wide Web, I'll show in Chapter 17, *Using Toolkits for Multimedia Programming*, and Chapter 19, *Some Sample Multimedia Applications*, that they can also be used for standalone hypertext multimedia applications.

HTML Browsers

We briefly looked at Web browsers in Chapter 5, *Hypertext, Hypermedia, and the World Wide Web*. There are many different browsers available for Linux, each having its own strengths and limitations. These programs generally only support the display of graphics and text; other forms of multimedia such as sound and video require external viewer programs. Typically the MIME typing mechanism is used to associate a multimedia URL with the appropriate external viewers.

This means that the multimedia viewing takes place outside of the Web browser (i.e., in a different window). Perhaps in the future we will see some browsers adopt a standardized protocol that enables external viewers to work within the browser itself (Netscape calls these "plug-ins"). An alternative approach to solving this problem is to use Java.

Unlike many of the applications described in this book, many of these browsers are not freely redistributable software. They may be distributed as binaries only, use non-freely available toolkits such as Motif, or have restrictions on their distribution, preventing them from being included on Linux CD-ROM distributions, for example.

As HTML is still evolving, the browsers support different subsets of the HTML specification and various proprietary extensions. Most graphical browsers have a similar user interface, so in the following sections I will only show a few representative screen shots.

Mosaic

> Author: National Center for Supercomputing Applications
> (*mosaic-x@ncsa.uiuc.edu*)
> Available from: *ftp://ftp.ncsa.uiuc.edu/Mosaic/*

Mosaic is the program that started the World Wide Web explosion with the first easy-to-use graphical browser. Both the source code and precompiled binaries for Linux are freely available from the NCSA ftp site. In order to compile Mosaic you need the Motif toolkit (Motif is not needed to run the precompiled versions because they are statically linked with the Motif libraries). Figure 12-1 shows a typical Mosaic screen.

Some of the notable features of the current release (version 2.7 beta 2 at time of writing) are:

- Support for some HTML 3.0 features

- Access to ftp and Usenet news

- Kerberos authentication

Several precompiled versions of Mosaic for different Linux configurations can be found at *ftp://sunsite.unc.edu/pub/Linux/system/Network/info-systems/www/Mosaic/*. Mosaic is still actively being developed, but the NCSA doesn't have the resources of larger software vendors like Netscape. So Mosaic seems to be lagging behind in terms of features when compared to commercial Web browsers, although it's still probably the best freely available package. Several commercial vendors licensed the Mosaic source code and enhanced it to produce commercialized versions.

Netscape Navigator

> Author: Netscape Communications
> Available from: *ftp://ftp.netscape.com/*

Netscape Communications was founded by Marc Andreessen, the primary author of Mosaic. *Netscape* is, without doubt, the most sophisticated Web browser available and has become an industry standard that others are measured against for features. Some of the features of the 2.0 release include:

- Support for numerous HTML extensions

- Frames (scrollable regions within Web pages)

- Motif graphical user interface

- Support for applets written in Java language

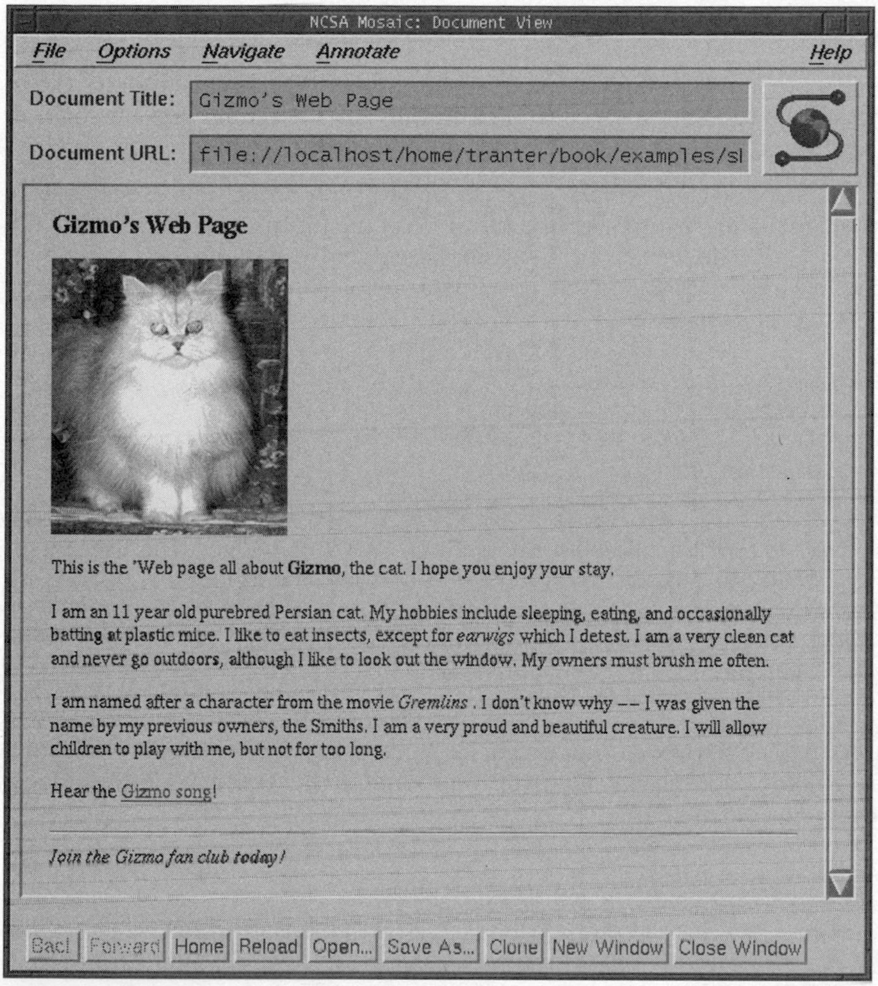

Figure 12-1: Mosaic browser

- RSA encryption, decryption, and authentication

- Hierarchical bookmarks

- All options configurable from menus

- Access to mail, news, ftp, and Gopher

- Background loading (you don't have to wait for entire page or images to download)

Netscape is a commercial software product distributed in binary form only. Users can download the software for evaluation purposes but are required to purchase it after the evaluation period (Netscape is free for educational users).

Because it is shipped as a binary statically linked with Motif, the executable is large (almost four megabytes), and there can be compatibility problems if you do not use the appropriate version of the Linux kernel and C libraries. At the time of this writing, a Linux version of Netscape was available on the Internet but it was not being officially supported.

Chimera

> Author: John Kilburg (*john@cs.unlv.edu*)
> Available from: *ftp://ftp.cs.unlv.edu/pub/chimera/*

Chimera is an X-based Web browser for UNIX. It uses the freely available MIT Athena widget set and a modified form of the NCSA HTML widget. The user interface is very similar to Mosaic. As of version 1.65 Chimera supports HTML forms, inline images, and access to Gopher, ftp, HTTP, and local files. It can work with *term*, *SOCKS*, and proxy servers. External viewer programs can be invoked using the standard MIME protocol and configured using mailcap files.

While it's not sophisticated, Chimera does provide all of the basic features needed in a graphical Web browser, and it can be built using free software (no Motif toolkit is needed). More information can be found at the World Wide Web page *http://www.unlv.edu/chimera/*.

Arena

> Author: Dave Raggett, Hakon Lie, Henrik Frystyk, Phill Hallam-Baker
> (*arena@w3.org*)
> Available from: *ftp://ftp.w3.org/pub/arena*

Arena is being developed by the World Wide Web Consortium as a test bed for the HTML 3.0 language. While not intended as a full-featured browser (it lacks a hot list, for example), it may still be acceptable to some users, particularly those who want to experiment with the new features of HTML 3.0.

As of the pre-release version 0.98 of Arena, the main features of HTML 3.0 supported were tables, math equations, and style sheets. The pre-release versions are distributed only as precompiled binaries for a number of platforms, including Linux. The pre-release source code can be obtained on request, and the source for version 1.0 is expected to be made freely available. More information can be found at the Arena Web page at *http://www.w3.org/WWW/Arena/*.

Lynx

Author: University of Kansas (*lynx-dev@ukanaix.cc.ukans.edu*)
Available from: *ftp://ftp2.cc.ukans.edu/pub/lynx*

Not everyone runs the X Window System, and some sites desire a text-based Web browser for dial-up access to a Linux system configured as a computer bulletin board system. *Lynx* is a World Wide Web browser that requires only a cursor-addressable character terminal.

Developed at the University of Kansas, the source code and precompiled binaries are freely available by anonymous ftp. Figure 12-2 shows Lynx running within an *xterm* terminal emulator (it also runs fine on a Linux virtual console).

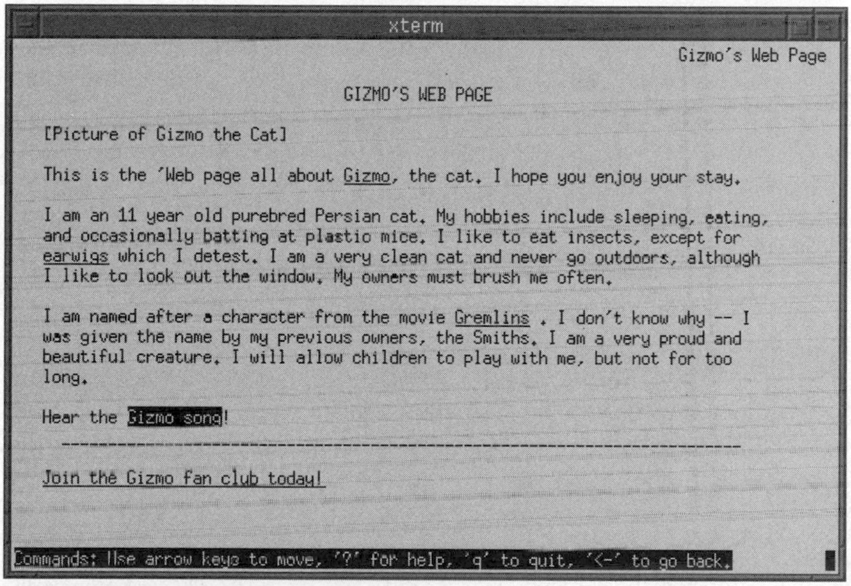

Figure 12–2: Lynx Web browser

Some of the features of version 2.4.2 of Lynx include:

- Use of character attributes like bold and underline (where available)

- Support for Latin-1 character set (where available)

- Support for HTML forms

- Access to Gopher, HTTP, ftp, WAIS, and NNTP

- Can call external viewers for sound, video, etc. (configured using MIME)

- Online help

- Single-key commands

- Can call external programs for mail and news access

- *emacs*, *vi*, or user-defined key bindings

- Bookmarks

- Can upload/download binary files to local terminal via *zmodem* or *kermit*

- Can be configured to restrict specific features (e.g., for a BBS or public access FreeNet environment)

Because it offers Web, email, Usenet news, and filesystem access, Lynx could easily be used as the user interface for a dial-up BBS system offering Internet access. A single Linux system with a multi-port serial card and a bank of modems could likely support a dozen users.

TkWWW

> Author: Joseph Wang (*joe@mit.edu*)
> Available from: *ftp://ftp.aud.alcatel.com/tcl/extensions/tkWWW-0.12.tar.gz*

TkWWW is a Web browser and WYSIWYG HTML editor that runs under X. It uses the Tcl language and the Tk toolkit to implement a Motif-like user interface. The user interface is much like other browsers but has the added capability of allowing users to edit HTML pages using pull-down menus. This feature allows you to create Web pages with little or no knowledge of the underlying HTML language. Since the entire user interface is written in an interpreted language, it is easy to make modifications and extensions to the program.

TkWWW requires Tcl and the Tk toolkit; both are included with most Linux distributions. The tkWWW program can be built as either a Tcl script or an executable binary.

TkWWW is released under the GNU general public license. The Free Software Foundation is hoping to make this program the official GNU Web browser, further developing it to support the features of HTML 3.0.

ASHE

> Author: John R. Punin (*puninj@cs.rpi.edu*)
> Available from: *ftp://ftp.cs.rpi.edu/pub/puninj/ASHE/ASHE-1.3/src/*
> *xhtml-1.3.tar.gz*

This program is invoked as *xhtml* but is really called *ASHE*—A Simple HTML Editor. It is, as the name implies, a text editor designed for writing HTML documents. It uses the Motif toolkit and runs under X11.

The top half of the screen is a text area with all of the usual features of a typical text editor including cut and paste, file load and save, printing, and undo. You can enter HTML manually or with the help of menu options.

The bottom half of the interface is a previewer that shows how the HTML being edited would be displayed by a Web browser. This screen gives immediate feedback on the text being edited. The previewer supports most HTML features including forms, in-line images, and tables. Multiple HTML files can be edited simultaneously in separate windows. The user interface is similar to Mosaic (it uses the same HTML widget and Motif toolkit). Online help is implemented as an HTML file. Figure 12-3 shows a typical *xhtml* screen.

Ross C. Linder (*ross@mecalc.co.za*) has compiled *xhtml* for Linux and released a statically linked binary that doesn't require Motif in order to run. It can be found at *ftp://sunsite.unc.edu/pub/Linux/X11/xapps/editors/xhtml.tar.gz*.

If you want to recompile *xhtml* yourself you will need the Motif toolkit. This is recommended if you have Motif, because the resulting executable will be much smaller. More information can be found on the ASHE Web page: *http://www.cs.rpi.edu/˜puninj/ASHE/*.

tkHTML

Author: Liem Bahneman (*roland@cac.washington.edu*)
Available from: *ftp://ftp.ssc.com/pub/ssc/roland/tkHTML/*

TkHTML is another HTML document editor for X11. It operates like a standard text editor with additional menu functions tailored to HTML. A document preview window shows how a browser would format the Web page. Figure 12-4 shows the tkHTML main and preview windows.

TkHTML was written in Tcl using the Tk toolkit, resulting in a graphical Motif-like interface. More information can be found on the Web at the site *http://www.ssc.com/˜roland/tkHTML/tkHTML.html*.

Java Browsers

The 2.0 release of Netscape Navigator for Linux supports Java. It is interesting to note that the Microsoft Windows 3.1 and Macintosh versions of Netscape do not support Java because of limitations in these operating systems.

We'll look at some of the tools for developing Java applications under Linux in Chapter 17.

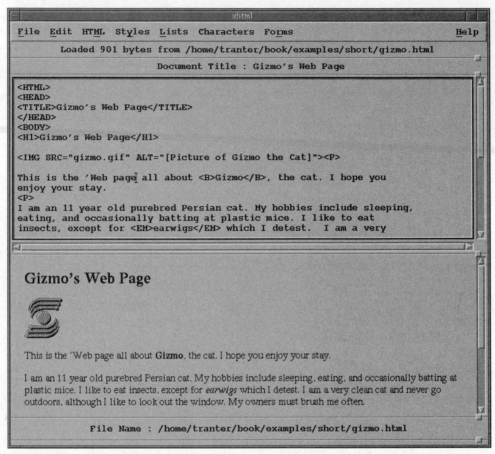

Figure 12–3: ASHE—a simple HTML editor

VRML Browsers

Like Java, VRML is still in its early stages, and applications for Linux are lagging behind some of the other platforms, but this is rapidly changing. As I write this chapter, there are at least two freely available VRML viewers supported or soon-to-be supported under Linux, and more in development.

VRweb is a VRML viewer developed as a joint project between the Institute for Information Processing and Computer Supported New Media (IICM, part of Graz University of Technology, Austria), the National Center for Supercomputing Applications (NCSA, a unit of the University of Illinois at Urbana-Champaign), and the University of Minnesota (home of Gopher). It claims to be the only VRML browser that is freely available in source code form for noncommercial use and does not require commercial packages such as *Inventor* or Motif. Under Linux it uses the

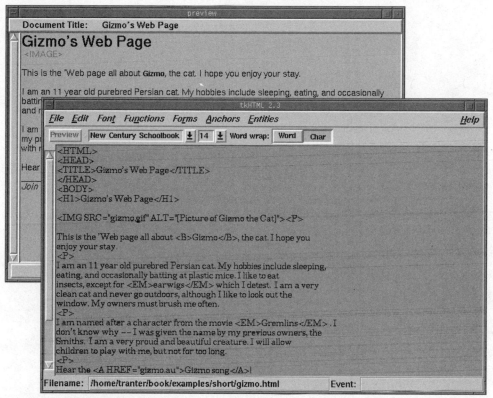

Figure 12–4: TkHTML HTML editor

Mesa library, a free workalike of the *OpenGL* 3D graphics library. More information can be found on the Web at *http://www.iicm.tu-graz.ac.at/vrweb/*.

WebOOGL is a free VRML browser developed by The Geometry Center at the University of Minnesota. It is a "quasi-compliant" browser, meaning that most of the VRML spec is implemented, but a few features (such as texture mapping) are silently ignored. It is built on top of the Center's 3D viewer *Geomview*. WebOOGL currently runs on Sun and SGI workstations, and a Linux port is in the works. For more information check *http://www.geom.umn.edu/software/weboogl/*.

Additional VRML viewers and development tools undoubtedly will be available by the time you read this book. More information can be found on the Web sites and other references listed in Appendix B, *Linux Resources*.

CHAPTER THIRTEEN
GAMES

For most of us, Linux is a hobby and a source of enjoyment. I spend much of my working day in front of a UNIX system. When I come home and log on to my Linux machine I sometimes have to remind myself that I'm not at work. Linus Torvalds once said that the driving force behind Linux was that it should be fun.* What better way to have fun, relax, and reduce stress than to play a computer game?

On a more serious note, games are also important because they push the state of the art of computing and multimedia with their requirements for real-time response, graphics, sound, and animation. Video games have historically been a key factor in bringing multimedia into the mainstream and bringing down the cost of the technology. Many of the first computers in the home were video games, and chances are good that the first time you saw a virtual reality visor or glove, it was part of a game.

Developing a new game or studying the source code of an existing game can be instructive for learning about multimedia application development. A successful game often presents a very good user interface. A co-worker once mused that if you wanted to see the user interface of the future, you should look at *DOOM*. With recent interest in technologies like VRML, that may not be far from the truth. The metaphor of a three-dimensional virtual world with high resolution images rendered in real-time and controlled by the user using input from a mouse, joystick, or "glove," combined with high-quality audio, could be the ultimate in intuitive user interfaces.

In this chapter I'll look at some of the games available for Linux. As usual, I've attempted to categorize them, and have room for only a small sample of what is available. Check the references in Appendix B, *Linux Resources*, for the most up-to-date information.

---

* I have to admit that I have difficulty explaining to my spouse why hacking the Linux kernel is fun.

These games run natively under Linux. There are some options for running popular MS-DOS-based games under Linux as well. The Linux DOS emulator allows running most MS-DOS programs, including those with graphics, under Linux. Microsoft Windows applications are not supported under the emulator, but the Linux WINE project is working to provide this support. A commercial solution for running Windows programs under Linux is also available from Willows Software.

For many Linux users, games are the only DOS programs they run.

Classic UNIX Games

The UNIX operating system originally was developed to write a space war game for an old minicomputer that was lying around unused. Traditionally UNIX has had a */usr/games* directory and allocated section 6 of the manpages to games.[*] Therefore, it's appropriate that I look at some of these old classics that have been around UNIX systems for almost as long as UNIX itself. Many of these were originally written in BASIC, Pascal, Fortran, or other more obscure languages but have since been converted to C.

Curt Olson (*curt@sledge.mn.org*) and Andy Tefft (*teffta@engr.dnet.ge.com*) have ported a collection of about 35 classic games from BSD UNIX to Linux, providing both source code and precompiled binaries. These aren't exactly state of the art arcade games, but some are very entertaining (or nostalgic, depending on your age). There is no support for graphics or sound; they just use text and sometimes the cursor positioning and formatting capabilities of the *termcap* or *curses* libraries.

A number of other classic UNIX games are also available separately from Internet archive sites. The Colossal Cave text adventure and Star Trek are two good examples. Many of these games are included with Linux distributions. If they aren't on your system, you can find them on Internet archive sites. A good starting point is *ftp://sunsite.unc.edu/pub/Linux/games/*.

X11-Based Games

Games that use only text are limited. A number of games have been written to run under the the X Window System, allowing the use of graphics, animation, and in some cases sound. These programs have the advantage of being generally portable to most systems running X, so while not written specifically for Linux, most will compile and run with little or no porting.

---

[*] I've noticed in at least one commercial operating system derived from UNIX that one of the "enhancements" made by the vendor was to remove all games.

Some of the games in this category include:

golddig
> similar to the commercial game LodeRunner

manix
> clone of Pacman

Xasteroids
> based on the vector graphics video game

xtetris
> X11 version of Tetris

fly
> graphical billiards game

xnetmine
> X11 version of Minesweeper

xmille
> Milles Bournes card game

gnuchess
> GNU chess program with optional graphical user interface

xlander
> lunar lander simulation

xmahjongg
> ancient Chinese tile matching game

Figure 13-1 shows a screen from *xboing* by Justin Kibel (*jck@citri.edu.au*). Similar to the commercial game known as *breakout*, this challenging game offers dozens of levels, colorful animation, and sound.

Again, many of these games are offered as part of Linux distributions, or can be found on archive sites such as either *ftp://sunsite.unc.edu/pub/Linux/games/x11/* or *ftp://ftp.x.org/contrib/games/*.

Linux-Specific Games

Writing a game can be a good way to learn multimedia programming under Linux. In the days of 8-bit computers and video games, developing a good graphical game often required expensive software development tools and had to be written in assembly language. The speed of PC hardware today makes it feasible to write games in C or C++, and they can be developed using Linux.

A number of video games have been written specifically for Linux. Some are loosely based on games that the authors enjoyed on older computers, and some

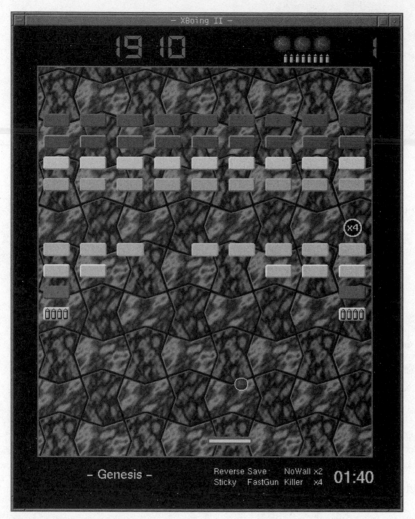

Figure 13-1: XBoing

are entirely new. Many of these games use the *svgalib* graphics library because it is simple, small, efficient, and easy to learn. Users of other operating systems are out of luck because most of these games run only under Linux.

Some of my favorite games in this category include *koules*, an original action game; *sasteroids*, based on the arcade game Asteroids; and *bdash*, inspired by BoulderDash.

Another game that can be included in this category is the shareware hit *DOOM* by Id software. Two Linux versions of this game exist: one that uses the *svgalib* library and one that runs under X11. You'll find *DOOM* and most of these games on archive sites such as *ftp://sunsite.unc.edu/pub/Linux/games/*.

Multiuser and Network Games

Historically UNIX systems have been multiuser, although most Linux systems running on personal computers don't make of use of this capability.* Games like the Colossal Cave text adventure evolved to support multiple users, allowing players to interact with other humans. As networking advanced, the games added support for players on a local area network, and then on the Internet. Today, with many Linux systems having low-cost access to the Internet via modem and a service provider, network games are possible with many millions of users around the world.

Dozens of different MUDs (MUD stands for Multiple User Dimension, Multiple User Dungeon, or Multiple User Dialogue) have been developed and are running with players distributed across the Internet. Some run continuously, with players joining and leaving the game over the course of a day. Older games had a pre-defined virtual world in which users interacted. Newer systems allow the players to construct their own areas of the world and define the behavior. Many of the games have developed their own rules of conduct and linguistic terms, in effect becoming virtual communities.

Some Linux software can be found by searching either or both of the following two ftp sites: one is *ftp://sunsite.unc.edu/pub/Linux/games/actionrpg/* and the other is *ftp://sunsite.unc.edu/pub/Linux/games/muds/*. Also see Appendix B for other sources of software and information.

Most MUDs today are text-based, but as computing power and network bandwidth increase, technologies such as VRML are expected to allow the creation of worlds with elaborate multimedia interfaces supporting three-dimensional rendered graphics, sound, music, and graphical user interfaces. The result may be very close to the "Cyberspace" envisioned by science fiction authors such as William Gibson, a prospect I find exciting, fascinating, and perhaps a bit frightening.

---

* As I write this chapter my son is playing *moria* on an external terminal connected to my Linux system.

PART FOUR

MULTIMEDIA PROGRAMMER'S GUIDE

If you want to develop your own multimedia applications, you will find Part IV to be the most useful part of this book. It covers programming of the multimedia devices using the facilities provided by the Linux kernel. We then look at the various toolkits that can be used to build complete applications. Finally, I develop several small but functional multimedia applications.

CHAPTER FOURTEEN

PROGRAMMING SOUND DEVICES

In this chapter we look at sound programming under Linux. The examples use the C programming language, as that is by far the most commonly used language under Linux.

C is also the obvious choice as a matter of convenience. Linux, like UNIX systems, is built around a kernel and libraries written in C. Using the operating system facilities from other programming languages usually requires additional effort. The examples will also compile using the GNU C++ compiler, g++.

If you have experience with C, but are not familiar with UNIX (or POSIX) compatible programming environments, don't despair. The next section should cover enough of the basics to allow you to understand the examples. But you should also consider supplementing the material with other references that cover UNIX programming.

If you are already familiar with programming devices under Linux or other UNIX-like systems, you may choose to skim through or skip the next section entirely.

Keep in mind that not all multimedia applications will need to program at this level. In Chapter 17, *Using Toolkits for Multimedia Programming*, I will explore some toolkits that can avoid, or at least minimize, having to program at the device level. Often, though, toolkits do not provide the functionality or efficiency that is needed, and C programming is required.

The Linux Sound Driver

Under Linux, like any UNIX-compatible system, user programs rarely access the hardware devices directly. The kernel has *drivers* for all hardware devices. At the kernel driver level, controlling hardware involves bit manipulation of hardware registers in a highly hardware-dependent and often time-critical manner. The kernel shields this from user programs. To an application, the devices appear as (somewhat special) files in the filesystem. This unified high-level view of devices is mostly hardware-independent. For example, usually you don't need to know what kind of sound card is installed in order to write applications to control it.

The Linux sound driver has an interesting history behind it. In 1992 Hannu Savolainen wrote a Linux kernel driver for the original 8-bit SoundBlaster card. Later, partly at the request of users, he added support for more sound cards. The sound driver has been included as a standard part of the kernel since the early days of Linux (that is, prior to the version 1.0 kernel).

The same driver was adapted to work with several other Intel-based UNIX and compatible operating systems. As the drivers could be used independently of UNIX, they were given a distinct name—Voxware. Unfortunately the same name was later registered by Voxware Incorporated and could no longer be used. For a period of time the package was known as TASD, the Temporarily Anonymous Sound Driver.

For some time Hannu had been looking for assistance from sound card vendors to help sponsor the development of the driver. Some vendors did provide cards, programming information, and funding, but it was still mostly a part-time effort for Hannu. In March 1996 it was announced that the sound driver was "going commercial." The company 4Front Technologies is now offering a commercial sound card driver for a number of UNIX and compatible operating systems for PCs and workstations, based on the former Voxware, called the UNIX Sound System (USS). It is sold and supported commercially, and like most commercial software products, is distributed in binary form.

At the same time the free version continues to be offered for Linux with similar conditions as before (e.g., freely redistributable source code). This version is called USS Lite. While it will not be supported by 4Front Technologies, it will continue to be maintained by Hannu Savolainen. The commercial and free versions will be compatible with each other, although the commercial USS release may include additional features (for example, support for sound cards from vendors who don't release programming information). If USS is widely accepted, it may become the standard sound programming API for UNIX systems. As I write this book, however, USS is in its first beta release and is available only for the Linux platform.

All of the programming information and examples in this chapter are based on the sound driver included in the Linux kernel version 2.0. They should work with later versions, but new features are being continually added to the sound driver. To be sure, you should check the latest driver *README* files for changes, new features, and possible incompatibilities.

Alternative device drivers are available as kernel patches. These drivers operate independently of the Linux sound driver, typically providing some functionality that the "official" kernel sound driver does not support. Using these sound drivers is not recommended, because they make your applications less portable. If you are contemplating writing drivers for new sound cards, you are urged to add the functionality to the kernel sound drivers, and ask the author to merge them into the standard driver source code (and ultimately, the standard Linux kernel sources).

While the examples in this chapter are specifically for Linux, the Linux sound drivers are supported on a number of other Intel UNIX platforms, making your code potentially portable to other operating systems. The examples are also aimed at the Intel version of Linux. At the time of writing, this was the only architecture that supported the Linux sound drivers.

Basic Device Programming

Typical usage for controlling a device under Linux consists of using a small set of function calls, usually called *system calls*, because they are implemented by the operating system's kernel. The interface is virtually identical to the one used for regular disk files. This standardized method of accessing devices means programmers don't need to learn new functions for each type of device. Programs can be written that will work with many different types of devices as well as disk files.

The *open* system call establishes access to the device, returning a file descriptor to be used for subsequent calls. The *read* and *write* functions receive data from and send data to a device, respectively. The *ioctl* routine is a catch-all function to perform other operations that do not fit the read/write model. For instance, to set mixer gains, the mixer driver offers an *ioctl* command that would be meaningless in any other devices.

Finally, *close* is used to notify the operating system that the device is no longer in use. The operating system normally closes all open devices when a program exits, but it is good practice to explicitly close them in your application. Most devices support a subset of these operations. For example, some devices may be read only, and not support the *write* function.

Some C programmers may not be familiar with the *read* and *write* functions. File and terminal access typically uses the buffered input/output routines such as *printf* and *scanf*. These are usually more efficient for files because the reads and writes are buffered in memory and performed later in larger blocks, reducing the overhead associated with calling the kernel read and write routines repeatedly. For low-level access to multimedia devices, you normally do not want this—you generally want data to be serviced immediately and have explicit control over buffer sizes. I will now look at each of these system calls in more detail.

The open System Call

This system call follows the format:

```
int open(const char *pathname, int flags, int mode);
```

This function is used to gain access to a device so you can subsequently operate on it with other system calls. The device or file can be an existing one that is to be opened for reading, writing, or both. It can also be used to create a new file.

The `pathname` parameter is the name of the file to be operated on. It can be a regular file, or a device file such as */dev/dsp*. The `flags` parameter indicates the mode to be used for opening the file, and takes one of the following values:

O_RDONLY
> open for read only

O_WRONLY
> open for write only

O_RDWR
> open for both read and write

In addition, some flags can be "bitwise OR" with the ones above to control other aspects of opening the file. A number of flags are defined, most of which are device-specific and not important to our discussion here.

The third `mode` parameter is optional—it specifies file permissions to be used when creating a new file and is only used when the O_CREAT option is given.

The *open* call, if successful, returns an integer file descriptor (a small positive number) to be used in subsequent system calls to reference the file. If the *open* fails for some reason, the call returns -1 and sets the variable `errno` to a value indicating the reason for failure.

There are some other more obscure options not relevant to our purposes; see the *open(2)* manpage for details.

The read System Call

The format of this function is:

```
int read(int fd, char *buf, size_t count);
```

This call returns data from a file or device. The first parameter is a file descriptor, obtained from a previous call to open. The buf parameter points to a buffer in which to hold the data returned—a sequence of bytes. The `char *` definition for the buffer is a convenience to cover all kinds of data. The argument is often cast to another data type, such as a data structure, that represents the particular kind of data you're dealing with. The count parameter indicates the *maximum* number of bytes to be read. If successful, the function returns the actual number of bytes read, which is sometimes less than count. On error, the value -1 is returned and the global variable `errno` is set to a value indicating the error cause.

Calling *read* can cause a process to block until the data is available.

The write System Call

Writing data uses the *write* system call, which takes the form:

```
size_t write(int fd, const char *buf, size_t count);
```

This function is analogous to read, but sends data to a file or device. Parameter `fd` is the open file descriptor, `buf` points to the data to be written, and `count` indicates the number of bytes to be written. The function returns the number of bytes actually written, or -1 if an error occurred. Like the read call, the process may be blocked by the kernel until the data has been successfully written.

The ioctl System Call

The *ioctl* system call, a catch-all function, takes the form:

```
int ioctl(int fd, int request, ...);
```

This function is used for performing miscellaneous operations on a file or device that does not fit into the read or write calls. Each request may set some behavior of the device, return information, or both. It is device-specific.

The first parameter is a file descriptor, obtained when the device was opened. The second is an integer value indicating the type of *ioctl* request being made. There is usually a third parameter, which is dependent on the specific *ioctl* request being made.

Later in the chapter I will show some examples of using *ioctl* on multimedia sound devices.

The close System Call

The last of the basic functions follows this format:

```
int close(int fd);
```

The *close* system call notifies the kernel that access to a file or device is no longer required, allowing any related resources to be freed up.

As there is a limit on the number of files that any one process can have open at one time, it is good practice to close files or devices when you are finished with them.

Example Program

The simple program in Example 14-1 illustrates most of the concepts discussed so far.

Example 14-1: Example of Linux System Calls

```c
/*
 * syscalls.c
 * Program to illustrate common system calls. Doesn't actually
 * perform any useful function, but will later be expanded into
 * a program which does.
 */

#include <unistd.h>
#include <stdio.h>
#include <fcntl.h>
#include <sys/types.h>
#include <sys/ioctl.h>
#include <linux/soundcard.h>

int main()
{
  int fd;                   /* device file descriptor */
  int arg;                  /* argument for ioctl call */
  unsigned char buf[1000];  /* buffer to hold data */
  int status;               /* return status of system calls */

  /* open device */
  status = fd = open("/dev/dsp", O_RDWR);
  if (status == -1) {
    perror("error opening /dev/dsp");
    exit(1);
  }

  /* set a parameter using ioctl call */
  arg = 8000; /* sampling rate */
  status = ioctl(fd, SOUND_PCM_WRITE_RATE, &arg);
  if (status == -1) {
    perror("error from SOUND_PCM_WRITE_RATE ioctl");
    exit(1);
  }

  /* read some data */
  status = read(fd, buf, sizeof(buf));
  if (status == -1) {
    perror("error reading from /dev/dsp");
    exit(1);
  }

  /* write some data */
  status = write(fd, buf, sizeof(buf));
  if (status == -1) {
    perror("error writing to /dev/dsp");
    exit(1);
  }
```

Example 14–1: Example of Linux System Calls (continued)

```
/* close the device */
status = close(fd);
if (status == -1) {
  perror("error closing /dev/dsp");
  exit(1);
}

/* and exit */
return(0);
}
```

First I include the header files that define the library routines used in the program. An easy way to identify these is to read the relevant manpages for the functions. I then start the function *main*, the only one in this small program, and define the variables needed to hold the file descriptor, the argument to *ioctl*, the data buffer, and the status returned by the system calls used.

I open the device file */dev/dsp*, indicating to open for both read and write. The third parameter is not needed as I am not creating a new file. After calling *open*, I check the return value, which displays an error message and exits if the call was not successful. I then use the *ioctl* call to set a parameter of the device. The meaning and type of the argument is specific to this *ioctl* function, but can be ignored for now. I'll cover it later.

Next I call *read* to obtain some data bytes from the device. I again check the return status. Then the same data is written back in a similar manner using the *write* system call.

The last step is to close the device, and again I check the status of the call to *close*, although some programmers might consider this level of checking a bit paranoid.

If you are new to C programming under Linux, I recommend that you enter the example program on your system and run it. Don't worry yet about *what* it does, just concentrate on successfully compiling it and verifying that it runs without errors. Try changing the program so that it attempts to operate on a nonexistent device and check that an error message is produced. Can you think of ways to produce any other error messages from the sample program?

Sound Programming Basics

The Linux sound driver tries to present an idealized sound card interface to the application programmer. It takes care of the hardware differences between cards although you do sometimes have to worry about whether a specific function is supported or not (e.g., whether a MIDI interface exists).

Figure 14-1 shows a block diagram of the idealized model of a sound card that the Linux sound driver provides. The diagram is somewhat simplified, and not all sound cards support all of the devices shown.

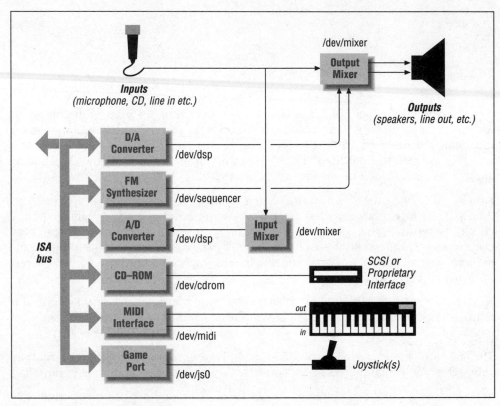

Figure 14–1: Sound card block diagram

The various hardware blocks (D/A converter, synthesizer, etc.) are controlled by the CPU via the ISA[*] bus. The ISA bus consists of data, address, and control signals that connect to the sound card via the slot in which the sound card is inserted. The bus allows the CPU to control the devices on the sound card, but it has no support for analog inputs or outputs; these are typically supported by connectors on the rear panel of the card.

There are several analog inputs on the left-hand side—microphone, CD audio, and line level input are the most common. On the right side are the analog outputs—usually speaker and line level as a minimum. An output mixer combines the various signal sources and sends them to the output devices. The signal sources may include input devices, to support playing the input signals through

---

[*] Sound cards could use buses other than ISA, such as EISA and PCI, but these are not in common use.

the speakers (a common example is playing audio CDs through the sound card using a CD-ROM drive).

Similarly, an input mixer accepts several analog signals, combines them, and feeds the output to an analog to digital converter to be digitized. Many sound cards also provide CD-ROM, MIDI, and joystick interfaces.

Applications that access the sound devices should include the sound header file *linux/soundcard.h*. Some additional functions specific to the Gravis UltraSound card are defined in *linux/ultrasound.h*.

In the next sections I will step through each of the sound driver device files, exploring the application programming interface, and looking at some small code examples. I recommend trying the code out on your system and modifying it, to fully illustrate the concepts.

Programming /dev/sndstat

The device */dev/sndstat/* is the simplest device provided by the sound driver. A read-only device file, its only purpose is to report information about the sound driver in human-readable form. It is much like the files found in the */proc* filesystem (and arguably should be found there).

The device is really meant for human use; it will probably never be read from a program, as you can get the same information more easily using *ioctl* calls. It is useful for checking your hardware configuration (DMA channel, IRQ number, etc.) and for finding out the version of the sound driver being used.

Included in the output are some "magic numbers" you can pass to a kernel loader program such as LILO to configure the sound driver at run-time.

Here is a sample output, produced using the shell *cat* command:

```
% cat /dev/sndstat
Sound Driver:3.5.2-960330 (Tue May 21 19:08:17 EDT 1996 root,
Linux fizzbin 2.0.0 #1 Tue May 21 19:22:57 EDT 1996 i386
Kernel: Linux fizzbin 2.0.0 #1 Tue May 21 19:22:57 EDT 1996 i386
Config options: a80002

Installed drivers:
Type 1: OPL-2/OPL-3 FM
Type 2: SoundBlaster
Type 6: SoundBlaster 16bit
Type 7: SB MPU

Card config:
SoundBlaster at 0x220 irq 5 drq 1,5
(SB MPU at 0x0 irq 1 drq 0)
OPL-2/OPL-3 FM at 0x388 irq 0 drq 0
```

```
Audio devices:
0: SoundBlaster Pro 3.2

Synth devices:
0: Yamaha OPL-3

Midi devices:
0: SoundBlaster

Timers:
0: System clock

Mixers:
0: SoundBlaster
```

The shell command above is the usual way of reading this device.* I won't write any code that uses it, and in fact I recommend against developing any software that relies on the format of the output. In the future, it is likely to change as the sound driver is enhanced.

Programming /dev/dsp

/dev/dsp is the digital sampling and digital recording device, and probably the most important for multimedia applications. Writing to the device accesses the D/A converter to produce sound. Reading the device activates the A/D converter for sound recording and analysis.

The name *DSP* comes from the term *digital signal processor*, a specialized processor chip optimized for digital signal analysis. Sound cards may use a dedicated DSP chip, or may implement the functions with a number of discrete devices. Other terms that may be used for this device are *digitized voice* and *PCM*.

Some sounds cards provide more than one digital sampling device; in this case a second device is available as */dev/dsp1*. Unless noted otherwise, this device operates in the same manner as */dev/dsp*.

The DSP device is really two devices in one. Opening for read-only access allows you to use the A/D converter for sound input. Opening for write only will access the D/A converter for sound output. Generally speaking you should open the device either for read only or for write only. It is possible to perform both read and write on the device, albeit with some restrictions; this will be covered in a later section.

Only one process can have the DSP device open at a time. Attempts by another process to open it will fail with an error code of EBUSY.

---

* Incidentally, trying to browse the device using *less* produces an error message. Surprisingly, the *more* program does work.

Reading from the DSP device returns digital sound samples obtained from the A/D converter. Figure 14-2(a) shows a conceptual diagram of this process. Analog data is converted to digital samples by the analog to digital converter under control of the kernel sound driver and stored in a buffer internal to the kernel. When an application program invokes the *read* system call, the data is transferred to the calling program's data buffer. It is important to understand that the sampling rate is dependent on the kernel driver, and not the speed at which the application program reads it.

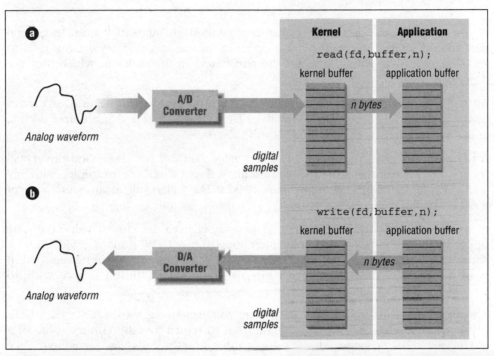

Figure 14-2: Accessing /dev/dsp

When reading from */dev/dsp* you will never encounter an end-of-file condition. If data is read too slowly (less than the sampling rate), the excess data will be discarded, resulting in gaps in the digitized sound. If you read the device too quickly, the kernel sound driver will block your process until the required amount of data is available.

The input source depends on the mixer setting (which I will look at shortly); the default is the microphone input. The format of the digitized data depends on which *ioctl* calls have been used to set up the device. Each time the device is opened, its parameters are set to default values. The default is 8-bit unsigned samples, using one channel (mono), and an 8 kHz sampling rate.

Writing a sequence of digital sample values to the DSP device produces sound output. This process is illustrated in Figure 14-2(b). Again, the format can be defined using *ioctl* calls, but defaults to the values given above for the *read* system call (8-bit unsigned data, mono, 8 kHz sampling).

If the data are written too slowly, there will be dropouts or pauses in the sound output. Writing the data faster than the sampling rate will simply cause the kernel sound driver to block the calling process until the sound card hardware is ready to process the new data. Unlike some devices, there is no support for non-blocking I/O.

If you don't like the defaults, you can change them through *ioctl* calls. In general you should set the parameters *after* opening the device, and *before* any calls to *read* or *write*. You should also set the parameters in the order in which they are described below.

All DSP *ioctl* calls take a third argument that is a pointer to an integer. Don't try to pass a constant; you must use a variable. The call will return -1 if an error occurs, and set the global variable `errno`.

If the hardware doesn't support the exact value you call for, the sound driver will try to set the parameter to the closest allowable value. For example, with my sound card, selecting a sampling rate of 9000 Hz will result in an actual rate of 9009 Hz being used.

If a parameter is out of range, the driver will set it to the closest value (i.e., the upper or lower limit). For example, attempting to use 16-bit sampling with an 8-bit sound card will result in the driver selecting 8 bits, but no error will be returned. It is up to you, the programmer, to verify that the value returned is acceptable to your application.

All of the *ioctl* calls for the DSP device are names starting with SOUND_PCM. Calls in the form SOUND_PCM_READ_*XXX* are used to return just the current value of a parameter. To change the values, the *ioctl* calls are named like SOUND_PCM_WRITE_*XXX*. As discussed above, these calls also return the selected value, which is not necessarily the same as the value passed to the sound driver.

The *ioctl* constants are defined in the header file *linux/soundcard.h*. Let's examine each of them in detail.

SOUND_PCM_WRITE_BITS
  Sets the sample size, in bits. Valid choices are 8 and 16, but some cards do not support 16.

SOUND_PCM_READ_BITS
  Returns the current sample size, which should be either 8 or 16 bits.

SOUND_PCM_WRITE_CHANNELS

Sets the number of channels—1 for mono, 2 for stereo. When running in stereo mode, the data is interleaved when read or written, in the format left-right-left-right.... Remember that some sound cards do not support stereo; check the actual number of channels returned in the argument.

SOUND_PCM_READ_CHANNELS

Returns the current number of channels, either 1 or 2.

SOUND_PCM_WRITE_RATE

Sets the sampling rate in samples per second. Remember that all sound cards have a limit on the range; the driver will round the rate to the nearest speed supported by the hardware, returning the actual (rounded) rate in the argument. Typical lower limits are 4 kHz; upper limits are 13, 15, 22, or 44 kHz.

SOUND_PCM_READ_RATE

Returns just the current sampling rate. This is the rate used by the kernel, which may not be exactly the rate given in a previous call to SOUND_PCM_WRITE_RATE, because of the previously discussed rounding.

Sample Program

I will now illustrate programming of the DSP device with a short example. I call the program in Example 14-2 *parrot*. It records a few seconds of audio, saving it to an array in memory, then plays it back.

Example 14–2: Reading and Writing the /dev/dsp Device

```
/*
 * parrot.c
 * Program to illustrate /dev/dsp device
 * Records several seconds of sound, then echoes it back.
 * Runs until Control-C is pressed.
 */

#include <unistd.h>
#include <fcntl.h>
#include <sys/types.h>
#include <sys/ioctl.h>
#include <stdlib.h>
#include <stdio.h>
#include <linux/soundcard.h>

#define LENGTH 3     /* how many seconds of speech to store */
#define RATE 8000    /* the sampling rate */
#define SIZE 8       /* sample size: 8 or 16 bits */
#define CHANNELS 1   /* 1 = mono 2 = stereo */

/* this buffer holds the digitized audio */
unsigned char buf[LENGTH*RATE*SIZE*CHANNELS/8];
```

Example 14–2: Reading and Writing the /dev/dsp Device (continued)

```
int main()
{
  int fd;      /* sound device file descriptor */
  int arg;     /* argument for ioctl calls */
  int status;  /* return status of system calls */

  /* open sound device */
  fd = open("/dev/dsp", O_RDWR);
  if (fd < 0) {
    perror("open of /dev/dsp failed");
    exit(1);
  }

  /* set sampling parameters */
  arg = SIZE;     /* sample size */
  status = ioctl(fd, SOUND_PCM_WRITE_BITS, &arg);
  if (status == -1)
    perror("SOUND_PCM_WRITE_BITS ioctl failed");
  if (arg != SIZE)
    perror("unable to set sample size");

  arg = CHANNELS;  /* mono or stereo */
  status = ioctl(fd, SOUND_PCM_WRITE_CHANNELS, &arg);
  if (status == -1)
    perror("SOUND_PCM_WRITE_CHANNELS ioctl failed");
  if (arg != CHANNELS)
    perror("unable to set number of channels");

  arg = RATE;     /* sampling rate */
  status = ioctl(fd, SOUND_PCM_WRITE_RATE, &arg);
  if (status == -1)
    perror("SOUND_PCM_WRITE_WRITE ioctl failed");

  while (1) { /* loop until Control-C */
    printf("Say something:\n");
    status = read(fd, buf, sizeof(buf)); /* record some sound */
    if (status != sizeof(buf))
      perror("read wrong number of bytes");
    printf("You said:\n");
    status = write(fd, buf, sizeof(buf)); /* play it back */
    if (status != sizeof(buf))
      perror("wrote wrong number of bytes");
    /* wait for playback to complete before recording again */
    status = ioctl(fd, SOUND_PCM_SYNC, 0);
  if (status == -1)
    perror("SOUND_PCM_SYNC ioctl failed");
  }
}
```

The source file starts by including a number of standard header files, including *linux/soundcard.h*. Then some constants are defined for the sound card settings used in the program, which makes it easy to change the values used. A static buffer is defined to hold the sound data.

I first open the DSP device for both read and write and check that the open was successful. Next I set the sampling parameters using *ioctl* calls. Notice that a variable must be used because the driver expects a pointer. In each case I check for an error from the *ioctl* call (a return value of -1), and that the values actually used are within range. This programming may appear to be overly cautious, but I consider it good coding practice that pays off when trying to debug the code. Note that I do not check that the actual sampling rate returned matches the selected rate because of the sampling rate rounding previously described.

I then run in a loop, first prompting the user to speak, then reading the sound data into the buffer. Once the data is received, I warn the user, then write the same data back to the DSP device, where it should be heard. This repeats until the program is interrupted with Control-C.

The SOUND_PCM_SYNC *ioctl* has not yet been mentioned. I'll show what this is used for in the section titled "Advanced Sound Programming," later in this chapter.

Try compiling and running this program. Then make some enhancements:

1. Make the parameters selectable using command-line options (sample rate, size, time). See the effect on sound quality with different sampling rates.

2. Reverse the sound samples (and listen for hidden messages), or play them back at a different sampling rate from the one at which they were recorded.

3. Automatically start recording when the voice starts and stop when silence occurs (or a maximum time is reached). Hints: for 8-bit unsigned data the zero value is 0x80, but you will likely see values that vary around this level due to noise. Set a noise threshold (or better yet, measure the background noise level at the start of the program).

4. Bonus question: modify the program so that it can recognize the words that are spoken.

Programming /dev/audio

The */dev/audio* device is similar to */dev/dsp*, but is intended for compatibility with the audio device on workstations made by Sun Microsystems, where it has the same name. The device uses μ-law encoding. It does not support the SunOS *ioctl* functions (in principle it could, though). The main purpose is to support user commands such as **cat file.au >/dev/audio** to play Sun μ-law encoded files.

It is not recommended that you use */dev/audio* for new application programs. The μ-law encoding adds software overhead and some distortion. It is better to use the

/dev/dsp interface instead. Only one of */dev/audio* and */dev/dsp* is available at any one time, as they are just different software interfaces to the same hardware device. There is also a */dev/audio1* device available for those cards that have a second sampling device.

Programming /dev/mixer

In Chapter 2, *Digital Audio*, I briefly discussed mixers—electronic circuits that combine or add several signals together. The capabilities of mixers provided on sound cards vary. The */dev/mixer* device (and */dev/mixer1*, if a second mixer is supported) presents an idealized model of a sound card mixer; it is shown in block diagram form in Figure 14-3.

The mixer really contains two mixer circuits. The input mixer (shown near the bottom of the diagram) accepts analog inputs from a number of different signal sources. The sources are sometimes referred to as mixer channels or mixer devices. An electronic gain control, a software-controlled "volume control," adjusts the level of the signal from each mixer channel before it goes into the input mixer. Electronic switches control which channels have their signals connected to the mixer. Some sound cards only allow one channel to be connected as a recording source (the inputs are exclusive choices), while others allow any combination of inputs. The signals are then fed to the mixer, which essentially adds them together. There is usually one final gain control that adjusts the level of the signals coming out of the mixer (labelled *Reclev*, for recording level, in Figure 14-3). The resulting signal is fed to the analog to digital converter where it can be digitized for further signal processing (e.g., written to a sound file). Note that up until the analog to digital converter, all of the signals are in analog form.

The output mixer works in a similar manner. Various input signals are fed to the input mixer, usually passing through gain controls first. In this case all channels are normally connected to the mixer. To effectively remove an input signal from the mixer, its gain control should be set to zero gain. After the output mixer combines the analog signals, there is one final gain control to adjust the overall volume level, and there may be tone controls. The last step is to send the resulting output signal to the speakers or other analog outputs.

This is an idealized mixer; any or all of the inputs, outputs, and level controls may or may not be present. Some sound cards, most notably the original SoundBlaster, have no programmable mixer channels at all. The audio paths may be stereo, mono, or a mixture of both. As the capabilities and design of sound cards vary, there may be slight differences between the diagram and a specific card—for example, on some cards the CD level setting may affect both record and playback, while on others it is only a playback level control. Software applications should determine the capabilities of the mixer at run-time using calls to the sound driver, so that the applications are not dependent on the capabilities of any one sound card. I will illustrate how to do this shortly.

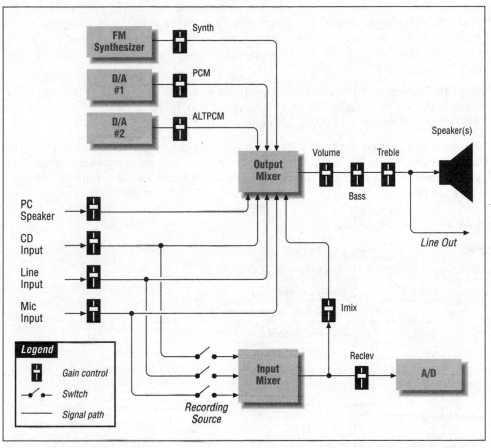

Figure 14-3: /dev/mixer block diagram

Programming the mixer consists of setting the desired levels for the gain controls and the switches for the recording source. Other than that, the mixer operates continuously, taking no computing resources to operate.

The mixer doesn't fit into the typical UNIX device model, and therefore does not support the *read* and *write* system calls. Other than *open* and *close*, all functions are performed using the *ioctl* call.

Unlike the DSP device, more than one process can open the mixer at one time. Furthermore, any mixer settings remain in effect after the mixer device is closed. This capability is desirable, because you generally want to be able to set a parameter, such as the volume level, and have it remain in effect after the program setting it has completed. When the kernel first initializes, the mixer is set to reasonable default values.

You can also take one shortcut when programming: the mixer *ioctl* calls can be used on *any* sound device (to access the first mixer only). For example, if an application has opened */dev/dsp*, there is no need to open */dev/mixer* to change mixer settings. Just use the file descriptor that was returned when you opened */dev/dsp*.

All of the mixer *ioctl* commands are prefixed with SOUND_MIXER or MIXER_. Like the DSP device *ioctl* calls, the third parameter should be a pointer to an integer. The driver will return a value in this parameter.

The devices currently supported by the sound driver are shown in Table 14-1. The names in the first column are the symbolic names used as parameters to the *ioctl* system calls that control the mixer. The second column lists the purpose of each mixer channel.

Table 14–1: Mixer Channels

Name	Description
SOUND_MIXER_VOLUME	master output level
SOUND_MIXER_BASS	bass tone control
SOUND_MIXER_TREBLE	treble tone control
SOUND_MIXER_SYNTH	FM synthesizer
SOUND_MIXER_PCM	D/A converter
SOUND_MIXER_SPEAKER	PC speaker output level
SOUND_MIXER_LINE	line input
SOUND_MIXER_MIC	microphone input
SOUND_MIXER_CD	audio CD input
SOUND_MIXER_IMIX	playback volume from recording source
SOUND_MIXER_ALTPCM	secondary D/A converter
SOUND_MIXER_RECLEV	master recording level
SOUND_MIXER_IGAIN	input gain level
SOUND_MIXER_OGAIN	output gain level
SOUND_MIXER_LINE1	card-specific input #1
SOUND_MIXER_LINE2	card-specific input #2
SOUND_MIXER_LINE3	card-specific input #3

The main function of a mixer is to set gain levels. Different sound cards may provide 8 or 16 bits of gain control. As an application programmer you do not have to worry about this; the sound driver scales all levels to a percentage, a value from 0 to 100. The macro MIXER_READ is the recommended way to read the current level setting of a channel. It accepts a parameter corresponding to the bitmask for the channel in question. For example, the call to read the current microphone input level could look like this:

```
int vol;
ioctl(fd, MIXER_READ(SOUND_MIXER_MIC), &vol);
printf("Mic gain is at %d %%\n", vol);
```

The channel may support stereo, so the returned volume includes two values, one for each channel. The least significant byte holds the left channel volume, and the next significant byte holds the right channel volume. Decoding can be performed like this:

```
int left, right;
left  = vol & 0xff;
right = (vol & 0xff00) >> 8;
printf("Left gain is %d %%, Right gain is %d %%\n", left, right);
```

For mono devices (one channel), the gain value is in the lower order byte (the same as the left channel above).

The gain levels can be set using the MIXER_WRITE macro. The volume settings are encoded in the same manner as when reading, like this:

```
vol = (right << 8) + left;
ioctl(fd, MIXER_WRITE(SOUND_MIXER_MIC), &vol);
```

The volume parameter passed to the *ioctl* is both an input and an output. As the capabilities of the mixer hardware channels vary, the sound driver will have to scale the percentage value to the nearest value supported by the hardware. The *ioctl* call returns the actual value used.

Most *ioctl* calls to the mixer either act on a mixer channel (one of the level controls shown in Table 14-1) or make use of a bit field containing information for all channels. The sound driver header file provides symbolic names for each of these channels. The actual names are subject to change during future development of the mixer driver, but the total number of channels will be equal to the value SOUND_MIXER_NRDEVICES (i.e., they will range from zero through SOUND_MIXER_NRDEVICES - 1). In addition, you can obtain symbolic names for these channels if you define arrays such as the following:

```
const char *labels[] = SOUND_DEVICE_LABELS;
const char *names[]  = SOUND_DEVICE_NAMES;
```

The first set of names are in a format suitable for labeling the controls of a mixer program. The second set are in a format better suited for command-line options (i.e., they are all single words in lowercase).

Several *ioctl* calls are used for finding out information about the mixer. These all return an integer bitmask in which each bit corresponds to a particular mixer channel. SOUND_MIXER_READ_DEVMASK returns a bitmask where a bit is set for each channel that is supported by the mixer. SOUND_MIXER_READ_RECMASK has a bit set for each channel that can be used as a recording source. For example, we could check if the CD input was a valid mixer channel using the following code:

```
ioctl(fd, SOUND_MIXER_READ_DEVMASK, &devmask);
if (devmask & SOUND_MIXER_CD)
  printf("The CD input is supported");
```

We could also find out if it was available as a recording source using this code:

```
ioctl(fd, SOUND_MIXER_READ_RECMASK, &recmask);
if (recmask & SOUND_MIXER_CD)
  printf("The CD input can be a recording source");
```

Remember to use the bitwise operator (&) here, not the boolean operator (&&).

SOUND_MIXER_READ_RECSRC indicates which channels are currently selected as the recording source. More than one source may be selected, if the sound card permits. SOUND_MIXER_READ_STEREODEVS has bits set if a channel supports stereo. If cleared, it supports only one channel (mono).

A similar *ioctl* call returns information about the sound card as a whole: SOUND_MIXER_READ_CAPS. Each bit corresponds to a capability of the sound card. Currently only one capability exists: SOUND_CAP_EXCL_INPUT. If this bit is set, the recording source channels are mutually exclusive choices. If cleared, then any or all can be set at one time.

The *ioctl* SOUND_MIXER_WRITE_RECSRC sets the current recording source channel. Following the earlier example, we could now set the CD input as a recording source using:

```
devmask = SOUND_MIXER_CD;
ioctl(fd, SOUND_MIXER_WRITE_DEVMASK, &devmask);
```

Make sure you pass a variable as the argument. Passing an immediate value won't work because the kernel function expects a pointer.

Example Program

The sample program shown in Example 14-3 illustrates most of the functions of the mixer. It lists all of the mixer channels, indicating which are available on the currently installed sound card. It shows which channels can be inputs, which input channels are currently selected, whether the channels are stereo, and the current gain setting. It also lists whether the input channels are a mutually exclusive choice. If the input channels are mutually exclusive, then only one input channel may be selected at any one time. If the choice is not mutually exclusive, then you may select more than one simultaneous input source channel.

Example 14-3: Accessing /dev/mixer

```
/*
 * mixer_info.c
 * Example program to display mixer settings
 */

#include <unistd.h>
#include <stdlib.h>
#include <stdio.h>
#include <sys/ioctl.h>
#include <fcntl.h>
#include <linux/soundcard.h>

/* utility function for printing status */
void yes_no(int condition)
{
  condition ? printf("  yes      ") : printf("  no       ");
}

int main(int argc, char *argv[])
{
  int fd;        /* file descriptor for mixer device */
  int i;         /* loop counter */
  int level;     /* volume setting */
  char *device;  /* name of device to report on */
  int status;    /* status of system calls */
  /* various device settings */
  int recsrc, devmask, recmask, stereodevs, caps;
  /* names of available mixer channels */
  const char *sound_device_names[] = SOUND_DEVICE_LABELS;

  /* get device name from command line or use default */
  if (argc == 2)
    device = argv[1];
  else
    device = "/dev/mixer";

  /* open mixer, read only */
  fd = open(device, O_RDONLY);
  if (fd == -1) {
    fprintf(stderr, "%s: unable to open '%s', ", argv[0], device);
    perror("");
    return 1;
  }

  /* get all of the information about the mixer */
  status = ioctl(fd, SOUND_MIXER_READ_RECSRC, &recsrc);
  if (status == -1)
    perror("SOUND_MIXER_READ_RECSRC ioctl failed");
  status = ioctl(fd, SOUND_MIXER_READ_DEVMASK, &devmask);
  if (status == -1)
```

Example 14-3: Accessing /dev/mixer (continued)

```
     perror("SOUND_MIXER_READ_DEVMASK ioctl failed");
  status = ioctl(fd, SOUND_MIXER_READ_RECMASK, &recmask);
  if (status == -1)
    perror("SOUND_MIXER_READ_RECMASK ioctl failed");
  status = ioctl(fd, SOUND_MIXER_READ_STEREODEVS, &stereodevs);
  if (status == -1)
    perror("SOUND_MIXER_READ_STEREODEVS ioctl failed");
  status = ioctl(fd, SOUND_MIXER_READ_CAPS, &caps);
  if (status == -1)
    perror("SOUND_MIXER_READ_CAPS ioctl failed");

  /* print results in a table */
  printf(
        "Status of %s:\n\n"
        "Mixer     Device    Recording Active    Stereo    Current\n"
        "Channel   Available Source    Source    Device    Level\n"
        "--------- --------- --------- -------- --------- ---------\n",
        device
        );

  /* loop over all devices */
  for (i = 0 ; i < SOUND_MIXER_NRDEVICES ; i++) {
    /* print number and name */
    printf("%2d %-7s", i, sound_device_names[i]);
    /* print if available */
    yes_no((1 << i) & devmask);
    /* can it be used as a recording source? */
    yes_no((1 << i) & recmask);
    /* it it an active recording source? */
    yes_no((1 << i) & recsrc);
    /* does it have stereo capability? */
    yes_no((1 << i) & stereodevs);
    /* if available, display current level */
    if ((1 << i) & devmask) {
      /* if stereo, show both levels */
      if ((1 << i) & stereodevs) {
        status = ioctl(fd, MIXER_READ(i), &level);
        if (status == -1)
          perror("SOUND_MIXER_READ ioctl failed");
        printf("  %d%% %d%%", level & 0xff, (level & 0xff00) >> 8);
      } else { /* only one channel */
        status = ioctl(fd, MIXER_READ(i), &level);
        if (status == -1)
          perror("SOUND_MIXER_READ ioctl failed");
        printf("  %d%%", level & 0xff);
      }
    }
    printf("\n");
  }
  printf("\n");
```

Example 14-3: Accessing /dev/mixer (continued)

```
    /* are recording sources exclusive? */
    printf("Note: Choices for recording source are ");
    if (!(caps & SOUND_CAP_EXCL_INPUT))
      printf("not ");
    printf("exclusive.\n");
    /* close mixer device */
    close(fd);
    return 0;
}
```

Note how the sample program avoids hardcoding any particular channel names or numbers in the source. This independence keeps the program portable as new channels are added to the sound driver. On my system, this output is produced:

```
    Status of /dev/mixer:
```

Mixer Channel	Device Available	Recording Source	Active Source	Stereo Device	Current Level
0 Vol	yes	no	no	yes	90% 90%
1 Bass	no	no	no	no	
2 Trebl	no	no	no	no	
3 Synth	yes	no	no	yes	75% 75%
4 Pcm	yes	no	no	yes	75% 75%
5 Spkr	no	no	no	no	
6 Line	yes	yes	no	yes	75% 75%
7 Mic	yes	yes	yes	no	16%
8 CD	yes	yes	no	yes	75% 75%
9 Mix	no	no	no	no	
10 Pcm2	no	no	no	no	
11 Rec	no	no	no	no	
12 IGain	no	no	no	no	
13 OGain	no	no	no	no	
14 Line1	no	no	no	no	
15 Line2	no	no	no	no	
16 Line3	no	no	no	no	

```
    Note: Choices for recording source are exclusive.
```

You can verify that the mixer functions also operate using another sound device by running the program with */dev/dsp* as the device file given on the command line.

The previous program is instructive, but not particularly useful because it does not allow you to change the mixer settings. Example 14-4 is a simple program that allows setting the mixer levels.

Example 14–4: Simple Mixer Program

```c
/*
 * mixer.c
 * Example of a simple mixer program
 */

#include <unistd.h>
#include <stdlib.h>
#include <stdio.h>
#include <sys/ioctl.h>
#include <fcntl.h>
#include <linux/soundcard.h>

/* names of available mixer devices */
const char *sound_device_names[] = SOUND_DEVICE_NAMES;

int fd;                     /* file descriptor for mixer device */
int devmask, stereodevs;    /* bit masks of mixer information */
char *name;                 /* program name */

/* display command usage and exit with error status */
void usage()
{
  int i;

  fprintf(stderr, "usage: %s <device> <left-gain%%> <right-gain%%>\n"
         "       %s <device> <gain%%>\n\n"
            "Where <device> is one of:\n", name, name);
  for (i = 0 ; i < SOUND_MIXER_NRDEVICES ; i++)
    if ((1 << i) & devmask) /* only display valid devices */
      fprintf(stderr, "%s ", sound_device_names[i]);
  fprintf(stderr, "\n");
  exit(1);
}

int main(int argc, char *argv[])
{
  int left, right, level;  /* gain settings */
  int status;              /* return value from system calls */
  int device;              /* which mixer device to set */
  int i;                   /* general purpose loop counter */
  char *dev;               /* mixer device name */

  /* save program name */
  name = argv[0];

  /* open mixer, read only */
  fd = open("/dev/mixer", O_RDONLY);
  if (fd == -1) {
    perror("unable to open /dev/mixer");
    exit(1);
```

Example 14-4: Simple Mixer Program (continued)

```
    }

    /* get needed information about the mixer */
    status = ioctl(fd, SOUND_MIXER_READ_DEVMASK, &devmask);
    if (status == -1)
      perror("SOUND_MIXER_READ_DEVMASK ioctl failed");
    status = ioctl(fd, SOUND_MIXER_READ_STEREODEVS, &stereodevs);
    if (status == -1)
      perror("SOUND_MIXER_READ_STEREODEVS ioctl failed");

    /* check that user passed two or three arguments on command line */
    if (argc != 3 && argc != 4)
      usage();

    /* save mixer device name */
    dev = argv[1];

    /* figure out which device to use */
    for (i = 0 ; i < SOUND_MIXER_NRDEVICES ; i++)
      if (((1 << i) & devmask) && !strcmp(dev, sound_device_names[i]))
        break;
    if (i == SOUND_MIXER_NRDEVICES) { /* didn't find a match */
      fprintf(stderr, "%s is not a valid mixer device\n", dev);
      usage();
    }

    /* we have a valid mixer device */
    device = i;

    /* get gain values */
    if (argc == 4) {
      /* both left and right values given */
      left  = atoi(argv[2]);
      right = atoi(argv[3]);
    } else {
      /* left and right are the same */
      left  = atoi(argv[2]);
      right = atoi(argv[2]);
    }

    /* display warning if left and right gains given for non-stereo device */
    if ((left != right) && !((1 << i) & stereodevs)) {
      fprintf(stderr, "warning: %s is not a stereo device\n", dev);
    }

    /* encode both channels into one value */
    level = (right << 8) + left;

    /* set gain */
    status = ioctl(fd, MIXER_WRITE(device), &level);
```

Example 14-4: Simple Mixer Program (continued)

```
    if (status == -1) {
      perror("MIXER_WRITE ioctl failed");
      exit(1);
    }

    /* unpack left and right levels returned by sound driver */
    left  = level & 0xff;
    right = (level & 0xff00) >> 8;

    /* display actual gain setting */
    fprintf(stderr, "%s gain set to %d%% / %d%%\n", dev, left, right);

    /* close mixer device and exit */
    close(fd);
    return 0;
}
```

A typical use of the program to set the external CD input levels would look like:

```
% mixer cd 80 90
cd gain set to 80% / 90%
```

Going briefly through the program's source code, function *main* starts by opening the mixer and getting information about it that will be needed later. We get the user's first command-line argument, then loop through all of the valid mixer channels looking for a match to the given channel name. If there is no match then the command line is in error, and we quit.

Otherwise, we get either one or two gain parameters from the command line, convert them to integers, and encode them into the single number format used by the mixer functions. We then set the level using a mixer *ioctl* call. Finally, we unpack and display the actual gain values that were returned by the sound driver.

Note that all *ioctl* calls are checked for successful return codes. Another nicety is to check that when the user specifies different left and right gain values, the channel really supports stereo. If not, we warn the user. Another helpful feature is that the command usage line lists the valid mixer channel names:

```
% mixer
usage: mixer <device> <left-gain%> <right-gain%>
       mixer <device> <gain%>

Where <device> is one of:
vol synth pcm line mic cd
```

Otherwise the user would have to guess or read the documentation to determine the valid mixer channel names. A useful enhancement to this program, to turn it into a full-featured mixer program, would be to add the ability to set the mixer recording source. I leave that as an exercise for you, the reader.

Programming /dev/sequencer

The *dev/sequencer* device allows you to program the FM or wavetable synthesizer built into the sound card or external devices on a MIDI bus. It is intended for computer music applications.

The word *sequencer* refers to an application that controls MIDI devices, sending messages to them in an appropriate sequence to play music.

The interface to this device is quite complex. It uses commands loosely based on the events used by the MIDI protocol. A typical command might start playing a note using a particular instrument voice.

Before using the on-board synthesizer, you have to download patches to define one or more instruments. These can be individual patches loaded on a per-instrument basis or, more commonly, a full set such as the 128 standard MIDI voices. These patches are usually contained in files.

I'm not going to cover this device in any more detail. It is of less interest to most multimedia application developers because it is limited to music, and applications already exist that can play most computer music files (these were covered in Part III).

There is a higher-level interface to the synthesizer and MIDI bus, */dev/sequencer2*, but it is not yet available in the current sound driver. A higher-level interface for managing patches for the */dev/sequencer* devices is planned, but not yet complete. Called */dev/patmgr*, it is quite specialized and probably not of interest to most multimedia application developers, so I won't explore it further.

The device */dev/midi* will provide low-level access to the MIDI bus. It is not currently fully implemented, and the API is in the process of changing. The MIDI interface is somewhat specialized and normally used only by musicians.

If you are interested in computer music, I urge you to look at the source code for some of the existing software applications such as *mp02*, *adagio*, and *glib*, in order to gain an understanding of the programming interface.

Example Program

For what it's worth, in Example 14-5 I offer a small example program that illustrates how to determine the sequencer devices supported by a sound card.

Example 14–5: Example of Accessing /dev/sequencer

```
/*
 * seq_info.c
 * Example program for /dev/sequencer
 */
#include <unistd.h>
```

Example 14-5: Example of Accessing /dev/sequencer (continued)

```
#include <stdlib.h>
#include <stdio.h>
#include <fcntl.h>
#include <sys/types.h>
#include <sys/ioctl.h>

#include <sys/soundcard.h>

/* return string given a MIDI device type */
char *midi_device_type(int type)
{
  switch (type) {
  case SNDCARD_ADLIB:       return("Adlib");
  case SNDCARD_SB:          return("SoundBlaster");
  case SNDCARD_PAS:         return("ProAudioSpectrum");
  case SNDCARD_GUS:         return("GravisUltraSound");
  case SNDCARD_MPU401:      return("MPU401");
  case SNDCARD_SB16:        return("SoundBlaster16");
  case SNDCARD_SB16MIDI:    return("SoundBlaster16 MIDI");
  case SNDCARD_UART6850:    return("6850 UART");
  case SNDCARD_GUS16:       return("Gravis UltraSound 16");
  case SNDCARD_MSS:         return("Microsoft Sound System");
  case SNDCARD_PSS:         return("Personal Sound System");
  case SNDCARD_SSCAPE:      return("Ensoniq SoundScape");
/* these require a more recent version of the sound driver */
#if SOUND_VERSION >= 301
  case SNDCARD_PSS_MPU:     return("Personal Sound System + MPU");
  case SNDCARD_PSS_MSS:     return("Personal Sound System/Microsoft Sound
                                   System");
  case SNDCARD_TRXPRO_MPU:  return("MediaTrix Pro + MPU");
  case SNDCARD_MAD16:       return("MAD16");
  case SNDCARD_MAD16_MPU:   return("MAD16 + MPU");
  case SNDCARD_CS4232:      return("CS4232");
  case SNDCARD_CS4232_MPU:  return("CS4232 + MPU");
  case SNDCARD_MAUI:        return("Maui");
  case SNDCARD_PSEUDO_MSS:  return("Pseudo-MSS");
#endif /* SOUND_VERSION >= 301 */
#if SOUND_VERSION >= 350
  case SNDCARD_GUSPNP:      return ("Gravis UltraSound PlugNPlay");
#endif /* SOUND_VERSION >= 301 */
  default:                  return("unknown");
  }
}
/* return string given a synthesizer device type */
char *synth_device_type(int type)
{
  switch (type) {
  case SYNTH_TYPE_FM:     return("FM");
  case SYNTH_TYPE_SAMPLE: return("Sampling");
  case SYNTH_TYPE_MIDI:   return("MIDI");
```

Example 14-5: Example of Accessing /dev/sequencer (continued)

```
  default:                 return("unknown");
  }
}

/* return string given a synthesizer device subtype */
char *synth_device_subtype(int type)
{
  switch (type) {
  case FM_TYPE_ADLIB:   return("Adlib");
  case FM_TYPE_OPL3:    return("OPL-3");
  case SAMPLE_TYPE_GUS: return("GUS");
  default:              return("unknown");
  }
}

int main(int argc, char *argv[])
{
  int i, status, numdevs;
  struct synth_info sinfo;
  struct midi_info minfo;
  int fd;        /* file descriptor for /dev/sequencer */
  char *device; /* name of device to report on */

  /* get device name from command line or use default */
  if (argc == 2)
    device = argv[1];
  else
    device = "/dev/sequencer";

  /* try to open device */
  fd = open(device, O_WRONLY);
  if (fd == -1) {
    fprintf(stderr, "%s: unable to open `%s', ", argv[0], device);
    perror("");
    return 1;
  }

  status = ioctl(fd, SNDCTL_SEQ_NRSYNTHS, &numdevs);
  if (status == -1) {
    perror("ioctl failed");
    exit(1);
  }
  printf("%s:\n%d synthesizer device%s installed\n", device, numdevs,
        numdevs == 1 ? "" : "s");

  for (i = 0 ; i < numdevs ; i++) {
    sinfo.device = i;
    status = ioctl(fd, SNDCTL_SYNTH_INFO, &sinfo);
    if (status == -1) {
      perror("ioctl failed");
```

Example 14–5: Example of Accessing /dev/sequencer (continued)

```
        exit(1);
    }
    printf("Device %d: '%s' type: '%s' subtype: '%s' voices: %d\n",
            i,
            sinfo.name,
            synth_device_type(sinfo.synth_type),
            synth_device_subtype(sinfo.synth_subtype),
            sinfo.nr_voices);
}
status = ioctl(fd, SNDCTL_SEQ_NRMIDIS, &numdevs);
if (status == -1) {
  perror("ioctl failed");
  exit(1);
}
printf("%d MIDI device%s installed\n", numdevs,
        numdevs == 1 ? "" : "s");
for (i = 0 ; i < numdevs ; i++) {
  minfo.device = i;
  status = ioctl(fd, SNDCTL_MIDI_INFO, &minfo);
  if (status == -1) {
    perror("ioctl failed");
    exit(1);
  }
  printf("Device %d: '%s' type: '%s'\n",
          i,
          minfo.name,
          midi_device_type(minfo.dev_type));
}
/* close file and exit */
close(fd);
return 0;
}
```

On my system, the program reported one FM synthesizer present and one MIDI interface, and produced the following output:

```
/dev/sequencer:
1 synthesizer device installed
Device 0: 'Yamaha OPL-3' type: 'FM' subtype: 'OPL-3' voices: 18
1 MIDI device installed
Device 0: 'SoundBlaster' type: 'SoundBlaster'
```

Advanced Sound Programming

This section describes some miscellaneous sound programming issues that require special consideration or are less commonly used.

We saw earlier that */dev/dsp* operates using unsigned data, either 8 or 16 bits in size, while */dev/audio* uses μ-law encoded data. It is possible to change the data formats a device uses with the SOUND_PCM_SETFMT *ioctl* call. A number of data formats are defined in the *soundcard.h* header file, all prefixed with the string AFMT_. For example, to set the coding format to µ-law, you could use:

```
fmt = AFMT_MU_LAW;
ioctl(fd, SOUND_PCM_SETFMT, &fmt);
```

The argument will be returned with the coding format that was selected by the kernel (which will be the same as the one selected unless the device does not support it). The special format AFMT_QUERY will return default format for the device. To find out all of the formats that a given device supports, you can use the SOUND_PCM_GETFMTS *ioctl*. It returns a bitmask that has bits set for each of the supported formats.

The *SNDCTL_DSP_GETBLKSIZE ioctl* returns the block size that the sound driver uses for data transfers. The returned value is an integer, indicating the number in bytes. This information can be useful in an application program for selecting a buffer size that ensures that the data passed to the driver is transferred in complete blocks.

The SNDCTL_DSP_GETCAPS *ioctl* returns a bitmask identifying various capabilities of a sound card DSP device. They are listed in *soundcard.h* with labels prefixed by DSP_CAP. A typical capability is DSP_CAP_DUPLEX, a boolean flag indicating whether the device supports full duplex mode (simultaneous record and play-back).

Example 14-6 illustrates these system calls, displaying information about a DSP device (*/dev/dsp* by default).

Example 14-6: Determining DSP Capabilities

```
/*
 * dsp_info.c
 * Example program to display sound device capabilities
 */

#include <unistd.h>
#include <stdlib.h>
#include <stdio.h>
#include <string.h>
#include <sys/ioctl.h>
#include <fcntl.h>
#include <linux/soundcard.h>

/* utility function for displaying boolean status */
static char *yes_no(int condition)
{
  if (condition) return "yes"; else return "no";
}

/*
 * Set sound device parameters to given values. Return -1 if
```

Example 14-6: Determining DSP Capabilities (continued)

```
 * values not valid. Sampling rate is returned.
 */
static int set_dsp_params(int fd, int channels, int bits, int *rate) {
  int status, val = channels;

  status = ioctl(fd, SOUND_PCM_WRITE_CHANNELS, &val);
  if (status == -1)
    perror("SOUND_PCM_WRITE_CHANNELS ioctl failed");
  if (val != channels) /* not valid, so return */
    return -1;
  val = bits;
  status = ioctl(fd, SOUND_PCM_WRITE_BITS, &val);
  if (status == -1)
    perror("SOUND_PCM_WRITE_BITS ioctl failed");
  if (val != bits)
    return -1;
  status = ioctl(fd, SOUND_PCM_WRITE_RATE, rate);
  if (status == -1)
    perror("SOUND_PCM_WRITE_RATE ioctl failed");
  return 0;
}

int main(int argc, char *argv[])
{
  int rate;
  int channels;            /* number of channels */
  int bits;                /* sample size */
  int blocksize;           /* block size */
  int formats;             /* data formats */
  int caps;                /* capabilities */
  int deffmt;              /* default format */
  int min_rate, max_rate;  /* min and max sampling rates */
  char *device;            /* name of device to report on */
  int fd;                  /* file descriptor for device */
  int status;              /* return value from ioctl */

  /* get device name from command line or use default */
  if (argc == 2)
    device = argv[1];
  else
    device = "/dev/dsp";

  /* try to open device */
  fd = open(device, O_RDWR);
  if (fd == -1) {
    fprintf(stderr, "%s: unable to open '%s', ", argv[0], device);
    perror("");
    return 1;
  }
```

Example 14–6: Determining DSP Capabilities (continued)

```
  status = ioctl(fd, SOUND_PCM_READ_RATE, &rate);
  if (status == -1)
    perror("SOUND_PCM_READ_RATE ioctl failed");
  status = ioctl(fd, SOUND_PCM_READ_CHANNELS, &channels);
  if (status == -1)
    perror("SOUND_PCM_READ_CHANNELS ioctl failed");
  status = ioctl(fd, SOUND_PCM_READ_BITS, &bits);
  if (status == -1)
    perror("SOUND_PCM_READ_BITS ioctl failed");
  status = ioctl(fd, SNDCTL_DSP_GETBLKSIZE, &blocksize);
  if (status == -1)
    perror("SNFCTL_DSP_GETBLKSIZE ioctl failed");

  printf(
        "Information on %s:\n\n"
        "Defaults:\n"
        "  sampling rate: %d Hz\n"
        "  channels: %d\n"
        "  sample size: %d bits\n"
        "  block size: %d bytes\n",
        device, rate, channels, bits, blocksize
        );

/* this requires a more recent version of the sound driver */
#if SOUND_VERSION >= 301
  printf("\nSupported Formats:\n");
  deffmt = AFMT_QUERY;
  status = ioctl(fd, SOUND_PCM_SETFMT, &deffmt);
  if (status == -1)
    perror("SOUND_PCM_SETFMT ioctl failed");
  status = ioctl(fd, SOUND_PCM_GETFMTS, &formats);
  if (status == -1)
    perror("SOUND_PCM_GETFMTS ioctl failed");
  if (formats & AFMT_MU_LAW) {
    printf("  mu-law");
    (deffmt == AFMT_MU_LAW) ? printf(" (default)\n") : printf("\n");
  }
  if (formats & AFMT_A_LAW) {
    printf("  A-law");
    (deffmt == AFMT_A_LAW) ? printf(" (default)\n") : printf("\n");
  }
  if (formats & AFMT_IMA_ADPCM) {
    printf("  IMA ADPCM");
    (deffmt == AFMT_IMA_ADPCM) ? printf(" (default)\n") : printf("\n");
  }
  if (formats & AFMT_U8) {
    printf("  unsigned 8-bit");
    (deffmt == AFMT_U8) ? printf(" (default)\n") : printf("\n");
  }
  if (formats & AFMT_S16_LE) {
```

Example 14-6: Determining DSP Capabilities (continued)

```
      printf("  signed 16-bit little-endian");
      (deffmt == AFMT_S16_LE) ? printf(" (default)\n") : printf("\n");
  }
  if (formats & AFMT_S16_BE) {
    printf("  signed 16-bit big-endian");
    (deffmt == AFMT_S16_BE) ? printf(" (default)\n") : printf("\n");
  }
  if (formats & AFMT_S8) {
    printf("  signed 8-bit");
    (deffmt == AFMT_S8) ? printf(" (default)\n") : printf("\n");
  }
  if (formats & AFMT_U16_LE) {
    printf("  unsigned 16-bit little-endian");
    (deffmt == AFMT_U16_LE) ? printf(" (default)\n") : printf("\n");
  }
  if (formats & AFMT_U16_BE) {
    printf("  unsigned 16-bit big-endian");
    (deffmt == AFMT_U16_BE) ? printf(" (default)\n") : printf("\n");
  }
  if (formats & AFMT_MPEG) {
    printf("  MPEG 2");
    (deffmt == AFMT_MPEG) ? printf(" (default)\n") : printf("\n");
  }

  printf("\nCapabilities:\n");
  status = ioctl(fd, SNDCTL_DSP_GETCAPS, &caps);
  if (status == -1)
    perror("SNDCTL_DSP_GETCAPS ioctl failed");
  printf(
          "  revision: %d\n"
          "  full duplex: %s\n"
          "  real-time: %s\n"
          "  batch: %s\n"
          "  coprocessor: %s\n"
          "  trigger: %s\n"
          "  mmap: %s\n",
          caps & DSP_CAP_REVISION,
          yes_no(caps & DSP_CAP_DUPLEX),
          yes_no(caps & DSP_CAP_REALTIME),
          yes_no(caps & DSP_CAP_BATCH),
          yes_no(caps & DSP_CAP_COPROC),
          yes_no(caps & DSP_CAP_TRIGGER),
          yes_no(caps & DSP_CAP_MMAP));

#endif /* SOUND_VERSION >= 301 */

  /* display table heading */
  printf(
          "\nModes and Limits:\n"
          "Device    Sample    Minimum    Maximum\n"
```

Example 14-6: Determining DSP Capabilities (continued)

```
        "Channels  Size      Rate      Rate\n"
        "--------  --------  --------  --------\n"
        );

  /* do mono and stereo */
  for (channels = 1; channels <= 2 ; channels++) {
    /* do 8 and 16 bits */
    for (bits = 8; bits <= 16 ; bits += 8) {
      /* To find the minimum and maximum sampling rates we rely on
         the fact that the kernel sound driver will round them to
         the closest legal value. */
      min_rate = 1;
      if (set_dsp_params(fd, channels, bits, &min_rate) == -1)
        continue;
      max_rate = 100000;
      if (set_dsp_params(fd, channels, bits, &max_rate) == -1)
        continue;
      /* display the results */
      printf("%8d  %8d  %8d  %8d\n", channels, bits, min_rate, max_rate);
    }
  }
  close(fd);
  return 0;
}
```

Typical output from the *dsp_info* program looks like this:

```
Information on /dev/dsp:

Defaults:
  sampling rate: 8000 Hz
  channels: 1
  sample size: 8 bits
  block size: 4096 bytes

Supported Formats:
  mu-law
  unsigned 8-bit (default)

Capabilities:
  revision: 1
  full duplex: no
  real-time: no
  batch: no
  coprocessor: no
  trigger: yes
  mmap: yes

Modes and Limits:
Device    Sample   Minimum  Maximum
Channels  Size     Rate     Rate
```

```
--------   --------   --------   --------
   1          8         4000       43478
   2          8         4000       21739
```

I mentioned earlier that you can't record and play back at the same time with one sound device. You can, however, change parameters such as sampling rate and sample size "on the fly." First, you need to open the PCM device for read and write. Then, before changing any parameters, use the *ioctl* call

```
ioctl(fd, SOUND_PCM_SYNC, 0);
```

in order to inform the sound driver that it should complete any data transfers that are in progress. You can now change parameters, or even switch between recording and playback. I used this feature earlier in the *parrot* example program.

You can also stop record or playback immediately using

```
ioctl(fd, SOUND_PCM_RESET, 0).
```

Unfortunately, a true bidirectional mode that allows simultaneous recording and playback is not supported (it likely will be in the future, though). This mode would be useful, for example, for implementing a computerized telephone utility that allows users to communicate using a sound card. There is one other alternative: some sound cards, such as the ProAudioSpectrum, have two independent PCM devices—*/dev/dsp* and */dev/dsp1*. You can use one for read and one for write, resulting in simultaneous recording and playback. In order to perform the simultaneous data transfers, it would probably be best to implement the system as two separate processes.

Some applications are time critical. The sound driver transfers data using DMA buffers, a typical buffer size being 64 kilobytes. This can impact real-time applications because of the time needed to fill up buffers for transfer. Transferring 64K of data at 8 kHz would take eight seconds. If a multimedia application was performing an animation, for example, it would be unacceptable to have the display stop for eight seconds while the process was waiting for a full buffer of sound data. You can reduce the buffer size using the *ioctl* call in this form:

```
ioctl(fd, SOUND_PCM_SUBDIVIDE, &divisor);
```

The divisor parameter takes the value 1, 2, or 4; it reduces the DMA buffer size by the corresponding factor. Note that the divisor operates on the default buffer size, not the current value, so you cannot call the function repeatedly to keep reducing the divisor.

For some applications, the smaller DMA buffer size may still not be enough. When the program *DOOM* was ported to Linux, the performance of the game was impacted by the pauses required to play sound effects. A new real-time *ioctl* was added to address applications such as this one. The *ioctl* call is called SNDCTL_DSP_SETFRAGMENT, and is explained in the file *experimental.txt* included in the kernel sound driver source.

The PC Speaker Sound Driver

Chapter 8, *The CD-ROM Driver*, covered the installation and testing of the sound driver for the built-in PC speaker. Currently this driver is distributed as a kernel patch. This driver doesn't require a sound card, only the standard PC speaker. It tries to be as compatible as possible with the real sound driver, supporting a subset of the kernel sound API. It also supports some homebrew sound hardware you can build yourself.

Not surprisingly it does not support emulation of an FM synthesizer or MIDI interface. It does support replacements for the */dev/audio* and */dev/dsp* devices, but for sound output only. There is also limited */dev/mixer* support.

The driver uses unique device files and can co-exist with the real sound driver. Users that do not have a sound card typically create the standard sound device files as symbolic links to the PC speaker devices, so that sound applications will be able to open the expected devices. The driver includes a *soundcard.h* header file, which is necessary only if the user does not already have the standard sound header file installed. I'll briefly look at all of the supported devices.

/dev/pcsp

> This device emulates the */dev/dsp* device, for output only. Attempts to read from it will always return the error EINVAL. It accepts all of the standard */dev/dsp ioctl* calls (although some are simply ignored), including the mixer *ioctl* functions. Some additional *ioctl* calls exist for setting parameters specific to the PC speaker driver. You'll find it easier to use the *pcsel* program (included with the driver source distribution) to set these parameters.

/dev/pcsp16

> This device simulates a 16-bit sound card. The driver is optional, selected when configuring the kernel driver. Internally the driver is 8-bit, but it is included for applications that insist on a 16-bit sound device (most notably, the game *DOOM*).

/dev/pcaudio

> This device is the analog of */dev/audio*, the μ-law device. It has the same limitations as */dev/pcsp*.

/dev/pcmixer

> This device accepts all of the kernel mixer *ioctl* calls. Only a master volume control is supported, and there are no recording source devices. There is support for stereo if a stereo DAC device is used.

You can run the *mixer_info* and *dsp_info* programs listed earlier to display the devices' capabilities.

The PC speaker driver is quite an accomplishment, considering the limitations of the hardware it has to work with. Many applications designed for the real sound card will work with the driver without changes. Results vary depending on the type of speaker installed and the speed of the system, but given a fast enough machine, you can even play MOD files.

CHAPTER FIFTEEN

PROGRAMMING JOYSTICK DEVICES

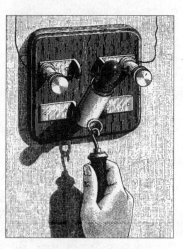

While not a multimedia device *per se*, a joystick port is commonly provided on sound cards, and can be used as an input for multimedia applications, particularly games. The driver works equally well with the joystick interfaces provided on multi-function game interface cards.

I covered the installation and testing of the Linux joystick driver, and where to obtain it, in Chapter 9, *The Joystick Driver*. It is currently distributed separately from the Linux kernel source and is installed as a kernel-loadable module.

Devices

The joystick devices are conventionally named */dev/js0* and */dev/js1* (most interface cards support two joysticks). Programs that access the joysticks should include the header file *joystick.h*. This header file is typically placed under the standard */usr/include* or */usr/include/linux* directories when the joystick driver package is installed. Let's look at each of the system calls supported by the device.

The joystick device should be opened for reading only. The driver attempts to determine if a joystick interface is present when the device is opened (a joystick need not be plugged in to the interface). If no joystick interface is present, the driver returns an error of ENODEV. Only one process may have a joystick open for reading at one time. Attempting to open a device when it is in use will fail with an error code of EBUSY. If more than one joystick is installed, then each joystick device has its own device file.

The *read* system call returns the joystick data in a data structure of type JS_DATA_TYPE, defined in *joystick.h* as:

```
struct JS_DATA_TYPE {
    int buttons;
    int x;
    int y;
}
```

The number of bytes read should be equal to JS_RETURN, which is defined as `sizeof(struct JS_DATA_TYPE)`. Perform this in one call to the *read* function. Don't try to read more or less than JS_RETURN bytes of data at a time, otherwise the call to *read* will fail with an error of EOVERFLOW.

The structure element x contains the X axis value, which increases as the joystick is moved from left to right. The y value is the Y axis, which increases as the joystick is moved from top to bottom. The *buttons* field indicates the on/off status of the joystick fire buttons. Bit zero is set if button 0 is pressed, and cleared otherwise. Bit 1 similarly reflects the current state of button 1. Currently only two buttons are supported.

The following code shows how to read the current joystick values. I assume that the joystick device has already been opened.

```
struct JS_DATA_TYPE js;
int x, y, button0, button1;

read(fd, &js, JS_RETURN);
x = js.x;
y = js.y;
button0 = js.buttons & 0x01;
button1 = js.buttons & 0x02;
```

We call *read* with a parameter that is a pointer to a variable of type JS_DATA_TYPE. The number of bytes to be read is JS_RETURN. When the system call returns, the joystick state is stored in the variable that was passed. The X and Y positions and button status can then be extracted from the data structure. I use hexadecimal numbers when getting the button status to emphasize that these are bitmasks used to extract the status of individual bits.

In a real application, it would be good practice to check that the *read* system call was successful, returning a value equal to the number of bytes that was read. It doesn't make sense to write data to the joystick, so using the *write* system call will return an error code. Several *ioctl* calls are supported and are shown in Table 15-1.

The values returned for joystick X and Y axes range from approximately zero to a value that varies from one joystick to another. Applications often need to know the range of values, or at least the values when the stick is centered. Thus, a form of calibration is required for each joystick.

Table 15–1: Joystick ioctl Functions

Name	Argument Type	Description
JS_SET_CAL	struct JS_DATA_TYPE	set calibration factor
JS_GET_CAL	struct JS_DATA_TYPE	get calibration factor
JS_SET_TIMEOUT	long	set timeout value
JS_GET_TIMEOUT	long	get timeout value
JS_SET_TIMELIMIT	long	set time limit value
JS_GET_TIMELIMIT	long	get time limit value
JS_SET_ALL	struct JS_DATA_SAVE_TYPE	set all parameters
JS_GET_ALL	struct JS_DATA_SAVE_TYPE	get all parameters

A common method of calibration is to prompt the user to move the stick to the extreme positional ranges, and sometimes the center as well. The joystick readings corresponding to these values can be stored in variables and used in the application to determine, for example, if the joystick is above or below the center position.

Storing the calibration values in a file to avoid having to calibrate each time the application is run is a useful enhancement, although there is no standardized file format for doing this.

Another calibration method is to normalize the joystick values to fit within a specific data range. Typically they are adjusted so that the joystick returns an 8-bit value (i.e., a total range of roughly 0 to 255). The JS_SET_CAL and JS_GET_CAL *ioctl* calls set and return such a calibration factor. After the kernel measures the joystick position, the results are scaled by shifting them to the right the number of bits given by the calibration factor. The default value is 0 (no shifting), and you cannot shift the data to the left. The advantage of this scheme is that, once set up, the kernel performs the scaling. The disadvantage is that the overall range of values is reduced, resulting in less accuracy in the joystick measurement.

Here is a simple example. Suppose for a given joystick the range for the X axis is found experimentally to vary from 0 to 883 and the Y axis from 0 to 1179. You want to determine the calibration values that will scale the joystick values to fit within an 8-bit byte.

The value 883 in hexadecimal is 0x373 or 001101110011 in binary. We need to shift this to the right two positions to fit it within 8 bits, so then the correction factor is 2.

Similarly for the Y axis, 1179 is 0x49b hex or binary 010010011011. We need to shift this three bit positions, so the correction factor is 3. The code to set the factor would look like the following example.

```
struct JS_DATA_TYPE js;
js.x = 2;
js.y = 3;
ioctl(fd, JS_SET_CAL, &js);
```

Now when reading the joystick position the kernel driver will scale the data so that the returned values fit within one byte.

The joystick driver source code comes with the sample program *jscal*, which calibrates a joystick for an 8-bit range. Note that the calibration values are reset each time the device is opened, so you need to perform the calibration within your own application. The basic algorithm used by the program is the following:

1. Prompt user to move joystick to lower right (maximum X and Y position)

2. Read joystick X and Y values

3. Shift X value to the right until result is no longer > 255

4. Count how many bits we shifted

5. Shift Y value to the right until result is no longer > 255

6. Count how many bits we shifted

7. Set calibration value to number of X and Y bits shifted above

Because this method of calibration reduces the accuracy of the joystick readings, and because it must be done each time the joystick is opened, I don't recommend using it. In most cases it would be better to implement the calibration algorithm in your own application.

It takes time to read the joystick data, and a user can move the joystick only so fast. Reading the joystick values too often would be a waste of CPU time. The JS_SET_TIMELIMIT parameter indicates the minimum time to wait before reading a new set of joystick values. If the joystick is read before this time has elapsed, the previous values are returned. The default is ten jiffies or one hundred milliseconds.

The joystick works using a one-shot timer. The time required for the timer to trigger indicates the joystick value. If no joystick is present, the timer will take a very long time to trigger. The JS_SET_TIMEOUT *ioctl* indicates how many attempts to read the joystick should be made before deciding that no joystick is connected. In this case, the *read* call will fail with an ENODEV error. The default is 4864 (0x1300 in hexadecimal), an arbitrary value that works.

The functions JS_GET_ALL and JS_SET_ALL allow you to read or set all of the above parameters at once. They use a parameter of type JS_DATA_SAVE_TYPE, which is defined as:

```
struct JS_DATA_SAVE_TYPE {
    int JS_TIMEOUT;                 /* timeout */
    int BUSY;                       /* joystick is in use */
    long JS_EXPIRETIME;             /* time after which stick must be re-read*/
    long JS_TIMELIMIT;              /* max time before data is invalid */
    struct JS_DATA_TYPE JS_SAVE;    /* last read data */
    struct JS_DATA_TYPE JS_CORR;    /* correction factor */
};
```

This *close* function operates as you would expect. It closes the connection between the application and joystick device, making it available to other processes.

Example Program

Now let's look at a small example program. Example 15-1 is a somewhat simplified version of a program included with the kernel joystick driver.

Example 15–1: Example Joystick Program

```
/*
 * joystick.c
 * Example program for joystick driver. Returns status of first
 * joystick.
 */
#include <unistd.h>
#include <stdlib.h>
#include <stdio.h>
#include <sys/ioctl.h>
#include <fcntl.h>
#include <linux/joystick.h>

int main()
{
    int fd, status;
    struct JS_DATA_TYPE js;
    struct JS_DATA_SAVE_TYPE jsd;

    /* open device file */
    status = fd = open("/dev/js0", O_RDONLY);
    if (status < 0) {
        perror("open of /dev/js0 failed");
        exit(1);
    }

    /* display current settings */
    status = ioctl(fd, JS_GET_ALL, &jsd);
    if (status == -1) {
        perror("error from ioctl");
        exit(1);
    }
```

Example 15–1: Example Joystick Program (continued)

```
printf(
        "timeout: %d  busy: %d  expire time: %ld  time limit: %ld\n"
        "buttons: %d  x: %d  y: %d  x corr: %d  y corr: %d\n"
        "Current joystick settings: (interrupt to exit)\n",
        jsd.JS_TIMEOUT, jsd.BUSY, jsd.JS_EXPIRETIME,
        jsd.JS_TIMELIMIT, jsd.JS_SAVE.buttons,
        jsd.JS_SAVE.x, jsd.JS_SAVE.y,
        jsd.JS_CORR.x, jsd.JS_CORR.y);

while (1) {
  status = read(fd, &js, JS_RETURN);
  if (status != JS_RETURN) {
    perror("error reading /dev/js0");
    exit(1);
  }
  printf("button 0: %s  button 1: %s  X axis: %4d  Y axis: %4d\r",
        (js.buttons & 0x01) ? "on " : "off",
        (js.buttons & 0x02) ? "on " : "off",
        js.x,
        js.y);
  fflush(stdout); /* make sure line is output */
  usleep(100); /* don't run too fast */
}
exit(0);
}
```

I open the first joystick device, checking for errors. Then the JS_GET_ALL *ioctl* call is used to obtain information about the joystick interface, which is then displayed in a suitable format.

Next I start a loop that will not end until the user interrupts the program. I obtain the stick settings using a call to *read*, checking that the expected number of bytes is received. The data, contained in a JS_DATA_TYPE structure, is displayed. I then flush the output, to ensure it is written to the display, and then delay for a short time (there is no point in reading the joystick any more quickly than this). This loop continues, providing a continuous display of the joystick settings.

On my system, with the joystick centered, the output looks like this:

```
timeout: 4864  busy: 1  expire time: 687486  time limit: 10
buttons: 0  x: 0  y: 0  x corr: 0  y corr: 0
Current joystick settings: (interrupt to exit)
button 0: off  button 1: off  X axis:  640  Y axis:   99
```

If you have a joystick, try running the program on your system (remember to load the joystick driver first!). See what range of X and Y values you obtain. Try adding *ioctl* calls to change some of the joystick driver parameters and see what effect it has.

CHAPTER SIXTEEN

PROGRAMMING CD-ROM DEVICES

This chapter covers programming of CD-ROM devices, concentrating on the functions likely to be used for multimedia applications. The techniques for programming a CD-ROM depend on whether you're using it as:

- A storage device for files

- A source of analog audio

- A source of digital audio data

Thanks to the Linux kernel drivers, the different types of CD-ROM drives appear the same from a software point of view, even though there are vast differences in the way they are programmed at the hardware level. Whether the drives use SCSI, IDE, or proprietary interfaces, you can program them in the same way (with only a few exceptions).

Definitions for the CD-ROM specific *ioctl* calls and other functions are found in the header file *linux/cdrom.h*. Some additional header files (e.g., *sbpcd.h*, *cdu31a.h*) have drive-specific information that is mainly intended for use by the kernel drivers, but may also include some drive-specific *ioctl* functions. Don't use these functions if you want your applications to be portable.

CD-ROM Data Access

A CD-ROM device functions much like other block-oriented devices such as hard and floppy disks. Applications can open, read, and close the device. For example, the following shell command will read the raw data from a CD-ROM and display it:

```
% cat -v /dev/cdrom
```

This command is not particularly useful because the raw data is not in a human-readable form. In practice, CD-ROMs containing filesystems are mounted using the *mount* system call. They differ from other disk devices in that they are mounted read-only and almost always use an ISO 9660 filesystem.

Only the superuser can perform a *mount* system call, although a *mount* program that is setuid to *root* can allow users to mount. The *mount* command is generally used to mount filesystems; there is a corresponding system call and command to unmount filesystems, both called *umount.** Once a CD-ROM filesystem is mounted, the files on the disc can be accessed just like those on any other device, except that they are read only.

Multimedia applications are very unlikely to perform mounting or unmounting themselves as the standard *mount* and *umount* commands are almost universally used to do this, so I won't look at any programming examples.

I will look at a simple but basic function. Most drives, in addition to offering a front panel switch, allow software to eject a CD-ROM disc. Example 16-1 shows a simple eject program that will perform this function.

Example 16–1: Simple CD-ROM Eject Program

```
/*
 * eject.c
 * Example program to eject CD
 */
#include <unistd.h>
#include <stdlib.h>
#include <sys/ioctl.h>
#include <fcntl.h>
#include <linux/cdrom.h>

/* CD-ROM device file name */
#define DEVICE "/dev/cdrom"

int main()
{
  int fd;          /* file descriptor for CD-ROM device */
  int status;      /* return status for system calls */

  /* open device */
  status = fd = open(DEVICE, O_RDONLY);
  if (status < 0) {
    perror("unable to open "DEVICE);
    exit(1);
  }
  /* eject */
  status = ioctl(fd, CDROMEJECT);
  if (status != 0) {
    perror("CDROMEJECT ioctl failed");
```

---

* A piece of UNIX trivia: some manpages list the fact that *umount* is misspelled under the BUGS section.

Example 16–1: Simple CD-ROM Eject Program (continued)

```
    exit(1);
}
/* close device */
status = close(fd);
if (status != 0) {
  perror("unable to close "DEVICE);
  exit(1);
}
exit(0);
}
```

The program is quite straightforward. I first open the device for read only (you can change the definition of DEVICE as needed to match your CD-ROM device name). I then use the CDROMEJECT *ioctl* call, which does not require any additional parameters. Lastly I close the device. The example, like any well-behaved program, checks the status of each system call and displays any errors that occur.

This simple program suffers from a few limitations. As I noted above, the device name is hard-coded. Of more concern is the fact that some CD-ROM drives will allow programs to eject a mounted disc, which is sure to produce errors when the disc is subsequently accessed. Some drives won't allow this practice, and may even disable the front panel eject switch. In any case you really should check to see if a disc is mounted before trying to eject.

The SBPCD kernel CD-ROM driver also has an interesting auto-eject feature. When enabled, the driver will automatically eject the disc whenever the device is closed or unmounted. This feature can come in handy, because you usually want to remove the disc after unmounting or playing an audio CD. However this behavior does not work well with some audio CD player programs that start playing a disc and then close the device. Another irritation is that when you halt a Linux system before powering it down, the CD-ROM filesystem will usually become unmounted, resulting in an open disc tray when the system is turned off.

The auto-eject feature is controlled using an *ioctl* call. You can create a program to enable or disable it by replacing one line of the program in Example 16-1 with either of the following two:

```
status = ioctl(fd, CDROMEJECT_SW, 1); /* to enable */
status = ioctl(fd, CDROMEJECT_SW, 0); /* to disable */
```

Currently this feature is supported only for the drives that use the SBPCD, Aztech, and IDE CD drivers, so attempting to use it with others types will cause the *ioctl* to return an error.

There is a more functional eject program that handles the check for mounted devices and can control the auto-eject feature. It is included in some Linux distributions and can also be obtained from the Internet archive sites listed in Appendix B, *Linux Resources.*

CD Audio

A second application for CD-ROM drives is as a source of analog audio. Virtually all CD-ROM drives support playing standard Compact Disc Digital Audio discs, either through a headphone jack or via a sound card.

An audio CD cannot be mounted, and attempting to read from the device will return an error. All functions are controlled by *ioctl* calls. Table 16-1 lists the currently supported CD-ROM functions.

SCSI CD-ROM drives also support a number of *ioctl* calls for performing most of these functions via SCSI commands, but this method works only for SCSI drives. Use the calls defined in *linux/cdrom.h*, as these work with all drives, independent of interface type.

Some of the more esoteric *ioctl* calls (e.g., CDROMVOLREAD) may not be supported by all drives. So for maximum portability you should attempt to handle errors from these calls, or avoid them entirely. There is a movement towards standardizing the functions across the different CD-ROM device drivers, so this situation should improve over time.

I will now discuss each of the *ioctl* calls in turn, then illustrate most of them with an example program.

Table 16-1: CD-ROM ioctl Calls

Name	Argument	Purpose
CDROMEJECT	–	eject CD-ROM media
CDROMEJECT_SW	0 or 1	control auto-eject feature
CDROMSTART	–	turn the motor on
CDROMPLAYTRKIND	struct cdrom_ti	play given track/index
CDROMPLAYMSF	struct cdrom_msf	play given min/sec/frame
CDROMSTOP	–	stop playback
CDROMPAUSE	–	pause (valid when playing)
CDROMRESUME	–	resume (valid when paused)
CDROMVOLCTRL	struct cdrom_volctrl	set volume
CDROMVOLREAD	struct cdrom_volctrl	read volume
CDROMREADTOCHDR	struct cdrom_tochdr	read TOC header
CDROMREADTOCENTRY	struct cdrom_tocentry	read TOC entry
CDROMSUBCHNL	struct cdrom_subchnl	read Q sub-channel data
CDROMREADMODE1	struct cdrom_read	read mode 1 data

Table 16–1: CD-ROM ioctl Calls (continued)

Name	Argument	Purpose
CDROMREADMODE2	struct cdrom_read	read mode 2 data
CDROMREADAUDIO	struct cdrom_read_audio	read digital audio data
CDROMMULTISESSION	struct cdrom_multisession	return multisession info
CDROMRESET	–	reset drive
CDROM_GET_UPC	–	return disc Universal Product Code
CDROMAUDIOBUFSIZ	int	set audio buffer size (in frames)
CDROMREADFROMSLOT	int	select slot for multi-disc changers
DDIOCSDBG	int	set driver debug flag
BLKRASET	int	set read-ahead buffer size

I have already looked at the CDROMEJECT call and the related CDROMEJECT_SW function in the previous section. These are really the only calls that are not specific to audio CDs.

The next few functions shown in Table 16-1 are for playing audio. Note that basic audio playing does not require any CPU intervention once started. With a single command the drive can play a range of audio tracks. While this is happening, no data are being read by the CPU; the drive is simply sending an analog audio signal to the headphones or speakers via a sound card. More sophisticated features such as handling play lists of songs obviously require some software programming.

On each audio CD is a table of contents data area that lists the number of tracks on the disc and their locations. This information can be used by audio CD player programs to display the disc information and allow the user to select the tracks to be played. Unfortunately, the table of contents does not provide the names of the tracks, lyrics, or other such information. The data in the table of contents are virtually guaranteed to be unique for a given CD though, so some audio CD player programs use the data to identify a CD and use an external database to display track names and other information.

Locations on an audio CD can be represented by three methods. The simplest is using track and index numbers. A track is a logical position on the disc and generally corresponds to a song (not to be confused with tracks as used on floppy disk drives; compact discs actually store the data in one long continuous spiral). Within these tracks, some CDs provide index marks that correspond to specific locations of interest. The liner notes for a CD should indicate what the index marks represent (in my experience, index marks are rare).

The second way to identify locations on a CD is using minute/second/frame (MSF) values, which correspond to the elapsed time as the disc is played. The finest resolution is one frame, which corresponds to 1/75 of a second.

The third method is known as a logical block address (LBA), which is a count of frames since the start of the disc. The logical block address can be calculated from the minute/second/frame value using the following formula:

$$lba = minutes * 60 * 75 + seconds * 75 + frames - 150;$$

Similarly, given a logical block address, one can calculate the corresponding minutes, seconds and frames using:

$$minutes = (lba + 150) / (60 * 75);$$
$$seconds = (lba + 150) / 75 - minutes * 60;$$
$$frames = (lba + 150) - seconds * 75 - minutes * 60 * 75;$$

The value 150 is the fixed offset of the first logical frame (two seconds) and is defined in the CD-ROM header file as `CD_BLOCK_OFFSET`.

Each audio CD provides a table of contents, which lists the location of each track in either LBA or MSF format. Thus, all three addressing schemes can be converted from one to another.

The *ioctl* call CDROMPLAYTRKIND is particularly useful: it plays a range of audio tracks. The argument is of type `struct cdrom_ti`, defined as follows:

```
struct cdrom_ti {
    u_char       cdti_trk0; /* start track */
    u_char       cdti_ind0; /* start index */
    u_char       cdti_trk1; /* end track */
    u_char       cdti_ind1; /* end index */
};
```

You must specify start and end tracks to play, and can optionally specify index marks. To play entire tracks, set the index mark values to 0. The function call will return once the CD starts playing. To know whether the last track has finished playing, you need to use the CDROMSUBCHNL function, which is discussed later.

A similar call, CDROMPLAYMSF, will play a range of tracks specified as minute/second/frame values. The argument is of the following type:

```
struct cdrom_msf {
    u_char cdmsf_min0;    /* start minute */
    u_char cdmsf_sec0;    /* start second */
    u_char cdmsf_frame0; /* start frame */
    u_char cdmsf_min1;    /* end minute */
    u_char cdmsf_sec1;    /* end second */
    u_char cdmsf_frame1; /* end frame */
};
```

You should issue the CDROMPLAYTRKIND or CDROMPLAYMSF commands only when the drive is in the stopped state, otherwise it probably will ignore the command. Also note that when the drive completes playing the last track or frame specified, it will not automatically go back into the stopped state.

If you want to do more than just play a range of tracks (for example, to play a list of specific tracks) then you need to handle this in software. Typically you would monitor the state of the CD-ROM drive to determine when a track has completed playing, then send a command to play the next track in the list.

The CDROMSTOP *ioctl* call is used to stop playing. It should be used after any of the CDROMPLAY *ioctl* calls. Using CDROMPAUSE will pause the playing of a track, so that it can be resumed later using the CDROMRESUME call.

Most CD drives let you set the output volume level. The CDROMVOLCTRL call is used to control volume; it takes a parameter of type `struct cdrom_volctrl`:

```
struct cdrom_volctrl {
  u_char  channel0; /* left channel */
  u_char  channel1; /* right channel */
  u_char  channel2;
  u_char  channel3;
};
```

The data structure offers four channels of gain. The last two are for future four-channel CDs and sound cards; they should be set to zero. The volume has an 8-bit range (0 to 255), and only controls the level coming from the CD-ROM drive's analog audio output.

The *ioctl* call CDROMVOLREAD returns the current volume settings. It is currently supported only by the SBPCD and IDE-CD drivers.

I discussed the table of contents provided on audio CDs. Two *ioctl*s are provided to read this information. CDROMREADTOCHDR reads the header of summary information, which indicates the start and end tracks, in a parameter of type `struct cdrom_tochdr`:

```
struct cdrom_tochdr {
  u_char  cdth_trk0; /* start track */
  u_char  cdth_trk1; /* end track */
};
```

This information is needed to use the CDROMREADTOCENTRY call, which returns information about individual tracks. The *ioctl* parameter uses the data structure shown below:

```
struct cdrom_tocentry {
  u_char  cdte_track;
  u_char  cdte_adr   :4;
  u_char  cdte_ctrl :4;
  u_char  cdte_format;
```

```
    union {
      struct {
        u_char   minute;
        u_char   second;
        u_char   frame;
      } msf;
      int lba;
    } cdte_addr;
    u_char   cdte_datamode;
};
```

You must pass the track number (the first track is 1) in the **cdte_track** field. To obtain information for the end of the last track this value must be the magic number given by CDROM_LEADOUT.

In the **cdte_format** field, you indicate in which format you wish the data to be returned, either CDROM_LBA for logical block address, or CDROM_MSF for minute/second/frame. You then use the appropriate portion of the data structure: either lba or msf.

I have now covered enough background material to write a simple program to play audio CD tracks. The program in Example 16-2 supports playing tracks, stopping, pausing, resuming, setting the volume levels, and displaying the table of contents.

Example 16–2: Simple Audio CD Player Program

```
/*
 * playcd.c
 * Example of simple audio CD player
 *
 */

#include <unistd.h>
#include <stdlib.h>
#include <stdio.h>
#include <sys/ioctl.h>
#include <fcntl.h>
#include <linux/cdrom.h>

/* display command usage and exit */
void usage(void)
{
  fprintf(stderr,
          "usage: playcd <options>\n"
          "valid options:\n"
          "   play <first-track> <last-track>\n"
          "   stop\n"
          "   pause\n"
          "   resume\n"
          "   volume <left-vol> <right-vol>\n"
```

Example 16-2: Simple Audio CD Player Program (continued)

```
             "   toc\n");
  exit(1);
}


/*
 * Utility routine to print error message and exit if given
 * non-zero status
 */
void status_check(int status, const char *ioctl)
{
  char buf[255];
  if (status != 0) {
    sprintf(buf, "%s ioctl failed", ioctl);
    perror(buf);
    exit(1);
  }
}

int main(int argc, char *argv[])
{
  const char *device = "/dev/cdrom";   /* CD-ROM device file name */
  int fd;                              /* CD-ROM file descriptor */
  int status;                          /* hold status of system calls */
  struct cdrom_ti ti;                  /* track/index info */
  struct cdrom_tochdr tochdr;          /* TOC header */
  struct cdrom_tocentry tocentry;      /* TOC entry */
  struct cdrom_volctrl volctrl;        /* volume settings */

  /* there should be at least one command line argument */
  if (argc < 2)
    usage();
  /* open device */
  status = fd = open(device, O_RDONLY);
  if (status < 0) {
    perror("open failed");
    exit(1);
  }
  if (!strcmp(argv[1], "play")) {
    if (argc != 4)
      usage();
    ti.cdti_trk0 = strtol(argv[2], 0, 10);
    ti.cdti_ind0 = 0;
    ti.cdti_trk1 = strtol(argv[3], 0, 10);
    ti.cdti_ind1 = 0;
    status = ioctl(fd, CDROMPLAYTRKIND, &ti);
    status_check(status, "CDROMPLAYTRKIND");
  } else if (!strcmp(argv[1], "stop")) {
    status = ioctl(fd, CDROMSTOP);
    status_check(status, "CDROMSTOP");
  } else if (!strcmp(argv[1], "pause")) {
```

Example 16–2: Simple Audio CD Player Program (continued)

```
    status = ioctl(fd, CDROMPAUSE);
    status_check(status, "CDROMPAUSE");
} else if (!strcmp(argv[1], "resume")) {
    status = ioctl(fd, CDROMRESUME);
    status_check(status, "CDROMRESUME");
} else if (!strcmp(argv[1], "volume")) {
    if (argc != 4)
      usage();
    volctrl.channel0 = strtol(argv[2], 0, 0);
    volctrl.channel1 = strtol(argv[3], 0, 0);
    volctrl.channel2 = 0;
    volctrl.channel3 = 0;
    status = ioctl(fd, CDROMVOLCTRL, &volctrl);
    status_check(status, "CDROMVOLCTRL");
} else if (!strcmp(argv[1], "toc")) {
    int track;
    status = ioctl(fd, CDROMREADTOCHDR, &tochdr);
    status_check(status, "CDROMREADTOCHDR");
    printf("Track mn/sc/frm   Track mn/sc/frm   Track mn/sc/frm
      Track mn/sc/frm\n");
    for (track = 1 ; track <= tochdr.cdth_trk1 ; track++) {
      tocentry.cdte_track = track;
      tocentry.cdte_format = CDROM_MSF; /* want info in MSF format */
      status = ioctl(fd, CDROMREADTOCENTRY, &tocentry);
      status_check(status, "CDROMREADTOCENTRY");
      printf("%5d %02d:%02d.%03d %c ",
            tocentry.cdte_track,
            tocentry.cdte_addr.msf.minute,
            tocentry.cdte_addr.msf.second,
            tocentry.cdte_addr.msf.frame,
            (tocentry.cdte_ctrl & CDROM_DATA_TRACK) ? 'D' : 'A');
      if ((track % 4) == 0 || (track == tochdr.cdth_trk1))
        printf("\n");
    }
    /* now print info for end of last track */
    tocentry.cdte_track = CDROM_LEADOUT;
    status = ioctl(fd, CDROMREADTOCENTRY, &tocentry);
    status_check(status, "CDROMREADTOCENTRY");
    printf("(end) %02d:%02d.%03d\n",
            tocentry.cdte_addr.msf.minute,
            tocentry.cdte_addr.msf.second,
            tocentry.cdte_addr.msf.frame);
} else {
    usage();
}

/* close device */
status = close(fd);
if (status != 0) {
    perror("close failed");
```

Example 16–2: Simple Audio CD Player Program (continued)

```
    exit(1);
  }
  exit(0);
}
```

After you try running the above program, make some small modifications to it. For example, have it display the table of contents in LBA format instead of MSF. This simple program is still quite crude and could use more checking and additional features. Some of the existing CD player programs such as *workman* do a much better job at simulating a consumer CD player.

The CDROMSUBCHNL *ioctl* returns information about an audio CD, including the current address, in both absolute and relative form, and the current state (e.g., playing, paused, completed, in error). This information is contained in a data area known as the Q channel, and can be useful in a CD player program to display status information or determine what state the drive is in. The function accepts a parameter of type `struct cdrom_subchnl`, defined as:

```
struct cdrom_subchnl
{
  u_char  cdsc_format;
  u_char  cdsc_audiostatus;
  u_char  cdsc_adr:  4;
  u_char  cdsc_ctrl: 4;
  u_char  cdsc_trk;
  u_char  cdsc_ind;
  union cdrom_addr cdsc_absaddr;
  union cdrom_addr cdsc_reladdr;
};
```

You pass the function the desired format for the results, either CDROM_MSF or CDROM_LBA, in the `cdsc_format` field. It returns the current track and index number (if any) in the `cdsc_trk` and `cdsc_ind` fields. The absolute address (relative to the beginning of the disc), is returned in the `cdsc_absaddr` field, in the selected data format. The relative address (relative to the start of the current track), is returned in the `cdsc_reladdr` field. The field `cdsc_audiostatus` identifies the current status of the drive (stopped, playing, paused, etc.). Finally, the `cdsc_status` and `cdsc_ctrl` fields provide some additional low-level information from the Q channel.

The program in Example 16-3 shows an example of using the call to display the CD state, track, and position in both absolute and relative format.

Example 16–3: Read CD Subchannel Data

```
/*
 * subchnl.c
 * Example program to display audio CD subchannel data
```

Example 16–3: Read CD Subchannel Data (continued)

```c
 */
#include <unistd.h>
#include <stdlib.h>
#include <stdio.h>
#include <sys/ioctl.h>
#include <fcntl.h>
#include <linux/cdrom.h>

/* return audio status as a string */
char *audiostatus(int status)
{
  switch (status) {
  case CDROM_AUDIO_INVALID:   return "Invalid";
  case CDROM_AUDIO_PLAY:      return "Playing";
  case CDROM_AUDIO_PAUSED:    return "Paused";
  case CDROM_AUDIO_COMPLETED: return "Completed";
  case CDROM_AUDIO_ERROR:     return "Error";
  case CDROM_AUDIO_NO_STATUS: return "Stopped";
  default:                    return "Unknown";
  }
}

int main()
{
  const char *device = "/dev/cdrom";  /* CD-ROM device file name */
  int fd;                             /* CD-ROM file descriptor */
  int status;                         /* hold status of system calls */
  struct cdrom_subchnl subchnl;       /* parameter for ioctl call */

  /* open device */
  status = fd = open(device, O_RDONLY);
  if (status < 0) {
    perror("open failed");
    exit(1);
  }

  while (1) {
    /* read subchannel data */
    subchnl.cdsc_format = CDROM_MSF; /* want results in MSF format */
    status = ioctl(fd, CDROMSUBCHNL, &subchnl);
    if (status < 0) {
      perror("CDROMSUBCHNL ioctl failed");
      exit(1);
    }
    printf("Status: %s Track: %d Position: %02d:%02d:%02d
      (%02d:%02d:%02d)\r",
           audiostatus(subchnl.cdsc_audiostatus),
           subchnl.cdsc_trk,
           subchnl.cdsc_reladdr.msf.minute,
           subchnl.cdsc_reladdr.msf.second,
```

Example 16–3: Read CD Subchannel Data (continued)

```
            subchnl.cdsc_reladdr.msf.frame,
            subchnl.cdsc_absaddr.msf.minute,
            subchnl.cdsc_absaddr.msf.second,
            subchnl.cdsc_absaddr.msf.frame);
      fflush(stdout);
      usleep(100000);
   }
   exit(0);
}
```

If you are doing more CD programming, a useful tool is the *cdtester* program, included with the kernel source code in the README file for the SBPCD kernel driver. This program makes use of all of the CD-ROM *ioctl* calls from a command-line interface. You can use it to experiment with your drive interactively without writing any code.

Reading Digital Audio

In the previous section we played audio using a CD-ROM drive. Even though the audio was stored in digital format on the CD, it left the drive in analog form. Why not get at the digital audio data directly? Surprisingly, this is not a simple thing to do. With some CD-ROM drives it is simply not possible, and with others it requires some elaborate and sometimes undocumented programming.

Some of the first CD-ROM kernel drives for Linux implemented support for reading the digital audio data, but the method was driver-dependent. Recent kernel revisions are working towards a standardized method that will operate identically for all supported drives. That method is described in this section. The CDROMREADAUDIO *ioctl* call reads audio data. The argument is of the data type:

```
struct cdrom_read_audio
{
   union cdrom_addr addr; /* frame address */
   u_char addr_format; /* CDROM_LBA or CDROM_MSF */
   int nframes; /* number of 2352-byte-frames to read at once */
   u_char *buf; /* frame buffer (size: nframes*2352 bytes) */
};
```

Before making the call, you must set `addr_format` to the type of addressing to be used—CDROM_LBA or CDROM_MSF. Then fill in either the `msf` or `lba` fields of `addr`, as appropriate for the addressing mode selected. Next fill in the `nframes` field to indicate the number of frames to read, each of which takes 2352 bytes. Make sure that the `buf` parameter points to a storage area of appropriate size.

With the SBPCD driver you must also use the CDROMAUDIOBUFSIZ *ioctl* to set the audio buffer size, in frames, before reading the audio data. The other drivers do not require this step.

Example 16-4 is a short program that illustrates reading data from an audio CD.

Example 16–4: Example of Reading Digital Audio Data

```
/*
 * readaudio.c
 * Example program to read digital audio data from CD
 *
 * usage: readaudio <min> <sec> <frame> <# frames> <device>
 *    e.g. readaudio 1 2 3 4 /dev/cdrom
 *
 */
#include <unistd.h>
#include <stdlib.h>
#include <stdio.h>
#include <sys/ioctl.h>
#include <fcntl.h>
#include <linux/cdrom.h>
#include <linux/sbpcd.h>

int main(int argc, char *argv[])
{
  int fd;                            /* CD-ROM file descriptor */
  int status;                        /* hold status of system calls */
  struct cdrom_read_audio read_audio; /* parameter for ioctl call */
  unsigned char *buffer;             /* buffer for audio data */
  int i;                             /* loop index */
  int minute, second, frame;         /* where to start reading */
  int nframes;                       /* number of frames to read */
  char *device;                      /* CD-ROM device name */

  /* check and parse command line arguments */
  if (argc != 6) {
    fprintf(stderr,
        "usage: readaudio <min> <sec> <frame> <# frames> <device>\n"
        "  e.g. readaudio 1 2 3 4 /dev/cdrom\n");
    exit(1);
  }
  minute  = strtol(argv[1], 0, 10);
  second  = strtol(argv[2], 0, 10);
  frame   = strtol(argv[3], 0, 10);
  nframes = strtol(argv[4], 0, 10);
  device  = argv[5];
  /* open device */
  status = fd = open(device, O_RDONLY);
  if (status < 0) {
    perror("open failed");
    exit(1);
  }
  /* set audio buffer size - only needed for SBPCD drives */
  status = ioctl(fd, CDROMAUDIOBUFSIZ, nframes);
  if (status <= 0) {
```

Example 16–4: Example of Reading Digital Audio Data (continued)

```
    perror("CDROMAUDIOBUFSIZ ioctl failed (ignore for non-SBPCD drives)");
    /* don't exit, in case it is a non-SBPCD drive */
  }
  /* dynamically allocate buffer for audio data */
  buffer = (unsigned char*) malloc(CD_FRAMESIZE_RAW * nframes);
  if (buffer == 0) {
    perror("malloc failed");
    exit(1);
  }
  read_audio.addr_format = CDROM_MSF; /* use MSF format */
  read_audio.addr.msf.minute = minute;
  read_audio.addr.msf.second = second;
  read_audio.addr.msf.frame  = frame;
  read_audio.nframes = nframes;
  read_audio.buf = buffer;
  printf("Reading %d frames from %s starting from %02d:%02d.%03d
            (%d bytes)\n",
       nframes, device, minute, second, frame, CD_FRAMESIZE_RAW * nframes);
  status = ioctl(fd, CDROMREADAUDIO, &read_audio);
  if (status != 0) {
    perror("CDROMREADAUDIO ioctl failed");
    exit(1);
  }
  /* display data in hex, 24 bytes per line */
  for (i = 0 ; i < CD_FRAMESIZE_RAW * nframes ; i++) {
    printf("%02X ", buffer[i]);
    if ((i+1) % 24 == 0)
      printf("\n");
  }
  exit(0);
}
```

This program simply displays a hex dump of the sound data for the specified frames. A logical extension would be to save the data to a sound file. The CDROM-READAUDIO function is currently supported only by the SBPCD, Sony CDU31A, and IDE-CD kernel drivers. The data is also not read in real time.

In addition, drives that use the SBPCD driver have an extra quirk. The data read is not synchronized to the beginning of each audio frame. Thus, you'll find either some overlap or some missing data when reading data from consecutive frames. The raw data won't sound correct unless some higher-level software analyzes it and correctly fits the overlapping pieces together. The *cdda2wav-sbpcd* program mentioned in Part III attempts to do this, but (at least in my experience) isn't totally reliable. Possibly in the future the kernel driver will perform this function.

Unlike analog recording schemes, reading digital audio data from a CD allows one to make a "perfect" copy. This technique can be useful for obtaining very clean audio data from a CD for the purpose of signal processing, analysis, or recording. Because this process may violate copyright restrictions, you should do so only for your own personal use.

Miscellaneous Functions

I overlooked a few of the *ioctl* functions in Table 16-1. The CDROMMULTISESSION *ioctl* returns information for multisession discs. In order to understand its use, I need to cover some background information.

Multisession discs can have data added to them after the initial disc creation. The most common example of this is a PhotoCD. Initially the disc might contain images from one roll of film. At a later date, you can add additional images to the disc. This process can be repeated, up to the total capacity of the disc.

The original data on the disc cannot be changed, only added to; this means that the original table of contents will only list the first set of images. When new images are added to the disc, a new table of contents is also written, which lists the locations of the old images as well as the new ones. Images can effectively be deleted by omitting them from the new table of contents, so they will no longer be listed (they can still be retrieved using the previous table of contents).

Each cluster of data written to at one time is called a session. Multisession drives are able to read the data from multiple sessions, including the table of contents. In order to read a multisession disc, you just have to read the last table of contents.

The CDROMMULTISSESSION *ioctl* will tell you the address of this last session. It returns a data structure that indicates if a CD is multisession, and if so, the address (in LBA or MSF format) of the start of the last session. The program shown in Example 16-5 illustrates the use of this call.

Example 16–5: Multisession Example

```
/*
 * multisess.c
 * Example program to display CD multi-session information
 */
#include <unistd.h>
#include <stdlib.h>
#include <stdio.h>
#include <sys/ioctl.h>
#include <fcntl.h>
#include <linux/cdrom.h>

int main()
{
  const char *device = "/dev/cdrom";   /* CD-ROM device file name */
  int fd;                              /* CD-ROM file descriptor */
  int status;                          /* hold status of system calls */
  struct cdrom_multisession arg;       /* parameter for ioctl call */

  /* open device */
  status = fd = open(device, O_RDONLY);
  if (status < 0) {
```

Example 16–5: Multisession Example (continued)

```
    perror("open failed");
    exit(1);
}
/* get multisession info */
arg.addr_format = CDROM_LBA; /* want results in LBA format */
status = ioctl(fd, CDROMMULTISESSION, &arg);
if (status < 0) {
    perror("CDROMMULTISESSION ioctl failed");
    exit(1);
}
if (arg.xa_flag) {
    printf("Last session is at logical block address %d.\n", arg.addr.lba);
} else {
    printf("Not a multi-session disc.\n");
}
exit(0);
}
```

I ran the program on a PhotoCD, and it correctly identified the disc as multisession, with the last (and only) session starting at logical block address zero.

This low-level function is generally not necessary, as the Linux kernel drivers that support multisession will automatically return the table of contents for the last session when you use the CDROMREADTOCHDR and CDROMRADTOCHDR calls. You can use this *ioctl* to look at previous tables of contents in order to find deleted files or to trace the history of changes.

The CDROMREADMODE1 *ioctl* call reads mode 1 data from the CD. This is the low-level format of the data stored on a CD-ROM. Given an address in LBA format, the call returns the raw data in a buffer. Similarly, the CDROMREADMODE2 *ioctl* call reads mode 2 data. This is a format used on CD/XA, an extended form of CD-ROM similar to CD-I. Currently only the Aztech driver supports this function.

A rarely used *ioctl* is the CDROMSTART. It takes no parameters, and its purpose is to turn on the CD drive motor. This is normally not necessary, as most *ioctl* commands will activate the motor as required when it is needed. Most drives will also automatically turn the spindle motor off if the drive is not used for several minutes.

The CDROM_GET_UPC function reads the Universal Product Code (UPC) from a disc and returns it as an eight-byte value. It seems that very few CD-ROMs store the UPC code, and most of the Linux kernel drivers do not support this call, so in most cases the value returned has all zeroes.

CDROMRESET performs a drive reset for SBPCD drives. DDIOCSDBG sets the SBPCD kernel debug flag under program control (it can also be set when compiling the driver). BLKRASET sets the read-ahead buffer size, an *ioctl* call that is also supported by most of the other block devices, including hard disks.

The CDROMREADFROMSLOT function is used with multi-disc CD changers to select a specific disc slot. It takes a single integer parameter corresponding to the disc slot to be selected (the first slot is zero). A simple program illustrating the use of this *ioctl* call is included in the documentation for the IDE-CD kernel driver.

Some of these functions are somewhat specialized, and won't work with all CD-ROM drives. One way to gain a better understanding of what they do is to read the kernel source code.

Future Directions

Not all Linux CD-ROM kernel drivers support all of the *ioctl* functions listed in this chapter, and there are minor differences in the way that some of the drivers behave. For example, some drivers lock the front panel eject button when a CD is mounted while others do not. This situation is largely due to the fact that the drivers were written by different authors. David van Leeuwen, author of one of the kernel drivers, has proposed a standard for implementing CD-ROM kernel drivers, which would ensure commonality by using a new hardware-independent software layer. As of the 2.0 kernel this is just a proposal, but it has the backing of most of the CD-ROM driver authors and is expected to be implemented in the future. From an application writer's point of view, the changes would be relatively minor, and would make it much easier to write code that would work consistently with all types of CD-ROM drivers. The proposal document is included with the kernel source code in the file */usr/src/linux/Documentation/cdrom/cdrom-standard.tex*.

CHAPTER SEVENTEEN

USING TOOLKITS FOR MULTIMEDIA PROGRAMMING

In the previous chapter I looked at programming multimedia devices in the C language using the device level interface provided by the Linux kernel. Many applications have been written entirely using this approach, but there are often advantages to using a toolkit.

In this chapter I look at several of the programming toolkits available under Linux that are applicable to multimedia programming. The purpose is not to explain in detail how to use each toolkit, but rather to give an overview of the capabilities and applicability of each, so that the multimedia application developer can make an informed choice of which tool to use.

General Issues

A *software toolkit* is a package intended to assist in the development of software applications. It may include subroutine libraries, tools for creating and manipulating data and source code, language interpreters and translators, and complete applications.

There are both advantages and disadvantages to using toolkits. The decision of when to use them depends on a number of factors, and usually involves tradeoffs. The most common reason for using a toolkit is to reduce development time and effort. Usually the kit provides low-level features that the programmer does not have to implement, giving him more time to focus on the high-level functions of the application. Less code needs to be written and debugged, reducing the time to market for the new design.

The toolkit may also provide more features and functionality than the application developer would have been able to implement for a specialized application. Some toolkits are supported on several programming platforms, making the resulting applications portable. It may also enforce a standardized user interface, reducing the learning curve for users already familiar with other applications developed using the same toolkit.

There are some potential disadvantages as well. The developer must invest time in learning how to use the toolkit, although this effort is rewarded if the same environment is used for several applications. An unreliable toolkit may require the developer to debug the code in the toolkit itself (assuming the source code is available). For applications in which efficiency is critical, a toolkit may add an extra layer of software between the application and device, possibly causing unacceptable penalties in execution time, code size, or other resources.

In some cases, required functionality may be missing from a toolkit, and it may be difficult to extend the tools or program around it. Some toolkits allow you to get at the underlying lower level functions on which the toolkit is based, while others try to hide this from the user. Another disadvantage is that if a toolkit is not portable, it will restrict the platforms on which the resulting applications can run.

Some toolkits are commercial products, and the cost may be a significant factor, particularly if there are run-time licensing fees for the resulting applications that use the tools. Support and maintenance may also be a significant ongoing cost. Freeware tools, on the other hand, may be poorly documented and unsupported.[*]

As is often the case, the best solution depends on the requirements of your specific application. You should consider the relative importance of factors such as run-time efficiency, development time, reliability, compatibility, experience, and cost. Don't overlook the possibility of using more than one toolkit to develop your application. In some cases, several tools may work well together: for example, a graphics library and a sound toolkit.

True to the spirit of Linux, most of the packages reviewed here are free software of some sort, or at least low cost. I did contact the vendors of two popular commercial multimedia authoring systems for UNIX platforms to inquire if they had or were planning to develop Linux ports of their products. Neither vendor had plans to do so, citing as reasons the fact that most Linux users used freeware and that the unstable state of Linux (rapidly changing kernel versions, different distributions, etc.) made it difficult to support. As these are expensive products (approximately US$10,000), this reason is perhaps not surprising.

In this chapter, I will take a brief look at a number of toolkits. They will be loosely categorized into multimedia toolkits (those that attempt to cover all multimedia needs), graphics toolkits, and sound toolkits. In some cases the classification is somewhat arbitrary.

At the start of each section I list the toolkit name, the primary developer, where it can be obtained, and what the distribution status is (i.e., commercial, free software, shareware). I will give a brief description of the package and its capabilities, and attempt to describe where the toolkit would be applicable for use, and what its strengths and limitations are.

---

* Not necessarily, though. Many free software packages have excellent "unofficial" support via the Internet, and some commercial packages offer extremely poor (and expensive) support.

There are so many graphics toolkits available that one could fill a book describing them, so I describe only a few here. The criteria for selection were that they had to be supported under Linux and be low-cost or free of charge. I also tried to pick those that were somewhat unique in some way in order to give a better picture of the different types of toolkits.

I have tried to be impartial in reviewing each product, making an effort to point out both strengths and weaknesses. Some comments may inadvertently reflect some of my own biases.

Multimedia Toolkits

While somewhat arbitrary, my guideline for categorizing a package in this section was that it had to provide facilities for graphics, sound, animation, and hypertext. In theory, that should be adequate for implementing multimedia applications without the need for any additional tools. In practice you probably will need to combine these with other tools to meet all your needs.

HTML

While not a multimedia toolkit per se, a simple but viable option for developing multimedia applications is to use the hypertext technology used by the World Wide Web, which I described in Chapter 5, *Hypertext, Hypermedia, and the World Wide Web*. The application can be written as a series of HyperText Markup Language (HTML) pages. As well as formatted text, the pages can include small inline graphics. External programs can be invoked to support playback of sound files, large graphic images, and full-motion video such as MPEG. The pages are linked to other pages using HTML's hypertext capability.

The information can be displayed using any of the widely available browser tools such as Mosaic or Netscape. For users with Internet access, it may be feasible to export the pages to the World Wide Web. Alternatively, the system can run using the local filesystem on one computer, or over a local area network.

The Mosaic viewer has a "kiosk" mode that operates with restricted features. A small standalone Linux system in a suitable enclosure could be used to implement a low-cost public information kiosk. More ambitious developers might want to make use of a touch screen as a pointing device.

HTML has sophisticated features such as fill-in forms to accept user input. The data entered can be processed by scripts on a server and the results returned. This process allows the user to access databases, fill out survey forms, and link to other information systems. The possibilities are endless.

The major advantage of this approach is that no traditional "programming" is required. HTML is easy to learn, requiring only a text editor. It is also low-cost; all of the necessary software is freely available. If the material is electronically "published" via the World Wide Web, it becomes immediately available to millions of readers.

This method is good for computer-based training and information dissemination applications. It is also platform-independent, with viewer programs available for virtually every computing platform.

There are limitations, however, in what can be done with HTML. In the past, functions such as animation have been limited to external viewer programs. With the availability of Java-enabled Web browsers, animation and interactive applications can now be implemented as Java applets, which are portable, quickly downloaded, and run locally on the user's computer.

The HTML language is still being developed and one has to be careful that the features used are compatible with the end user's browser programs (this is not as much of a problem if you have control over the browser, as in a kiosk application). The creation of forms is easily implemented in HTML, but the software to manipulate the data from the forms requires more traditional programming, although usually in higher-level languages such as Perl and Tcl.

Andrew

Name: Andrew
Author: Carnegie Mellon University
Available from: *ftp://ftp.andrew.cmu.edu/pub/AUIS/*
Distribution policy: Unrestricted

The Andrew System is the result of a joint venture undertaken in 1982 between IBM and Carnegie Mellon University, with the goal of developing an advanced workstation and distributed computing environment. Since 1992 the system, known as the Andrew User Interface System (AUIS), has been freely distributed and supported by the Andrew Consortium.

AUIS consists of three main components. The first is the Andrew User Environment (AUE), which is made up of a number of powerful integrated tools, most notably:

- A multimedia text editor/word processor (started by typing *ez*)

- A hypertext help system (*help*)

- A shell interface (*typescript*)

- A multimedia mail reader (*messages*)

- A graphical filesystem browser (*bush*)

At a lower level is the Andrew ToolKit (ATK). This is the object-oriented programming environment with which the AUE tools were created. The system provides powerful high-level objects for supporting graphics, spreadsheets, text editors, equation formatters, and a facility for simple animation. All of these objects can be embedded in other objects that the programmer creates, using a facility for dynamically loading objects when needed.

As well as the AUE tools, several other specialized applications (such as GUI builders) are provided to assist in developing applications, known collectively as the Andrew Development Environment Workbench (ADEW). Andrew applications are written in C, with the help of a tool called *class* that supports object-oriented programming. Classes containing data structures and functions, possibly inherited from other classes, are defined using a language vaguely similar to C++, which is then preprocessed to produce C header files. The system comes with a number of example applications illustrating how to write programs using *class*. Also provided is a script language called *ness*, which can be used for implementing complete applications, or be embedded in objects or documents.

The third component is the Andrew Message System (AMS), a multimedia interface for mail and bulletin board systems. It supports many advanced features including user authentication, return receipts, automatic mail sorting, vote collection and tabulation, enclosures, audit trails of related messages, and subscription management. Much of this system formed the basis for what is now the MIME standard for multimedia.

Andrew runs under the X Window System and has been ported to over a dozen different UNIX-based systems. Under Linux, an easy-to-install binary distribution has been put together by Terry Gliedt (*tpg@mr.net*). This feature avoids the time and effort of building the system from source code and allows the user to install only those components that are desired.

The system comes with extensive documentation, most of which can be accessed from the Andrew help system. Another good source is the book *Multimedia Applications Development with the Andrew Toolkit,* by Nathaniel Borenstein, published by Prentice-Hall. In addition, the August through November 1994 issues of *Linux Journal* included a series of articles on the Andrew System by Terry Gliedt.

The strength of the Andrew System, in my opinion, is its powerful set of integrated tools and high-level building blocks for developing multimedia applications. It has been available for several years and has been shown to be stable and reliable, yet it is still being enhanced. The system, and therefore the applications developed using it, is supported on many different platforms, which is a boon to portability. Andrew is freely available and is supported by the Andrew Consortium via the Internet.

The disadvantages of the system are that it is complex, and most users should expect quite a long learning curve before being comfortable enough with it to develop applications (although the AUE tools are quite easy and intuitive to use). Because the objects provided by the toolkit are very powerful, the resulting applications can be somewhat large. The full Andrew development system requires approximately 30 to 40 megabytes of disk space.

Andrew's approach to object-oriented programming is nonstandard. Many programmers would prefer to learn a more popular object-oriented language such as C++ (the Andrew System predates the development of C++), and see this as a disadvantage.

Support for animation is limited to some vector graphics–based animation. There is no direct support for full-motion video formats such as MPEG. The facilities for sound in the Andrew ToolKit are also quite limited.

I see two distinct ways in which multimedia developers can use this system. You could use the editor for writing C source code and documentation and utilize the other tools for enhancing productivity while following a traditional C programming approach. The Andrew User Environment creates a comfortable integrated graphical environment for doing this.

The other approach would be to use the building blocks provided by the Andrew ToolKit as the basis for developing multimedia applications. Once the programmer is familiar with the system, the development of sophisticated applications should be greatly aided by the system.

The Andrew System is freely available and applications developed using it can be freely distributed or sold. The only restrictions are that they cannot use the names of IBM, CMU, and other contributors in their advertising, and they cannot sue any contributors. Serious developers may wish to join the Andrew Consortium. Membership entitles them to receive more frequent software updates and programming support and consultation, depending on the level of membership.

The Andrew System is available by anonymous ftp from the Internet host *ftp.andrew.cmu.edu* in the directory */pub/AUIS*. A binary distribution for Linux is available at *ftp://sunsite.unc.edu/pub/Linux/X11/andrew/*. You can contact the Andrew Consortium by checking the World Wide Web site that's located at *http://www.cs.cmu.edu/afs/cs.cmu.edu/project/atk-ftp/web/andrew-home.html*, by sending email to *info-andrew@andrew.cmu.edu*, or by mail to:

> Wilfred J. Hansen, Director
> Andrew Consortium
> School of Computer Science
> Carnegie Mellon University
> 5000 Forbes Avenue
> Pittsburgh, PA 15213
> 412–268–6710

MetaCard

> Name: MetaCard
> Author: Metacard Corporation
> Available from: *ftp://ftp.metacard.com/MetaCard/*
> Distribution policy: licensed commercial product

MetaCard is a commercial multimedia development environment based on the HyperTalk scripting language made popular by Apple's *HyperCard* product (you could think of MetaCard as a UNIX clone of HyperCard). It is available for more than a dozen UNIX platforms, including Linux.

The system uses a model based on sets of hypertext pages, usually called *stacks*. You use the development environment to create stacks containing text, graphics, sound, animation, and hypertext links using WYSIWYG layout tools.

The script language used by MetaCard is MetaTalk, a superset of Apple's Hyper-Talk. Apple HyperCard stacks can be imported and executed, although they may require some changes. While it is compatible with HyperCard stacks, the design environment of MetaCard is completely different from HyperCard.

Events such as keyboard or mouse input can trigger the execution of scripts written in the MetaTalk language, enabling more complex functions to be implemented. If MetaTalk is not adequate, you can call external programs, or even software modules written in C. Alternatively, there is an embedded version of MetaCard that can be linked with and called from C programs.

The system supports text with various fonts, styles, and sizes. Tools are provided to generate graphics, or external files can be imported in most common formats. Animations in AVI, FLI/FLC, and QuickTime formats can be played (although they cannot be created). There is also support for playing sound files.

An evaluation copy of MetaCard can be downloaded by anonymous ftp from *ftp.metacard.com* in the directory */MetaCard* or by sending electronic mail to *support@metacard.com* (if you do not have Internet or email access, the software can be sent to you on floppy disk media). The demonstration version is fully functional, except that the save function has been disabled. If the product is purchased, a license key is supplied that turns the evaluation copy into the fully functional product. Licensing is on a per-user basis.

Executing MetaCard stacks requires a run-time version of the product. The run-time engine can be freely distributed, so there is no additional licensing cost. At the time of this writing, a single-user copy of MetaCard for Linux was US$195 (the cost for other platforms was somewhat higher).

In my opinion the key strength of MetaCard is that it is very functional, supporting the majority of the needs of multimedia programming. Most of the development tools and documentation are implemented using HyperTalk. The system doesn't require a knowledge of traditional programming languages such as C. It is low-cost, particularly when compared to other commercial multimedia systems. Because the script language is compatible with Apple's HyperTalk, there are many available books on the HyperCard product that can be used as reference. For those already familiar with HyperCard, the learning curve should be very short indeed. Because stacks can execute on any of the supported platforms, applications developed using it are quite portable.

Some users may see it as a disadvantage that the product is not freely available. Another drawback, in addition to the purchase cost, is the fact that source code is not provided, so the user cannot fix bugs or modify the product. Compatibility problems are also possible due to changes in the Linux kernel or differences between Linux distributions. Some users may find the card stack-based paradigm somewhat restrictive when compared to more general purpose graphical user interface toolkits.

There is both a mailing list for MetaCard and a list of frequently asked questions; information on these is included in the distribution. For more information on MetaCard, you can send email to *support@metacard.com*, or contact:

> MetaCard Corporation
> 4710 Shoup Pl.
> Boulder, CO 80303
> 303-447-3936 (phone)
> 303-499-9855 (fax)

MET++

> Name: MET++
> Authors: Philipp Ackermann, Dominik Eichelberg
> Available from: *ftp://ftp.ifi.unizh.ch/pub/projects/met++/*
> Distribution policy: freely available

MET++ is described as an object-oriented multimedia application framework. It was developed at the University of Zurich, Switzerland, by Philipp Ackermann and Dominik Eichelberg. MET++ provides a library of reusable objects for implementing two- and three-dimensional graphics, graphical user interface components, printing, audio, and music. The framework takes care of event handling and message passing for the application developer.

The system is implemented in C++ and consists of class libraries as well as some sample applications implemented using the framework. The example applications range from a simple "hello, world" application to a multimedia authoring tool and a multimedia text editor. Also included are a number of development tools including an object inspector, a class inheritance hierarchy viewer, a source code browser, and a program structure visualization tool.

The toolkit supports many standard file formats for text, two- and three-dimensional graphics, audio, and music. A hypertext/hypermedia link mechanism is provided, including a World Wide Web browser. The system is an extension of the ET++ application framework developed by Andre Weinand and Erich Gamma.

MET++ is currently considered a beta release. It runs on Sun, HP, and SGI workstations, and a Linux port is planned. The developers welcome volunteers to assist in the work of porting and testing.

The advantages of this system, in my opinion, are that it provides a number of highly functional building blocks for multimedia applications. It is based on standards (both the implementation language and the file formats supported), and runs on several UNIX platforms. The files and documentation are freely available by anonymous ftp from the Internet site *ftp.ifi.unizh.ch* in the directory */pub/projects/met++*.

The main disadvantage is that (at least at the time of writing) MET++ has not yet been ported to Linux. It is a large package, requiring roughly 100 megabytes of disk space. Because it is a beta release, bugs are to be expected, many changes are likely, and there is little documentation available.

You can obtain more information by sending email to *met@ifi.unizh.ch*, or also by contacting:

> University of Zurich
> Department of Computer Science
> Multimedia Laboratory
> P. Ackermann, D. Eichelberg
> Winterthurerstrasse 190
> CH-8057 Zurich
> Switzerland
> +41-1-257 4569 (phone)
> +41-1-363 0035 (fax)

MET++ shows a lot of potential as a multimedia toolkit, and by the time you read this chapter, the chances are good that it will be running under Linux (or if not, why not volunteer to help?).

Java

> Name: Java
> Author: Sun Microsystems and others
> Available from: *ftp://java.blackdown.org/pub/Java/linux/*
> Distribution policy: See licensing agreement for details

We discussed the Java programming language in Chapter 12, *Hypermedia Applications*. The Java Development kit, or JDK, was the first available toolkit for Java, consisting of a compiler, run-time interpreter, applet viewer, debugger, and class libraries. The JDK source code from Sun Microsystems has been ported to Linux by Randy Chapman (there may be other ports as well, but this seems to be the most popular). There is a Java on Linux HOWTO document that describes how to obtain and install the Linux JDK and has references to other Java resources.

To use Java you'll also need a Java-enabled Web browser. The Linux version of Netscape Navigator fully supports Java applets.

In May 1996, most of the major operating system vendors announced they would be adding native support for executing Java programs to their operating systems. A few weeks later that support was implemented for Linux, making it the first operating system to do so. As of the 1.3.100 Linux kernel, Java binaries and applets can be directly executed from the command line (provided that the JDK is installed).

Java is growing rapidly and a number of commercial and freeware Java tools have been announced for the Linux platform, with more expected to follow.

X11 Graphics Toolkits

In this section, I look at a number of toolkits that are designed for supporting graphics functions under the X Window System. Later I will look at systems not based on X.

The functions provided by the X Window System are quite low-level and do not enforce any particular look and feel. Most X11-based application developers make use of toolkits to reduce their development effort. Many different toolkits have been developed, based on the particular goals of the implementors. Some are designed for ease of use, some strive to be object-oriented, and others are tied to a specific implementation language. In this section I look at a number of common toolkits for X; if you look, you can undoubtedly find others. The common feature is that they can all be used under Linux.

SUIT

> Name: SUIT
> Author: Nathaniel Young
> Available from: *ftp://uvacs.cs.virginia.edu/pub/suit/*
> Distribution policy: Free for nonprofit organizations

SUIT is the Simple User Interface Toolkit, developed at the University of Virginia by Nathaniel Young and others. The goal of SUIT is to allow designers to create applications with sophisticated graphical user interfaces in C without the lengthy learning period associated with traditional toolkits.

All of the common graphical objects such as menus, lists, buttons, and text fields are provided, as well as higher-level objects such as text editors, file browsers, color choosers, formatted text, and even a graphical clock. Low-level drawing primitives are also provided.

The minimal application, consisting of a window with a "quit" button, can be coded with a function *main()* and three SUIT library calls. The package comes with a number of example programs that illustrate all of the basic widget types and library features. A 15-page tutorial document is provided to get the user quickly started using the toolkit. A 160-page reference guide covers all of the details. Both documents are distributed in PostScript format.

In my experience, one of the most tedious and time-consuming tasks in developing graphical applications can be getting all of the objects correctly positioned. One common solution to this task is to provide a GUI builder tool that lets the developer "draw" the interface. The SUIT toolkit takes a different approach—a "resource editor" is built in and is available while the application is executing. By holding down the shift and control keys you can select, move, and resize any graphical object. You can also change properties such as color and widget type, create and destroy objects, and access online help.

The widget settings (called *resources*) are saved in a data file when a SUIT application exits and are read back in when it starts up, making them permanent. When the developer is ready to ship the application to end users, one minor change can be made to the code to disable the resource editor, and the resource file (which happens to be C source code) is compiled and linked into the executable, effectively freezing the interface.

SUIT is also a multi-platform toolkit. As well as running on most X11-based UNIX platforms, it can be compiled for Macintosh, MS-DOS, and MS-Windows systems.

The full SUIT distribution including source code and documentation can be obtained by anonymous ftp from *ftp://uvacs.cs.virginia.edu/pub/suit/*. Precompiled binaries for most platforms (but not Linux) are also available there. A Linux port of SUIT can be found at *ftp://sunsite.unc.edu/pub/Linux/X11/devel/*. This package includes Linux binaries, header files, and the example programs, but no documentation.

Inquiries about SUIT can be sent by email to *suit@uvacs.cs.virginia.edu*. There is also a mailing list; send mail to *suit-users-request@uvacs.cs.Virginia.EDU* for information. The Usenet newsgroup *comp.windows.suit* is another forum for discussing SUIT issues.

The documentation states that SUIT, including all its source code, is available without charge to universities and other nonprofit institutions. For-profit organizations can license the software for a fee in the neighborhood of US$25,000. Anyone may download SUIT for evaluation purposes.

The advantages of SUIT are that it is free and quite simple to use, while providing reasonably good functionality in a small package. The learning curve should be shorter than many other toolkits (they claim users can be productive after two hours), and the documentation appears adequate. The integrated GUI builder is a boon to developers, while the multi-platform capability makes the resulting applications potentially portable to all of the major computing platforms. The resulting applications have a look and feel that is very close to the Motif toolkit, which is arguably the *de facto* standard for X11 applications.

On the downside, developers of commercial applications may find the licensing requirements too restrictive. The tool is available only via the Internet, and support is via Internet mail and Usenet news.

Those interested in a more object-oriented toolkit may prefer to look at alternatives, such as C++ based toolkits. Some functions are missing from the toolkit, most notably the ability to support applications with more than one base window.

SUIT was written in the early 1990s and is no longer being actively developed. Traffic in the Usenet newsgroup and mailing list is quite low.

The Linux distribution of SUIT provides statically linked libraries, which result in large executables (approximately 350 to 400 kilobytes). Creating dynamic libraries would help significantly.

InterViews

> Name: InterViews
> Author: Mark Linton
> Available from: *ftp://interviews.stanford.edu/pub/*
> Distribution policy: Unrestricted

InterViews is a C++ based software system for developing graphical applications. It was written by Mark Linton as a joint research project between Stanford University and Silicon Graphics, Inc. InterViews is also a library of C++ classes that provides an object-oriented programming environment for resolution-independent graphics, document formatting, and graphical connectivity.

As well as the toolkit libraries, the package includes some sample applications, including a structured drawing editor and a WYSIWYG document editor, both of which are useful applications in their own right. Documentation includes a reference manual, tutorials, and manpages for all utilities and library functions.

The *ibuild* tool is an interface builder, similar to the structured drawing editor, which assists the developer in designing applications based on InterViews. Applications developed with the toolkit have a unique look and feel, different from Motif or other standards.

InterViews is freely distributed under the same restrictions with which the MIT X Consortium distributes the X Window System. The software is copyrighted, but there are no restrictions on what can be done with it. It is available via anonymous ftp from *ftp://interviews.stanford.edu/pub/*.

The standard distribution requires some patches to compile under Linux. These are available in the *contrib* directory, as well as on many of the major Linux archive sites. The Slackware distribution of Linux includes InterViews, but not all of the tools required for software development are included in that package (it fits on one floppy disk). The Linux version of InterViews includes dynamic libraries.

There's a newsgroup, *comp.windows.interviews*, and a mailing list that mirrors the newsgroup, *interviews@interviews.stanford.edu*. To join the list, email *interviews-requests@stanford.edu*. Email *interviews-bugs@interviews.stanford.edu* to send bug reports.

InterViews has many powerful features and the graphics primitives are fast. A GUI builder tool assists in application development. Users who are looking for an object-oriented toolkit will be pleased with this system. It also supports printing via PostScript.

On the negative side, it is more complex than some of the simpler toolkits, and a significant learning curve is to be expected. Documentation is somewhat scattered, and some sections of the reference manual are incomplete.

The main argument against using InterViews is the fact that it is no longer actively being developed. The author is working on its successor, Fresco, discussed next.

Incidentally, a commercial version of InterViews is sold by Quest Windows Corporation under the name ObjectViews C++. It has a number of enhancements as well as commercial support, but at the time of this writing was not offered for the Linux platform.

Fresco

Name: Fresco
Author: Mark Linton
Available from: *ftp://ftp.faslab.com/pub/Fresco/*
Distribution policy: Unrestricted

Fresco is an object-oriented user interface system for the development of graphical applications. It is a design evolution of the InterViews toolkit, although it is not backwards-compatible with InterViews. Development is headed by the key developer of InterViews, Mark Linton.

The Fresco architecture provides user interface objects such as sliders, buttons, and text editors as well as the layout objects used to compose them. Objects can be embedded in other objects and can be saved in a machine-independent form to support persistence.

Fresco uses a standard object model, CORBA, which allows for object distribution and provides a standardized, high-level notation called IDL for object definition. While the sample MIT implementation of Fresco is implemented in C++, the API is defined in IDL, and bindings are being developed for other languages including Smalltalk and Python.

Fresco also provides support for Tcl-based scripting, multi-threading, resolution independence, and internationalization.

Fresco is currently undergoing the standardization process within the X Consortium. A version of Fresco was included in the X11R6 distribution. The code is subject to change (the Consortium calls it a "work in progress"). Newer versions are periodically made available on the Internet. Fresco is planned to be a multi-platform system, with support for X11, Windows NT, Windows 95, and Macintosh platforms.

The latest Fresco source code snapshots can be obtained by anonymous ftp from *ftp.faslab.com* in the directory */pub/Fresco*. An excellent source of information on Fresco is the World Wide Web site *http://www.faslab.com/fresco/HomePage.html*.

Fresco will compile under Linux. It requires X11R6 and GNU g++ version 2.6.3 or later. Pre-compiled binaries and up-to-date information on the Linux port can be found on the World Wide Web at *http://www.clark.net/pub/ecn/fresco.html*

The strength of Fresco is the rich level of functions offered. It builds on the technology of the popular InterViews toolkit. The interface specification and sample implementation are freely available. It makes use of the C++ language to support an object-oriented architecture. The look and feel should be compatible with industry standards such as Motif and Windows 95 (and in fact it can make use of underlying toolkits such as Motif).

The CORBA standard will allow applications to be distributed across different machines and operating systems. It currently runs on several computing platforms and operating systems. The toolkit is fully multi-threaded.

The disadvantages are that Fresco is still currently incomplete and subject to change. It is quite complex and has not yet been proven.

It is still too soon to see if Fresco will be successful, but I believe that it has the potential to become the *de facto* standard toolkit for X window–based systems, and also make inroads into Windows NT and Windows 95 markets.

XView

Name: XView
Author: Dan Heller
Available from: *ftp:/sunsite.unc.edu/pub/Linux/libs/X/xview/xview3L5.1.tar.gz*
Distribution policy: Unrestricted

XView (X Window System-based Visual/Integrated Environment for Workstations) is an implementation of OpenLook, which is a user interface specification jointly developed by Sun and AT&T. XView is included by Sun Microsystems as part of the SunOS operating system and was used for implementing many of the graphical tools provided by Sun's OpenWindows windowing environment. The source code, written in C, is freely available as part of the MIT X distribution, and it will compile under Linux with only minor changes.

The XView toolkit supports all the expected graphical objects, from buttons, menus, and windows, to more sophisticated objects such as text editors and command windows. Unlike most toolkits, the developer performs most operations using only five basic function calls. Though coded in C, the structure of the toolkit can be considered object-oriented, with a hierarchy of objects that inherit characteristics from others. UIT is a C++ class-library for developing OpenLook applications that sits on top of the XView toolkit and gives it an object-oriented interface.

In addition to the toolkit, several useful XView applications are provided in the distribution, including the *cmdtool* terminal emulator, *textedit* text editor, and *olwm* and *olvwm* window managers. The toolkit is extensible; some third parties have created additional objects. The SlingShot extensions are a freely available XView add-on that adds additional high-level objects such as tree diagrams and arrays of images. Sun users should note that some of the productivity tools provided by Sun as part of OpenWindows are *not* freely available, most notably the OpenLook file manager and mail tool. Sun's OpenLook DevGuide (Developers Graphical User Interface Design Editor) is also not available for Linux. However, the run-time libraries required by DevGuide generated applications are freely available, so source code produced by the tool can be recompiled for Linux systems.

The XView applications and development libraries (including shared libraries, UIT, and the SlingShot package) are included in the Slackware distribution of Linux as the XV series of disks, as well as on the major Linux archive sites.

The down side of XView is it's no longer being actively developed or supported. Sun essentially abandoned OpenLook and moved to Motif as the standard user interface for all new development. XView applications have a different look and feel from Motif, and can sometimes confuse users not familiar with them. XView does seem to be regaining some popularity as it is introduced to Linux users.

I find it strange that OpenLook—and XView—never became particularly successful. It was free, powerful, well-documented, and had the backing of two large vendors. Most software developers would agree that OpenLook is a more elegant interface for programming than Motif. The key reason seems to be that the other UNIX vendors aligned to oppose Sun by using Motif. Motif also has the advantage of being closer to the Microsoft Windows look and feel.

Motif

Name: Motif
Author: Open Software Foundation
Available from: Various commercial vendors
Distribution policy: Commercial product

In the battle for the *de facto* standard toolkit for X11-based systems, most would agree that Motif has won. Like many other popularity contests in the software world, the choice is not always based on technical superiority, but such is life.

Motif is intended for applications written in C, though it has some facilities for C++, and some third parties provide bindings for other languages. It's built on top of the X Toolkit Intrinsics, the Xt library that's part of X11. Motif offers a large number of different graphical objects (widgets) with a pleasing three-dimensional appearance. Most Motif packages include the *mwm* window manager, and some provide a GUI builder tool.

Motif is a commercial product developed by the Open Software Foundation. Third parties, such as workstation vendors, typically license the Motif source code and port it to specific platforms. They then sell development kits consisting of precompiled libraries, header files, and possibly additional development tools and documentation.

Linux users can buy Motif from a number of vendors at a reasonable cost. Note that these are binaries, as the cost of a Motif source license is out of reach for most Linux users.

The advantages of Motif are that it is (arguably) the *de facto* standard toolkit for X. It is functional, has a look and feel familiar to most users, and documentation is widely available. Motif applications that are statically linked can be freely distributed without cost. The toolkit is well-supported and continues to be enhanced by OSF. The Motif interface was used as the basis for the IEEE P1295 standard for user interfaces.

It is a somewhat low-level toolkit, with quite a long learning curve to be expected. While Linux versions of the toolkit are typically less expensive than for other platforms, it is not free. The source code is not available, so the user must rely on the vendor for bug fixes. The resulting applications are large unless they use shared libraries, which usually must be purchased by the end user.

One should keep in mind that there are other toolkits that support the Motif look and feel (but not the API) without using Motif. Some toolkits also build on Motif, adding value to it by making it easier to use, or object-oriented. There are some plans in the free software community to develop a free source-code-compatible implementation of Motif, but this is still in the early stages. One such project has been dubbed "LessTif." Information can be found on the Web at *http://www.cs.uidaho.edu:8000/hungry/microshaft/lesstif.html*.

Most of the Motif distributions for Linux do not include GUI builders. One freely available GUI builder is VXP (Visual X Window System Programming Interface). It runs on many UNIX platforms including Linux and is available from *http://www.shsu.edu/˜stdyxc05/VXP/* or *ftp://ftp.shsu.edu:/pub/VXP/*.

The following vendors offer Motif for Linux:

Moo-Tiff

USA: Europe:
InfoMagic   LaserMoon Ltd
P.O. Box 30370
Flagstaff, Arizona
USA 86003-0370
email: *info@infomagic.com*   email: *info@lasermoon.co.uk*
WWW: *http://www.infomagic.com*   tel: +44 (0)329-826444
tel: +1-602-526-9565
fax: +1-602-526-9573

Swim Motif
ACC Corporation Inc.
email: *info@acc-corp.com*
tel: 800-546-7274

MetroLink Motif
MetroLink Inc.
email: *sales@metrolink.com*
tel: 305-938-0283
WWW: *http://www.metrolink.com*

ObjectBuilder/OI

Name: ObjectBuilder/OI
Author: OpenWare Technologies (formerly ParcPlace Systems)
Available from: *ftp://sunsite.unc.edu/pub/Linux/devel/OI/*
Distribution policy: Commercial product/free Linux binaries

ObjectBuilder is a GUI builder for developing applications that use the Object Interface (OI) C++ Toolkit. OpenWare Technologies sells the package commercially for several UNIX workstation platforms. They have made a fully functional Linux version available for free in order to encourage developers to try the product and (they hope) purchase the workstation version.

The package consists of the ObjectBuilder GUI builder, OI libraries (both static and shared), include files, some example applications, and documentation in the form of PostScript files, online help, and manpages.

The GUI builder lets you create the user interface portion of your applications by dragging and dropping items from a palette of objects. Attributes of the objects are defined by filling in menus. ObjectBuilder generates a configuration file defining the design, C++ source files, and a makefile.

The OI toolkit is C++ based, and offers all of the expected graphical objects including root windows, menus, dialog boxes, and labels. The user interface is compliant with either OpenLook or Motif (selectable at run-time), but it does not use either of these toolkits for its implementation.

The package can be obtained by anonymous ftp from either of the following two sites: one is located at *ftp://sunsite.unc.edu/pub/Linux/devel/OI/* and the other at *ftp://tsx-11.mit.edu/pub/linux/attic/packages/OI/*. The second site has a few more patches and contributed code.

The toolkit is available from the vendor and is documented in the book *OI Programmer's Guide: Version 4, Second Edition*, by Amber Benson and Gary Aitken, published by Prentice-Hall. There is an independent electronic mailing list for ObjectBuilder/OI. Join by sending email to *oi-users-request@bbn.com*.

The vendor can be reached at:

> OpenWare Technologies
> 8000 Arlington Expressway
> Jacksonville, FL 32211
> Head Office: 904-725-7187
> Boulder, Colorado office: 303-440-9991

As I see it, the strengths of ObjectBuilder/OI are its cost (at least on the Linux platform), the standard OpenLook and Motif look and feel, and online documentation. The GUI builder offers the potential to significantly reduce development time. The developer, ParcPlace Systems, has a good reputation for their Smalltalk implementation.

The major issue (at least at the time of this writing) is that the toolkit was built for quite an old distribution of Linux. It may not work on your system due to changes in the C libraries, X server, and compiler version. (I was able to run the GUI builder, but could not compile or link the sample applications due to changes in g++.)

Also, disk space requirements are moderate (about 12MB), but a minimum of 16MB of RAM is required to use the system with reasonable performance.

The Linux version is not officially supported by the vendor and not all documentation is provided. While you can develop and ship applications for Linux using the toolkit, the main intent appears to be to convince you to buy the commercial version for one of the other workstation platforms.

The Linux version of ObjectBuilder was made publicly available when the product was owned by ParcPlace Systems. Since then the rights have been sold to OpenWare Technologies. When contacted, the vendor had no immediate plans to update the free Linux version.

Forms Library

Name: Forms Library
Authors: T.C. Zhao, Mark Overmars
Available from: *ftp://bloch.phys.uwm.edu/pub/xforms/*
Distribution policy: Free for noncommercial/nonprofit use

Forms Library, also known as XForms, is a C-based GUI toolkit built on top of X. The main goals of the design were simplicity and ease of use.

The toolkit consists of an object library and one header file. All of the standard graphical objects are provided, as well as some higher-level objects such as a clock, file browser, and facilities for graphical plotting. The user can extend the library with their own user-defined objects. While implemented in C, it can also be called from C++.

The included WYSIWYG GUI builder lets you design an interface and then generates the appropriate C source code. The user needs to add the code to implement callbacks and other application-specific functions. A test mode lets you try out the interface from within the GUI builder. The tool can be used even after making changes to the generated code.

Documentation consists of a 200-page reference manual supplemented by the online help provided from within the GUI builder. Over 50 example applications are included that illustrate all of the graphical objects and library functions.

The toolkit is available by ftp from *ftp://bloch.phys.uwm.edu/pub/xforms* and *ftp://ftp.cs.ruu.nl/pub/XFORMS*. The World Wide Web site that has information, including screen images, can be found at *http://bragg.phys.uwm.edu/xforms*. The archive sites include precompiled libraries (static and shared) for Linux, as well as other platforms.

You can join a mailing list by sending email to *xforms-request@cs.ruu.nl*.

In my opinion, the toolkit meets its design goal of being simple, small, and easy to use, while at the same time providing many highly functional graphical building blocks. It is well documented, and runs on all of the major UNIX platforms. While not object-oriented, it does support applications written in C++.

Purists may complain that the look and feel is not identical to real Motif applications, although it is close. The toolkit is also only free for noncommercial and nonprofit applications; commercial use requires a license arrangement. Unlike most free toolkits, the Forms Library is available only in binary form. The authors have chosen not to distribute the source code, but are committed to keeping the binaries freely available.

V

Name: V
Author: Bruce Wampler (*wampler@cs.unm.edu*)
Available from: *ftp://ftp.cs.unm.edu/pub/wampler/*
Distribution policy: GNU LGPL

V is a portable graphical user interface framework implemented in C++. Applications written with V are portable to X11/UNIX systems (using the Athena widgets) and to Microsoft Windows 3.1. The author is working on X11 Motif and Windows 95 support, and in future possibly OS/2 and Apple Macintosh as well. He has developed a number of successful commercial applications. He has made C freely available under the GNU library general public license.

V offers support for all of the common graphical objects. It uses a heavily object-oriented approach. The resulting applications take on the look and feel of the underlying native platform.

The main goal in developing V was ease of use. It is reputed to be small and easy to learn. It comes with a 150-page manual, manpages, and several example applications, including a full-featured drawing program.

The potential disadvantages of V are that, because it is reasonably small and simple, it imposes some constraints on functionality. Users cannot fall through to use features of the underlying toolkit. No GUI builder is offered. V has only recently been released to the Internet, but it has been in use at the University of New Mexico for some time. V is a GUI toolkit only—it does not offer other functions such as container classes or interprocess communication.

For more information see the author's World Wide Web page, located at *http://www.cs.unm.edu/~wampler*.

Grafix

Name: Grafix
Author: Wolfgang Koehler
Available from: *ftp://sunsite.unc.edu/pub/Linux/X11/devel/grafix.1.2.tgz*
Distribution policy: GNU GPL

Grafix is an X11-based toolkit originally designed for scientific visualization but also supporting most of the common objects needed for implementing graphical user interfaces. It's a small package, consisting of a library, include files, several demonstration programs, and some documentation. The package also includes a number of sample applications, ranging from a simple one-button demo to a three-dimensional plot of mathematical functions.

The library is implemented in about 3000 lines of C++ code. It should run on any UNIX-compatible system supporting X11 (it has been tested under Linux with X11R5 and X11R6).

It includes classes for implementing windows, several types of buttons, pulldown menus, help screens, scrollbars, and some more sophisticated objects for plotting using real-value coordinates, file selection, and a simple edit window. The most interesting object is a complete manager to handle the display of two-dimensional mathematical functions in arbitrary perspective with shadowing and zooming.

The advantages of this package are its small size and simplicity. The plotting routines may be useful to some users. It is low-cost and requires no other underlying toolkits.

On the negative side, the functionality is limited and it is not well documented. The author cannot guarantee support, so users should be prepared to fix bugs or extend the toolkit themselves.

Xtpanel

Name: Xtpanel
Authors: Steve Cole, Dave Nichols, Stanford University
Available from: *ftp://sunsite.unc.edu/pub/Linux/X11/devel/xtpnl-lx.tgz*
Distribution policy: Free for noncommercial use

Xtpanel is a utility for creating graphical interfaces from the shell command line or an *xtpanel* script file. It lets you create an interactive program without the need for conventional programming.

The package comes with a number of sample *xtpanel* scripts demonstrating all of the available graphical objects. They include text fields, messages, buttons, toggles, sliders, scrollbars, and lists, with the ability to group the objects in order to control placement.

The script language is simple and is fully documented in the manpage. To make scripts even easier to write, a script generator (itself implemented in *xtpanel*) is supplied that automates most of the effort in building and testing script files.

The program uses the X toolkit and the MIT Athena widget set. The Athena widgets look rather plain, but this is improved if the three-dimensional Athena replacements are used. The script generator also requires the *tcsh* shell program.

This is an excellent tool for simple applications. It is especially suited for adding a GUI to existing command line–based programs, and is small, fast, and easy to use.

Being based on a script language, it has limitations in speed and what can be implemented. Complex graphical applications are probably better off using a C or C++ based toolkit. The look and feel of the Athena toolkit is also not as polished as some others.

Libsx

Name: Libsx
Author: Dominic Giamapolo
Available from: *ftp://sunstte.unc.edu/pub/Linux/X11/devel/libsx.tar.gz*
Distribution policy: GNU GPL

Libsx is a graphics library built on top of the Athena widget set. It is intended to make writing X applications easier than using the Xt toolkit directly. It packages the commonly performed functions so one library call can replace 10 to 20 lines of X code. Unlike some toolkits, Libsx does not the hide the underlying window system, so you have access to all of the low-level X functions if needed.

The toolkit provides support for labels, buttons, text fields, scrollbars, lists, drawing areas, and other commonly needed graphical objects. The contributed code also includes a file chooser, color browser, and some other higher-level functions.

The package includes libraries and header files. There is a binary distribution for Linux with precompiled static and shared libraries. Documentation (in the form of ASCII text files) describes how to use the system, in conjunction with a number of example programs. The examples range from a two-line "hello, world" program to a text file viewer implemented in only 200 lines of code.

Libsx makes writing X applications much less painful, and results in small, fast executables, particularly if the shared libraries are used. Documentation appears adequate, it is portable to most systems that support X, and it has had a few years of testing and enhancements.

It uses the traditional programming approach—no GUI builder tools and no object-oriented features. This may be a weakness or a benefit depending on your point of view. The Athena widgets have a less polished look than toolkits such as Motif, although the 3D Athena replacement library helps a lot in this regard. Finally, there are some limitations imposed by the underlying Athena widgets, but these are likely not important for most applications.

WxWindows

Name: WxWindows
Author: Julian Smart, University of Edinburgh
Available from: *ftp://ftp.aiai.ed.ac.uk/pub/packages/wxwin/*
Distribution policy: Freely available

WxWindows is a multi-platform GUI toolkit implemented in C++. Applications written using WxWindows can run on X11-based systems including Linux (using XView or Motif), Microsoft Windows 3.1, and Windows NT. Apple Macintosh and text-based versions are also in development.

WxWindows was originally developed at the Artificial Intelligence Applications Institute, University of Edinburgh, to develop a hypertext-based knowledge acquisition and diagramming tool. It was made publicly available in the hope that others would also find it useful.

The package provides class libraries for implementing all of the usual graphical objects provided by the underlying toolkits, as well as hypertext capability, printing to PostScript printers, and an inter-process communication facility.

Documentation consists of a FAQ, user manual, and reference manual, all provided in both PostScript and hypertext format. A number of example programs are also included.

The package includes some development tools and applications including a hypertext help system and a GUI builder tool. A number of additional add-on packages also are available separately on the Internet.

There is a World Wide Web site, *http://www.aiai.ed.ac.uk/~jacs/wxwin.html*, and a mailing list (send email to *wxwin-users-request@auai.ed.ac.uk* to join).

The main advantage this toolkit offers is the ability to write an application that can run on multiple platforms with little or no source code changes. The object-oriented programming interface is arguably superior to that of the underlying toolkits.

The downside is that this is quite a complex package and requires some effort to learn. It requires an underlying toolkit (Motif or XView under Linux). Because of its size, you will need considerable disk space and adequate memory to perform compiles without swapping. The resulting executable programs are quite large, although this can be greatly improved by using shared libraries.

Under X11 the GUI builder is supported by the Motif version but not XView, due to limitations in the XView toolkit (this may be corrected in the future).

For those without Internet access, the software can also be obtained on floppy disk directly from the author:

> Dr. Julian Smart
> Artificial Intelligence Applications Institute
> University of Edinburgh
> 80 South Bridge
> Edinburgh, Scotland
> EH1 1HN.
> email: *J.Smart@ed.ac.uk*
> tel. 031-650-2746

Xtent

> Name: Xtent
> Author: Doug Blewett and others, AT&T Bell Laboratories
> Available from: *ftp://sunsite.unc.edu/pub/Linux/X11/devel/xtent3.2.tgz*
> Distribution policy: Freely available

Xtent is a script language for creating X Toolkit-based applications. The syntax of the language is based on the format used for X11 resource files, with features of C and C++ and some aspects of Lisp. The interpreter may be used standalone or embedded within a C program.

Xtent is built on top of an X11 widget set and provides access to all of the features of the underlying widgets. It currently supports the MIT Athena, Motif, HP, and OpenLook.[*]

The package includes the library and header files and a standalone version of the interpreter. A 150-page manual documents the system, and several sample programs are included.

---

[*] This is a different implementation of OpenLook from the XView toolkit discussed earlier in this chapter.

Developers should find the script language relatively easy to use. Because it is an interpreter, changes can be made quickly with no recompilation. The resulting applications have the same look and feel as the underlying widget set.

Using the package requires a knowledge of the underlying widgets, and you have to program for a specific widget set. Less functionality is available when using the Athena widgets. It is a reasonably low-level toolkit because it works at the widget level. While simple, it requires you to learn a new language.

QT

Name: Qt
Author: Troll Tech, Norway
Available from: *ftp://sunsite.unc.edu/pub/Linux/devel/lang/c++/qt-0.98.tar.gz*
Distribution policy: Free for noncommercial use

Qt (pronounced "cute") is an object-oriented framework for developing graphical user interface applications under X11. It provides approximately 100 C++ classes for implementing graphical user interfaces as well as more general purpose classes supporting strings, date and time functions, file input/output, and data structures. Qt supports a Motif-like look and feel, but only uses the X library.

A unique feature of the toolkit is a meta-object system that extends C++ with new concepts the developers call "signals" and "slots." The developer claims that these allow you to define clean and natural object interfaces for creating independent objects. The extensions are implemented using a preprocessor called *moc*—Meta Object Compiler.

Documentation is provided in the form of HTML pages. The same information is available on the World Wide Web from *http://www.troll.no/*. The package includes several example programs, ranging from the obligatory "hello, world" program to a full implementation of the game Tetris.

The Linux version of Qt is freely available for noncommercial use. Object libraries (in both *a.out* and *elf* format) and include files are provided, but not the library source code. At the time of writing, Qt was considered a beta release. The vendor reports that the final release will be sold as a commercial product for several workstation platforms, but the Linux version will continue to be freely distributed.

There is a mailing list for Qt. Send a message containing the single word "subscribe" to *qt-interest-request@nvg.unit.no* to join. The vendor can also be contacted by email at *info@troll.no* or by postal mail at:

Troll Tech
Postboks 6133 Etterstad
N-0602 Oslo
Norway

Qt appears to be an easy-to-use and complete C++ based toolkit. The C++ extensions are intriguing, but nonstandard. Yet, it is a new package, still in beta test, and with no proven track record. Source code is not available, and the license agreement states that it is not to be used for commercial programs.

Tcl/Tk

Name: Tcl/Tk
Author: John Ousterhout
Available from: *ftp://sunsite.unc.edu/pub/Linux/devel/lang/tcl/*
Distribution policy: freely available

Tcl (usually pronounced "tickle") stands for Tool Command Language, written by Dr. John Ousterhout while at the University of California, Berkeley. Tcl is a simple script language interpreter originally intended to be embedded within applications. It offers all of the features you would expect from a programming language, including variables, string and mathematical operators, control flow constructs, and user defined procedures.

Rather than being used as a standalone shell, Tcl is actually a library that is meant to be embedded in applications written in traditional languages like C or C++. The library provides the command parser, which can be called from an application. The philosophy of Tcl is that large applications can be made more powerful and flexible by embedding a script language within them to allow the user to customize the tool and add new functions.

Tk is an extension to Tcl that provides an interface to the X Window System. Tk adds commands that allow you to build graphical user interfaces with a Motif look and feel. Because the programming is at a higher level than traditional C toolkits and can be easily modified without recompilation, graphical applications can be quickly developed and tested. *wish* is a simple shell program that lets you write standalone scripts using Tcl and Tk. Many applications can be written using *wish* without the need for any traditional C code.

The home ftp site for the Tcl and Tk source code is the directory *ftp://ftp.cs.berkeley.edu/ucb/tcl/*. The Slackware distribution of Linux includes pre-compiled Tcl and Tk libraries, *wish*, and several other Tcl extensions. Linux binaries can also be found at major Linux archive sites such as the one listed at the beginning of this section.

The source distribution includes manpages and some example programs. The source archive site also includes a number of conference papers and other documents. The Usenet newsgroup *comp.lang.tcl* is devoted to the language, and a comprehensive FAQ list is posted there regularly. The FAQ is an excellent source for information on Tcl applications and extensions.

The definitive reference for Tcl and Tk is Dr. John Ousterhout's book, *Tcl and the Tk Toolkit*. A number of other Tcl books are also in print.

John Ousterhout is now working for Sun Microsystems on Tcl and Tk related projects. He is leading a small development team that is reported to be working on enhancements as well as ports of Tcl and Tk to the Apple Macintosh and Microsoft Windows platforms. Sun would like to make Tcl/Tk for UNIX what Visual Basic is for Microsoft Windows. At the same time they promise that the core software will remain freely available.

Tcl and the Tk extensions are highly functional and have been proven to be reliable. Sophisticated graphical applications can be quickly developed. The software is free, has the industry standard Motif look and feel, and is supported by many extensions. With care, Tcl/Tk scripts can be portable across many different computer platforms. It is without doubt one of the most popular tools for implementing GUIs under UNIX today, and is being used for hundreds of freeware applications and several commercial products.

Tcl/Tk has few disadvantages. There is a need to learn a new script language, and some beginners may find some of the language features confusing. Because it is an interpreter, there is some performance penalty, but the user always has the option of coding critical functions in C.

Xt and the Athena Widgets

Many of the toolkits I have described are built on the Xt intrinsics library included as part of the standard X11 distribution. Programming at this level typically requires more effort than using a toolkit, but is certainly possible and may be a viable option for applications that are simple or for efficiency reasons cannot incur the overhead of an extra toolkit layer.

Another option is to use the Athena widgets, also included with the X distribution. This widget set was meant as an example implementation and lacks the more polished look and feel of toolkits such as Motif. However, there is a freely available "drop-in" replacement for the Athena library that adds a three-dimensional appearance that is much like Motif. Applications can be statically linked with the 3D library, or, better yet, installing the dynamic 3D Athena library replacement causes all Athena-based applications to take on the new appearance.

One commonly used program that is implemented using the Athena widgets is the GNU *ghostview* PostScript previewer.

You can find the 3D Athena widget library on any major Linux archive site, including *ftp://sunsite.unc.edu/pub/Linux/libs/* (look for files with "Xaw" in the filename).

Wine

Name: Wine
Author: various (more than 50 contributors)
Available from: *ftp://sunsite.unc.edu/pub/Linux/ALPHA/wine/*
Distribution policy: freely available

Wine is an application that lets you run Microsoft Windows 3.1 programs under Linux and X11. It offers two possibilities for multimedia applications. First, it could conceivably be used for running commercial Windows multimedia applications in emulation mode under Linux.

Wine can also be used as a Microsoft Windows compatible library. Applications that were written for the Windows API could be compiled and linked natively using the Linux compiler to run under X11. This requires that the source code for the applications be available, which is generally not the case for commercial or shareware programs.

At the time of this writing, wine was still in the early stages of development and ran only a few small Windows applications. It is unclear whether wine will ever reach the point where it could run Windows-based multimedia authoring applications. This capability would likely require that it also support some of the Windows multimedia APIs, probably a significant development effort.

The home page for the wine project can be found at the following URL: *http://daedalus.dra.hmg.gb/gale/wine/wine.html*.

COSE and CDE

UNIX has long been criticized for the lack of compatibility between its many different variants. This discrepancy has hindered application development, added to user training, and made system administration of heterogeneous systems more complex.

COSE, the Common Open Software Environment, is an initiative by the major UNIX vendors to standardize UNIX systems in a number of different areas. The first component of COSE is CDE, the Common Desktop Environment, which specifies a standard user interface for UNIX systems, including a window system, window manager, guidelines for look and feel, and some key graphical applications. The COSE desktop is based on the Motif toolkit and window manager with a number of features and tools adapted from Sun's OpenLook window system and Hewlett Packard's Visual User Environment (VUE).

The second major component of the COSE specification is for the UNIX API and includes the kernel system calls and library functions. It has been dubbed Spec1170 because it initially consisted of about 1,170 functions (it now contains more). With a standardized UNIX API, developers can write software that is portable across COSE compliant systems at the source level. The common UNIX API is based on a number of existing standards such as POSIX and XPG4.

Several vendors are now shipping systems that are compliant or partially compliant with CDE and the common UNIX API. At least two vendors are also offering CDE for Linux as a commercial product.

Future COSE work hopes to address other areas including graphics and multimedia. One interesting initiative is PWI, the Public Windows Interface. It is an attempt to make the API for Microsoft Windows a freely available specification. PWI would allow, for example, vendors to develop Windows-compatible toolkits running on UNIX.

Non-C Based X Toolkits

Most of the graphics toolkits mentioned up to now support applications written in C or C++. They are the most commonly used languages for software development under Linux, but there are a number of other languages available, several of which support graphics as part of the development environment. I only briefly mention them here.

Smalltalk is one of the so-called "pure" object-oriented languages, and traditionally is implemented as a graphical design environment. STIX (Small Talk Interface to X) adds support for the X protocol to GNU Smalltalk. Both of these are freely available from the Free Software Foundation and are also included in the Slackware distribution of Linux. Smalltalk/X is another Smalltalk implementation, which has a graphical user interface similar to commercial Smalltalk environments and is free for educational use.

Lisp was originally designed for text processing, and a Lisp interpreter forms the basis of GNU *emacs*. Several packages add graphical support to Lisp, including CLX (Common Lisp to X11 Interface), GNU Common Lisp, *Stk* (a Scheme interpreter with access to Tk), and *Winterp* (a Lisp-based prototyping environment for Motif).

SWI Prolog is a freely available package for the language that has support for X11.

Non-X11 Graphics Toolkits

While X11 is the most common window system under Linux, it is not the only one. There are some other graphics systems in use that are sometimes termed kernel-based graphics. The graphics primitives are provided in an object library that is linked to the application. The term "kernel" here refers not to the Linux kernel, but to the graphics library.

These graphics libraries typically write directly to the display hardware, giving them a speed advantage. They are also generally quite small and simple to program for, too.

The disadvantages of kernel-based graphics are that they are hardware-dependent, and the display and application must run on the same machine. Each library has a different API, and generally the functionality is much less than that provided by X. These are problems that the X Window System overcomes, at the expense of more complexity, speed, and memory requirements.

MGR

Name: MGR
Author: Stephen Uhler, Bellcore
Available from: *ftp://sunsite.unc.edu:/pub/Linux//apps/MGR/*
Distribution policy: Freely available

MGR (for ManaGeR) is a graphical windowing system. It consists of a window manager with graphics terminal emulation on a bitmapped display. MGR offers a mouse and keyboard-driven graphical user interface with multiple overlapping windows. Client programs are written for the MGR API, which supports *termcap*-like terminal control functions, graphics primitives, and a message-based client/server architecture.

MGR originated on older 8-bit and 16-bit machines such as Macintoshes, Ataris, and PCs running Minix and Coherent. It is also supported on various UNIX systems, including Linux.

In comparison to X, MGR requires fewer resources. The MGR program itself uses less than 500K of memory, and the full distribution requires only about five megabytes of disk space for all binaries, fonts, and documentation.

Included in the distribution are a number of applications, many of which have X11 counterparts. MGR-aware versions of common tools such as *emacs*, *vi*, and *Ghostscript* are also available.

Documentation consists of manpages and a reference manual. Many sample programs are included. Vincent Broman has written a MGR HOWTO document which addresses Linux-related issues; this document can be found at the ftp site, *ftp://sunsite.unc.edu/pub/Linux/docs/HOWTO/MGR-HOWTO*.

MGR's strengths are its small size, speed, and meager memory and disk space requirements.

However, there are few MGR applications, and the user base is quite small (especially on the Linux platform). With most graphics cards, only low-resolution modes are supported (320x200 mode is really ugly). In my opinion MGR is essentially an obsolete system, and really should not be considered as a viable option unless perhaps you have an old 386SX-16 system with four megabytes of RAM sitting idle, and you simply must run a windowing system on it.

SVGALib

Name: SVGALib
Author: Harm Hanemaayer
Available from: *ftp://sunsite.unc.edu:/pub/Linux/libs/graphics/svgalib125.tar.gz*
Distribution policy: Freely available

SVGALib is a low-level graphics library for VGA graphics adaptors. It originally started as VGALib, but now supports most VGA and SuperVGA video cards, including those with accelerated chipsets.

Programming of the cards is chip-specific, but the library can detect the card type at run-time and use the appropriate driver. SVGALib supports basic graphics functions for pixel plotting, line drawing, mouse and keyboard support, and virtual console switching. It can use most of the graphics modes supported by the video cards.

The package consists of header files and source code that is compiled to produce both static and shared libraries (precompiled libraries are also available). Included is a small amount of documentation, and some example programs.

Also included is GL (not to be confused with a graphics library of the same name developed by Silicon Graphics), a library of higher-level functions to draw lines, circles, boxes, and text characters. For users with EGA graphics, EGALib is an equivalent package for this older graphics card.

A number of applications for Linux have been developed or ported to run under Linux with VGALib. These include some MPEG, JPEG, and GIF graphic viewers, a frontend for GNU *Ghostscript*, and a number of games (including the shareware game *DOOM*).

The advantages of SVGALib are that it is fast, small, and quite simple to use. It is ideal for games and other "real-time" applications.

Its main disadvantage is the limited functionality: it only provides rudimentary graphics functions. Applications running under SVGALib take over the full screen, and therefore cannot integrate with other tools as is done in the multi-window X environment (it is possible to run SVGALib and X applications concurrently in separate virtual consoles, though).

Programs running under SVGALib need to be setuid to *root* in order to access the video memory. Applications must also handle the fact that end users may use graphics cards that support different graphics modes and resolutions.

Finally, the documentation is minimal and assumes some knowledge of bitmapped graphics and VGA programming techniques.

Sound Toolkits

In Chapter 14, *Programming Sound Devices*, I looked at sound programming using the API provided by the Linux kernel. Programming at this level has some disadvantages. It is low-level, requiring considerable code to implement basic sound functions. It is also non-portable, being restricted to Linux (and some other UNIX platforms, provided they use the same kernel sound drivers).

The kernel driver also does not directly support the playing of several samples simultaneously, or sharing the sound resource between different applications. It also does not lend itself well to applications that use a client/server architecture. For example, under the X Window System, an application may run on one machine but be displayed on another. If this is a multimedia application, the audio needs to be presented to the user, but with the traditional programming approach, instead the audio may come out on a server sitting in a computer room.

These are some of the problems that a sound toolkit can try to address. While nowhere near as mature and common as graphics toolkits, there are some packages available for Linux.

SoundIt

Name: SoundIt
Author: Brad Pitzel
Available from: *ftp://sunsite.unc.edu:/pub/Linux/devel/soundIt0.03.tar.gz*
Distribution policy: Freely available

SoundIt is a real-time sound mixer library. Mainly intended for adding sound effects to games, it provides a facility for playing digitized sounds. Multiple sounds can be mixed and played simultaneously up to the limit of the number of channels programmed.

The library is currently limited to 8-bit mono channels with no support for volume control, and sound files must be in raw format. It uses the real-time features of the Linux sound driver, and forks a subprocess so the calling process isn't delayed during sound playing (a necessity for real-time applications such as games).

The simple API consists of only five function calls and the library is implemented in about 500 lines of C code. It was written to add sound support for the author's *sasteroids* game.

Included are some example applications, including one that plays the unforgettable "Rapping Linus" song, which features vocals by a famous software designer from Finland.

The related package RawSeq expands on the ideas in these example applications by implementing a simple but quite powerful sequencer program for playing music using sound samples and a simple script language. Included is yet another version of "Rapping Linus." RawSeq is by Christian Bolik and can be found at *ftp://sunsite.unc.edu/pub/Linux/apps/sound/mixers/rawseq-0.1.tar.gz*.

The SoundIt library is small and efficient. While limited to playing sound samples, it can be useful for applications such as games or multimedia applications requiring simple sound effects. The documentation mentions possible enhancements; hopefully the author or others will implement some of these and make the package even more useful.

sfxserver

Name: sfxserver
Author: Terry Evans
Available from: *ftp://sunsite.unc.edu:/pub/Linux/apps/sound/players/
sfxserver-0.02.tgz*
Distribution policy: Freely available

Similar to SoundIt, the sfxserver package provides the capability for playing sound samples using multiple channels. It differs in that it is implemented as a server program, with which applications communicate using standard input and output. sfxserver supports simultaneously playing up to eight channels from a group of up to 100 sound sample files (these limits can be changed when compiling). Only 11 kHz mono raw sound sample files are supported. It also provides for stereo volume control of the samples played.

In the same directory is the sfxclient program, which illustrates how to communicate with the sfxserver program.

The capabilities of sfxserver are comparable to SoundIt, and even though it was developed independently, it comes with sound samples taken from the SoundIt package.

RPlay

Name: RPlay
Author: Mark Boyns
Available from: *ftp://ftp.sdsu.edu:/pub/rplay/*
Distribution policy: GNU GPL

The two previously described sound toolkits addressed the problem of playing multiple sounds simultaneously, but only on a single machine. Modern windowing systems such as X11 support a client/server approach in which the applications are separated into a client program that is separate from, and may be running on a different machine than the one with which the user interacts. A windowing environment also allows multiple applications to run simultaneously. For multimedia, several applications may wish to use the sound hardware simultaneously.

The RPlay toolkit attempts to solve these problems. It provides a sound server that runs as a daemon process, and accepts requests to play sound files from client programs. The sound server, much like an X server, can be located on a different machine from the client programs. The sound server accepts requests from multiple applications at one time.

Applications can communicate with the RPlay server using either of two protocols. Both are based on Berkeley sockets.

RPlay is a UDP protocol. It is a simple, unidirectional protocol with minimal overhead. The basic command to play a sound file requires only five bytes in addition to the sound file name. The API consists of seven core functions. This protocol is good for applications such as games or for low-bandwidth connections.

The RPTP protocol is based on TCP. It is a reliable bidirectional protocol in which the server sends back responses to commands. This allows finer control, for example, when defining sound file formats. The API has only four core functions.

Both protocols provide similar functionality. Sound files can be played, stopped, paused, and resumed, and parameters such as volume can be changed. Applications that use the RPlay API need to include the RPlay C header files and are linked with the RPlay library.

The distribution includes the rplayd sound sever daemon, which is typically set up to be started by the *inetd* super-daemon whenever sound requests are issued. Also included are a number of utilities and contributed applications. The documentation lists a number of X11 games that support the RPlay protocol for sound effects. Manpages and GNU info files document the API.

There is an RPlay mailing list that you join by sending email to *rplay-request@sdsu.edu* containing a line in the form "subscribe username@hostname".

RPlay successfully solves the problem of separating applications from the sound hardware and making it a shared resource. It has a simple API, runs on most common workstation platforms, and is freely available.

Its weak areas are that the functions provided are still quite low-level. It is essentially limited to playing sound files, with no support for sound input or other non-file sound sources. There is only minimal support for playing multiple sounds simultaneously.

Network Audio System

Name: Network Audio System
Authors: Jim Fulton, Greg Renda, and Dave Lemke, Network Computing
     Devices, Inc.
Available from: *ftp://ftp.x.org:/contrib/audio/nas/*
Distribution policy: Freely available

The Network Audio System (NAS) is a device-independent protocol for playing, recording, and manipulating audio over a network. It uses a client/server model, similar to the X Window System, in which a sound server acts as a shared resource for managing sound input and output devices.

It was developed by Network Computing Devices, a vendor of X terminals and X server software, and is distributed freely. The source distribution supports most major workstation platforms including Linux.

NetAudio supports playing sound files in most of the standard file formats. The server can cache sounds locally for better performance, and the API allows applications to control mixing of the audio data from the various devices. Multiple applications can share the audio devices simultaneously.

The package includes the sound server, C language library and header files, and a number of utilities and sample applications. Documentation consists of manpages and some PostScript manuals and conference papers. There is also a mailing list: send email to *nas-request@ncd.com* to find out how to join.

For users who do not wish to build the system from source code, the site *ftp://sunsite.unc.edu:/pub/Linux/apps/sound/nas-1.2p1a.bin.tar.gz* holds precompiled Linux binaries.

Some applications that support NetAudio are the games *xboing*, *xpilot*, and the Sun workstation version of the commercial game *SimCity*.

In summary, Network Audio provides a network-transparent client/server model for supporting sound, much like the X11 window system. It provides a rich library of API functions for application programmers, runs on most UNIX platforms and X terminals, and is free.

The cost of a sophisticated system is complexity—the API has over 130 functions, although basic operations can be implemented with just a few calls.

AudioFile

Name: AudioFile
Author: Digital Equipment Corporation, Cambridge Research Lab
Available from: *ftp://crl.dec.com/pub/DEC/AF/*
Distribution policy: Freely available

AudioFile is another network-transparent audio server. It was heavily influenced by the X11 model, one of the developers being part of the original X Window System design team.

Like RPlay and Network Audio, it includes a sound server, a programming API, and some contributed applications. Both the sound output and the input devices are supported.

Currently AudioFile supports only DEC, Sun, and SGI workstations. At the time of this writing, a port to FreeBSD had just been announced, but to my knowledge no Linux port has been made. There was interest on the mailing list in doing so, and it should be reasonably straightforward, but as far as I know no one has stepped forward to take on the task.

For more up-to-date information you can join the mailing list by sending email to *af-request@crl.dec.com*.

A standard sound server for X11-based UNIX systems would be very desirable, but at the time of writing there was no clear leader between RPlay, Network Audio, or AudioFile, and most workstation vendors were not shipping any sound server with their systems. It is even more unfortunate that these systems cannot co-exist with each other (and most cannot co-exist with applications that access the sound devices directly). Hopefully there will be some standardization in this area as multimedia applications become more common on UNIX systems. One interim solution taken by some software developers is to support several of the sound servers as a compile-time option, although this requires more programming effort.

CHAPTER EIGHTEEN

INTERFACE AND DEVELOPMENT CONSIDERATIONS

When starting a new software application, most developers will first do some high-level design. Often the starting point will be the user interface. At some stage coding will then start, followed by a long period of debugging, then possibly a realization that the basic design was flawed, at which point it's back to design again . . . .

Finally, at some point, your creation will be completed, and you will want to document and package it and distribute it to the world.

In this chapter I will briefly look at some of the user interface issues that should be considered when developing multimedia applications. I will then discuss some issues related to coding, packaging, and distributing your creation.

User Interface Issues

Multimedia applications by their nature often make use of a graphical user interface, which places more demands on the application developer. The event-driven style of programming graphical applications is significantly different from the more traditional data processing model that experienced programmers may be accustomed to. The application typically ends up being a collection of event handling routines that are driven by the end user's actions in no predetermined order.

Making the user interface simple for the user is one of the most difficult tasks for the programmer, but it is important because the user interface can make or break an application. A good interface will be intuitive, minimizing the need for documentation or training. A bad interface will be confusing, causing users to throw up their hands in disgust and try another application.

I'll now offer a number of guidelines and areas for you to consider when designing and implementing your interface. As every application is different, most of these are general in nature. Feel free to break the rules if you feel it is justified.

You should start by thinking about your intended audience. Is this a development tool for experienced programmers or is it aimed at non-computer users? Tailor the interface and nomenclature used to the end user's level of experience.

Is there a metaphor for a real-life object or process that you can mimic to make the interface more intuitive? One common example is a sound recording program that works like an audio tape recorder.

There is often a trade-off between ease of learning versus features for power users. One solution is to hide the more advanced, complex, or rarely used features from the main interface, either by relegating them to other windows or menus, or having different user interfaces for different types of users (with the end user able to select and change her user type).

Don't expect to design the final user interface the first time. You should be prepared to rework it based on feedback from users. If you have suitable tools, consider developing a working prototype of the GUI to get a feel for how it will work.

The use of color can add information to a user interface and can highlight important messages. It is generally a safe assumption that the end user will have a color display. You should, however, take into account differing screen resolutions. Try to ensure your program is usable whether the end user has a 640x480 256-color display or 1280x1024 24-bit video. If practical, allow the user to resize the windows to match their display. You should also allow the end user to customize the colors used. Under X11, programs usually do this by consulting the resource database—a user simply puts directives in his or her *.Xdefaults* file.

It is good practice to check for all types of errors, not only bad user input, but even things that should never happen. The C library function *assert* is one approach for checking for fatal errors, which should never occur.

You should give the user some form of feedback when performing any operations that will take a noticeable length of time, so they do not think the application has locked up or crashed. Use a pop-up window, a busy mouse cursor, or other similar methods.

You can learn a lot about user interfaces (both good and bad) by looking at other applications. You may want to imitate the look and feel of applications that are similar to, or used in conjunction with, your own. It you are using a toolkit such as Motif or OpenLook that has a published style guide, you should check your application for conformance against the standard.

Finally, finish off your application with a professional polish. Implement some form of online help, create an attractive icon, and add an "About" box listing the program version, author, and email address.

Development Guidelines

The GNU project has a coding standard document, which can be useful for Linux development, although you may not agree with all of its recommendations. You probably have it online as part of the GNU *emacs* information system. If not, it can be found on GNU ftp sites and CD-ROM archives.

The Linux kernel distribution includes a short document describing Linus Torvalds' opinions on coding standards. It can be found in the file that is called */usr/src/linux/Documentation/CodingStyle*.

Old-time C programmers should be sure to write ANSI style C code (i.e., with function prototypes), unless they need portability with the non-ANSI C compilers offered by some commercial UNIX vendors.

It is worthwhile to spend some time learning how to use the multimedia utilities for manipulating sound and image files. These include *xv*, *ImageMagick*, *sox*, and others discussed in Part III of this book. These utilities offer some audio and video effects that can make your application look more polished.

Eventually your application will reach the stage where it appears to be working. Don't neglect to spend some time testing it. As well as testing the code yourself, you might want to ask a limited group of people to act as testers to iron out any major problems before the code is released to the general public. Many developers use the notion of alpha and beta releases. Alpha releases are generally intended for potential users to get an idea of what the application will eventually do. It will typically be only partly functional, is not intended to be really usable, and the author is usually not interested in bug reports. Beta releases are for code that is thought to be working, but has been tested only by the author. Beta testers are encouraged to find and report bugs. Labeling code as a beta release also provides the developer with a good excuse to hide behind when the end users find the inevitable bugs.

Once you have tested your application, you need to package it properly for end users. The assumption here is that you are developing a free software package and will be distributing source code. Most applications are distributed as *gzip* compressed *tar* files. You should include some documentation on what the software is (typically in a README file) and how to build and install it (usually an INSTALL file). You should document it in a manpage and in longer documents if appropriate.

A *make* file should be provided to build the code, as well as install it. Normally the production version of the software should be compiled with full optimization and no debug information. When installing you should follow the recommendations of the Linux filesystem standard.

Shipping binaries is usually not a good idea because the end user may have object libraries with different and incompatible versions. This procedure is usually only acceptable if the build process requires some nonstandard compiler or other tools, and an incrementally linked object file that just needs a final link is probably the best option in this case.

You should clearly indicate the distribution policy for your software in order to protect yourself from legal liabilities and to stop others from restricting the redistribution of your code or profiting from it (if this is important to you). Many different policies are in use, and you can create your own, but some of the more common ones are:

Simple Copyright Statement
> This statement may or may not be necessary depending on the local copyright laws, but is generally a good idea if you want to keep ownership of the source code.

GNU General Public License
> Also known as the GPL or copyleft, this is the GNU distribution policy, described in the file COPYING; you probably have a copy of this in */usr/src/linux*. The Linux kernel and most utilities are released under the GPL, although some authors feel it is too restrictive. Ownership of code released under the GPL can be transferred to the Free Software Foundation, or kept under the author's copyright.

GNU Library General Public License
> This policy, the LGPL, is less restrictive that the GPL and is intended for software such as libraries that are linked with applications. The GNU C library and some GUI toolkits use this policy.

Simple Legal Disclaimer
> This is typically a statement that the software is provided without warranty, and the author is not responsible for what happens if someone uses the software.

Public Domain
> This means you give up all rights of ownership to the software. Even though the term "public domain" is often used when referring to free software, this type of distribution policy is actually quite rare.

Distribution as shareware, in which the user is requested to send a payment if the software is found useful, is not very common in the UNIX software world. What is sometimes done is to distribute the source code freely, but offer support and consulting services for a fee, generally for commercial users. Several companies have made a successful business out of supporting GNU software in this way.

Once the software is tested, and you have decided on the distribution policy, it is time to distribute it. Generally the best method is to upload it to the major Internet archive sites, assuming you have Internet ftp access. Most ftp sites have uploading policies that you should read and follow to ensure your software is accepted. You should also include a Linux Software Map entry, so it will be added to the database of Linux software. Finally, you should announce your creation with a posting to the *comp.os.linux.announce* newsgroup (and possibly others, if your software is not Linux-specific).

If you're lucky, Linux users will start trying out your application. Expect to receive email messages about bugs or suggestions for enhancements. Try to be patient with "newbies" who can't run or build your code and email you for help.

No matter how much testing you did, expect to make bug fixes. One nice thing about free software, though, is that you don't have to support it if you don't want to, and someone else might even improve it if you don't.

Who knows? If your software is useful enough, it may make its way into one of the Linux distributions and be used by hundreds or even thousands of users. If it is installed on one of the major archive sites, as a minimum, it will end up being published on the CD-ROM versions of the archive sites. Good software packages sometimes begin to develop a life of their own, continuing to evolve long after the original author has lost interest.

In the next chapter I will develop some real multimedia applications. Feel free to try the programs out, but remember, these are only beta releases, so there may be bugs!

CHAPTER NINETEEN
SOME SAMPLE MULTIMEDIA APPLICATIONS

In this chapter I present some real multimedia applications that tie together the programming concepts from previous chapters. The applications are reasonably small in order to allow them to be presented in the book, but at the same time they are meant to be large enough to be illustrative of complete working applications. I've tried to cover several very different types of applications and use different approaches in terms of the toolkits, programming languages, and overall complexity.

For each example I describe the problem being solved and some of the design decisions that led to the approach that was used, and then I outline the implementation. I'll discuss the strengths, benefits, and trade-offs of the resulting application, and suggest some potential enhancements. I encourage you to compile and run the examples and create some changes and enhancements of your own.

Complete listings are given in Appendix C, *Source Code Listings*. If you have Internet access, you can save typing and pick up any more recent changes or enhancements by loading the code from the O'Reilly & Associates ftp site referenced in the "Example Programs" section of the Preface.

MusicMachine

The Problem

The goal of this application was to create a program for playing rhythms by programming sequences of sound samples. Essentially intended for fun, it was based on what I thought an electronic drum machine might do, never having seen one.

With suitable sound sample files, it can produce drum rhythms. With other samples, it can be more akin to a rap music generator. I call it *MusicMachine*. I leave it up to you to decide whether to call it a game, a toy, or a musical instrument.

Requirements

The main requirement of the program was that it be easy and fun to use. A graphical user interface running under the X Window System was desired, allowing it to be used along with other tools like sound mixers.

As always, I would like it to be portable and low-cost, and the development effort should be minimized. I would like to be able to make use of sound files available from the Internet or on CD-ROM.

The Solution

Two key design decisions were made. The first was to use the Xforms toolkit to implement the graphical user interface. I chose to use Xforms because it is a very functional X11 toolkit and is actively being supported and enhanced by its developers. It appeared to offer graphical objects that could implement the features I required. The GUI builder also promised to reduce the development effort, and it is supported on multiple computer platforms. An additional consideration was that I had never used this toolkit for a complete application before and wanted to learn more about it.

The second major decision was to use the SoundIt toolkit to help implement the sound sample file playing capability. This toolkit supports playing and mixing multiple sound voices, which was a basic requirement of the application. The toolkit offered to save considerable development effort over coding the same functionality in C.

The user interface was initially designed on paper, going through a number of iterations as the decision proceeded. Reading through the Xforms documentation, I selected graphical objects that would be used to implement the needed features.

The next step was to create the initial prototype of the user interface using the *fdesign* GUI builder tool included with the Xforms toolkit. I found this tool very easy to use. It saved countless time that would have been spent tweaking the user interface. The code generation capability also allowed me to have a working prototype once the GUI was designed using *fdesign*. This generated skeleton code was also used as the basis for implementing the application.

As minor changes were made to the user interface, the GUI builder continued to be used. The code generated by the tool was kept in a separate file from the hand-written code, making this process very easy.

The SoundIt library, while only about 500 lines of C code, simplified the implementation significantly. It took care of loading and playing the sound samples.

One initial concern was whether the Xforms and SoundIt toolkits would work together. I encountered no problems. A related problem was how to implement the playing of sound samples at regular intervals. Here the Xforms timer object proved to be the ideal solution.

Program Description

Figure 19-1 shows some of the *MusicMachine* program in action.

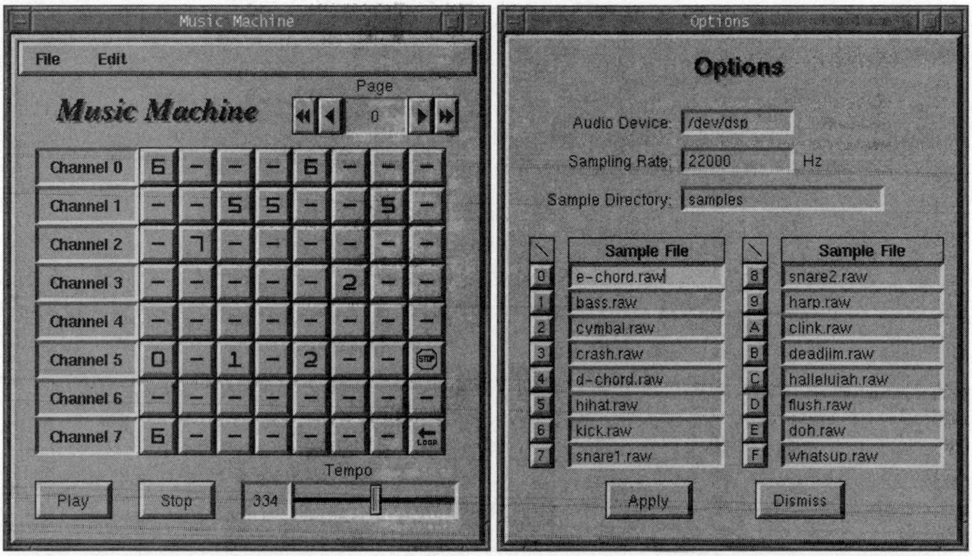

Figure 19–1: MusicMachine user interface

The application is divided into five C source files. File *soundit.c* is simply the SoundIt library source with only a few minor changes. Any statements that wrote to standard error or output were removed, as the application was to have a completely graphical user interface. One bug, described later, was also found and corrected. I made use of some of the sound samples that came with the toolkit, as well as some others from an Internet archive on CD-ROM. The *sox* tool was used to convert the sound files to the 8-bit unsigned raw format required by SoundIt. I also had to convert all samples to one common sample rate.

File *mm.c* is the code generated by the *fdesign* application generator to create the Xforms graphical objects needed. This file was regenerated several times as the GUI was modified. The 400 lines of code are quite straightforward and easy to read.

File *mm_cb.c* implements all of the callback functions for graphical objects in the application. The *fdesign* tool created the initial skeleton for this file, and the functionality was then augmented with hand-written C code.

File *mm_util.c* contains various utility functions used by the application. These could have been placed in one of the other files but were broken out into a separate source in order to reduce the amount of compilation needed during development and to make the code more modular.

The last file, *mm_main.c*, is the main program for the application. This file was also initially generated by *fdesign* and then subsequently modified slightly in order to set some fields to default values and handle some simple command-line options. Several bitmaps, used for labels on buttons, were created using the X11 *bitmap* tool.

Conclusions

I found one problem with the SoundIt library, which occurred only when used in conjunction with the Xforms toolkit. While easy to correct, it was rather subtle, so I will describe it in some detail.

I had most of the *MusicMachine* application implemented and functioning, but there was one mysterious problem. Whenever I reloaded a new set of sound samples, the program crashed with some X protocol errors. This difficulty was a concern, because the source code for Xforms was not available to me, so any problems with the toolkit itself could not easily be traced.

I knew that the problem occurred only when the SoundIt toolkit was initialized for the second time. Looking at the SoundIt source revealed that it operated by forking a child process to play the sounds. When the toolkit was reinitialized, the child process was killed and a new one created. Running my application under *strace* revealed that it was quitting because of an exception caused by writing to a closed socket. I suspected some sort of interaction between the killing of the child process used by the SoundIt libraries and the socket used for the X server, but again I did not have the source for Xforms to trace what it was doing.

Looking again at the SoundIt source, the problem became clear. The child process created to play sounds would detect the closing of the pipe that it used to communicate with its parent and would quit by calling *exit()*. However, calling *exit()* initiates a clean-up by closing all open file descriptors. In this case, this included the parent process's socket connection to the X server! This is a classic error under UNIX systems—the correct method is for the child process to call *_exit()* which does not close all open file descriptors. A simple change to the SoundIt library fixed the problem. Note that this was a problem only because I was using X11 and wanted to be able to initialize the *soundit* library more than once.

As this was an example program, I tried to keep it reasonably small. A number of enhancements easily could be made. Currently only a simple looping capability is provided. More sophisticated functions for branching, looping a specific number of times, and calling sound subroutines could easily be implemented to make the program more powerful and flexible.

Rather than creating a new sound file format (as was done here), I feel a better approach for a real-world application would be to use the existing MOD file format. Extending this application into a complete MOD file editor would make it a much more useful tool. To my knowledge no Linux-based (or UNIX-based) MOD file editors exist, so there would be considerable interest in such a project.

Overall I feel *MusicMachine* was a success. The two toolkits significantly reduced development time. Even though it is a limited example program, it is quite fun to use.

One disadvantage is the fact that the source for Xforms is not available, even though the toolkit is freely available in binary form. Fortunately I found it to be reliable and had no need to debug the toolkit. Another disadvantage is that the graphical user interface is nonstandard, but I like the look of it.

The SoundIt library also proved to be very useful. The only criticism I could note is that it is not portable to other operating systems (although you could write a compatible library). Some additional functions, such as control of volumes for each voice, would be useful.

Scope

The Problem

The concept behind this application was to take digitized sound data from a sound card and display it graphically as a plot of amplitude versus time. In effect, the program should implement a software-based oscilloscope for displaying sound waveforms, which led to its name—*scope*.

Requirements

The program had one essential requirement: to display the data in real time. In other words, the graphed data should match what was being digitized by the sound card with little or no delay.

Secondary requirements were to accept input from a sound file, to be able to control sound recording parameters such as sampling rate, and to control the display. Again, the basic requirement for speed outweighed all other factors.

The Solution

The X Window System uses a client/server architecture where the application and display can be distributed across different systems. X11-based applications also typically use several software layers, most often the Xlib library, the Xt intrinsics, and a top-level toolkit. These features make the system portable and distributed, but one of the costs is the overhead in software layers that reduces its speed and increases memory requirements. For this application I suspected that the overhead of using X would have too much impact on the real-time requirements.

Instead, I opted to use the SVGALib graphics library, which offers a much simpler and faster interface to the underlying VGA graphics hardware than X. While the functions it provides are quite low-level, they appeared adequate for this simple application.

For efficiency, the display implements the sound waveform plot and little else. Some basic features to control it were implemented as command-line options, including choosing the display color, video mode, sampling rate, and DMA divisor.

A simple graticule (a fancy name for a border around the display) can optionally be shown. The user can choose between point and line display modes to trade off speed versus display quality. A simple trigger function (a feature common on real oscilloscopes) allows waiting until the input exceeds a threshold level before displaying the waveform. The manpage, included with the software, describes all of these features and options in more detail.

I also added some enhancements over the original requirements. The ability to read from a file rather than the sound device was easy to implement. It can actually be interesting to look at non-sound files graphically.

I added support for input from a joystick. While not particularly useful, it was mainly meant to illustrate joystick programming. If you were to use, say, an appropriate thermistor in place of a joystick you might be able to use it as a chart recorder for temperature measurement.[*]

The last feature added was a screen shot option. The contents of the display can be written to a file in X bitmap format. This feature was added for one very important reason. As I was writing this chapter I realized I wanted to incorporate a screen shot of the *scope* display in the book. All of the other examples programs ran under X11 and could use standard screen shot tools. But how to dump what is on the VGA screen? I didn't find any existing tools to do this, so I implemented the functionality in the program itself. Figure 19-2 shows such a screen shot.

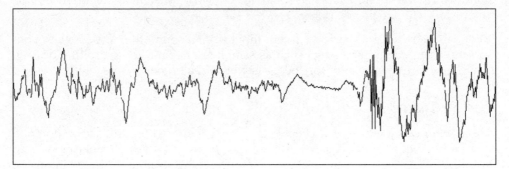

Figure 19-2: Screen shot from Scope program

---

[*] A thermistor is an electronic component that varies its electrical resistance with temperature.

Program Description

The complete program was small enough to implement as one source file of about 600 lines of C (the first working prototype was about 50 lines).

The program itself should be self-explanatory if you read the SVGALib documentation. It starts off by defining some global variables used to hold just about anything of interest in the program (we can blame this lack of structure on efficiency).

Some utility functions come next, to support showing command usage, displaying verbose output, parsing command-line options, and initializing the data points.

The function *draw_graticule* illustrates the level of graphics functions provided by SVGALib. A graticule is drawn by clearing the screen, selecting a color, and then drawing four lines. The *init_sound_card* function is illustrative of many of the sound card functions described in Chapter 14, *Programming Sound Devices*.

The *screen_dump* function generates an X bitmap file corresponding to the display by looking at each pixel. The code is a bit tedious because of the need to pack the pixels into 8-bit values in the correct order.

The function *handle_key* gets a keystroke and performs the appropriate function. It uses the convenience function *vga_getkey()* provided by SVGALib, which gets a keystroke without blocking.

Function *get_data* obtains a block of data (enough to fill the display) from a sound card or file (the function doesn't care which, as it's just a file descriptor). The trigger function, if enabled, is also implemented here, by waiting for a value outside the trigger threshold before reading the data.

A separate function, *get_joy_data*, is used to get data from the joystick because of the unique format that this device driver returns.

Function *graph_data* implements the display. If in point mode, we draw points; otherwise, we use line segments. It is necessary to first erase the previous data from the display, so we keep both the current data and the previous screen of data. This function was made inline (a GNU C language extension equivalent to the C++ keyword) in hopes of improving execution speed when the function is called.

Finally we have function *main*, which performs initialization, then runs in a loop checking for key commands, getting data, and plotting it.

Conclusions

Displaying real-time sound data takes considerable processing power, but by using SVGALib, avoiding floating-point math, and keeping the code simple, the application runs quite well even on a low-end 386 machine.

A number of enhancements could be made. A fancier display with on-screen controls and mouse support would make it look more professional. These would likely also introduce overhead that would negatively impact the performance.

It would be an interesting exercise to recode the application to use the X Window System and see if the anticipated overhead really was significant. Some optimizations, such as using the shared memory X server extensions, might overcome this problem.

It occurred to me that a frequency spectrum plot using fast Fourier transforms would be an interesting variant of this program. Before I had a chance to implement such a tool, Andrew Veliath wrote and released his excellent *svgafft* program that does just this. He also chose to use SVGALib for his implementation.

GuitarTutor

The Problem

The concept for this application was a tool to assist in learning how to play chords on the guitar. The user should be able to select a guitar chord and see a graphical display diagramming the fingering for the chord. By clicking on a button, the user can hear the sound of a guitar playing the chord.

Requirements

The basic requirements for the application were to support the functions:

- It should graphically display guitar chords using the standard notation used by most guitar chord books and sheet music.

- The program should allow chords to be defined using some sort of data file (i.e., the user must be able to add new chords without changing the source code).

- The application must play life-like guitar chords using a sound card.

- It should provide an easy-to-use graphical user interface running under the X11 windowing system.

A secondary design goal was to implement the application in C++ to gain experience in object-oriented programming.

The Solution

After looking at the requirements and thinking about some of the possible features of the application, I realized that it was an ambitious project (at least for a one-person design team). I decided to use an approach commonly used in larger projects—break the application down into several releases, each having an increasing level of functionality. This process reduces the time required to have a working application, minimizing the risk of failure.

Release 1 would support only the minimum level of functionality required for a useful tool. These features were determined to be the following:

- It would offer a graphical user interface.

- It would implement a display of chords.

- It would support playing chords (using separate sound samples for each chord).

- It would support a small number of guitar chords (approximately 20).

- It would allow the user to create new chords by editing an ASCII data file.

The following additional features would be implemented in Release 2:

- The ability to edit and create new chords from the GUI

- More sophisticated chord diagrams

- The ability to print chord diagrams to a PostScript file or printer

- A larger database of chords (approximately 100)

- A method to allow the user to hear either a complete guitar chord or the individual notes making up the chord

The most complex and least critical features were slated for a possible Release 3. Some features were quite vague and possibly impractical to implement. This was the feature list:

- An online help system

- The ability to annotate the chord diagrams with arbitrary text

- Printing of multiple chord diagrams in a nicely formatted "book" form

- Synthesized sound (e.g., chords generated by scaling and mixing sound samples rather than one sample for each chord)

- The ability to change the characteristics of the played sound (e.g., electric vs. acoustic guitar, volume, and various effects)

- Support for a larger database of chords (potentially several thousand)

- Support for multiple fingerings (different ways of playing the same chord)

- The ability to show chords while playing songs, possibly using MIDI files

- Ports to other operating systems such as SunOS and Microsoft Windows

Shortly before the project was started, I saw an announcement on the Internet for a new GUI toolkit called *V*. As this toolkit was C++ based and supported X11, it looked like a good solution for implementing the design. It also offered multiple platform support, potentially allowing the application to run under other windowing systems, and it was released under the GNU library general public license.

After defining the requirements and the toolkit being used, I proceeded with the design. I first spent some time reviewing the capabilities of the V toolkit and understanding its programming model. I then created a sketch of the user interface on paper, working out the graphical buttons, menus, and other objects needed.

The recommended way to start a V application is to start with the "tutor" example application included with the toolkit. I did this, modifying it to create a mostly nonfunctional but executable version of the *GuitarTutor* user interface. Being able to play with the user interface allowed me to try some different approaches to see what was workable. For example, the chord selection function was tested using the V list, spinner, and combo box objects to see which was preferable.

Design then shifted to the key functions needed, starting with the format for the data file defining the guitar chord database. I designed a C++ class to manage the guitar chord and sound data, including support to load and save the data files. A member function was written to support the playing of digitized sound files. This class I tested and debugged on its own by writing a small main program that exercised the data structures and member functions.

With the GUI and chord data functions implemented, the two were integrated together, and the remainder of the functionality was implemented. When possible, one feature at a time was implemented and tested before moving on to another.

Program Description

All of the features for release 1 were implemented. Most of the source code is listed in Appendix C. The full distribution, available from the Internet, includes sound sample files, *make* file, and everything else needed to build the application. Figure 19-3 shows the main window of the application.

The source code resides in five C++ source files and associated header files, totaling less than 1000 lines of code. The structure of the application closely follows the V tutor application that was used as a starting point.

Some simple sound samples were created to make the application usable. They use 8-bit unsigned data with an 8 kHz sampling rate and were recorded using a microphone and an acoustic guitar.

At a high level the code uses the V toolkit's object-oriented design philosophy. I still used some C programming techniques, such as the use of `char *` strings rather than the *String* class provided by the GNU g++ library. I did make use of the C++ *iostream* class for input and output.

Figure 19–3: GuitarTutor main window

Conclusions

Overall I consider *GuitarTutor* to be a success. I found the V toolkit easy to use, reliable, well documented, and without a steep learning curve. It does perhaps lack a few of the more obscure features that some toolkits offer (e.g., non-rectangular buttons and being able to specify the exact placement of objects). The well-commented *tutor* application made a very good starting point for creating my program.

Even though V has no GUI builder (the source code hints that one is in the works), I found it easy to design the user interface. The toolkit takes care of most of the placement and scaling of objects on the screen. It was not very difficult to implement scaling of the guitar chords to the screen when the window was resized by the user. With some toolkits, this rescaling is difficult or impossible to do.

The multiplatform capability of the toolkit is a potentially useful feature, allowing applications to run on other operating systems and windowing systems.

CHAPTER TWENTY
CONCLUSIONS

By now you should have a good understanding of what multimedia is and the key technologies involved. You've most likely configured your system for sound and CD-ROM support and looked at some of the existing Linux multimedia applications. I hope you've also tried some of the example programs listed in the book and perhaps modified them to test your understanding. If you've managed to stay with me this far, I hope that you now feel confident and motivated to develop some new multimedia applications of your own for Linux. Or perhaps you just have a better appreciation of the areas where you need to do more study.

Both Linux and multimedia technology are moving quickly. In this last chapter I was tempted to make some predictions on where I thought multimedia and Linux are headed in the future. Fortunately, I resisted the temptation, realizing that by the time you read this book, most of my predictions would likely already either be proven right (making them useless) or wrong (making me look foolish).

It is clear, however, that processor speeds and disk capacities will continue to increase and that multimedia applications are going to expand to make use of this new horsepower. The Internet will also continue to grow in popularity and evolve to support the increased number of users and demand for greater bandwidth.

What is less clear is how Linux will fit into the future of computing, and of multimedia in general. Will it die? Will it take over the world? In my opinion, probably neither. The momentum of Linux is such that I believe it cannot be stopped. I see a number of challenges ahead for Linux as a multimedia platform, though.

As new hardware devices such as MPEG decoding cards become more common, new Linux kernel drivers will be needed. Developing these drivers will be difficult if the hardware vendors refuse to open up their designs and make programming information available. I can see three possible scenarios for the future.

In the worst-case scenario, vendors will refuse to document their new hardware, or do so only under non-disclosure agreements, offering drivers for commercial operating systems only. These restrictions will effectively make support for these devices impossible, locking Linux out of the newest and most exciting developments in multimedia hardware.

In a second scenario, the situation could continue much as it is today, where some vendors agree (possibly after much pleading from Linux users) to provide the necessary information so that some unpaid but enterprising Linux developers can write the necessary drivers for Linux.

In an ideal world the hardware vendors themselves would offer and support Linux kernel drivers for their new devices, or at least sponsor the development of the drivers by others with donations of hardware and software development kits. Some progressive hardware vendors have already done this, realizing that the Linux platform can be a significant market. I hope that this trend continues.

Another important issue that will affect Linux (and other operating systems) is the development of standards. Using CD-ROM interfaces as an example, the first generation of drives used proprietary interfaces. In order for Linux to support six different types of CD-ROM drives, six different hardware interfaces needed to be understood and kernel drivers written for each of them. Linux users with an unsupported drive were either out of luck, or had to write a kernel driver themselves, which is a significant undertaking.

Most second-generation CD-ROM drives now use the enhanced IDE ATAPI standard. By adopting a single standard, only one kernel driver need be written to support dozens of models of hardware. More effort can be spent on developing and enhancing this one driver. Everyone benefits—the users, the software developers, and the hardware vendors. Some vendors, however, still cling to the belief that a proprietary product will generate more revenue by reducing their competition.

Another reason for proprietary solutions is emerging technologies. When a vendor develops a new product it typically offers some new technological advance. If successful, the technology can become a *de facto* standard in a short period of time. Formal standards developed by standards bodies generally take longer to be finalized (some people would even argue that the approval of a standard indicates that a technology has become obsolete).

Standards need not be *de facto*. More recent multimedia standards developed by groups such as MPEG actually precede products that implement the technology. I believe this is the approach that will help the industry move ahead.

Thus, the greatest challenge I see for Linux as a multimedia platform is the fight for open standards and resistance to proprietary solutions so that software drivers and successful applications can be developed.

Up until now, Linux has developed at a rapid pace, while still generally being of exceptionally high reliability and offering some unique architectural features, thanks to the many talented software designers who contributed to it. In order for Linux to continue to be on the leading edge of technology, this support needs to continue. With the growing popularity of Linux, particularly among educational institutions and researchers, I believe this process will continue.

Where Linux goes now is in the hands of the users and developers, who, in many cases, are one and the same. In this respect, the best way to predict the future is to invent it.

PART FIVE

APPENDIXES

Included here is some additional reference material. Appendix A, *What Is Linux?*, is a brief description of what Linux is, where it originated, and what it contains. Appendix B, *Linux Resources*, lists a number of resources related to Linux and multimedia, including the names of CD-ROM vendors, Internet-related information sources, and printed documentation. Appendix C, *Source Code Listings*, contains source code listings for the complete multimedia applications described in Chapter 19, *Some Sample Multimedia Applications*. Finally, there's a glossary of terms used in the book.

WHAT IS LINUX?

L inux is a computer operating system, a piece of software that manages computing resources and acts as the foundation on which to run application software, the computer programs that are used to serve some useful purpose.

The heart of Linux, the kernel, was developed by Finnish university student Linus Torvalds with help from many volunteers around the world working together and communicating via the Internet.

Linux is based on the UNIX operating system, but does not contain any source code from UNIX. It is mostly compatible with the IEEE POSIX standards as well as many common extensions taken from BSD and System V versions of UNIX. Linux also sports a number of unique features.

Linux is a multiuser, multitasking operating system that supports a 32-bit demand-paged virtual memory system. It runs on Intel PCs that have a 386 or better processor. It supports virtually all of the common PC hardware including hard and floppy disks, video cards, and network interfaces. Linux is also in various stages of being ported to a number of other common computer architectures including Motorola 68K, MIPS, DEC Alpha, Power PC, and Sun SPARC.

The key feature that distinguishes Linux from other operating systems is that the source code is freely available under the terms of the GNU General Public License, or GPL. While the authors still retain copyright to the source code, the GPL ensures that Linux can be freely distributed, modified, and even sold provided that the source code remains freely redistributable.

Linux is most commonly acquired as a distribution on floppy disk, CD-ROM, tape, or by anonymous ftp over the Internet. Distributions typically include language compilers, editors, utilities, documentation, a graphical user interface—in short, everything needed for a working system. Virtually all of the software is freely available. Many of the utilities were developed by the Free Software Foundation as part of the GNU project. A number of commercial software applications are also offered for Linux. Most applications written for UNIX systems are also easily ported to run under Linux.

Over 2000 pages of freely available documentation has been created by the Linux Documentation Project, and several books have been published on the subject. More than a dozen vendors sell Linux distributions on CD-ROM.

Linux compares favorably to commercial UNIX and offers many advantages over alternative operating systems for PCs. There is estimated to be at least several hundred thousand Linux users world-wide, possibly several million, and the number is growing.

LINUX RESOURCES

L isted here are a number of resources that are relevant either to Linux or multimedia. I've arranged them according to the type of material. Many of these references come from the Internet. Most of the development and discussion of Linux occurs over the Internet, so being plugged into the Net is practically mandatory for serious users and developers.

The Internet related references are all subject to change and cannot be guaranteed to be valid due to the dynamic nature of the Net. It is recommended you also use one of the many World Wide Web search engines to help find information specific to your needs.

Linux and Multimedia CD-ROM Vendors

The following companies sell Linux distributions on CD-ROM. Most also offer one or more of multimedia-related CD-ROMs, Linux and UNIX books, software, T-shirts, technical support, and consulting services. O'Reilly & Associates sells Linux on two CD-ROMs with the book entitled *Running Linux Companion CD-ROM*.

> ACC Bookstore
> 136 Riverside Avenue
> Westport, CT 06880
> USA
> email: *info@acc-corp.com*
> WWW: *http://www.redhat.com/*
> TEL: 1-800-546-7274, 1-203-454-5500
> FAX: 1-203-454-2582

> Caldera, Inc.
> 931 W. Center St.
> Orem, Utah 84057
> USA
> email: *info@caldera.com*
> WWW: *http://www.caldera.com/*
> TEL: 1-800-850-7779, 1-801-342-3455
> FAX: 1-801-342-3401

CHAOS Computing
8450 Ann Mari Tr.
Intver Grove Heights, MN 55077
USA
email: *info@chaoscomp.com*
WWW: *http://www.chaoscomp.com/*
FTP: *ftp://ftp.chaoscomp.com/*
TEL: 1-612-552-1920

CraftWork Solutions
4320 Stevens Creek Blvd, Suite 170
San Jose, CA 95129
USA
email: *info@craftwork.com*
WWW: *http://www.craftwork.com/*
TEL: 1-800-985-1878

DoubleDisk
19 rue des Oiseaux
91130 Ris Orangis
France
TEL: (33 1) 42 78 64 64
FAX: (33 1) 69 06 80 15

Infomagic
11950 N. Highway 89
Flagstaff, AZ 86004
USA
email: *info@infomagic.com*
WWW: *http://www.infomagic.com/*
FTP: *ftp://ftp.infomagic.com/*
TEL: 1-800-800-6613
FAX: 1-520-526-9573

Just Computers!
P.O. Box 751414
Petaluma, CA 94975-1414
USA
email: *sales@justcomp.com*
WWW: *http://www.justcomp.com/*
TEL: 1-800-800-1648, 1-707-586-5600
FAX: 1-707-586-5606

Lasermoon Ltd.
The Forge
Fareham Road
Wickham, Hants PO16 0QB
England
email: *info@lasermoon.co.uk*
FTP: *ftp://ftp.lasermoon.co.uk/*
TEL: 1329 834 944

O'Reilly & Associates, Inc.
103A Morris Street
Sebastapol, CA 95472
USA
email: *nuts@ora.com*
WWW: *http://www.ora.com/*
FTP: *ftp://ftp.ora.com/*
TEL: 1-800-998-9938
FAX: 1-707-829-0104

Pacific HiTech
3855 South 500 West, Suite M
Salt Lake City, Utah 84115
USA
email: *info@pht.com*
WWW: *http://www.pht.com/*
FTP: *ftp://ftp.pht.com/*
TEL: 1-800-765-8369, 1-801-261-1024
FAX: 1-801-261-0310

Prime Time Freeware
370 Altair Way, Suite 150
Sunnyvale, CA 94086
USA
email: *ptf@cfcl.com*
WWW: *http://www.ptf.com/ptf/*
TEL: 1-408-433-9662
FAX: 1-408-433-0727

Red Hat Software, Inc.
Durham, NC
USA
email: *info@redhat.com*
WWW: *http://www.redhat.com/*
TEL: 1-800-454-5502, 1-203-454-5500
FAX: 1-203-454-2582

SSC, Inc.
P.O. Box 55549
Seattle, WA 98155
USA
email: *sales@ssc.com*
WWW: *http://www.ssc.com/*
TEL: 1-206-782-7733
FAX: 1-206-782-7191

S.u.S.E Linux
Gebhardtstrasse 2
D-90762 Furth
Germany
email: *suse@suse.de*
WWW: *http://www.suse.de/*
TEL: +49-911-7405331
FAX: +49-911-7417755

Trans-Ameritech Systems
2342A Walsh Ave.
Santa Clara, CA 95051
USA
email: *order@trans-am.com*
TEL: 1-408-727-3883
FAX: 1-408-727-3882

Walnut Creek CD-ROM
4041 Pike Lane, Suite D-902
Concord, CA 94520
USA
email: *info@cdrom.com*
WWW: *http://www.cdrom.com/*
FTP: *ftp://ftp.cdrom.com/*
TEL: 1-510-674-0783
FAX: 1-510-674-0821

Workgroup Solutions
P.O. Box 460190
Aurora, CO 80046-0190
USA
email: *info@wgs.com*
WWW: *http://www.wgs.com/*
FTP: *ftp://ftp.wgs.com/*
TEL: 1-303-699-7470
FAX: 1-303-699-2793

Yggdrasil Computing, Inc.
4880 Stevens Creek Blvd., Suite 205
San Jose, California 95129-1034
USA
email: *info@yggdrasil.com*
WWW: *http://www.yggdrasil.com/*
TEL: 1-800-261-6630, 1-408-261-6630
FAX: 1-408-261-6631

Usenet News Groups

Listed here are some Usenet newsgroups relevant to Linux and multimedia. Where there is a whole hierarchy of relevant groups, I've indicated a wildcard (e.g., *comp.os.linux.**). Depending on your news feed you may or may not receive these groups and others. Also check for any regional newsgroups in your area.

alt.binaries.multimedia
Multimedia binaries

alt.cd-rom.*
Unofficial CD-ROM groups

alt.uu.comp.os.linux.questions
Part of Usenet University

comp.emulators.ms-windows.wine
The WINE project

comp.graphics.*
Various computer graphics groups

comp.infosystems.*
Includes WWW, Gopher, WAIS

comp.lang.java
Java language

comp.multimedia
General multimedia topics

comp.music.midi
MIDI and computer music

comp.os.linux.*
All the Linux specific groups

comp.publish.cdrom.*
CD-ROM publishing

comp.soft-sys.*
    Various software toolkits

comp.sources.unix
    UNIX source code

comp.std.unix
    UNIX standardization

comp.sys.ibm.pc.soundcard.*
    PC sound card information

comp.unix.*
    All the UNIX-specific groups

comp.windows.*
    Various GUI toolkits

comp.windows.x.*
    X11 news groups

gnu.*
    GNU groups

Internet ftp Sites

These are some of the primary archive sites for Linux software. Sunsite is the largest and is often very slow because of heavy use. You can use one of the alternate sites that mirrors sunsite (see the file MIRRORS), preferably one that is geographically close to you.

ftp://ftp.x.org/
    X Consortium home site

ftp://nic.funet.fi/pub/OS/Linux/
    Linus' home site in Finland

ftp://prep.ai.mit.edu/pub/gnu/
    Primary GNU site

ftp://rtfm.mit.edu/pub/usenet/
    Archive of Usenet news FAQ documents

ftp://sunsite.unc.edu/pub/Linux/
    Largest Linux archive

ftp://tsx-11.mit.edu/pub/linux/
    Another large Linux archive

World Wide Web Sites

Listed here are some primary sites on the World Wide Web for information related to Linux, UNIX, and multimedia.

Linux Sites

http://www.cs.helsinki.fi/linux/
  University of Helsinki, Finland

http://gandalf.pht.com/linux-int/
  Linux International

http://sunsite.unc.edu/mdw/linux.html
  Linux Documentation Project

http://www.blackdown.org/java-linux.html
  The Java-Linux Porting Project

http://www.linux.org/
  The Linux Home Page

http://www.redhat.com/lg/gazette_toc.html
  The Linux Gazette

http://www.silkroad.com/lds/lds.html
  Linux Users Directory

Sound Card Vendors

http://www.aztechca.com/
  Aztech Labs

http://www.creaf.com/
  Creative Labs

http://www.diamondmm.com/
  Diamond Multimedia

http://www.ensoniq.com/
  Ensoniq

http://www.gravis.com/
  Advanced Gravis

http://www.mediavis.com/
  Mediavision

http://www.orchid.com/
    Orchid

http://www.tbeach.com/
    Turtle Beach

Multimedia Related

http://personal.eunet.fi/pp/voxware/
    Hannu Savolainen's UNIX Sound System Lite home page

http://www.4front-tech.com/
    4Front Technologies home page

http://java.sun.com/
    Sun Java Site

http://rosebud.sdsc.edu/vrml/
    VRML Repository

http://viswiz.gmd.de/MultimediaInfo/
    Index of Multimedia Information Sources

http://vrml.wired.com/
    Virtual Reality Modeling Language (VRML) Forum

http://www.cen.com/mw3/
    Motif on the World Wide Web

http://www.debian.org/
    The Debian Project

http://www.ncsa.uiuc.edu/General/VRML/VRMLHome.html
    NCSA VRML Home Page

http://www.osf.org/
    OSF Home Page

http://www.smli.com/research/tcl/
    Tcl/Tk Project at Sun Microsystems

http://www.x.org/
    X Consortium Home Page

http://www.xfree86.org/
    XFree86 Home Page

http://www.iuma.com/
    Internet Underground Music Archive

Miscellaneous

http://www.ieee.org/
   IEEE home page

http://www.ora.com/
   O'Reilly & Associates, Inc. home page

Printed Documentation

The following books were referenced in the main body of this book:

Linux Network Administrator's Guide
   by Olaf Kirch, O'Reilly & Associates

Multimedia Applications Development with the Andrew Toolkit
   by Nathaniel Borenstein, Prentice-Hall

OI Programmer's Guide: Version 4, Second Edition
   by Amber Benson and Gary Aitken, Prentice-Hall

Running Linux, Second Edition
   by Matt Welsh and Lar Kaufman, O'Reilly & Associates

Tcl and the Tk Toolkit
   by John Ousterhout, Addison-Wesley

A number of introductory books on Linux are available from several publishers. A few of them are very well-written, but in my experience many of them appear to have been quickly thrown together, are full of errors and out of date information, and are often just a rehash of an existing UNIX book. One should also watch out for CD-ROMs included in these books; they often contain incomplete and/or obsolete versions of Linux. *Caveat emptor.*

If Linux is your first exposure to UNIX-like operating systems, most good books on UNIX are useful for learning the basics, and most of the information should be applicable to Linux.

In my biased opinion, the best introductory Linux book is *Running Linux*. It covers just about everything, from installation to programming tools. The *Linux Network Administrator's Guide* provides detailed coverage of networking under Linux, including connecting to the Internet, electronic mail, and news.

Linux Journal is a monthly magazine devoted entirely to Linux. I highly recommend getting a subscription; it's an excellent way to keep up-to-date on the latest Linux developments. *Linux Journal* is published by SSC, Inc. See the CD-ROM vendor section for their address.

A more general publication devoted to multimedia is *IEEE Multimedia*. See the previous section for a pointer to its Web site. You may be able to borrow a copy from a local university or corporate library. The articles can be quite technical, so for something lighter and of more general interest you might want to check out *Wired* magazine. You can reach them by email at *info@wired.com*.

The Linux Documentation Project is a group of volunteers devoted to developing free documentation for Linux. Documentation currently includes:

- More than 50 HOWTOs—short documents on specific Linux topics (e.g., setting up a printer)

- Several full-length books, including *Linux Installation and Getting Started*, which covers just about everything the Linux newbie needs to know

- The Linux manpages

The Sound and CD-ROM HOWTOs are particularly relevant for multimedia users.

In all, there are over 2000 pages of documentation, not including the manpages. Most of these documents are available in ready-to-print PostScript format, ASCII text, and HTML via the Internet. You also usually find them on Linux CD-ROM distributions. Several companies sell printed copies under various names (e.g., *The Linux Bible*). If you want hard copies, buying them can save a lot of wear and tear on your printer.

Other Sources

It is almost impossible to keep up with the articles posted to the Linux Usenet newsgroups. Most of the developers communicate using a number of email mailing lists on various topics (sometimes called "channels"). The lists with high traffic can also be subscribed as a digest, a compilation of all the day's email messages, which is only sent once per day. You can find out how to join the lists by sending a mail message with the work "help" as the message body to *MajorDomo@vger.rutgers.edu.*[*]

The Linux software map is an attempt to create a database of all Linux software. If you have browsed any archive sites, you have probably seen these "lsm" files. The latest database file can be found at *ftp://sunsite.unc.edu/pub/Linux/docs/LSM.gz*.

Finally, find out if there is a local Linux user group in your area. Some of these groups are very active and can be of invaluable help to new users. If there is no user group, consider starting one.

---

[*] At the time of this writing, these mailing lists were extremely overloaded, and the maintainer was looking for an alternate site.

SOURCE CODE LISTINGS

This section includes source listings for the complete multimedia applications described in Chapter 19, *Some Sample Multimedia Applications*. Some support files are not included, because they are too long or can't be easily shown in printed form. The files I left out include items such as icon bitmaps, make files, documentation, and sound samples. All of the files, including any later updates or corrections, are available by anonymous ftp from the O'Reilly & Associates' site, located at *ftp://ftp.ora.com/pub/examples/linux/multimedia*. Directions for obtaining the examples are in the "Example Programs" section of the Preface. Information on this book in particular, and O'Reilly & Associates' publications in general, can be found on the World Wide Web at *http://www.ora.com/*. All of the source code is released under the terms of the GNU General Public License.

MusicMachine

This is the source for *MusicMachine*. If you want to run it, get the code from the Internet site listed above. It includes the sound samples, bitmaps, and sample songs that can't be listed here. It also has the data file for the *fdesigner* GUI builder tool used in conjunction with the XForms toolkit. Due to space restrictions, I have omitted the files that were generated by the GUI builder and the source for the *SoundIt* toolkit.

Example C-1: mm_cb.c

```
/*
 * This file contains the callback routines for MusicMachine
 */

#include <assert.h>

#include "forms.h"
#include "mm.h"
#include "soundit.h"
#include "mm_util.h"

/* array containing notes for all channels */
int notes[NUM_CHANNELS][NUM_PAGES*NUM_CHANNELS];
```

Example C-1: mm_cb.c (continued)

```c
/* current position in notes array for each channel */
int pos[NUM_CHANNELS];

/* flags indicating if a channel is stopped */
int stopped[NUM_CHANNELS];

/* main window file menu */
void file_menu_cbk(FL_OBJECT *ob, long data)
{
  const char *filename;

  switch (fl_get_menu(ob)) {
  case 1: /* load */
    filename = fl_show_fselector("Load from file:", "", "", "");
    if (filename != 0)
      load_sample_file(filename);
    break;
  case 2: /* save */
    filename = fl_show_fselector("Save to file:", "", "", "");
    if (filename != 0) {
      save_sample_file(filename);
      fl_invalidate_fselector_cache();
    }
    break;
  case 3: /* new */
    if (fl_show_question("Clear the current patterns?", 0, 0)) {
      clear_samples();
      update_bitmaps();
    }
    break;
  case 4: /* about */
    fl_show_form(about_window, FL_PLACE_CENTER, FL_FULLBORDER, "About");
    break;
  case 5: /* quit */
    if (fl_show_question("Do you want to quit?", 0, 0)) {
      Snd_restore();
      exit(0);
    }
    break;
  default:
    assert(0); /* should never happen */
  }
}

/* main window edit menu */
void edit_menu_cbk(FL_OBJECT *ob, long data)
{
  /* only menu item is "options" */
  fl_show_form(sample_window, FL_PLACE_CENTER, FL_FULLBORDER, "Options");
}
```

Example C-1: mm_cb.c (continued)

```c
/* play button */
void play_button_cbk(FL_OBJECT *ob, long data)
{
  int i;

  /* reset position to the start for all channels */
  for (i = 0 ; i < NUM_CHANNELS ; i++) {
    pos[i] = 0;
    stopped[i] = 0;
  }

  /* start timer object by giving it a very small non-zero value */
  fl_set_timer(timer, 0.001);
}


/* tempo slider */
void tempo_slider_cbk(FL_OBJECT *ob, long data)
{
  /* nothing to do */
}


/* used by callbacks for rhythm buttons for all channels */
void channel_callback(FL_OBJECT *ob, long data, int channel)
{
  /* get current value */
  int i = (int) data + SAMPLES_PER_PAGE * (int) fl_get_counter_value(page);

  /* see which mouse button was pushed */
  switch (fl_get_button_numb(ob)) {
  case 1:
    /* increment value */
    notes[channel][i]++;
    break;
  case 2:
    /* note value becomes a rest */
    notes[channel][i] = REST;
    break;
  case 3:
    /* decrement value */
    notes[channel][i]--;
    break;
  default:
    assert(0); /* should never happen */
  }

  /* wrap around when first or last value reached */
  if (notes[channel][i] == STOP-1)
    notes[channel][i] = 16;
  if (notes[channel][i] > NUM_SAMPLES)
    notes[channel][i] = STOP;
```

Example C-1: mm_cb.c (continued)

```
    update_bitmap(ob, notes[channel][i]);
}

/* rhythm buttons for channel 0 */
void channel_0_cbk(FL_OBJECT *ob, long data)
{
    channel_callback(ob, data, 0);
}

/* rhythm buttons for channel 1 */
void channel_1_cbk(FL_OBJECT *ob, long data)
{
    channel_callback(ob, data, 1);
}

/* rhythm buttons for channel 2 */
void channel_2_cbk(FL_OBJECT *ob, long data)
{
    channel_callback(ob, data, 2);
}

/* rhythm buttons for channel 3 */
void channel_3_cbk(FL_OBJECT *ob, long data)
{
    channel_callback(ob, data, 3);
}

/* rhythm buttons for channel 4 */
void channel_4_cbk(FL_OBJECT *ob, long data)
{
    channel_callback(ob, data, 4);
}

/* rhythm buttons for channel 5 */
void channel_5_cbk(FL_OBJECT *ob, long data)
{
    channel_callback(ob, data, 5);
}

/* rhythm buttons for channel 6 */
void channel_6_cbk(FL_OBJECT *ob, long data)
{
    channel_callback(ob, data, 6);
}

/* rhythm buttons for channel 7 */
void channel_7_cbk(FL_OBJECT *ob, long data)
{
    channel_callback(ob, data, 7);
}
```

Example C-1: mm_cb.c (continued)

```c
/* page button */
void page_button_cbk(FL_OBJECT *ob, long data)
{
  /* the button itself updates the page number, we just need to update
     the display */
  update_bitmaps();
}

/* stop button */
void stop_button_cbk(FL_OBJECT *ob, long data)
{
  /* stop timer by giving it a zero value */
  fl_set_timer(timer, 0);
}

/* callback for timer */
void timer_cbk(FL_OBJECT *ob, long data)
{
  int ch;

  for (ch = 0 ; ch < NUM_CHANNELS ; ch++)
    /* play sound for this channel if it is a note and channel has not
       been stopped */
    if (notes[ch][pos[ch]] > 0 &&
        notes[ch][pos[ch]] <= NUM_SAMPLES &&
        !stopped[ch])
      Snd_effect(notes[ch][pos[ch]] - 1, ch);

  /* advance to next position */
  for (ch = 0 ; ch < NUM_CHANNELS ; ch++) {
    pos[ch]++;

    /* wrap around at end */
    if (pos[ch] >= NUM_PAGES*SAMPLES_PER_PAGE)
      pos[ch] = 0;

    /* check for loop back to start */
    if (notes[ch][pos[ch]] == LOOP)
      pos[ch] = 0;

    /* check for stop */
    if (notes[ch][pos[ch]] == STOP)
      stopped[ch] = 1;
  }

  /* set timer for next time, tempo is in beats per minute */
  fl_set_timer(ob, 60.0 / fl_get_slider_value(tempo));
}

/* sample file entry */
```

Example C-1: mm_cb.c (continued)

```c
void sample_file_cbk(FL_OBJECT *ob, long data)
{
  char file[256];
  char msg[256];

  /* make sure file exists */
  strcpy(file, fl_get_input(sample_dir));
  strcat(file, "/");
  strcat(file, fl_get_input(ob));

  if (!file_exists(file)) {
    sprintf(msg, "Sample file \"%s\" does not exist.", file);
    fl_show_alert("Warning:",
                  msg,
                  "Enter a valid sample file name and try again.",
                  0);
  }
}


/* apply button */
void samples_apply_cbk(FL_OBJECT *ob, long data)
{
  /* reload new set of samples and parameters */
  init_samples();
}

/* options dismiss button */
void samples_dismiss_cbk(FL_OBJECT *ob, long data)
{
  /* make window go away */
  fl_hide_form(sample_window);
}

/* audio device entry field */
void audio_device_cbk(FL_OBJECT *ob, long data)
{
  char msg[256];
  const char *file = fl_get_input(ob);

  if (!file_exists(file)) {
    sprintf(msg, "Sample device \"%s\" does not exist.", file);
    fl_show_alert("Warning:",
                  msg,
                  "Enter a valid sample device file name and try again.",
                  0);
  }
}

/* sampling rate entry field */
void sampling_rate_cbk(FL_OBJECT *ob, long data)
```

Example C-1: mm_cb.c (continued)

```
{
  /* do a simple range check */
  int rate = atoi(fl_get_input(sampling_rate));
  if (rate < 4000 || rate > 45000)
    fl_show_alert("Warning:",
                  "Invalid sample rate.",
                  "Enter a decimal number between 4000 and 45000",
                  0);
}


/* buttons next to each sample file */
void test_sample_cbk(FL_OBJECT *ob, long data)
{
  /* play the sample passed to callback */
  Snd_effect(data, data % NUM_CHANNELS);
}


/* callback for sample directory entry field */
void sample_dir_cbk(FL_OBJECT *ob, long data)
{
  const char *file = fl_get_input(ob);
  char msg[256];

  if (!file_exists(file)) {
    sprintf(msg, "Sample directory \"%s\" does not exist.", file);
    fl_show_alert("Warning:",
                  msg,
                  "Enter a valid directory name and try again.",
                  0);
  }
}


/* about dismiss button */
void about_dismiss_cbk(FL_OBJECT *obj, long data)
{
  /* make window go away */
  fl_hide_form(about_window);
}
```

Example C-2: mm_main.c

```
/*
 * Music Machine application main program
 */

#include "forms.h"
#include "mm.h"
#include "mm_util.h"

int main(int argc, char *argv[])
```

Example C-2: mm_main.c (continued)

```
{

  /* initialize xforms toolkit */
  fl_initialize(argv[0], "Mm", 0, 0, &argc, argv);

  /* create the forms for windows */
  create_the_forms();

  /* set fields to default values */
  fl_set_input(audio_device, "/dev/dsp");
  fl_set_input(sampling_rate, "22000");
  fl_set_input(sample_dir, ".");
  fl_set_slider_bounds(tempo, 60, 600);
  fl_set_slider_value(tempo, 240);
  fl_set_slider_step(tempo, 1);
  fl_set_slider_precision(tempo, 0);
  fl_set_counter_bounds(page, 0, 31);
  fl_set_counter_value(page, 0);
  fl_set_counter_step(page, 1, 8);
  fl_set_counter_precision(page, 0);
  fl_set_menu(file_menu, "Load|Save|New|About%l|Quit");
  fl_set_menu(edit_menu, "Options");
  fl_set_goodies_font(FL_NORMAL_STYLE, FL_NORMAL_SIZE);
  update_bitmaps();

  /*
   * error if more than one command line parameter (forms library has
   * already swallowed any parameters it recognizes)
   */
  if (argc > 2) {
    fprintf(stderr, "usage: mm [song-file]\n");
    exit(1);
  }

  /* load any filename on command line */
  if (argc == 2)
    load_sample_file(argv[1]);

  /* show the first form */
  fl_show_form(main_window,FL_PLACE_CENTER,FL_FULLBORDER,"Music Machine");

  /* call event handler loop */
  fl_do_forms();

  return 0;
}
```

Example C-3: mm_util.h

```
#ifndef MM_UTIL_H
#define MM_UTIL_H

/*
 * Prototypes for functions in mm_util.c and other definitions for
 * Music Machine application.
 */

/* number of sound sample files */
#define NUM_SAMPLES 16

/* number of sound player channels */
#define NUM_CHANNELS 8

/* number of pages of sound data */
#define NUM_PAGES 32

/* number of sound samples on one page of sound editor */
#define SAMPLES_PER_PAGE 8

/* constants for rest (silence), loop,  and stop commands */
#define REST 0
#define LOOP -1
#define STOP -2

/* array holding notes for the "song" */
extern int notes[NUM_CHANNELS][NUM_PAGES*SAMPLES_PER_PAGE];

/*** FUNCTION PROTOTYPES ***/

/* load in sound sample files and initialize */
extern void init_samples(void);

/* update bitmap buttons to match current page of sound data */
void update_bitmap(FL_OBJECT *ob, int i);

/* update all bitmaps to reflect current page of sound data */
void update_bitmaps(void);

/* save song to file */
void save_sample_file(const char *filename);

/* load song from file */
void load_sample_file(const char *filename);

/* zero out all rhythm mmory */
void clear_samples(void);

/* return whether a file exists */
int file_exists(const char *filename);
```

Example C-3: mm_util.h (continued)

```
#endif /*MM_UTIL_H*/
```

Example C-4: mm_util.c

```
/*
 * Utility functions for Music Machine application
 */

#include <unistd.h>
#include <signal.h>
#include <stdio.h>
#include <string.h>
#include <assert.h>
#include <forms.h>

#include "soundit.h"
#include "mm.h"
#include "mm_util.h"

/* bitmaps for the buttons */
#include "bitmaps/stop.xbm"
#include "bitmaps/loop.xbm"
#include "bitmaps/rest.xbm"
#include "bitmaps/zero.xbm"
#include "bitmaps/one.xbm"
#include "bitmaps/two.xbm"
#include "bitmaps/three.xbm"
#include "bitmaps/four.xbm"
#include "bitmaps/five.xbm"
#include "bitmaps/six.xbm"
#include "bitmaps/seven.xbm"
#include "bitmaps/eight.xbm"
#include "bitmaps/nine.xbm"
#include "bitmaps/ten.xbm"
#include "bitmaps/eleven.xbm"
#include "bitmaps/twelve.xbm"
#include "bitmaps/thirteen.xbm"
#include "bitmaps/fourteen.xbm"
#include "bitmaps/fifteen.xbm"

/* array containing sound sample data */
Sample snd[NUM_SAMPLES];

/* load in sound sample files and initialize SoundIt library */
void init_samples(void)
{
  int i, status, rate;
  const char *device;
  char file[256];
```

Example C-4: mm_util.c (continued)

```c
/* stop playing and clear previous sound samples, if any */
Snd_restore();

/*
 * free up any memory previously allocated - otherwise we'll have a
 * major memory leak
 */
for (i = 0 ; i < NUM_SAMPLES ; i++)
  if (snd[i].data != 0) {
    free(snd[i].data);
    snd[i].data = 0;
  }

/* load each sample file */
for (i = 0 ; i < NUM_SAMPLES ; i++) {

  /* check for empty filename */
  if (!strcmp(fl_get_input(sample_file[i]), "")) {
    fl_show_alert("Error",
                  "One or more sample files are empty.",
                  "Enter valid sample file names and try again.",
                  0);
    return;
  }

  /* get directory and add filename to it */
  strcpy(file, fl_get_input(sample_dir));
  strcat(file, "/");
  strcat(file, fl_get_input(sample_file[i]));

  /* make sure file exists */
  if (!file_exists(file)) {
    char msg[256];
    sprintf(msg, "Sample file \"%s\" does not exist.", file);
    fl_show_alert("Warning:",
                  msg,
                  "Enter a valid sample file name and try again.", 0);
    return;
  }

  status = Snd_loadRawSample(file, &snd[i]);
  if (status) {
    char msg[256];
    sprintf(msg, "Sample file \"%s\" could not be loaded.", file);
    fl_show_alert("Error:",
                  msg,
                  "Check the sample file and try again.",
                  0);
    return;
  }
```

Example C-4: mm_util.c (continued)

```
  }

  /* get sampling rate and sound device from window */
  rate = atoi(fl_get_input(sampling_rate));
  device = fl_get_input(audio_device);

  /* initialize sound library */
  status = Snd_init(NUM_SAMPLES, snd, rate, NUM_CHANNELS, device);
  if (status == EXIT_FAILURE)
    fl_show_alert("Error",
                  "Unable to initialize SoundIt library",
                  "Check parameters in options menu and try again",
                  0);
}

/* update bitmaps for one channel to reflect current page of sound data */
void update_bitmap(FL_OBJECT *ob, int i)
{
  switch (i) {
  case STOP:
    fl_set_bitmapbutton_data(ob, stop_width, stop_height, stop_bits);
    break;
  case LOOP:
    fl_set_bitmapbutton_data(ob, loop_width, loop_height, loop_bits);
    break;
  case REST:
    fl_set_bitmapbutton_data(ob, rest_width, rest_height, rest_bits);
    break;
  case 1:
    fl_set_bitmapbutton_data(ob, one_width, one_height, zero_bits);
    break;
  case 2:
    fl_set_bitmapbutton_data(ob, one_width, one_height, one_bits);
    break;
  case 3:
    fl_set_bitmapbutton_data(ob, two_width, two_height, two_bits);
    break;
  case 4:
    fl_set_bitmapbutton_data(ob, three_width, three_height, three_bits);
    break;
  case 5:
    fl_set_bitmapbutton_data(ob, four_width, four_height, four_bits);
    break;
  case 6:
    fl_set_bitmapbutton_data(ob, five_width, five_height, five_bits);
    break;
  case 7:
    fl_set_bitmapbutton_data(ob, six_width, six_height, six_bits);
    break;
  case 8:
```

Example C-4: mm_util.c (continued)

```
        fl_set_bitmapbutton_data(ob, seven_width, seven_height, seven_bits);
        break;
    case 9:
        fl_set_bitmapbutton_data(ob, eight_width, eight_height, eight_bits);
        break;
    case 10:
        fl_set_bitmapbutton_data(ob, nine_width, nine_height, nine_bits);
        break;
    case 11:
        fl_set_bitmapbutton_data(ob, ten_width, ten_height, ten_bits);
        break;
    case 12:
        fl_set_bitmapbutton_data(ob, eleven_width, eleven_height, eleven_bits);
        break;
    case 13:
        fl_set_bitmapbutton_data(ob, twelve_width, twelve_height, twelve_bits);
        break;
    case 14:
        fl_set_bitmapbutton_data(ob, thirteen_width, thirteen_height,
            thirteen_bits);
        break;
    case 15:
        fl_set_bitmapbutton_data(ob, fourteen_width, fourteen_height,
            fourteen_bits);
        break;
    case 16:
        fl_set_bitmapbutton_data(ob, fifteen_width, fifteen_height,
            fifteen_bits);
        break;
    default:
        assert(0); /* should never happen */
        break;
    }
}


/* update all bitmaps to reflect current page of sound data */
void update_bitmaps(void)
{
    int i;
    int j = SAMPLES_PER_PAGE * (int) fl_get_counter_value(page);

    /* optimization: "freeze" the form during updating */
    fl_freeze_form(main_window);

    /* update all of the note buttons */
    for (i = 0 ; i < SAMPLES_PER_PAGE ; i++){
        update_bitmap(channel_0[i], notes[0][i+j]);
        update_bitmap(channel_1[i], notes[1][i+j]);
        update_bitmap(channel_2[i], notes[2][i+j]);
        update_bitmap(channel_3[i], notes[3][i+j]);
```

Example C-4: mm_util.c (continued)

```c
    update_bitmap(channel_4[i], notes[4][i+j]);
    update_bitmap(channel_5[i], notes[5][i+j]);
    update_bitmap(channel_6[i], notes[6][i+j]);
    update_bitmap(channel_7[i], notes[7][i+j]);
  }
  fl_unfreeze_form(main_window);
}

/* save song to a file */
void save_sample_file(const char *filename)
{
  int i, j;
  FILE *fp;

  /* open file for write */
  fp = fopen(filename, "w");

  /* error if can't open */
  if (fp == 0) {
    char msg[256];
    sprintf(msg, "Unable to save song file \"%s\".", filename);
    fl_show_alert("Error:",
                  msg,
                  strerror(errno),
                  0);
    return;
  }

  /* write data to file */
  fprintf(fp, "Music Machine version 1.0\n");
  fprintf(fp, "Audio Device: %s\n", fl_get_input(audio_device));
  fprintf(fp, "Sampling Rate: %d\n", atoi(fl_get_input(sampling_rate)));
  fprintf(fp, "Sample Directory: %s\n", fl_get_input(sample_dir));
  fprintf(fp, "Tempo: %.0f\n", fl_get_slider_value(tempo));
  for (i = 0; i < NUM_SAMPLES ; i++)
    fprintf(fp, "File%d: %s\n", i, fl_get_input(sample_file[i]));
  fprintf(fp, "Sample Data: %d channels %d samples\n",
          NUM_CHANNELS, NUM_PAGES*SAMPLES_PER_PAGE);
  for (i = 0; i < NUM_PAGES*SAMPLES_PER_PAGE ; i++)
    for (j = 0 ; j < NUM_CHANNELS ; j++)
      j == NUM_CHANNELS-1 ?
        fprintf(fp, "%d\n", notes[j][i])
          : fprintf(fp, "%d ", notes[j][i]);

  /* close file */
  i = fclose(fp);

  /* error if can't close */
  if (i != 0) {
    char msg[256];
```

Example C-4: mm_util.c (continued)

```
      sprintf(msg, "Unable to close song file \"%s\".", filename);
      fl_show_alert("Error:",
                    msg,
                    strerror(errno),
                    0);
  }
}

/* load song from a file */
void load_sample_file(const char *filename)
{
  int i, st;
  float version;
  float f;
  FILE *fp;
  char s1[256], s2[256];

  /* open file for read */
  fp = fopen(filename, "r");

  /* error if can't open */
  if (fp == 0) {
    char msg[256];
    sprintf(msg, "Unable to open song file \"%s\".", filename);
    fl_show_alert("Error:",
                    msg,
                    strerror(errno),
                    0);
    return;
  }

  st = fscanf(fp, "Music Machine version %f\n", &version);
  if (st != 1) {
    fl_show_alert("Error:",
                    "This is not a music machine song file.",
                    "Check the file and try again.",
                    0);
    return;
  }
  if (version != 1.0) {
    fl_show_alert("Error:",
                    "Incompatible version of music machine song file.",
                    "Should be version 1.0",
                    0);
    return;
  }

  st = fscanf(fp, "Audio Device: %s\n", s1);
  if (st != 1) {
    fl_show_alert("Error:",
```

Example C-4: mm_util.c (continued)

```c
                    "Invalid song file.",
                    "Audio device field is bad",
                    0);
    return;
  }
  fl_set_input(audio_device, s1);

  st = fscanf(fp, "Sampling Rate: %s\n", s1);
  if (st != 1) {
    fl_show_alert("Error",
                    "Invalid song file.",
                    "Sampling rate field is bad.",
                    0);
    return;
  }
  fl_set_input(sampling_rate, s1);

  st = fscanf(fp, "Sample Directory: %s\n", s1);
  if (st != 1) {
    fl_show_alert("Error:",
                    "Invalid song file.",
                    "Sample directory section is bad.",
                    0);
    return;
  }
  fl_set_input(sample_dir, s1);

  st = fscanf(fp, "Tempo: %f\n", &f);
  if (st != 1) {
    fl_show_alert("Error",
                    "Invalid song file.",
                    "Tempo field section is bad.",
                    0);
    return;
  }
  fl_set_slider_value(tempo, f);

  for (i = 0; i < NUM_SAMPLES ; i++) {
    sprintf(s2, "File%d: %%s\n", i);
    st = fscanf(fp, s2, s1);
    if (st != 1) {
      fl_show_alert("Error:",
                      "Invalid song file.",
                      "Sample file section is bad.",
                      0);
      return;
    }
    fl_set_input(sample_file[i], s1);
  }
```

Example C-4: mm_util.c (continued)

```c
    st = fscanf(fp, "Sample Data: %d channels %d samples\n", &i, &i);
    if (st != 2) {
      fl_show_alert("Error:",
                    "Invalid song file.",
                    "Sample data header section is bad.",
                    0);
      return;
    }

    for (i = 0; i < NUM_PAGES*SAMPLES_PER_PAGE ; i++) {
      st = fscanf(fp, "%d %d %d %d %d %d %d %d\n",
                  &notes[0][i], &notes[1][i], &notes[2][i], &notes[3][i],
                  &notes[4][i], &notes[5][i], &notes[6][i], &notes[7][i]);
      if (st != 8) {
        fl_show_alert("Error:",
                      "Invalid song file.",
                      "Sample data section is bad.",
                      0);
        return;
      }
    }

    /* close file */
    i = fclose(fp);

    /* error if can't close */
    if (i != 0) {
      char msg[256];
      sprintf(msg, "Unable to close song file \"%s\".", filename);
      fl_show_alert("Error:",
                    msg,
                    strerror(errno),
                    0);
    }

    /* update the display */
    update_bitmaps();

    /* load the new sound samples */
    init_samples();
}

/* clear out all rhythm mmory */
void clear_samples(void)
{
    int i, j;
    for (i = 0 ; i < NUM_CHANNELS ; i++)
      for (j = 0 ; j < NUM_PAGES*SAMPLES_PER_PAGE ; j++)
        notes[i][j] = REST;
}
```

Example C-4: mm_util.c (continued)

```c
/*
 * return whether a file exists (could be a regular file, directory, *
 * or even device file)
 */
int file_exists(const char *filename)
{
  FILE *fp = fopen(filename, "r");
  if (fp != 0) {
    fclose(fp);
    return 1;
  } else {
    return 0;
  }
}
```

Scope

This is the code for the *scope* program. It uses the *svgalib* graphics library.

Example C-5: scope.c

```c
/*
 *                      Software Oscilloscope
 *
 * Copyright (C) 1994-96 Jeff Tranter (Jeff_Tranter@Mitel.COM)
 *
 * This program is free software; you can redistribute it and/or modify
 * it under the terms of the GNU General Public License as published by
 * the Free Software Foundation; either version 2 of the License, or
 * (at your option) any later version.
 *
 * This program is distributed in the hope that it will be useful,
 * but WITHOUT ANY WARRANTY; without even the implied warranty of
 * MERCHANTABILITY or FITNESS FOR A PARTICULAR PURPOSE.  See the
 * GNU General Public License for more details.
 *
 * You should have received a copy of the GNU General Public License
 * along with this program; if not, write to the Free Software
 * Foundation, Inc., 675 Mass Ave, Cambridge, MA 02139, USA.
 *
 ***********************************************************************
 *
 * See the man page for a description of what this program does and what
 * the requirements to run it are.
 *
 * It was developed using:
 * - Linux kernel 1.0 (also 1.2 and 1.3)
 * - gcc 2.4.5 (and 2.6.3)
 * - svgalib version 1.05 (and 1.2)
```

Example C-5: scope.c (continued)

```
 * - SoundBlaster Pro
 * - Trident VGA card
 * - 80386DX40 CPU with 8MB RAM
 *
 * Revision History:
 * 0.1 - first version put up on internet
 * 0.2 - added -i option and a few minor changes
 * 0.3 - incorporated speedup option by La Monte H Yarroll
 *        (piggy@baqaqi.chi.il.us)
 *      - added joystick support
 *      - added image dump to file support
 */


#include <unistd.h>
#include <stdlib.h>
#include <stdio.h>
#include <sys/types.h>
#include <sys/ioctl.h>
#include <fcntl.h>
#include <vga.h>
#include <sys/soundcard.h>
#ifndef NO_JOY
#include <linux/joystick.h>
#endif

/* global variables */
int quit_key_pressed;        /* set by handle_key() */
int snd;                     /* file descriptor for sound device */
unsigned char b1[1024];      /* buffer for sound data */
unsigned char b2[1024];      /* previous buffer for sound data */
unsigned char *buffer = b1;  /* use pointers to buffers to avoid copies */
unsigned char *old = b2;
unsigned char *tmp;          /* holder for swapping pointers */
int offset;                  /* vertical offset */
int sampling = 8000;         /* selected sampling rate */
int actual;                  /* actual sampling rate */
int mode = G640x480x16;      /* graphics mode */
int colour = 2;              /* colour */
int dma = 4;                 /* DMA buffer divisor */
int point_mode = 0;          /* point v.s. line segment mode */
int verbose = 0;             /* verbose mode */
int v_points;                /* points in vertical axis */
int h_points;                /* points in horizontal axis */
int trigger = -1;            /* trigger level (-1 = disabled) */
int graticule = 0;           /* show graticule */
int file_read = 0;           /* reading from a file */
int joy_read = 0;            /* reading from a joystick */
char filename[255];          /* file name to read */

/* display command usage on standard error and exit */
```

Example C-5: scope.c (continued)

```c
void usage()
{
  fprintf(stderr,
          "usage: scope -r<rate>'-m<mode> -c<colour> -d<dma divisor>\n"
          "              -d<trigger> -p -l -g -v -i<file>\n"
          "Options:\n"
          "-r <rate>        sampling rate in Hz\n"
          "-m <mode>        graphics mode\n"
          "-c <colour>      trace colour\n"
          "-d <dma divide>  DMA buffer size divisor (1,2,4)\n"
          "-t <trigger>     trigger level (0 - 255)\n"
          "-p               point mode (faster)\n"
          "-l               line segment mode (slower)\n"
          "-g               draw graticule\n"
          "-v               verbose output\n"
          "-i <file>        read from file instead of /dev/dsp\n"
#ifndef NO_JOY
          "-j <device>      read from joystick device\n"
#endif
          );
  exit(1);
}

/* if verbose mode, show current parameter settings on standard out */
inline void show_info() {
  if (verbose) {
    printf("graphics mode: %d\n", mode);
    printf("       colour: %d\n", colour);
    if (!file_read && !joy_read)
      printf("  DMA divisor: %d\n", dma);
    if (point_mode)
      printf(" drawing mode: point\n");
    else
      printf(" drawing mode: line segment\n");
    if (graticule)
      printf("    graticule: on\n");
    else
      printf("    graticule: off\n");
    if (trigger == -1)
      printf("trigger level: disabled\n");
    else
      printf("trigger level: %d\n", trigger);
    if (!file_read && !joy_read) {
      printf("sampling rate: %d\n", sampling);
      printf("  actual rate: %d\n", actual);
    }
    if (file_read || joy_read)
      printf(" reading from: %s\n", filename);
    else
      printf(" reading from: /dev/dsp\n");
```

Example C-5: scope.c (continued)

```
    }
}

/* handle command line options */
void parse_args(int argc, char **argv)
{
#ifndef NO_JOY
  const char      *flags = "r:m:c:d:t:plgvi:j:";
#else
  const char      *flags = "r:m:c:d:t:plgvi:";
#endif
  int             c;

  while ((c = getopt(argc, argv, flags)) != EOF) {
    switch (c) {
    case 'r':
      sampling = strtol(optarg, NULL, 0);
      break;
    case 'm':
      mode = strtol(optarg, NULL, 0);
      break;
    case 'c':
      colour = strtol(optarg, NULL, 0);
      break;
    case 'd':
      dma = strtol(optarg, NULL, 0);
      break;
    case 't':
      trigger = strtol(optarg, NULL, 0);
      break;
    case 'p':
      point_mode = 1;
      break;
    case 'l':
      point_mode = 0;
      break;
    case 'g':
      graticule = 1;
      break;
    case 'v':
      verbose = 1;
      break;
    case 'i':
      file_read = 1;
      strcpy(filename, optarg);
      break;
#ifndef NO_JOY
    case 'j':
      joy_read = 1;
      strcpy(filename, optarg);
```

Example C-5: scope.c (continued)

```
        break;
#endif
    case '?':
      usage();
      break;
    }
  }
  if (joy_read && file_read) {
    fprintf(stderr, "scope: -i and -j options are mutually exclusive\n");
    exit(1);
  }
}

/* initialize screen data to zero level */
void init_data()
{
  int i;

  for (i = 0 ; i < 1024 ; i++) {
    buffer[i] = 128;
    old[i] = 128;
  }
}

/* draw graticule */
inline void draw_graticule()
{
  vga_clear();

  /* draw a frame */
  vga_setcolor(colour+1);
  vga_drawline(0, offset-1, h_points-1, offset-1);
  vga_drawline(0, offset+256, h_points-1, offset+256);
  vga_drawline(0, offset-1, 0, offset+256);
  vga_drawline(h_points-1, offset, h_points-1, offset+256);

  /* draw a tick mark where the trigger level is */
  if (trigger != -1) {
    vga_drawline(0, offset+trigger, 3, offset+trigger);
  }
}

/* initialize graphics screen */
void init_screen()
{
  vga_disabledriverreport();
  vga_init();
  vga_setmode(mode);
  v_points = vga_getydim();
  h_points = vga_getxdim();
```

Example C–5: scope.c (continued)

```
  offset = v_points / 2 - 127;
  if (graticule)
    draw_graticule();
}

/* cleanup: restore text mode and close sound device */
void cleanup()
{
  /* restore text screen */
  vga_setmode(TEXT);

  /* close input device */
    close(snd);
}

/* initialize /dev/dsp */
void init_sound_card()
{
  int parm;
  int status;

  /* open DSP device for read */
  snd = open("/dev/dsp", O_RDONLY);
  if (snd < 0) {
    perror("scope: cannot open /dev/dsp");
    cleanup();
    exit(1);
  }

  /* set mono */
  parm = 1;
  status = ioctl(snd, SOUND_PCM_WRITE_CHANNELS, &parm);
  if (status < 0) {
    perror("scope: error from sound device ioctl");
    cleanup();
    exit(1);
  }

  /* set 8-bit samples */
  parm = 8;
  status = ioctl(snd, SOUND_PCM_WRITE_BITS, &parm);
  if (status < 0) {
    perror("scope: error from sound device ioctl");
    cleanup();
    exit(1);
  }

  /* set DMA buffer size */
  status = ioctl(snd, SOUND_PCM_SUBDIVIDE, &dma);
  if (status < 0) {
```

Example C-5: scope.c (continued)

```
      perror("scope: error from sound device ioctl");
      cleanup();
      exit(1);
    }

    /* set sampling rate */
    parm = sampling;
    status = ioctl(snd, SOUND_PCM_WRITE_RATE, &parm);
    if (status < 0) {
      perror("scope: error from sound device ioctl");
    }
    ioctl(snd, SOUND_PCM_READ_RATE, &actual);
}

/* initialize input file */
void init_input_file()
{
  /* open file for read */
  snd = open(filename, O_RDONLY);
  if (snd < 0) {
    perror("scope: cannot open input file");
    cleanup();
    exit(1);
  }
}

#ifndef NO_JOY
/* initialize joystick */
void init_joystick()
{
  /* open device for read */
  snd = open(filename, O_RDONLY);
  if (snd < 0) {
    perror("scope: cannot open joystick device");
    cleanup();
    exit(1);
  }
}
#endif

/* dump image on screen to file scope.xbm in X bitmap format */
void screen_dump(void)
{
  int x, y, bit, bits;
  int x_max = vga_getxdim();
  int y_max = vga_getydim();
  int l = 0;
  FILE *fp;

  fp = fopen("scope.xbm", "w");
```

Example C-5: scope.c (continued)

```
   if (fp == 0) {
     perror("scope: unable to open scope.xbm");
     cleanup();
     exit(1);
   }

   fprintf(fp, "#define scope_width %d\n", x_max);
   fprintf(fp, "#define scope_height %d\n", y_max);
   fprintf(fp, "static unsigned char scope_bits[] = {\n   ");

   for (y = 0 ; y < y_max ; y++) {
     for (x = 0 ; x < x_max; x+= 8) {
       l++;
       bits = 0;
       for (bit = 0 ; bit < 8 ; bit++) {
         if (vga_getpixel(x + bit, y) != 0)
           bits += 1 << bit;
       }
       if (l == y_max*x_max/8)
         fprintf(fp, "0x%02x};\n", bits);
       else if (l % 12 ==  0)
         fprintf(fp, "0x%02x,\n   ", bits);
       else
         fprintf(fp, "0x%02x, ", bits);
     }
   }
   fclose(fp);
}

/* handle single key commands */
inline void handle_key()
{
  switch (vga_getkey()) {
  case 0:
  case -1:
    /* no key pressed */
    return;
    break;
  case 'q':
  case 'Q':
    quit_key_pressed = 1;
    return;
    break;
  case 'R':
    if (!file_read && !joy_read) {
      sampling = sampling * 10 / 9;
      ioctl(snd, SOUND_PCM_SYNC, 0);
      ioctl(snd, SOUND_PCM_WRITE_RATE, &sampling);
      ioctl(snd, SOUND_PCM_READ_RATE, &actual);
    }
```

Example C–5: scope.c (continued)

```
      break;
  case 'r':
    if (!file_read && !joy_read) {
      sampling = sampling * 9 / 10;
      ioctl(snd, SOUND_PCM_SYNC, 0);
      ioctl(snd, SOUND_PCM_WRITE_RATE, &sampling);
      ioctl(snd, SOUND_PCM_READ_RATE, &actual);
    }
    break;
  case 'T':
    if (trigger != -1) {
      trigger += 10;
      if (trigger > 255)
        trigger = 255;
      if (graticule)
        draw_graticule();
    }
    break;
  case 't':
    if (trigger != -1) {
      trigger -= 10;
      if (trigger < 0)
        trigger = 0;
      if (graticule)
        draw_graticule();
    }
    break;
  case 'l':
  case 'L':
    if (point_mode == 1) {
      point_mode = 0;
      vga_clear();
      if (graticule)
        draw_graticule();
    }
    break;
  case 'p':
  case 'P':
    if (point_mode == 0) {
      point_mode = 1;
      vga_clear();
      if (graticule)
        draw_graticule();
    }
    break;
  case 'C':
    colour++;
    if (graticule)
      draw_graticule();
    break;
```

Example C-5: scope.c (continued)

```
    case 'c':
      if (colour > 0) {
        colour--;
        if (graticule)
          draw_graticule();
      }
      break;
    case 'G':
      if (graticule == 0) {
        graticule = 1;
        draw_graticule();
      }
      break;
    case 'g':
      if (graticule == 1) {
        graticule = 0;
        vga_clear();
      }
      break;
    case ' ':
      /* pause until key pressed */
      while (vga_getkey() == 0)
        ;
      break;
    case 'd':
    case 'D':
      screen_dump();
      break;
    default:
      break;
    }
}

/* get data from sound card */
inline void get_data()
{
  unsigned char datum;
  int status;

  /* simple trigger function */
  if (trigger != -1) {
    /* positive trigger */
    if (trigger >128)
      do {
        read(snd, &datum, 1);
      } while (datum < trigger);
    else
      /* negative trigger */
      do {
        read(snd, &datum, 1);
```

Example C-5: scope.c (continued)

```
      } while (datum > trigger);
  }
  /* now get the real data */
  status = read(snd, buffer, h_points-2);
  if (status == 0) {
    fprintf(stderr, "scope: end of file\n");
    cleanup();
    exit(1);
  }
  if (status == 1) {
    perror("scope: error reading input");
    cleanup();
    exit(1);
  }
}


#ifndef NO_JOY
/* get data from joystick */
inline void get_joy_data()
{
  struct JS_DATA_TYPE js;
  int i, status;

  for (i = 0 ; i < h_points-1 ; i++) {
    status = read(snd, &js, JS_RETURN);
    if (status != JS_RETURN) {
      perror("scope: error reading joystick");
      cleanup();
      exit(1);
    }
    buffer[i] = js.y / 5; /* arbitrary scale factor */
  }
}
#endif

/* graph the data */
inline void graph_data()
{
  register int i;

  if (point_mode) {
    for (i = 1; i < h_points-1 ; i++) {
      /* erase previous point */
      vga_setcolor(0);
      vga_drawpixel(i, old[i] + offset);
      /* draw new point */
      vga_setcolor(colour);
      vga_drawpixel(i, buffer[i] + offset);
    }
  } else { /* line mode */
```

Example C-5: scope.c (continued)

```c
    for (i = 1; i < h_points-2  ; i++) {
      /* erase previous point */
      vga_setcolor(0);
      vga_drawline(i, old[i] + offset, i+1, old[i+1] + offset);
      /* draw new point */
      vga_setcolor(colour);
      vga_drawline(i, buffer[i] + offset, i+1, buffer[i+1] + offset);
      old[i] = buffer[i];
    }
  }
  /* swap the buffers for next time  */
  tmp = buffer;
  buffer = old;
  old = tmp;
}
/* main program */
int main(int argc, char **argv)
{
  parse_args(argc, argv);
  init_screen();
  init_data();
  if (file_read)
    init_input_file();
#ifndef NO_JOY
  else if (joy_read)
    init_joystick();
#endif
  else
    init_sound_card();
  show_info();

  if (joy_read) {
#ifndef NO_JOY
    while (!quit_key_pressed) {
      handle_key();
      get_joy_data();
      graph_data();
    }
#endif
  } else {
    while (!quit_key_pressed) {
      handle_key();
      get_data();
      graph_data();
    }
  }
  cleanup();
  exit(0);
}
```

GuitarTutor

This is the code for the *GuitarTutor* program. It uses the V GUI toolkit. Additional files needed to run the complete application can be obtained from the Internet.

Example C-6: tutapp.h

```
// tutapp.h

// definitions for guitar tutor application

#ifndef TUTAPP_H
#define TUTAPP_H

#ifdef vDEBUG
#include <v/vdebug.h>
#endif

#include <v/vapp.h>
#include <v/vawinfo.h>

#include "tcmdwin.h"

class tutApp : public vApp
{
   friend int AppMain(int, char **);

public:
   tutApp(char* name) : vApp(name) { }
   virtual ~tutApp() { }
   virtual vWindow* NewAppWin(vWindow *win, char *name, int h, int w,
                        vAppWinInfo *winInfo);
   virtual void Exit(void);
   virtual void CloseAppWin(vWindow *win);
   virtual void AppCommand(vWindow *win, ItemVal id, ItemVal val,
                     CmdType cType);
protected:

private:

};
#endif
```

Example C-7: tutapp.cpp

```
//   tutapp.cpp

// top level code for guitar tutor application

#include "tutapp.h"
```

Example C-7: tutapp.cpp (continued)

```cpp
vWindow *tutApp::NewAppWin(vWindow *win, char *name, int h, int w,
                           vAppWinInfo *winInfo)
{
  UserDebug1(Build,"tutApp::NewAppWin(%s)\n", name);
  vWindow *thisWin = win;
  vAppWinInfo *awinfo = winInfo;
  char *myname = name;

  if (!*name)
    myname = "Guitar Tutor";

  if (!thisWin)
    thisWin = new tCmdWindow(myname, h, w);

  if (!awinfo)
    awinfo = new vAppWinInfo(myname);

  return vApp::NewAppWin(thisWin,name,h,w,awinfo);
}

void tutApp::Exit(void)
{
  UserDebug(Build,"tutApp::Exit()\n");
  vApp::Exit();
}

void tutApp::CloseAppWin(vWindow *win)
{
  UserDebug(Build,"tutApp::CloseAppWin()\n");
  vApp::CloseAppWin(win);
}

void tutApp::AppCommand(vWindow *win, ItemVal id, ItemVal val,
                        CmdType cType)
{
  UserDebug1(Build,"tutApp::AppCmd(ID: %d)\n",id);
  vApp::AppCommand(win, id, val, cType);
}

static tutApp tut_App("TutorApp");

int AppMain(int argc, char **argv)
{
  (void) theApp->NewAppWin(0, "Guitar Tutor", 200, 300, 0);
  return 0;
}
```

Example C-8: tcmdwin.h

```
// tcmdwin.h

// definitions for command window

#ifndef TCMDWIN_H
#define TCMDWIN_H

#include <v/vcmdwin.h>
#include <v/vmenu.h>
#include <v/vstatusp.h>
#include <v/vcmdpane.h>

#ifdef vDEBUG
#include <v/vdebug.h>
#endif

#include "tcanvas.h"

class tCmdWindow : public vCmdWindow
{
    friend int AppMain(int, char **);

public:
    tCmdWindow(char *, int, int);
    virtual ~tCmdWindow();
    virtual void WindowCommand(ItemVal id, ItemVal val, CmdType cType);

protected:

private:
    vMenuPane *myMenu;
    tCanvasPane *myCanvas;
    vStatusPane *myStatus;
    vCommandPane *myCmdPane;
};
#endif
```

Example C-9: tcmdwin.cpp

```
//  tcmdwin.cpp

// command window functions

#include <string.h>
#include <errno.h>
#include <v/vnotice.h>
#include <v/vutil.h>
#include <v/vfilesel.h>
#include <v/vprinter.h>
#include <v/vynreply.h>
```

Example C-9: tcmdwin.cpp (continued)

```cpp
#include "tcmdwin.h"
#include "tchord.h"
#include "tutils.h"

typedef char string[255];

// local symbols
const ItemVal m_play    = 100;
const ItemVal m_chord   = 101;
const ItemVal m_rotated = 102;
const ItemVal m_notes   = 103;
const ItemVal m_status  = 104;

static vMenu FileMenu[] =
{
  {"New", M_New, notSens, notChk, noKeyLbl, noKey, noSub},
  {"Load...", M_Open, isSens, notChk, noKeyLbl, noKey, noSub},
  {"Save", M_Save, notSens, notChk, noKeyLbl, noKey, noSub},
  {"Save As...", M_SaveAs, notSens, notChk, noKeyLbl, noKey, noSub},
  {"Print...", M_Print, notSens, notChk, noKeyLbl, noKey, noSub},
#ifdef vDEBUG
  {"-", M_Line, notSens, notChk, noKeyLbl, noKey, noSub},
  {"Debug...", M_SetDebug, isSens, notChk, noKeyLbl, noKey, noSub},
#endif
  {"-", M_Line, notSens, notChk, noKeyLbl, noKey, noSub},
  {"Exit", M_Exit, isSens, notChk, noKeyLbl, noKey, noSub},
  {NULL}
};

static vMenu EditMenu[] =
{
  {"Undo", M_UnDo, notSens, notChk, noKeyLbl, noKey, noSub},
  {"Clear", M_Clear, notSens, notChk, noKeyLbl, noKey, noSub},
  {"Cut", M_Cut, notSens, notChk, noKeyLbl, noKey, noSub},
  {"Copy", M_Copy, notSens, notChk, noKeyLbl, noKey, noSub},
  {"Paste", M_Paste, notSens, notChk, noKeyLbl, noKey, noSub},
  {NULL}
};

static vMenu OptionsMenu[] =
{
  {"Rotated", m_rotated, notSens, notChk, noKeyLbl, noKey, noSub},
  {"Show Notes", m_notes, isSens, isChk, noKeyLbl, noKey, noSub},
  {NULL}
};

static vMenu HelpMenu[] =
{
  {"About...", M_About, isSens, notChk, noKeyLbl, noKey, noSub},
  {NULL}
```

Example C-9: tcmdwin.cpp (continued)

```
};

vMenu StandardMenu[] =
{
  {"File", M_File, isSens, notUsed, notUsed, noKey, &FileMenu[0]},
  {"Edit", M_Edit, isSens, notUsed, notUsed, noKey, &EditMenu[0]},
  {"Options", M_Options, isSens, notUsed, notUsed, noKey, &OptionsMenu[0]},
  {"Help", M_Help, isSens, notUsed, notUsed, noKey, &HelpMenu[0]},
  {NULL}
};

// list of chords, initially empty
chordList_t chord_list = { 0 };

// last file loaded or saved
static char filename[100] = "";

// database of chords
tutChords chords;

static CommandObject CommandBar[] =
{
  {C_Label, M_None, M_None, "Chord:", NoList, CA_None,
   isSens, NoFrame, 0, 0},
  {C_ComboBox, m_chord, m_chord, "Chord", (void*)chord_list, CA_Text,
   notSens, NoFrame, 0, 0},
  {C_Blank, M_None, M_None, "  ", NoList, CA_None,
   notSens, NoFrame, 0, 0},
  {C_Button, m_play, m_play, "Play", NoList, CA_None,
   notSens, NoFrame, 0, 0},
  {C_EndOfList, 0, 0, 0, 0, CA_None, 0, 0, 0}
};

static vStatus StatBar[] =
{
  {"No file loaded", m_status, CA_None, isSens, 0},
  {0, 0, 0, 0, 0}
};

tCmdWindow::tCmdWindow(char* name, int height, int width) :
  vCmdWindow(name, height, width)
{
  UserDebug1(Constructor, "tCmdWindow::tCmdWindow(%s) Constructor\n", name)
  myMenu = new vMenuPane(StandardMenu);
  AddPane(myMenu);
  myCanvas = new tCanvasPane;
  AddPane(myCanvas);
  myCmdPane = new vCommandPane(CommandBar);
  AddPane(myCmdPane);
  myStatus = new vStatusPane(StatBar);
```

Example C-9: tcmdwin.cpp (continued)

```
  AddPane(myStatus);
  ShowWindow();
}


tCmdWindow::~tCmdWindow()
{
  UserDebug(Destructor, "tCmdWindow::~tCmdWindow() destructor\n")
  delete myMenu;
  delete myCanvas;
  delete myStatus;
  delete myCmdPane;
}


void tCmdWindow::WindowCommand(ItemVal id, ItemVal val, CmdType cType)
{
  UserDebug1(CmdEvents, "tCmdWindow:WindowCommand(%d)\n", id)
  vNoticeDialog note(this);

  switch (id)
    {
      // File Menu commands
    case M_New:
      {
        UserDebug(CmdEvents, "tCmdWindow:WindowCommand(M_New)\n")
        vYNReplyDialog yesNo(this);
        int ans = yesNo.AskYN("Do you want to clear the loaded chords?");
        if (ans == 1) {
          chord_list[0] = 0;
          SetValue(m_chord, 0, ChangeList);
          SetString(m_status, "No file loaded");
          SetValue(m_chord, notSens, Sensitive);
          SetValue(m_play, notSens, Sensitive);
          SetValue(M_Save, notSens, Sensitive);
          SetValue(M_SaveAs, notSens, Sensitive);
          SetValue(M_Print, notSens, Sensitive);
          SetValue(M_New, notSens, Sensitive);
          strings_t strings = {0,0,0,0,0,0};
          myCanvas->DrawChord(strings, GetValue(m_notes));
        }
        break;
      }

    case M_Open:
      {
        UserDebug(CmdEvents, "tCmdWindow:WindowCommand(M_Open)\n")
        vFileSelect fsel(this);
        static char* filter[] = { "*.db", "*", 0 };
        int fI = 0;
        int ans = fsel.FileSelect("Load File", filename, 99, filter, fI);
```

Example C-9: tcmdwin.cpp (continued)

```cpp
    if (ans && *filename) {
      int status = chords.load(filename);
      if (status == -1) {
        string s;
        sprintf(s, "Unable to load file\n'%s'\n%s",
                filename, strerror(errno));
        note.Notice(s);
      } else {
        chords.chordNames(chord_list);
        SetValue(m_chord, 0, ChangeList); // notify that list has
          changed
        SetValue(m_chord, 0, Value); // select first item in list
        string s;
        sprintf(s, "File: %s", BaseName(filename));
        SetString(m_status, s);
        SetValue(m_chord, isSens, Sensitive);
        SetValue(m_play, isSens, Sensitive);
        SetValue(M_Save, isSens, Sensitive);
        SetValue(M_SaveAs, isSens, Sensitive);
        SetValue(M_Print, isSens, Sensitive);
        SetValue(M_New, isSens, Sensitive);
        strings_t strings;
        chords.fingering(chord_list[GetValue(m_chord)], strings);
        myCanvas->DrawChord(strings, GetValue(m_notes));
      }
    } else {
      note.Notice("No file selected.");
    }
    break;
  }

case M_Save:
  {
    UserDebug(CmdEvents, "tCmdWindow:WindowCommand(M_Save)\n")
     // see if file exists by trying to open for reading
      fstream fs(filename, ios::in);
    if (!fs.bad()) {
      fs.close();
      vYNReplyDialog yesNo(this);
      int ans = yesNo.AskYN("File already exists. Okay to overwrite?");
      if (ans != 1) {
        break;
      }
    }
    int status = chords.save(filename);
    if (status == -1) {
      string s;
      sprintf(s, "Unable to save file\n'%s'\n%s",
              filename, strerror(errno));
      note.Notice(s);
```

Example C-9: tcmdwin.cpp (continued)

```cpp
        }
        break;
      }

    case M_SaveAs:
      {
        UserDebug(CmdEvents, "tCmdWindow:WindowCommand(M_SaveAs)\n")
        vFileSelect fsel(this);
        static char* filter[] = { "*", 0 };
        int fI = 0;
        int ans = fsel.FileSelect("Save As", filename, 99, filter, fI);
        if (ans && *filename) {
          int status = chords.save(filename);
          if (status == -1) {
            string s;
            sprintf(s, "Unable to save file\n'%s'\n%s",
                    filename, strerror(errno));
            note.Notice(s);
          } else {
            string s;
            sprintf(s, "File: %s", BaseName(filename));
            SetString(m_status, s);
          }
        } else {
          note.Notice("No file name selected.");
        }
        break;
      }

    case M_Print:
      {
        UserDebug(CmdEvents, "tCmdWindow:WindowCommand(M_Print)\n")
        vPrinter printer;
        int status = printer.Setup();
        if (status) {
          note.Notice("Printing is not yet implemented.");
        }
        break;
      }

#ifdef vDEBUG
    case M_SetDebug:
      {
        UserDebug(CmdEvents, "tCmdWindow:WindowCommand(M_SetDebug)\n")
        vDebugDialog debug(this);
        debug.SetDebug();
        break;
      }
#endif
```

Example C-9: tcmdwin.cpp (continued)

```
case M_Exit:
  {
    UserDebug(CmdEvents, "tCmdWindow:WindowCommand(M_Exit)\n")
    theApp->Exit();
    break;
  }

// Edit Menu commands
case M_UnDo:
  break;

case M_Clear:
  break;

case M_Cut:
  break;

case M_Copy:
  break;

case M_Paste:
  break;

// Options Menu commands
case m_rotated:
  // not implemented yet
  break;

case m_notes:
  {
    UserDebug(CmdEvents, "tCmdWindow:WindowCommand(m_notes)\n")
    ItemVal curval = GetValue(id); // Get current status
    SetValue(m_notes, !curval, Checked); // Toggle check
    if (chord_list[0] != 0) {
      strings_t strings;
      chords.fingering(chord_list[GetValue(m_chord)], strings);
      myCanvas->DrawChord(strings, GetValue(m_notes));
    }
    break;
  }

// Help Menu commands
case M_About:
  {
    UserDebug(CmdEvents, "tCmdWindow:WindowCommand(M_About)\n")
    vNoticeDialog note(this, "About");
    note.Notice(
                "Guitar Tutor version 1.0\n"
                "by Jeff Tranter for\n"
                "The Linux Multimedia Guide\n"
```

Example C-9: tcmdwin.cpp (continued)

```
                        );
          break;
        }

      // Command Bar commands
      case m_chord:
        {
          UserDebug(CmdEvents, "tCmdWindow:WindowCommand(m_chord)\n")
          strings_t strings;
          chords.fingering(chord_list[val], strings);
          myCanvas->DrawChord(strings, GetValue(m_notes));
          break;
        }

      case m_play:
        {
          UserDebug(CmdEvents, "tCmdWindow:WindowCommand(m_play)\n")
          int index = GetValue(m_chord);
          UserDebug1(CmdEvents,
                    "tCmdWindow:WindowCommand() playing chord %s\n",
                    chord_list[index]);
          int status = chords.play(chord_list[index]);
          if (status == -1) {
            string s;
            sprintf(s, "Unable to play chord '%s'\n%s",
                    chord_list[index], strerror(errno));
            note.Notice(s);
          }
          break;
        }

      default:
        vCmdWindow::WindowCommand(id, val, cType);
        break;
    }
}
```

Example C-10: tcanvas.h

```
// tcanvas.h

// definitions for drawing canvas

#ifndef TCANVAS_H
#define TCANVAS_H

#include <v/vcanvas.h>

#include "tchord.h"
```

Example C–10: tcanvas.h (continued)

```
class tCanvasPane : public vCanvasPane
{
public:
  tCanvasPane();
  virtual ~tCanvasPane();
  virtual void Clear();
  virtual void Redraw(int, int, int, int);
  virtual void Resize(int, int);
  virtual void DrawChord(strings_t strings, int draw_notes);

protected:

private:
  strings_t strings;
  int drawNotes;
};
#endif
```

Example C–11: tcanvas.cpp

```
// tcanvas.cpp

// code for implementing drawing canvas

#include <iostream.h>
#include <v/vdebug.h>
#include <v/vwindow.h>

#include "tcanvas.h"
#include "tchord.h"
#include "tutils.h"

// names of notes on each string and fret
char *noteNames[numStrings][numFrets] = {
  { "E",  "F",  "F#", "G",  "G#", "A",  "A#", "B" },
  { "A" , "A#", "B",  "C",  "C#", "D",  "D#", "E" },
  { "D" , "D#", "E",  "F",  "F#", "G",  "G#", "A" },
  { "G" , "G#", "A",  "A#", "B",  "C",  "C#", "D" },
  { "B" , "C",  "C#", "D",  "D#", "E",  "F",  "F#"},
  { "E",  "F",  "F#", "G",  "G#", "A",  "A#", "B" }
};

tCanvasPane::tCanvasPane()
{
  strings[0] = strings[1] = strings[2] =
    strings[3] = strings[4] = strings[5] = 0;
  drawNotes = 1;
}

tCanvasPane::~tCanvasPane()
```

Example C–11: tcanvas.cpp (continued)

```cpp
{
  strings[0] = strings[1] = strings[2] =
    strings[3] = strings[4] = strings[5] = 0;
  drawNotes = 1;
}

void tCanvasPane::Clear()
{
  vCanvasPane::Clear();          // clear the canvas
}

void tCanvasPane::Redraw(int px, int py, int pw, int ph)
{
  UserDebug(WindowEvents, "tCanvasPane:Redraw()\n");

  int x0, y0; // upper left corner of diagram
  int w, h;   // distance between strings and frets
  int d;      // radius of dots

  // scale the diagram to fit the canvas
  w = h = Min(GetHeight()/(numFrets+3), GetWidth()/(numStrings+2));
  x0 = (GetWidth() - (numStrings-1)*w)/2;
  y0 = (GetHeight() - (numFrets)*h)/2;
  d = w/2;

  Clear(); // start with a clean slate

  // draw the horizontal lines (frets)
  for (int i = 0 ; i <= numFrets ; i++) {
    DrawLine(x0, y0+i*h, x0+(numStrings-1)*w, y0+i*h);
  }

  // draw the vertical lines (strings)
  for (int i = 0 ; i < numStrings ; i++) {
    DrawLine(x0+i*w, y0, x0+i*w, y0+(numFrets)*h);
  }

  // list the fret numbers
  for (int i = 1 ; i <= numFrets ; i++) {
    char s[2];
    sprintf(s, "%1d", i);
    DrawText(x0-w/2, y0+i*h, s);
  }

  // draw the fingering
  for (int i = 0 ; i < numStrings ; i++) {
    char s[2] = "X";
    s[0] = strings[i];
    switch (strings[i]) {
    case 'X':
```

Example C-11: tcanvas.cpp (continued)

```cpp
    case '0':
      {
        DrawText(x0+i*w-3, y0-5, s);
        break;
      }
    case '1': case '2': case '3': case '4':
    case '5': case '6': case '7': case '8':
      {
        int f = strings[i] - '0';
        DrawEllipse(x0+i*w-d/2, y0+f*h-d/2-w/2, d, d);
        break;
      }
    default:
      {
        UserDebug1(BadVals, "tCanvasPane::Redraw() bad string value '%c'",
                   strings[i]);
      }
    }
  }
}


  // note names
  if (drawNotes) {
    for (int s = 0 ; s < numStrings ; s++) {
      int f = strings[s] - '0';
      if (f >= 0 && f <= 8) {
        DrawText(x0+s*w-3, y0+(numFrets)*h+w-3, noteNames[s][f]);
      }
    }
  }
}

void tCanvasPane::Resize(int w, int h)
{
  UserDebug(WindowEvents, "tCanvasPane:Resize()\n");
  Redraw(0, 0, 0, 0);
  vCanvasPane::Resize(w,h);
}

void tCanvasPane::DrawChord(strings_t strings, int drawNotes)
{
  UserDebug(WindowEvents, "tCanvasPane:DrawChord()\n");
  for (int i = 0 ; i < numStrings ; i++) {
    tCanvasPane::strings[i] = strings[i];
  }
  tCanvasPane::drawNotes = drawNotes;
  Redraw(0, 0, 0, 0);
}
```

Example C-12: tchord.h

```
// tchord.h

// definitions for guitar chord database and sound functions

#ifndef TCHORD_H
#define TCHORD_H

// maximum number of chords, increase if needed
const int maxChords = 100;

// it's a 6 string guitar
const int numStrings = 6;

// show this many frets
const int numFrets = 8;

typedef char strings_t[numStrings];

// data structure for one guitar chord
typedef struct tutChord
{
  char longName[40];    // long name (e.g. "C Major"), must be unique
  char shortName[8];    // short name (e.g. "C")
                        // each string is either 0 (open), X (dead),
                        // or a fret number (first fret is 1)
  strings_t strings;    // finger for each string (ordered EADGBE)
  char sampleFile[80];  // sound sample filename
};

// type to hold array of chord names
typedef char *chordList_t[maxChords];

// class for a database of chords
class tutChords
{
public:
  tutChords() { fileName[0] = 0; numChords = 0; }
  tutChords(char *filename);
  ~tutChords() { fileName[0] = 0; numChords = 0; }
  void chordNames(chordList_t list);
  // these return -1 on error
  int load(char *fileName); // load chord file
  int save(char *fileName); // save chord file
  int play(char *longName); // play a chord
  int fingering(char *longName, strings_t &strings);

private:
  char fileName[80];         // database file name
  tutChord chord[maxChords]; // array of chords
  chordList_t chordList;     // list of long chord names
```

Example C-12: tchord.h (continued)

```
  int numChords;                  // current number of chords
};

#endif
```

Example C-13: tchord.cpp

```
//  tchord.cpp

// guitar chord database and sound functions

#include <fstream.h>
#include <string.h>
#include <v/vdebug.h>

#include "tchord.h"
#include "tutils.h"

// Constructor. Just calls load routine.
tutChords::tutChords(char *fileName)
{
  UserDebug1(Constructor, "tutChords::tutChords(%s)\n", fileName);
  load(fileName);
}

// Load chord database file. Returns -1 on error.
int tutChords::load(char *fileName)
{
  UserDebug1(Misc, "tutChords::load(%s)\n", fileName);
  fstream fs(fileName, ios::in);
  if (fs.bad()) {
    UserDebug1(BadVals, "tutChords::load(%s) can't open file\n", fileName);
    return -1;
  }

  // check for "magic number" at top of file
  char tmp[255];
  fs >> tmp;
  if (strcmp(tmp, "#GuitarTutor")) {
    UserDebug1(BadVals, "tutChords::load(%s) not a valid data file\n",
      fileName);
    return -1;
  }

  strcpy(tutChords::fileName, fileName);
  numChords = 0;
  char longName[255], shortName[255], strings[255], sampleFile[255];

  do {
    fs >> longName >> shortName >> strings >> sampleFile;
```

Example C-13: tchord.cpp (continued)

```cpp
      if (strlen(sampleFile)) {
         // sanity check on strings field
         if ((strlen(strings) != numStrings) ||
             (strspn(strings, "X012345678") != numStrings)) {
            UserDebug1(BadVals, "tutChords::load(%s) bad data in file\n",
                       fileName);
            return -1;
         }
         // input file uses underscore to indicate space
         StrSub(longName, '_', ' ');
         StrSub(shortName, '_', ' ');
         strcpy(chord[numChords].longName, longName);
         strcpy(chord[numChords].shortName, shortName);
         strcpy(chord[numChords].strings, strings);
         strcpy(chord[numChords].sampleFile, sampleFile);
         chordList[numChords] = chord[numChords].longName;
         numChords++;
         if (numChords >= maxChords) { // check for array overflow
            UserDebug1(BadVals, "tutChords::load(%s) too many chords in file\n",
                       fileName);
            return -1;
         }
         chordList[numChords] = 0; // clear next entry
      }
   } while (!fs.eof());

   UserDebug1(Misc, "tutChords::load() read %d chords\n", numChords);
   fs.close();
   if (numChords == 0)
      return -1;
   else
      return 0;
}

// Given chord name, return fingering info. Returns -1 on error.
int tutChords::fingering(char *longName, strings_t &strings)
{
   UserDebug1(Misc, "tutChords::fingering(%s)\n", longName);

   for (int i = 0 ; i < numChords ; i++) {
      if (!strcmp(longName, chord[i].longName)) {
         strings = chord[i].strings;
         return 0;
      }
   }
   UserDebug1(BadVals, "tutChords::fingering(%s) can't find chord\n",
      longName);
   return -1;
}
```

Example C-13: tchord.cpp (continued)

```cpp
// Save chord database to file.
int tutChords::save(char *filename)
{
  UserDebug1(Misc, "tutChords::save(%s)\n", fileName);
  fstream fs(filename, ios::out);
  if (fs.bad()) {
    UserDebug1(BadVals, "tutChords::save(%s) can't open file\n", fileName);
    return -1;
  }

  // write "magic number" at top of file
  fs << "#GuitarTutor" << endl;

  for (int i = 0 ; i < numChords ; i++) {
    char longName[255], shortName[255];
    strcpy(longName, chord[i].longName);
    strcpy(shortName, chord[i].shortName);
    // convert spaces to underscore
    StrSub(longName, ' ', '_');
    StrSub(shortName, ' ', '_');
    fs << longName << " " << shortName << " " <<
      chord[i].strings[0] << chord[i].strings[1] <<
      chord[i].strings[2] << chord[i].strings[3] <<
      chord[i].strings[4] << chord[i].strings[5] <<
      " " << chord[i].sampleFile << endl;
  }
  fs.close();
  return 0;
}

// Play a chord. Returns -1 on error.
int tutChords::play(char *chordName)
{
  UserDebug1(Misc, "tutChords::play(%s)\n", chordName);
  char *sampleFile = 0;
  const char *sound = "/dev/dsp"; // sound device

  // find the sample
  for (int i = 0 ; i < numChords ; i++) {
    if (!strcmp(chordName, chord[i].longName)) {
      sampleFile = chord[i].sampleFile;
      break;
    }
  }

  // this chord was not found
  if (sampleFile == 0) {
    UserDebug1(BadVals, "tutChords::play(%s) can't find chord\n",
      chordName);
    return -1;
```

Example C-13: tchord.cpp (continued)

```
    }

    // open sample file for read
    fstream in(sampleFile, ios::in);
    if (in.bad()) {
      UserDebug1(BadVals, "tutChords::play() can't open %s\n", sampleFile);
      return -1;
    }

    // open DSP for write
    fstream out(sound, ios::out);
    if (out.bad()) {
      UserDebug1(BadVals, "tutChords::play() can't open %s\n", sound);
      return -1;
    }

    // read sample file, write to DSP
    unsigned char buf;
    while (!in.eof()) {
      in >> buf;
      out << buf;
    }

    // close files
    out.close();
    in.close();

    return 0;
}

// return array of chord names
void tutChords::chordNames(chordList_t list)
{
    UserDebug(Misc, "tutChords::chordNames()\n");
    int i;
    for (i = 0 ; i < numChords ; i++)
      list[i] = chordList[i];
    list[i] = 0;
}
```

Example C-14: tutils.h

```
// tutils.h

// definitions for utility functions

// Convert all occurrences of character c1 to c2 in string s
void StrSub(char *s, int c1, int c2);

// Return the minimum of two values.
```

Example C-14: tutils.h (continued)

```
template <class T>
inline T Min(T x, T y)
{
  return (x < y) ? x : y;
}


// return base name of a file
// e.g. given "/foo/bar/file.c" return "file.c"
// assumes Unix style pathnames
char *BaseName(char *path);
```

Example C-15: tutils.cpp

```
// tutils.cpp

// miscellaneous utility routines

#include <string.h>

// Convert all occurrences of character c1 to c2 in string s
void StrSub(char *s, int c1, int c2)
{
  while (*s) {
    if (*s == c1)
      *s = c2;
    s++;
  }
}


// return base name of a file
// e.g. given "/foo/bar/file.c" return "file.c"
// assumes Unix style pathnames
char *BaseName(char *path)
{
  if (strrchr(path, '/'))
    return strrchr(path, '/')+1;
  else
    return path;
}
```

GLOSSARY

A

A/D
Analog to Digital; usually refers to the process of analog to digital conversion.

ADC
Analog to Digital Converter (or Conversion).

ADPCM
Adaptive Delta Pulse Code Modulation; a data compression scheme.

A-law
A companding algorithm commonly used in European telecommunications systems.

alpha
A term used to refer to an early pre-release version of software; contrast with beta; not to be confused with the DEC Alpha processor architecture.

analog
A continuously varying quantity; contrast with digital.

ANSI
American National Standards Institute; a standards body that develops (among others) standards for computer languages and hardware interfaces.

API
Application Programming Interface; the software protocol that defines how application software communicates with a specific piece of software, often a toolkit, library, or operating system kernel.

applet
A term commonly used to refer to a small application written in the Java programming language to perform functions on the World Wide Web.

ASCII
American Standard Code for Information Interchange; the 7-bit character code used by most modern computers.

ASIC
Application Specific Integrated Circuit; an IC designed for a specialized purpose.

ATA (AT Attachment interface)
IBM PC/AT Attachment interface; the official name for the ANSI standard for IDE disk interfaces.

ATAPI
ATA Packet Interface; a protocol for controlling mass storage devices, usually hard disks, CD-ROM, and tape drives.

ATM
Asynchronous Transfer Mode; a protocol for high-speed digital networks.

au
Common file extension for μ-law encoded sound files.

AVI
Audio Video Interleaved; a multimedia video format developed by Microsoft.

B

BBS
Bulletin Board System.

beta
The first test release of software to end users ("beta testers"); typically in a state where it is known to contain some bugs but is essentially complete; contrast with alpha.

bidirectional
Transferring information in two directions simultaneously.

binaries
Executable or other computer files that are unreadable by humans.

BIOS
Basic Input Output System; device driver software usually contained in read-only memory.

bit
Binary digit; a binary one or zero.

bit plane
A portion of a computer's video memory.

bitmapped
A video display in which individual pixels correspond to one or more bits of memory.

bmp
Common file extension for graphics files in bitmap format.

booting
The initial process of loading and starting a computer or operating system.

browser
A program for displaying World Wide Web documents.

C

CD
Compact Disc; usually intended to refer to CDDA discs.

CDDA
Compact Disc Digital Audio.

CD-ROM
Compact Disk Read Only Memory.

clone
A piece of hardware designed to be an exact copy of another.

codec
EnCOder-DECoder; hardware device or software algorithm for encoding and decoding data.

companding
A non-linear data compression scheme derived from compressing-expanding.

coprocessor
A specialized processing unit that complements the CPU; most commonly for floating point math or graphics operations.

copyleft
Popular term for the GNU General Public License.

CORBA
Common Object Request Broker Architecture; a standard for distributed object-based computing.

CPU
Central Processing Unit.

D

D/A
Digital to Analog; usually refers to the process of digital to analog conversion.

DAC
Digital to Analog Converter (or Conversion).

digital
A property having discrete values; contrast with analog.

disc
A storage method making use of cylindrical media; usually read/write.

disk
A storage method making use of cylindrical media; usually read-only.

DMA
Direct Memory Access; a process whereby data can be directly transferred between peripheral devices and main memory without CPU intervention.

DOS
Disk Operating System; usually refers to Microsoft's MS-DOS.

driver
Software for controlling a resource, usually a hardware device.

DSP
Digital Signal Processor; a specialized processor for manipulating digital data.

E

EIDE
Enhanced IDE; an interface for mass storage devices, usually disks.

EISA
Enhanced Industry Standard Architecture; a computer bus developed as an enhancement to the ISA bus; now generally considered obsolete.

F

FAQ
Frequently Asked Questions; usually refers to a document rather than the questions themselves.

FBM
Fuzzy BitMap/PixMap; a graphics file format used by Michael "Fuzzy" Mauldin's FBM image libary; usually used as an intermediate format when converting between other file formats.

FFT
Fast Fourier Transform; a mathematical technique for converting data from the time to frequency domain.

fizzbin
Card game played on the original Star Trek episode "A Piece of the Action"; the name of my home Linux system.

FM
Frequency Modulation; usually refers to the FM music synthesis technique.

Forth
A stack-based interpreted language.

FPS
Frames Per Second; used to characterize display speed of animation.

G

gcc
GNU C compiler; the most common C compiler on Linux systems.

gdb
GNU symbolic debugger; the most common debugger on Linux systems.

GIF
Graphics Interchange Format; a common graphics image file format.

GNU
GNU's Not UNIX; project initiated by Richard Stallman to develop a free UNIX-like operating system.

GPL
General Public License; GNU project license agreement.

grayscale
Video display capable of displaying several shades of a single color.

GUI
Graphical User Interface.

H

half-duplex
Communication scheme that transfers information in one direction at a time; in the context of multimedia, often used to refer to sound cards that can record or play back sound, but not both simultaneously.

HDTV
High Definition Television.

herring
Gregarious edible fish found in the colder areas of the North Atlantic, including Finland.

HFS

Hierarchical File System; usually refers to the filesystem used on Apple Macintosh systems.

High Sierra

Earlier name for the ISO 9660 standard.

HOWTO

A short document on a specific Linux-related topic; part of the Linux Documentation Project.

HTML

HyperText Markup Language; native language of documents on the World Wide Web.

Hyper-G

Hypermedia system much like the World Wide Web, but with support for distributed databases of documents, search tools, and user authentication.

HyTime

Hypermedia/Time-based Structuring Language; an extension of SGML to support hypertext and hypermedia.

HTTP

HyperText Transfer Protocol; used to transfer information between a Web server and a Web browser.

hybrid disc

A CD-ROM containing more than one type of filesystem (e.g., ISO 9660 and HFS); also used to refer to a CD containing both digital computer data and digital audio.

HyperCard

Hypertext system developed by Apple Computer.

hypermedia

Technology that combines hypertext and multimedia.

Hz

Hertz; cycles per second; sometimes used to refer to sampling rate (but strictly speaking, this is not correct).

I

IDE

Integrated Drive Electronics; a *de facto* standard for mass storage devices.

interleaving

Storage method that alternates between different types of data; typically used in multimedia files to preserve synchronization of audio and video streams or left and right stereo audio channels.

i/o address

Input/output address; a unique address used by the CPU to access an input or output device; usually expressed as a hexadecimal number.

ISA

Industry Standard Architecture; the hardware bus used by the IBM personal computer and compatibles.

ISDN

Integrated Services Digital Network; a fully digital system for telephone services supporting both voice and data.

ISO

International Organization for Standardization; an international standards body.

ISO 9660

ISO standard for data on CD-ROM.

J

Java

A general purpose programming language developed by Sun Microsystems; especially suited to portable, distributed applications over the Internet.

JPEG

Joint Photographic Experts Group; a standards body.

jukebox

A multi-disc CD-ROM drive; sometimes called a multi-disc changer.

K

kiosk
A standalone multimedia access terminal.

L

LBA
Logical Block Address; addressing scheme for Compact Disc audio data.

LED
Light Emitting Diode.

LGPL
The GNU Library General Public License; GNU project license agreement; applies to the GNU C library.

LILO
LInux LOader; program commonly used to boot Linux or other operating systems from floppy or hard disk.

line level
A hardware standard for analog signals distributed between audio devices.

LUN
Logical Unit Number; a form of addressing used by SCSI devices.

M

MIDI
Musical Instrument Digital Interface; a standard bus and protocol for communication between electronic musical instruments and controllers.

MIME
Multipurpose Internet Mail Extensions; a standard for sending multimedia data by email or other means.

mix
To combine two or more signals together; in the context of multimedia, usually refers to audio signals.

mixer
A hardware device that performs mixing; in the context of multimedia, usually refers to an audio mixer.

monochrome
A video display capable of displaying only two colors, typically black and white.

MPC
Multimedia PC; a standard for defining the minimum hardware requirements of a personal computer for running multimedia applications.

MPEG
Moving Pictures Experts Group; a standards body.

MPU-401
A *de facto* standard PC MIDI interface developed by Roland Corporation.

MSF
Minute/second/frame; addressing scheme for Compact Disc audio data.

MUD
Multi User Dungeon (or Dimension or Dialogue); a multi-player role-playing computer game.

mu-law
μ-law; a companding scheme commonly used in North America.

multi-session
A CD-ROM that has had data written (appended) to it at more than one point in time.

N

newbie
A newcomer or beginner; commonly used to refer to new Linux users.

news group
A Usenet news group.

NFS
Network File System; protocol for a filesystem distributed over a computer network.

NNTP
Net News Transfer Protocol; used for distributing Usenet news.

NTSC
The television standard used in North America and Japan.

O

OpenLook
A graphical user interface specification developed by Sun and AT&T.

OPL
A series of FM synthesizer chips developed by Yamaha and commonly used on sound cards.

oscilloscope
A device that displays electrical signals as a plot of voltage versus time.

P

patch
Parameters associated with the setup of one voice of an FM or Wavetable synthesizer; also a software update delivered in the form of listings of how two sets of files differ.

PBM
Portable BitMap; a graphics file standard commonly used as an intermediate form when converting between other formats; often used as an umbrella term to include several related formats: Portable BitMap (PBM) for monochrome images, Portable GrayMap (PGM) for grayscale images, Portable PixMap (PPM) for color images, and Portable Any Map (PNM) when referring to utilities that accept any of these file formats.

PCM
Pulse Code Modulation; a method of digital encoding for audio.

PDF
Portable Document Format; a file format developed by Adobe systems similar to PostScript with extensions for hypertext; sometimes called Adobe Acrobat files after the name of the Adobe file viewer program.

PhotoCD
A standard developed by Kodak for storing photographic images on CD-ROM.

pitch
Frequency; usually used in reference to computer music.

pixel
Picture Element; a single "dot" on a video display.

POSIX
Portable Operating System Interface; a series of IEEE standards for UNIX-compatible operating systems; Linux was designed against several of the POSIX standards, and at the time of this writing one Linux distribution had been officially certified as compliant with the POSIX.1 standard by an independent testing lab.

PostScript
A page description language developed by Adobe; often produced as output by computer programs and accepted by computer printers.

proprietary
Technology developed by a vendor that does not meet any recognized, published standard.

Q

QuickTime
Multimedia video format developed by Apple Computer.

R

ray tracing
Technique for generating realistic images using mathematical models of light.

RRIP
Rock Ridge Interchange Protocol; extensions to the ISO 9660 filesystem to support long filenames and other UNIX-like features.

S

SB
SoundBlaster; popular series of sound cards made by Creative Labs; a *de facto* standard.

SCSI
Small Computer Systems Interface; a standardized protocol for connecting computers and mass storage devices; pronounced "scuzzy."

sequencer
Hardware or software for controlling MIDI devices.

SGML
Standard Generalized Markup Language; standard language for describing document markup languages.

Slackware
A popular Linux distribution.

SOCKS
Commonly used protocol and software for Internet firewalls.

SunOS
UNIX operating system used on Sun workstations.

synthesizer
Hardware for creating sound using artificial techniques.

T

Tcl
Tool Command Language; a script language developed by John Ousterhout.

term
Software and protocol for accessing TCP/IP services over a serial link.

thumbnail
A reduced version of an image used for identification purposes.

TIFF
Tagged Image File Format; a graphics image file format.

Tk
Extensions to Tcl to support X11 graphics programming.

TOC
Table Of Contents; data structure on an audio CD.

U

URL
Uniform Resource Locator; naming convention for locating documents on the World Wide Web.

V

VCR
Video Cassette Recorder.

voice
An independent sound generator.

Voxware
Former name of the sound drivers in the Linux kernel; no longer used because the name is registered by the commercial company Voxware, Inc.

VRML
Virtual Reality Modeling Language; usually pronounced "vermel."

W

wavetable
Sound synthesis scheme making use of digital sound samples stored in dedicated memory.

Web
The World Wide Web.

Wine
WINdows Emulator; software that allows running Microsoft Windows programs under Linux.

Wish
Windowing shell; graphical shell program for Tk toolkit.

WWW

World Wide Web.

WYSIWYG

What You See Is What You Get; refers to an application program that displays a document as it would be printed.

X

X

The X Window System developed by MIT.

X11

Version 11 of the X Window System.

X11R6

Version 11 release 6 of the X Window System (similarly X11R4, X11R5).

INDEX

About the Author

When Jeff Tranter was first exposed to UNIX-based workstations about ten years ago, he dreamed of being able to afford a system with similar capabilities for home use. Today, he sees Linux as the realization of that dream, with the added bonus of being able to examine and modify all of the source code and even contribute to its development.

He's been using Linux since 1992 and is the author of the freely available Linux Sound and CD-ROM HOWTO guides. Jeff has also written a number of Linux utilities and several Linux-related magazine articles.

Jeff received his bachelor's degree in electrical engineering from the University of Western Ontario. He currently works as a software designer for a high-tech telecommunications company in Kanata, Ontario, Canada's Silicon Valley North.

When he's not busy compiling the latest Linux kernel, his personal interests include ham radio, Tae Kwon Do (he's a black belt), reading science fiction, and playing the guitar.

Colophon

Our look is the result of reader comments, our own experimentation, and feedback from distribution channels. Distinctive covers complement our distinctive approach to technical topics, breathing personality and life into potentially dry subjects.

Hanna Dyer designed the cover of *Linux Multimedia Guide*, based on a series design by Edie Freedman. The cover image, adapted from an engraving from the Dover Pictorial Archive, first appeared in *Frank Leslie's Illustrated Newspaper* on April 9, 1887. The newspaper engraving was based on a photograph by C.D. Kirkland. The cover layout was produced with Quark XPress 3.32 and Adobe Photoshop 3.0.4 software, using ITC Garamond fonts.

The interior layouts were designed by Edie Freedman and Jennifer Niederst, with modifications by Nancy Priest and Mary Jane Walsh. Chapter opening graphics are from the Dover Pictorial Archive and *Marvels of the New West: A Vivid Portrayal of the Stupendous Marvels in the Vast Wonderland West of the Missouri River*, by William Thayer (The Henry Bill Publishing Co., Norwich, CT, 1888). Interior fonts are Adobe ITC Garamond and Adobe Courier. Text was prepared by Erik Ray in SGML using the DocBook 2.4 DTD. The print version of this book was created by translating the SGML source into a set of gtroff macros using a filter developed at ORA by Norman Walsh. Steve Talbott designed and wrote the underlying macro set on the basis of the GNU gtroff -gs macros; Lenny Muellner adapted them to SGML and implemented the book design. The GNU groff text formatter version 1.09 was used to generate PostScript output. The illustrations that appear in the book were created in Macromedia Freehand 5.0 by Chris Reilley.

Graphics

Encyclopedia of Graphics File Formats
By James D. Murray & William vanRyper
2nd Edition April 1996
Includes CD-ROM 1154 pages
ISBN 1-56592-161-5

The *Encyclopedia of Graphics File Formats* is the definitive reference on graphics file formats; the first edition of the book has already become a classic for graphics programmers.

In this second edition, we have retrofitted the entire *Encyclopedia of Graphics File Formats* for display on the Internet's World Wide Web. Using the Enhanced Mosaic browser (included on the CD-ROM), you can navigate the book's contents on the CD-ROM and (if you have an Internet connection) link to the O'Reilly Web Center on the Internet where we maintain an online update service. There you'll find updates, descriptions of new formats, graphics news, and links to additional resources on the World Wide Web. On the CD-ROM, we've also included the updated printed book—still the most portable resource around.

Whether you're a graphics programmer, service bureau, or graphics designer who needs to know the low-level technical details of graphics files, this online resource/book is for you.

For each of more than 100 formats, the product provides quick summary information—How many colors are supported by the format? What type of compression does it use? What's the maximum image size? What's the platform, the numerical format, and the supporting applications? It also provides extensive text detailing how graphics files are constructed in a particular format.

The CD-ROM includes a collection of hard-to-find resources (many that have never before been available outside the organizations that developed them). We've assembled original file format specification documents (covering more than 100 formats) from such vendors as Adobe, Apple, IBM, Microsoft, and Silicon Graphics, along with test images and code examples for many of the formats. The CD-ROM also contains a set of publicly available software and shareware—for Windows, MS-DOS, OS/2, the Macintosh, and UNIX—that will let you convert, view, compress, and manipulate graphics files and images.

Technical requirements for the product: a CD-ROM drive; a PC running Microsoft Windows 3.1, 95, or NT; a Macintosh workstation, or a UNIX workstation supported by Spyglass Enhanced Mosaic. A 256-color monitor is highly recommended.

"At last!!! No more hunting, begging, borrowing, or stealing to find that particular file format information you need—here it is. . . in one place. If you work with graphics files, buy this book. . . . The *EGFF* is useful to file-dissecting neophytes and veterans alike. It is a well-written resource and reference book that you will wonder how you ever did without."
—*Microtimes (Product Spotlight)*

For information: **800-998-9938**, 707-829-0515; **info@ora.com; http://www.ora.com/**
To order: **800-889-8969** (credit card orders only); **order@ora.com**

Stay in touch with O'REILLY™

Visit Our Award-Winning World Wide Web Site

http://www.ora.com/

VOTED

"Top 100 Sites on the Web" —*PC Magazine*

"Top 5% Websites" —*Point Communications*

"3-Star site" —*The McKinley Group*

Our Web site contains a library of comprehensive product information (including book excerpts and tables of contents), downloadable software, background articles, interviews with technology leaders, links to relevant sites, book cover art, and more. File us in your Bookmarks or Hotlist!

Join Our Two Email Mailing Lists

LIST #1   NEW PRODUCT RELEASES: To receive automatic email with brief descriptions of all new O'Reilly products as they are released, send email to: listproc@online.ora.com and put the following information in the first line of your message (NOT in the Subject: field, which is ignored): **subscribe ora-news "Your Name" of "Your Organization"** (for example: **subscribe ora-news Kris Webber of Fine Enterprises)**

LIST #2   O'REILLY EVENTS: If you'd also like us to send information about trade show events, special promotions, and other O'Reilly events, send email to: **listproc@online.ora.com** and put the following information in the first line of your message (NOT in the Subject: field, which is ignored): **subscribe ora-events "Your Name" of "Your Organization"**

Visit Our Gopher Site

- Connect your Gopher to **gopher.ora.com**, or
- Point your Web browser to **gopher://gopher.ora.com/**, or
- telnet to **gopher.ora.com** (login: **gopher**)

Get Example Files from Our Books Via FTP

There are two ways to access an archive of example files from our books:

REGULAR FTP — ftp to: **ftp.ora.com** (login: **anonymous**—use your email address as the password) or point your Web browser to: **ftp://ftp.ora.com/**

FTPMAIL — Send an email message to: **ftpmail@online.ora.com** (write "help" in the message body)

Contact Us Via Email

order@ora.com — To place a book or software order online. Good for North American and international customers.

subscriptions@ora.com — To place an order for any of our newsletters or periodicals.

software@ora.com — For general questions and product information about our software.
  - Check out O'Reilly Software Online at **http://software.ora.com/** for software and technical support information.
  - Registered O'Reilly software users send your questions to **website-support@ora.com**

books@ora.com — General questions about any of our books.

cs@ora.com — For answers to problems regarding your order or our products.

booktech@ora.com — For book content technical questions or corrections.

proposals@ora.com — To submit new book or software proposals to our editors and product managers.

international@ora.com — For information about our international distributors or translation queries.
  - For a list of our distributors outside of North America check out: **http://www.ora.com/www/order/country.html**

O'REILLY™

101 Morris Street, Sebastopol, CA 95472 USA

TEL 707-829-0515 or 800-998-9938 (6 A.M. to 5 P.M. PST)

FAX 707-829-0104

Listing of Titles from O'REILLY™

INTERNET PROGRAMMING

CGI Programming on the
    World Wide Web
Designing for the Web
Exploring Java
HTML: The Definitive Guide
Web Client Programming with Perl
Learning Perl
Programming Perl, 2nd.Edition
    (Fall '96)
JavaScript: The Definitive Guide, Beta
    Edition (Summer '96)
Webmaster in a Nutshell
The World Wide Web Journal

USING THE INTERNET

Smileys
The Whole Internet User's Guide
    and Catalog
The Whole Internet for Windows 95
What You Need to Know:
    Using Email Effectively
Marketing on the Internet (Fall 96)
What You Need to Know: Bandits on the
    Information Superhighway

JAVA SERIES

Exploring Java
Java in a Nutshell
Java Language Reference
    (Fall '96 est.)
Java Virtual Machine

WINDOWS

Inside the Windows '95 Registry

SOFTWARE

WebSite™ 1.1
WebSite Professional™
WebBoard™
PolyForm™

SONGLINE GUIDES

NetLearning
NetSuccess for Realtors
NetActivism (Fall '96)

SYSTEM ADMINISTRATION

Building Internet Firewalls
Computer Crime:
    A Crimefighter's Handbook
Computer Security Basics
DNS and BIND
Essential System Administration,
    2nd ed.
Getting Connected:
    The Internet at 56K and Up
Linux Network Administrator's Guide
Managing Internet Information Services
Managing Usenet (Fall '96)
Managing NFS and NIS
Networking Personal Computers
    with TCP/IP
Practical UNIX & Internet Security
PGP: Pretty Good Privacy
sendmail
System Performance Tuning
TCP/IP Network Administration
termcap & terminfo
Using & Managing UUCP (Fall '96)
Volume 8: X Window System
    Administrator's Guide

UNIX

Exploring Expect
Learning GNU Emacs, 2nd Edition
    (Fall '96 est.)
Learning the bash Shell
Learning the Korn Shell
Learning the UNIX Operating System
Learning the vi Editor
Linux in a Nutshell (Fall '96 est.)
Making TeX Work
Linux Multimedia Guide (Fall '96)
Running Linux, 2nd Edition
Running Linux Companion
    CD-ROM, 2nd Edition
SCO UNIX in a Nutshell
sed & awk
Unix in a Nutshell: System V Edition
UNIX Power Tools
UNIX Systems Programming
Using csh and tsch
What You Need to Know:
    When You Can't Find Your
    UNIX System Administrator

PROGRAMMING

Applying RCS and SCCS
C++: The Core Language
Checking C Programs with lint
DCE Security Programming
Distributing Applications Across
    DCE and Windows NT
Encyclopedia of Graphics File
    Formats, 2nd ed.
Guide to Writing DCE Applications
lex & yacc
Managing Projects with make
ORACLE Performance Tuning
ORACLE PL/SQL Programming
Porting UNIX Software
POSIX Programmer's Guide
POSIX.4: Programming for
    the Real World
Power Programming with RPC
Practical C Programming
Practical C++ Programming
Programming Python (Fall '96)
Programming with curses
Programming with GNU Software
    (Fall '96 est.)
Pthreads Programming
    (Fall '96)
Software Portability with imake
Understanding DCE
Understanding Japanese Information
    Processing
UNIX Systems Programming for SVR4

BERKELEY 4.4 SOFTWARE DISTRIBUTION

4.4BSD System Manager's Manual
4.4BSD User's Reference Manual
4.4BSD User's Supplementary Docs.
4.4BSD Programmer's Reference Man.
4.4BSD Programmer's Supp. Docs.

X PROGRAMMING
THE X WINDOW SYSTEM

Volume 0: X Protocol Reference Manual
Volume 1: Xlib Programming Manual
Volume 2: Xlib Reference Manual
Volume. 3M: X Window System
    User's Guide, Motif Ed.
Volume. 4: X Toolkit Intrinsics
    Programming Manual
Volume 4M: X Toolkit Intrinsics
    Programming Manual, Motif Ed.
Volume 5: X Toolkit Intrinsics
    Reference Manual
Volume 6A: Motif Programming Man.
Volume 6B: Motif Reference Manual
Volume 6C: Motif Tools
Volume 8 : X Window System
    Administrator's Guide
Programmer's Supplement for Release 6
X User Tools (with CD-ROM)
The X Window System in a Nutshell

HEALTH, CAREER, & BUSINESS

Building a Successful Software Business
The Computer User's Survival Guide
Dictionary of Computer Terms
The Future Does Not Compute
Love Your Job!
Publishing with CD-ROM

TRAVEL

Travelers' Tales: Brazil (Summer '96 est.)
Travelers' Tales: Food (Summer '96)
Travelers' Tales: France
Travelers' Tales: Hong Kong
Travelers' Tales: India
Travelers' Tales: Mexico
Travelers' Tales: San Francisco
Travelers' Tales: Spain
Travelers' Tales: Thailand
Travelers' Tales: A Woman's World

TO ORDER: **800-889-8969** (CREDIT CARD ORDERS ONLY); **order@ora.com**; **http://www.ora.com/**
OUR PRODUCTS ARE AVAILABLE AT A BOOKSTORE OR SOFTWARE STORE NEAR YOU.

International Distributors

Customers outside North America can now order O'Reilly & Associates books through the following distributors. They offer our international customers faster order processing, more bookstores, increased representation at tradeshows worldwide, and the high-quality, responsive service our customers have come to expect.

EUROPE, MIDDLE EAST AND NORTHERN AFRICA *(except Germany, Switzerland, and Austria)*

INQUIRIES
International Thomson Publishing Europe
Berkshire House
168-173 High Holborn
London WC1V 7AA, United Kingdom
Telephone: 44-171-497-1422
Fax: 44-171-497-1426
Email: **itpint@itps.co.uk**

ORDERS
International Thomson Publishing Services, Ltd.
Cheriton House, North Way
Andover, Hampshire SP10 5BE,
United Kingdom
Telephone: 44-264-342-832 (UK orders)
Telephone: 44-264-342-806 (outside UK)
Fax: 44-264-364418 (UK orders)
Fax: 44-264-342761 (outside UK)
UK & Eire orders: **itpuk@itps.co.uk**
International orders: **itpint@itps.co.uk**

GERMANY, SWITZERLAND, AND AUSTRIA

International Thomson Publishing GmbH
O'Reilly International Thomson Verlag
Königswinterer Straße 418
53227 Bonn, Germany
Telephone: 49-228-97024 0
Fax: 49-228-441342
Email: **anfragen@arade.ora.de**

AUSTRALIA

WoodsLane Pty. Ltd.
7/5 Vuko Place, Warriewood NSW 2102
P.O. Box 935, Mona Vale NSW 2103
Australia
Telephone: 61-2-9970-5111
Fax: 61-2-9970-5002
Email: **info@woodslane.com.au**

NEW ZEALAND

WoodsLane New Zealand Ltd.
21 Cooks Street (P.O. Box 575)
Wanganui, New Zealand
Telephone: 64-6-347-6543
Fax: 64-6-345-4840
Email: **info@woodslane.com.au**

ASIA *(except Japan & India)*

INQUIRIES
International Thomson Publishing Asia
60 Albert Street #15-01
Albert Complex
Singapore 189969
Telephone: 65-336-6411
Fax: 65-336-7411

ORDERS
Telephone: 65-336-6411
Fax: 65-334-1617

JAPAN

O'Reilly Japan, Inc.
Kiyoshige Building 2F
12-Banchi, Sanei-cho
Shinjuku-ku
Tokyo 160 Japan
Telephone: 81-3-3356-5227
Fax: 81-3-3356-5261
Email: **kenji@ora.com**

INDIA

Computer Bookshop (India) PVT. LTD.
190 Dr. D.N. Road, Fort
Bombay 400 001
India
Telephone: 91-22-207-0989
Fax: 91-22-262-3551
Email: **cbsbom@giasbm01.vsnl.net.in**

THE AMERICAS

O'Reilly & Associates, Inc.
101 Morris Street
Sebastopol, CA 95472 U.S.A.
Telephone: 707-829-0515
Telephone: 800-998-9938 (U.S. & Canada)
Fax: 707-829-0104
Email: **order@ora.com**

SOUTHERN AFRICA

International Thomson Publishing Southern Africa
Building 18, Constantia Park
240 Old Pretoria Road
P.O. Box 2459
Halfway House, 1685 South Africa
Telephone: 27-11-805-4819
Fax: 27-11-805-3648

O'REILLY™